CYBERSPACE REGULATION:
A CRITICAL STUDY OF GLOBAL AND NATIONAL LAWS FROM THE PERSPECTIVE OF HUMAN RIGHTS

ACKNOWLEDGMENT

I am extremely delighted to express my sincere gratitude to my Guide, **Dr. P. Ishwara Bhat**, Professor, Chairman and Dean, Faculty of Law, Department of Studies and Research in Law, University of Mysore, Mysore. I am highly indebted to Dr. P. Ishwara Bhat for his constant encouragement and meticulous guidance in doing my research in a systematic way.

I am indeed grateful to **Dr. C. Basavaraju**, Reader and Chairman, Board of Studies, Department of Studies and Research in Law, University of Mysore, Mysore, for his valuable suggestions and support in carrying out my research work.

I also take his opportunity to acknowledge here the encouragement of the faculty members of Department of Studies and Research in Law, University of Mysore, Mysore, **Dr. M.D. Krishna, Dr. Ramesh** and **Dr. T.R. Maruthi**, I thank them for their extended support throughout my research work.

I sincerely acknowledge **Prof. T.M. Bhat**, Principal (Retd.), M. Krishna Law College, Hassan, for the encouragement and motivation which has helped me to a great extent in preparing this thesis.

I express my deep gratitude with respect for the encouragement and support of **Prof. J.M. Subramanya**, Former Director, SDM Institute for Management Development, Mysore.

I thank **Prof. Ramesh Venkateswaran**, Director, SDM Institute for Management Development, Mysore for his support.

Date:
Place: *C.S. Somu*

LIST OF CASES

Chapter 1

THE WORLD OF CYBERSPACE

"The ability of the World Wide Web (Internet) to penetrate every home and community across the globe has both positive and negative implications- while it can be an invaluable source of information and means of communication, it can also override community values and standards, subjecting them to whatever more may or may not be found online....The Internet is a challenge to the sovereignty of civilized communities, States, and nations to decide what is appropriate and decent behaviour."

Statement of Rep.Goodlatte in US Congress[1]

1.1 Introduction

Three times in the past 250 years the world has witnessed a major transformation affecting virtually every aspect of society. Founded on advances in science and fueled by innovations in technology, these industrial revolutions produced major leaps forward in human productivity and changed the way people work and interact with each other. By the time such a revolution runs its course, virtually every aspect of society has been affected in some significant way[2].

The first industrial revolution originated in Britain and lasted from roughly 1760 to 1830. It was founded on new methods of manufacturing based on iron and steam, and at its core were the first major advances since antiquity to use scientific reasoning to develop new products - in short, modern applied research[3]. These innovations ultimately spurred new forms of transportation such as the steamship

---

[1] Rep.Goodlatte is a member of House Judiciary Committee in US. This committee frequently weighs in on policy issues destined for implementation by the Federal Communication Commission (FCC).
[2] Bradford L. Smith, The Third Industrial Revolution: Policymaking for the Internet, 3 COLUM. SCI. & TECH. L. REV. 1, (Nov. 4, 2001) available at http://www.stlr.org/cite.cgi?volume=3&article=1 , visited on 14 Nov 2003.
[3] ibid

and the railroad, as well as the invention of mechanical looms and other machinery, which together prompted socio-economic changes such as the introduction of specialized labor and the factory system[4].Specialization and factories, in turn, led to widespread population shifts from rural to urban areas and to fundamental changes in the way people worked and interacted.

The second industrial revolution lasted from about 1875 to 1930. It was powered by inventions such as electricity, the telephone and the internal combustion engine and automobile, as well as new synthetics and alloys and new applications of steel and oil. These advances were made possible by the unprecedented availability of capital and the creation of the modern business organization. Among the revolution's many socio-economic effects were greater mobility, a growing middle class and the beginnings of more widespread leisure time[5].

Although different in many ways, these industrial revolutions shared certain characteristics. First, each was founded upon one or more new technologies that fundamentally changed manufacturing processes in a number of industries. Second, the adoption of these new technologies made it possible for manufacturers to improve productivity, which ultimately resulted in greater purchasing power and higher standards of living for broad segments of the population. Finally, these new technologies exerted profound and lasting effects on how people worked, socialized and used their leisure time.

Today the Internet is at the heart of a third industrial revolution. Made possible by technological advances in computer hardware, software, and telecommunications, the Internet has forced companies everywhere to reinvent themselves and the way they do business. This transformation in business practices has fueled unprecedented gains in productivity, generated both by improvements in efficiency and the creation of new markets. At the same time, the Internet is profoundly

---

[4] ibid
[5] ibid

changing the way people communicate with one another and express and enjoy themselves.

But as in any period of dramatic change, the Internet revolution raises several challenges and questions for legal systems around the world. To what extent do we need to adapt existing legal structures to facilitate efficient commercial practices while promoting innovation? How do we ensure that the law advances important social values that transcend these commercial interests? More fundamentally, what are the appropriate responsibilities of the public and private sectors in addressing these issues? Although several legal scholars -including David Post, James Boyle, Lawrence Lessig and others have offered insightful critiques of law's relationship to the Internet, these authors have been less successful in articulating a coherent model for resolving the many social and legal issues that arise online.

1.2 Law and Technology

Human history in a sense is a story of technology from flint stones to that of genetic. The tribulations and triumph of such a journey which will continue in the future, has one aspect, constant at its core – "the laws that govern them". Technology- if defined as 'set of refined processes' resulting in various application of daily use in our lives seems to be harmless marvel in its basic construct and explanation.

Technology has been an instrument of social change. Before the invention of automobiles there was no need for traffic signal lights and policemen and law to regulate the automobiles. Copyright law was created in the late Middle Ages in reaction to the invention and use of printing press. Similarly only after the invention of ship, maritime law developed. New technologies are human inventions. Technologies are a product of ingenious creativity forced by ecological, social or cultural pressures such as capitalist systems, economic pressures to increase productivity or political and military pressures such as warfare or ecological and demographic threats to a given society[6]. Technology, law, economic conditions and

---

[6] Lessig, Lawrence, Future of Ideas, The Penguin Press, New York, 2005

practices, social relations and cultural conceptions are different systems or contexts within which human beings act, alone and with others[7].

The rapid advances in science and medicine since 1950, and especially the advances in computer technology since 1980, have revolutionized the way society functions. It is widely recognized that our society is making a transition from the industrial manufacturing age to an information age. In contrast, law is struggling to keep pace with the technological advancements which are causing social changes in leaps and bounds[8].

Law has been slow to adapt to the choices posed by technology. It is accepted fact that knowledge, opportunities, and choices are inherently good, there are the possibilities of (i) prohibiting or restricting use of new technologies for no good reason or (ii) of misusing technology to harm people. Law that made sense in 1850, or even in 1950, can be inappropriate for today's problems and opportunities[9].

One of the important reasons why law takes its own time to adjust to new ideas and slow to change is that the evolved judicial principles. One of the basic principles of jurisprudence is *stare decisis*: the old decision stands as a precedent for the present and future. Such a principle gives society stable law, so that attorneys can predict the outcome of a case and advise their client. Therefore, judges are reluctant to make new law[10].

---

[7] Benklar Yochai, Technology, law Freedom and Development, The Indian Journal of Law and Technology , Vol.1, 2005

[8] Standler B Ronald, Response of Law to New Technology, available at http://www.rbs2.com/lt.htm, visited on 1 Jan 2004

[9] ibid
[10] ibid

Technology does not determine society, it embodies it. But nor does society determine technological innovations, it uses it. This dialectical interaction between society and technology has become part of the living society[11].

1.3 The Advent of Internet

The 'space race' has been identified as a catalyst for the development of personal computers, the argument being that the US had to minimize the size and weight of on board computers in order to compensate for the greater power of soviet rockets. The connection between the space race and the Internet is less well known, but may be equally significant[12].

The first artificial satellite, SPUTNIK, was launched in 1957 to great consternation in the US defense establishment. As part of its response, the Advanced Research Projects Agency (ARPA) was established under the auspices of the department of defense, with a remit of establishing US leadership in areas of science and technology which might posses military applications.[13]

The concept of a decentralized computer network had been considered in a number of countries, including the UK, but it was with the provision of substantial funding from ARPA in 1964 that a practical implementation was developed. The project was based upon ideas drawn up by Paul Baran of the RAND Corporation, an organization described as 'America's foremost cold war think tank. Its genesis lay in the desire to find a method of enabling the US military and government to maintain communications after a nuclear war. The assumption was that telecommunication control centers would be leading target for attack and that traditional telecommunications networks would be rendered unusable. The solution lay in reversing the conception that a telecommunications network should seek to be as reliable as possible by building in the assumption of unreliability. From this starting point, the system should be designed in such a way   as to enable messages

---

[11] Castells, Manuel, The Rise of Network Society, 2nd Edition, Blackwell Publishing Ltd., New York, 2002
[12] Lloyd J Ian, Information Technology Law,3rd edition, Butterworths, London,2000, at p 17

[13] ibid at p 17

to overcome obstacles. The system would link a number of computers or 'nodes'. Every message would be sent on their way and would pass from node to node until all arrived at the intended destination, where they would be reassembled to indicate the complete message. Although packets would be forwarded in approximately the correct direction the particular route taken by a packet would be dependent upon chance and network availability. If one section of the network had been damaged, the packets would be routed via other sections. A helpful illustration might be to analogize the system with the road network for transportation. The motorway network might be compared with a telecommunications network. It provides high capacity and high speed transport links. Disruption at a few key locations- by nuclear attack or less dramatic incidents- would render the system unusable. The Internet might be compared with the non- motorway road network. Travel may be slower and more circuitous, but the sheer variety of routes would make total disruption of service a most unlikely event[14] .

The initial network, ARPANET, which was named after its sponsors, was installed in 1969 with four nodes. By 1972, this figure had grown to 37. One of the next major developments was the evolution of the communication standard Transmission Control Protocol/Internet Protocol (TCP/IP). The TCP component was responsible for converting messages into streams of packets, whilst the IP is responsible for addressing and routing the packets to their destination. The TCP/IP protocols were developed in the 1970s, but it was with their adoption as the basis for ARPANET on 1st January 1983 that the Internet could be said to have originated[15] .

---

[14] ibid at p17
[15] ibid at p18

The word 'INTERNET' has been defined in a 1995 resolution of the US federal Networking Council as follows: 'Internet[16]' refers to the global information system that

---

[16] A description of the Internet set forth by Justice John Paul Stevens in the landmark Reno v. ACLU (Eastern District Court of Pennsylvania, civil action 98-5591, available at http://supreme.usatoday.findlaw.com/supreme_court/decisions/lower_court/98-5591.html, visited on 23 Feb 2002) decision, June 26, 1997 is as follows;

The Internet is an international network of interconnected computers. It is the outgrowth of what began in 1969 as a military program called Advanced Research Agency Project NETwork (ARPANET), which was designed to enable computers operated by the military, defense contractors, and universities conducting defense related research to communicate with one another by redundant channels even if some portions of the network were damaged in a war. While the ARPANET no longer exists, it provided an example for the development of a number of civilian networks that, eventually linking with each other, now enable tens of millions of people to communicate with one another and to access vast amounts of information from around the world. The Internet is "a unique and wholly new medium of worldwide human communication."

The Internet has experienced "extraordinary growth." The number of "host" computers--those that store information and relay communications--increased from about 300 in 1981 to approximately 9,400,000 by the time of the trial in 1996. Roughly 60% of these hosts are located in the United States. About 40 million people used the Internet at the time of trial, a number that is expected to mushroom to 200 million by 1999.

Individuals can obtain access to the Internet from many different sources, generally hosts themselves or entities with a host affiliation. Most colleges and universities provide access for their students and faculty; many corporations provide their employees with access through an office network; many communities and local libraries provide free access; and an increasing number of storefront "computer coffee shops" provide access for a small hourly fee. Several major national "online services" such as America Online, CompuServe, the Microsoft Network, and Prodigy offer access to their own extensive proprietary networks as well as a link to the much larger resources of the Internet. These commercial online services had almost 12 million individual subscribers at the time of trial.

Anyone with access to the Internet may take advantage of a wide variety of communication and information retrieval methods. These methods are constantly evolving and difficult to categorize precisely. But, as presently constituted, those most relevant to this case are electronic mail ("e mail"), automatic mailing list services ("mail exploders," sometimes referred to as "listservs"), "newsgroups," "chat rooms," and the "World Wide Web." All of these methods can be used to transmit text; most can transmit sound, pictures, and moving video images. Taken together, these tools constitute a unique medium--known to its users as "cyberspace"--located in no particular geographical location but available to anyone, anywhere in the world, with access to the Internet.

E mail enables an individual to send an electronic message--generally akin to a note or letter--to another individual or to a group of addressees. The message is generally stored electronically, sometimes waiting for the recipient to check her "mailbox" and sometimes making its receipt known through some type of prompt. A mail exploder is a sort of e-mail group. Subscribers can send messages to a common e-mail address, which then forwards the message to the group's other subscribers. Newsgroups also serve groups of regular participants, but these postings may be read by others as well. There are thousands of such groups, each serving to foster an exchange of information or opinion on a particular topic running the gamut from, say, the music of Wagner to Balkan politics to AIDS prevention to the Chicago Bulls. About 100,000 new messages are posted every day. In most newsgroups, postings are automatically purged at regular intervals. In addition to posting a message that can be read later, two or more individuals wishing to communicate more immediately can enter a chat room to engage in real time dialogue--in other words, by typing messages to one another that appear almost immediately on the others' computer screens. The District Court found that at any given time "tens of thousands of users are engaging in conversations on a huge range of subjects." It is "no exaggeration to conclude that the content on the Internet is as diverse as human thought."

The best-known category of communication over the Internet is the World Wide Web, which allows users to search for and retrieve information stored in remote computers, as well as, in some cases, to communicate back to designated sites. In concrete terms, the Web consists of a vast number of documents stored in different computers all over the world. Some of these documents are simply files containing information. However, more elaborate documents, commonly known as Web "pages," are also prevalent. Each has its own address--%rather like a telephone number." Web pages frequently contain information and sometimes allow the viewer to communicate with the page's (or "site's") author. They generally also contain "links" to other documents created by that site's author or to other (generally) related sites. Typically, the links are either blue or underlined text--sometimes images.

Navigating the Web is relatively straightforward. A user may either type the address of a known page or enter one or more keywords into a commercial "search engine" in an effort to locate sites on a subject of interest. A particular Web page may contain the information sought by the "surfer," or, through its links, it may be an avenue to other documents located anywhere on the Internet. Users

(i)   is logically linked together by a globally unique address space based on the internet protocol (IP)

(ii)   is able to support communications using the Transmission Control Protocol/Internet Protocol (TCP/IP) suite and

(iii)   provides, uses or makes accessible , either publicly or privately , high level services layered on the communications and related infrastructure described herein.

A feature of the TCP/IP protocols is that they enable any user to connect to the internet. These are no social or practical controls over the making of such connection and the cost implications are minimal. It is somewhat ironic that a system which was designed to enable the authorities to retain control over a nuclear wasteland should have metamorphosed into a system which is almost a byword for anarchy[17].

Cyberspace has developed with almost incredible speed, certainly when compared with other forms of communication technologies. In 1876, Alexander Graham Bell was awarded a patent for the telephone. Its impact on the world has been massive,

---

generally explore a given Web page, or move to another, by clicking a computer "mouse" on one of the page's icons or links. Access to most Web pages is freely available, but some allow access only to those who have purchased the right from a commercial provider. The Web is thus comparable, from the readers' viewpoint, to both a vast library including millions of readily available and indexed publications and a sprawling mall offering goods and services.

From the publishers' point of view, it constitutes a vast platform from which to address and hear from a worldwide audience of millions of readers, viewers, researchers, and buyers. Any person or organization with a computer connected to the Internet can "publish" information. Publishers include government agencies, educational institutions, commercial entities, advocacy groups, and individuals. Publishers may either make their material available to the entire pool of Internet users, or confine access to a selected group, such as those willing to pay for the privilege. "No single organization controls any membership in the Web, nor is there any centralized point from which individual Web sites or services can be blocked from the Web."

[17] Lloyd J Ian, Information Technology Law,3rd edition, Butterworths, London,2000, at p 18

but 74 years were to elapse before 50 million subscribers were connected. Radio took 38 years to reach the same figure. With the PC, only 16 years elapsed. From its inception in 1993, WWW (World Wide Web) required only four years to acquire 50 million users. In terms of statistics in 1989, the internet had some 100,000 host computers. By 1992, this figure had climbed to 1,000,000. In 1997, the figure had increased to some 13 million sites, with the internet maintaining a 100% annual growth rate through much of the decade[18].

Internet usage statistics from a recent survey conducted by www.internetworldstat.com is depicted below by a graph;

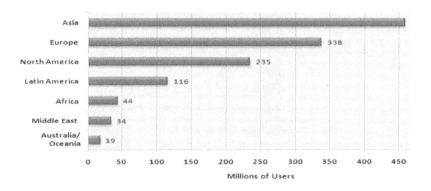

For users in the developed world, the internet is becoming a feature of our everyday lives. It is rare to find a newspaper which does not contain some feature on the internet. Most newspapers, and many television and radio programmes, maintain an electronic presence on the internet. Many advertisements and publicity documents refer readers to an internet site for further information[19].

The internet and the WWW are but one manifestation of a radical change in the nature of society which has been brought about by the computer. It is now a trite

---

[18] ibid
[19] See generally, Developments in the Law- The Law of Cyberspace, Harvard Law Review, Vol.112:1574, The Harvard Law Review Association, 1999

comment to say that we live in an 'Information Society', in which information in its many and various forms is becoming a more important commodity and measurement of prosperity than physical objects. The question arises what is the nature of this beast and how should it be regulated?

1.3.1 Nature of Internet

Internet today is a technology used by millions of surfers connecting millions of computer worldwide. The rate of growth of this technology is quantitatively and qualitatively different than its predecessors like telephone, radio or television. Internet is a single platform where all the others can converge - information, speech and visual combined as digital information. Unlike the other technologies often referred as 'push technologies' where the process is one-way from those who produce to those who consume, internet is referred as 'push and pull technology' offering interactive process.

Nevertheless, the social behaviour of 'netiquette' of the early group of users based on mutual trust and conditioning will also change in the various stages of the history of internet. The contemporary understating of this 'free space of the commons' is often debated on themes like cyber terrorism and cyber crime making the new jurisprudence of cyber laws and the great debate of 'freedom v regulation'.

Cyberspace[20] does not exist physically, except in the countless miles of electronic circuitry, fiber optic cables and silicon chips which make up our computers and our networks. Cyberspace, by its very nature, is everywhere and nowhere at once; it is the everythingness and nothingness of William Gibson's matrix, but it need not be realized only in futuristic dystopian novel. We exist in cyberspace today, everyday. Cyberspace is where we are, in our mind's eye, when we are on the phone with a loved one across the country. Cyberspace is where we are when we watch a movie, or wear headphones. It is where an architect's computer aided design exists before it

---

[20] The term 'CYBERSPACE' is coined by , William Gibson, in his novel, Neuromancer, and has been extensively used to denote virtual world.

is constructed. Cyberspace is an infinite, universal space, achieved by technology inhabiting minimal amount of physical space[21].

But immersive cyberspace as mediated through virtual interfaces, unlike the infinite reaches of physical space, is nothingness. It is a blank, black void until an artificial context is introduced. It is nothing, placeless and indescribable. The void of cyberspace has no gravity and no micro or macro climate of Sun, wind, earth and water. In cyberspace even a horizon is artificial. There are no building codes, no monetary budgets and no neighbors in cyberspace[22].

Furthermore, while three dimensional space exists in cyberspace, geography does not. We exist in physical space, in a physical place, in relation to all objects around us. Above, beyond, near and far. All of these words describe ourselves and other objects in relation to a context of other specific, distinct objects. Geography, the measure of three dimensional space, exists because objects in physical space bear physical presence, separated by physical distance. Geography cannot exist in cyberspace. To overlay cyberspace with a Cartesian coordinate system is futile, for its infinite reaches collapse into nothingness. Objects, despite their three-dimensionality, do not take up space. They have no place in relationship to other objects. Any virtual object, any world, any person can exist in the same space as any other at the same time. Conversely, any virtual object, world or person can exist in an infinite number of spaces simultaneously. All information, all environments, all ideas realized spatially and electronically will be available to all persons, everywhere, at all times in cyberspace[23].

1.3.2 Internet Infrastructure for Data Transfer

The Internet, and its communication miracles, results from a fundamental principle of network engineering: Keep It Simple. Every computer connected to the Internet is capable of doing a few, very simple tasks very quickly. By linking millions of comparatively simple systems together, complex functionality is achieved. The

---

[21] From the series Vers Une Architecture Virtuelle, The Nature of the Cyberspace, available at http://www.hitl.washington.edu/people/dace/porfoli/crit35.html, visited on 19 Aug 2004
[22] ibid
[23] ibid

Internet is an ingenious communications network in large part because it is so simple[24].

At the heart of any Internet transmission - sending an email, viewing a web page, or downloading an audio or video file - is the Internet Protocol (IP). Invented in 1974 by Vint Cerf and Robert Kahn, IP is a communications scheme that defines how data is sent across networks. IP has two key standardized elements that are involved in every transmission: (1) a common method for breaking each transmission down into small chunks of data, known as "packets", and (2) a unified global addressing system. IP gives every computer connected to the Internet a unique address, and a common definition of the packets of data that can be delivered to these addresses[25].

In other words, the Internet Protocol boils down to two simple rules:

1. Every computer connected to the Internet must be reachable via a numerical address of a specific form: four eight-bit numbers separated by periods - e.g., A.B.C.D where A, B, C, and D are between 0-255 (that's because each eight-bit string has $2^8=256$ different combinations). This address is called an "Internet Protocol address," or "IP address" for short. For example, the IP address for Google's homepage is 216.239.51.100[26].

2. Every computer connected to the Internet must be able to accept packets that have a 24 to 32 byte header and a packet size of up to 576 bytes. The header contains information on the origin[27].

Using IP, a computer first breaks down the message to be sent into small packets, each labeled with the address of the destination machine; the computer then passes those packets along to the next connected Internet machine, which looks at the

---

[24] Ethan Zuckerman & Andrew McLaughlin ,Introduction to Internet Architecture and Institutions , Berkman center for Internet and Society , visited on 2 May 2004, available at http://cyber.law.harvard.edu/digitaldemocracy/internetarchitecture.html#intro , visited on 28 Sep 2004

[25] ibid
[26] ibid
[27] ibid

destination address and then passes it along to the next connected Internet machine, which looks for the destination address and pass it along, and so forth, until the packets reach the destination machine. IP is thus a "best efforts" communication service, meaning that it does its best to deliver the sender's packets to the intended destination, but it cannot make any guarantees. If, for some reason, one of the intermediate computers "drops" (i.e., deletes) some of the packets, the dropped packets will not reach the destination and the sending computer will not know whether or why they were dropped[28].

By itself, IP can't ensure that the packets arrived in the correct order, or even that they arrived at all. That's the job of another protocol: TCP (Transmission Control Protocol). TCP sits "on top" of IP and ensures that all the packets sent from one machine to another are received and assembled in the correct order. Should any of the packets get dropped during transmission, the destination machine uses TCP to request that the sending machine resend the lost packets, and to acknowledge them when they arrive. TCP's job is to make sure that transmissions get received in full, and to notify the sender that everything arrived as sent[29].

An analogy can be drawn with the physical world to illustrate the working of TCP. Sending a communication (an email or web page or video file or whatever) via Internet Protocol packets is like sending a book by postcard. Figuratively speaking, the Internet Protocol allows your computer to take our book, cut out the pages, and glue each page onto a postcard. In order to allow the destination computer to reassemble the pages properly, your computer writes a number on each postcard, after all, there is no guarantee that the mailman will deliver the postcards in the exact right order[30].

Here's where it gets interesting. Because there's a danger that some postcards will be lost in the mail, the computer keeps a copy of each one, just in case it needs to resend a missing postcard. How will the computer know if it needs to resend some

---

[28] ibid
[29] ibid
[30] ibid

of the postcards? That's where TCP does its ingenious thing. TCP tells the destination computer to send a periodic confirmation postcard back to your computer, telling it that all postcards up to number X have been received. When the computer gets a confirmation postcard like that, it knows that it is safe to throw out the retained duplicate postcards up to number X. TCP also instructs the computer that, if no confirmation is received by a certain time, it should start to resend the postcards. The lack of a confirmation may mean that some postcards are missing, or that the confirmation itself got lost along the way. The computer is not too worried about sending unnecessary duplicates, because it knows that the destination computer is smart enough to recognize and ignore duplicates. In other words, TCP says that it's better to err on the side of over sending. TCP also helps computers to deal with the fact that there is a limit to how many postcards can be stuffed into a mailbox at one time. It allows the two computers to agree that the sender will only send perhaps 100 postcards and await a postcard confirming receipt of the first 100 before sending the next group[31].

Thus, TCP gives the sending and receiving computers a way to exchange information about the status of a communication, which packets have been received, which ones are missing. And it helps the two computers manage the rate of packet traffic, so as not to get overwhelmed[32].

1.3.3 Internet and Society

The Internet has revolutionized the way we live, work and communicate. It also changed the way we conduct and behave ourselves in the society. Most of the deviant conduct that may occur in cyberspace is not unknown to us or new, but the environment in which this happens is quite new and hence has to be dealt separately. Internet is a medium that remains poorly understood as result of change

---

[31] ibid
[32] ibid

15

of pace in our modern information environment and the lack of adequate supply of empirical studies of the internet[33].

All changes in systems of communication are important to the legal system and development of societies. Electronic communication has not only altered the way we communicate, it has also changed the way our societies work and are organized. The rise of the internet is a key to part of the social transformations taking place in late modernity. In order to understand this, and subsequent developments, we have to approach the internet as a modality of cultural transmission. As uncertainty about the impact of such a sophisticated communication technology undoubtedly exists, what we lack is a social theory of internet. We urgently need to find concepts and frameworks that can help us to develop a more critical understanding of the internet and continue to remain critical of what we find[34].

As far as the human rights of netizens are concerned a concrete international legal framework has to be put in place so that everyone is allowed to enjoy the benefits of this new communication medium.

1.4 Why Cyber Law?

The term cyber law has gained a wide recognition often spoke about in seminars, workshops and symposiums. Literature has been published using the terms like cyber law, Law of the Internet, Law Relating to Computers etc. In academic settings there are centers for Computer and the Law, Cyber law and research and son and so forth. The important question is whether these terms are used to denote a specific branch of study, or just a popular usage without coming to grips with what exactly is this branch of law, is it still evolving or is it a generic usage of dealing with varied existing laws on a glamorous pre-fix or suffix?

---

[33] Castells, Manuel , The Internet Galaxy-Reflections on the Internet, Business and Society, Oxford University Press, London, 2001
[34] Slevin, James, The internet and Society: Central Themes and Issues, Trojborgtrykkeriet, the Faculty of arts, University of Aarhus, The center for Internet Research, Aarhus, 2002

Judge Frank H. Easterbrook remarked at a conference on 'Law of Cyberspace', that they do not offer a course in "the Law of Horse'. He did not mean by this that Illinois specializes in grain rather than livestock. His point, rather, was that "Law and ..." courses should be limited to subjects that could illuminate the entire field of law. And that the best way to learn the law applicable to specialized endeavors is to study the general rules. Lots of cases deal with sales of horses; others deal with people kicked by horses; still more deal with the licensing and racing of horses, or with the care veterinarians give to horses, or with prizes at horse shows. Any effort to collect these strands into a course on "the Law of the Horse" is doomed to be shallow and to miss unifying principles. Teaching hundred percent of cases on people kicked by horses will not convey the law of torts well. Far better for most students- better , even, for those who plan to go into the horse trade- to take courses in property, torts, commercial transactions, and the like , adding to the diet of horse cases a smattering of transactions in cucumbers, cats, coals and cribs. Only by putting the law of the horse in the context of broader rules about commercial endeavors could one really understand the law about horses[35].

Judge Easterbrook is of the clear view that developing sound laws and applying them to cyberspace to makes sense. Cyberspace requires no new laws. For example, property in cyberspace can be best examined and applied with sound and robust development of intellectual property law[36].

In contrast to the views of Judge Easterbrook, Larence Lessig argues that there is an important general point that comes from thinking in particular about how law and cyberspace connect. This general point is about the limits on law as a regulator and about the techniques for escaping those limits. This escape, both in real space and in cyberspace, comes from recognizing the collection of tools that a society has at hand for affecting constraints upon behaviour. Law in its traditional sense- an order backed by a threat directed at primary behaviour- is just one of these tools. The general point is that law can affect these other tools- that they constrain behaviour

---

[35] Easterbrook H Frank, Cyberspace and the Law of the Horse, 1996 U.CHI.LEGAL.F 207, available at
http://www2.sims.berkeley.edu/courses/is205/s06/Readings/Easterbrook,%20Law%20of%20the%20 Horse.pdf , visited on 23 June 2005
[36] ibid

themselves, and can function as tools of the law. The choice among tools obviously depends upon their efficacy. But importantly, the choice will also raise a question about values.

Further Lessig, highlights two important cases which illustrates the requirement of separate law for cyberspace. The first one is about difficulty in distinguishing adult from child in internet transactions and the second one is about invasion of our privacy which is quite different from the real world. Lesigg describes them as follows;

(1) Zoning Speech – Porn in real space is zoned from kids. Whether because of laws (banning the sale of porn to minors) or norms (telling us to shun those who do sell porn to minors) or the market (porn costs money), it is hard in real space for kids to buy porn; hard, but not impossible. But on balance the regulations of real space have an effect. That effect keeps kids from porn[37].

These real space regulations depend upon certain features in the design of real space. It is hard in real space to hide that you are a kid. Age in real space is a self-authenticating fact. Sure a kid may try to disguise that he is a kid; he may don a mustache or walk on stilts. But costumes are expensive and not terribly effective. And it is hard to walk on stilts. Ordinarily a kid transmits that he is kid; ordinarily, the seller of porn knows a kid is a kid, and so the seller of porn, either because of laws or norms, can at least identify underage customers. Self-authentication makes zoning in real space easy[38].

In cyberspace, age is not similarly self-authenticating. Even if the same laws and norms did apply in cyberspace and even if the constraints of the market were the same (as they are not), any effort to zone porn in cyberspace would face a very difficult problem. Age is extremely hard to certify. To a website accepting traffic, all requests are equal. There is no simple way for a website to distinguish adults from kids, and likewise, no easy way for an adult to establish that he is an adult.

---

[37] Lessig, Lawrence, The lLaw of the Horse: What Cyberlaw Might Teach, 113 HARV.L REV.501(1999), available at http://www.lessig.org/content/articles/works/finalhls.pdf , vsisted 2 Feb 2003; See also 'Code and other Laws of Cyberpsace' by Lawrence Lessig published by Basic Books, 1999 for his arguments why he suggests 'CODE' should be law.
[38] ibid

This feature of the space makes zoning speech there costly- so costly, the Supreme Court concluded in Reno V ACLU that the constitution may prohibit it[39].

(2) Protected Privacy- if you walked into a store, and the guard at the store recorded your name; if cameras tracked your every step, noting what items you looked at and what items you ignored; if any employee followed you around, calculating the time you spent in any given aisle; if before you could purchase an item you selected, the cashier demanded that you reveal who you were; if any or all of these things happened in real space, you would notice. You would notice and could then make a choice about whether you wanted to shop in such a store. Perhaps the vain enjoy the attention; perhaps the thrifty are attracted by the resulting lower prices. They might have no problem with this data collection regime. But at least you would know. Whatever the reason, whatever the consequent choice, you would know enough in real space to know to make a choice[40].

In cyberspace, you would not. You would not notice such monitoring because such tracking in cyberspace is not similarly visible. When you enter a store in cyberspace, the store can record who you are; click monitors (watching what you choose with your mouse) will track where you browse, how long you view a particular page; an employee (if only a bot) can follow you around, and when you make purchases, it can record who you are and from where you came. All this happens in cyberspace- invisibly. Data is collected but without your knowledge. Thus you cannot choose whether you will participate in or consent to this surveillance. In cyberspace, surveillance is not self-authenticating. Nothing reveals whether you are being watched, so there is no real basis upon which to consent[41].

These examples mirror each other, and present a common pattern. In each, some bit of data is missing, which means that in each, some end cannot be pursued. In the first case, that end is collective (zoning porn); in the second, it is individual (choosing privacy). But in both, it is feature of cyberspace that interferes with the particular end. And hence in both, law faces a choice- whether to regulate to change this architectural feature, or to leave cyberspace alone and disable this collective or

---

[39] ibid
[40] ibid
[41] ibid

individual goal. Should the law change in response to these differences? Or should the law try to change the features of cyberspace, to make them conform to the law? And if the latter, then what constraints should there be on the law's effort to change cyberspace's nature? What principles should govern the law's mucking about this space? Or again, how should law regulate?

To many these questions will seem very odd. Many believe that cyberspace simply cannot be regulated. The anonymity and multi-jurisdictionality of cyberspace makes control by government in cyberspace impossible. The nature of the space makes behaviour there unregulable[42].

This belief about cyberspace is wrong, but wrong in an interesting way. It assumes either that the nature of cyberspace is fixed- that its architecture and the control it enables cannot be changed- or that government cannot take steps to change this architecture. Neither assumption is correct. Cyberspace has no nature; it has no particular architecture that cannot be changed. Its architecture is a function of its design or its code. This code can change, either because it evolves in a different way, or because government or business pushes it to evolve in a particular way and while particular versions of cyberspace do resist effective regulation, it does not follow that every version of cyberspace does so as well. Or alternatively, there are versions of cyberspace where beahaviour can be regulated and the government can take steps to increase this regulability[43].

There are several reasons why it is convenient to have a separate classification of law for computer and computer networks like internet:

(1) Solving legal problems that arose from the use of computers often requires some legal principles that are rarely encountered in the practice of law. For example:

(A) Disputes about e-mail and web pages on the Internet extend across state lines, and may even extend across national borders. For example, there are technical issues in personal jurisdiction and which state's law should be applied to the resolution of the dispute. To solve

---

[42] ibid
[43] ibid

these legal problems, one must understand principles of an abstruse area of law, called *Conflicts of Law*[44].

(B) Information stored on computers (e.g., software, data, trade secrets, confidential personal information) is generally much more valuable than the computer hardware. In order to protect this information, many of the concepts in the practice of computer law involve the specialized area of *Intellectual Property Law*, which includes copyrights, trademarks, and patents[45].

(2) Traditional concepts in law are being expanded by events in the area of computer law. For example:

(A) Computer software is legally considered a "good". Unlike other goods, the "purchaser" only owns the floppy diskette or compact disk that contains the software, plus a *license* to use the software. The Uniform Commercial Code was amended by including Article 2B to cover licensing of computer software[46].

(B) Computer databases that contain erroneous information (e.g., false credit reports) can be harmful to people, which may give rise to a new class of torts[47].

(C) Hackers who use a modem to enter a computer without authorization and either (1) use its services or (2) alter records are committing a crime similar to burglary, but the traditional notion of burglary requires the criminal personally to enter the victim's premises, which is not satisfied in the case of entry via data to/from a modem. Therefore, new laws were enacted to define computer crimes. (Personally, I think it would have been preferable to change the definitions in existing concepts, instead of create new concepts, but

---

[44] Standler B, Roland, What is Computer Law?, available at http://www.rbs2.com/cdefn.htm , visited on 1 Jan 2004
[45] ibid
[46] ibid
[47] ibid

no one would accuse the legal profession of honoring simplicity and economy.)

(D) Authentication of evidence contained in files on a computer presents some new problems, because of the ease with which data in the file can be altered, and also because it is easy to alter the operating system's date and time stamp in the directory[48].

(E) Searches of computer databases provide access to information that was difficult to locate in the pre-computer age, which makes computer databases a major new threat to privacy of individuals[49].

The Internet has been revolutionary in giving anyone with a website the equivalent of a printing press or television transmitter: now anyone can broadcast their information or opinion to the whole world, without first going through formal review by a publisher. Many governments have reacted to the Internet with new censorship of both websites and readers' access to the Internet. Furthermore, there has been widespread copyright infringement by people who post material at their website that was copied from other websites, or copied from books, without written permission of the copyright owner. Professor Hugh Gibbons at Franklin Pierce Law Center observes

"With the exception of the telephone and typewriter, the technological revolution of the past century has left the law untouched. Law has dealt at arm's length with technology, making new rules to cover air travel, genetic engineering, and the like, while the lawyers who do the work carry on with paper and pencil – until the advent of the computer."[50]

Law grows with ad hoc additions, which are often not consistent with a small

---

[48] ibid
[49] ibid
[50] ibid

collection of philosophical principles, in this way law is unlike science and engineering[51].

1.5 Regulation of Cyberspace

For every country, postal and telecommunications networks have long provided an infrastructure for the transmission of information. The publishing industry has provided mass dissemination of information since Gutenberg's invention of the printing press, whilst more recently, broadcasting has performed a similar role. The novel element in the vision of a super-highway is that there should be the capability for the two-way delivery of text, pictures, sound and video. The House of Lords Select Committee on Science and Technology, in its recent report on the Information Society[52], adopted the definition of a 'publicly accessible network capable of transferring large amounts of information at high speed between users'. Although the Internet is often regarded as a major component of the information superhighway, limitations in communications technologies have led to the suggestion that it constitutes 'little more than an electronic footpath[53]'.

If consideration is given to existing forms of information transfer, a variety of actors may initially be identified:

1) Cable, terrestrial and satellite broadcasters.
2) Publishers of printed, video and audio works.
3) Telephone and telecommunication companies.
4) Software producers.
5) Internet content producers and service providers.
6) Database Producers.

The activities involved may themselves be divided into a number of categories. Broadcasting services, for example, engage in a one-way transfer of information

---

[51] ibid
[52] The term 'information society' has been defined as a 'society dependent on information exchanges through the use of computers and telecommunications devices'. Definition given by Niels Brugger & Henrik bodker in their paper , The Internet and Society? Questioning Answers and Answering Questions, Ppaers from The Centre for Internet Research, Aarhus, Denmark 2002
[53] Supra note 12, p16

from broadcaster to viewer or listener. The model is one of simultaneous transmission to multiple users. Although some cable networks and systems 'pay per view' constitute exceptions to the rule, the user's only interaction with the system is, generally, to decide whether or not to receive a particular transmission. The same unidirectional transfer of the supply of books, newspapers, video and audio tapes will happen, but with the distinction that the customer has much more flexibility as to the time at which the materials will be read and used. Millions of viewers will simultaneously watch the evening television news. Although millions of persons may also buy a national newspaper, the element of synchronous transfer of data is less noticeable. Telephone companies provide an infrastructure which is used by customers to exchange data. The notion of two-way transfer is also present with on-line databases and many of the aspects of the internet[54].

More significantly, the activities have been subjected to radically different regulatory schema. Although there is a general trend towards liberlisation, driven in part by developments in digital technology, sectors such as broadcasting and telecommunications have traditionally been subject to much more stringent forms of regulation than has been the case with publishers. Until the 1980s, the need for massive investment in infrastructure, coupled with political requirements to provide a universal service, meant that telecommunications tended to be the subject of a de facto or de jure monopoly. Similar factors applied to the broadcasting sector, where state control might be exerted either through the establishment of monopoly or through the operation of a system of licenses. A further significant factor was the need to ration scarce resource. The development of satellite broadcasting and the emerging system of digital television removes any last vestiges of this consideration.

One of the more noticeable phenomena of the information society is that of convergence of technologies. A website may contain attributes of all three models. In a recent decision of the Court of Session, albeit issued only in the course of an action seeking an interim interdict, it has been held that in terms of copyright legislation, a website should be classed as a cable programme service. The massive

---

[54] Supra Note 12, p17

investment currently being undertaken to create cable networks in the UK means that television programmes are carried over the same wires as telephone calls. Trails have been conducted to establish the feasibility of introducing systems of 'video on demand', where the contents of a film or other programme will be transmitted to a viewer using the telephone system. Even television transmissions may soon become more interactive, so that, for example, a viewer will be able to place an order for goods or services advertised on television by pressing a few buttons on a television remote control device. As technologies converge, so pressures have emerged for the law to take a similar approach. Both the European Commission and the Department of Trade and Industry have published Green Papers on the topic. The latter document states that:

"Digital technology is rapidly being adopted for the reproduction, storage and transmission of information in all media. This means that any form of content (still or moving pictures, sound, text, data) can be made available via any transmission medium, eroding the traditional distinctions between telecommunications and broadcasting. Already it is possible to receive television or radio over the internet, while digital televisions will have some of the capabilities we currently find only in computers.

The greatly increased capacity and versatility of networks provides opportunities to improve the delivery of existing services and to create new ones. Consumers will have easier access to a wider range of content through various transmission media. They will be able to select the services they want at a time convenient to them and to benefit from enhanced two-way communication through interactivity. The potential benefits to the citizen/consumer, to business and to government are significant.

Our system of regulation faces new challenges as delivery systems adopt a common technology and assume common capabilities. Some new services fall within the remit of more than one regulator, creating a risk of excessive and/or inconsistent regulation. Where an identical service is transmitted over different delivery systems, it may be subject to different regulatory regimes. The development of new services, and their wide availability, must not be jeopardized by such regulatory overlaps and anomalies"[55].

The key initial document in European which moves towards the information society is the report of Commissioner Bangemann's 'group of prominent persons' to the meeting of the European Council in Corfu in June 1994. Entitled Europe and the Global Information society, the Bangemann Report added a political dimension to previously technically-driven moves towards convergence. Three topics are identified in the report as requiring legislative actions are[56]: 1) intellectual property rights; 2) privacy; and 3) security of information (encryption and information security

Therefore this international trend clearly indicates the need for regulatory framework in the area of free speech, intellectual property especially copyright, privacy and security which are core human rights.

1.5.1 Key Regulatory issues for Sovereign States

Sovereignty is a component that constitutes 'State' under international law along with the other components such as 'people' and territory'. Sovereignty is supreme authority, which on the international plane means not legal authority over all other states but rather legal authority which is not in law dependent on any other authority. Sovereignty in the strict and narrowest sense of the term implies, therefore, independence all round, within and without the borders of the country.

The word "sovereign" means that the state has power to legislate on any subject in conformity with constitutional limitations[57].

Cyberspace is basically a telecommunication network. It is borderless and has caused the 'death of distance'[58]. In relation to the telecommunications sovereignty of a state is governed by the International Telecommunication Convention, 1984.

---

[55] Supra Note 12, p18
[56] Supra Note 12, p19
[57] Synthetics & Chemicals Ltd V State of UP (1990) 1 SCC 109
[58] Cairncross, Francis, The Death of Distance: How Communication Revolution will Change our Lives, Harvard Business School Publication, 1997

The object of the convention is to facilitate relations and cooperation between the peoples by means of efficient telecommunication services. The term telecommunication has been defined in Annexure II of the convention as follows;

Telecommunication: Any transmission, emission or reception of signs, signals, writing, images and sounds or intelligence of any nature by wire, radio, optical or other electromagnetic systems. The definition clearly encompasses the cyberspace as it is now.

With the development of information technology, telecommunications have become much more complex and much more important. The Washington Convention, 1973 and the General Radio Communications attached to the International Telecommunication Convention concluded in Madrid on 9th December 1932 and the European Broadcasting conventions of 19th June 1933 and 15th September 1948 has marked the beginning of attempts to regulate a domain of human activity which by its very nature transcends the borders of territorial state.

India, as a sovereign state has every right to regulate cyberspace but technology makes it impossible for its regulation. For that matter, no country can regulate the cyberspace effectively on its own. One school of thought suggests that cyberspace must be allowed for self-regulation. That is, entities of cyberspace must regulate themselves. It is pertinent to note here the remarks made by John Perry Barlow-

"Governments of the Industrial world , you weary giants of flesh and steel, I come from Cyberspace, the new home of the Mind On behalf of the fiaure, I ask you of the past to leave us alone. You are not welcome among us. You have no sovereignty where we gather[59] ."

Another school suggests controlling the architecture of Internet for the purpose of regulation. That is Hardware Control and Software control for regulation the cyberspace by the government[60]. This essentially means regulating the manufacturers of computer hardware and developers of software. Regulation of hardware manufacturers might affect their right to trade or business and regulation

---

[59] John Perry Barlow, A Declaration of the Independence of Cyberspace
http://www.eff.org/pub/Publications/John_Perry_Barlow/barlow0296.declaration , visited 13 Feb 2002

[60] Lessig , Lawrence, 'Code and Other Laws of Internet', Basic Books, New York, 1999

of software developers might mean regulation of their right to expression as software is protected under copyright law.

1.5.2 Regulation via Hardware

Johnson and Post assert that because "individual electrons can easily, and without any realistic prospect of detection, 'enter' any sovereign's territory," controlling the flow of electronic information across borders is impossible[61]. It is not clear, however, how this conclusion follows from the premise. First of all, at least for the Internet, electrons are not the relevant unit but Internet Protocol ("IP') packets are. And in order for IP packets to enter a particular territory, certain physical components must be present there. By exercising control over the physical components required for Internet access, the state can regulate cyberspace. At the most basic level, a state can simply choose not to have any connection to the Internet. Of course this means that the state must forego the considerable benefits of Internet communications, including electronic commerce and the increased prosperity it may bring. Nevertheless, states that fear for their ability to regulate the Internet could choose this option. As of July 1996, at least thirty-three states were completely unconnected. At another level, the state can compel the creation of a hierarchical network and then impose control over the top level router in that hierarchy (the gateway host). By controlling the gateway to a subnet, the state can regulate the Internet in its territory. It does not seem relevant whether government control of the gateway components is direct (the government owns the components) or indirect (the government regulates Internet service providers). The point is that where widespread usage of the Internet depends on physical components, a government that controls these components can regulate cyberspace[62].

---

[61] See David R, .Jhonson & David Post, Law and Borders :Rise of Law in Cyberspace, 48 STA. L. REv. 1367 (1996). David Johnson is former chairman of the EFF, and David Post is a Policy Fellow of the ElF. Both are coauthors of the Cyberspace Law Institute. See Cyberspace Law Institute , available at http://www.cli.org, visited 12 Jan 2003

[62] Wu S Timothy, Cyberspace Sovereignty – The Internet and the International system, Harvard Journal of Law & Technology, Volume 10, Number 3 Summer 1997

Of course the barriers imposed by gateway servers may be overcome. First, the user can use normal telephone lines to dial up a provider outside the subnet in question. Second, the user can send or receive encrypted information. Because it is nearly impossible for the government to determine the content of encrypted messages, regulation of such content will be difficult. However, these "exit options" from state control are probably of such a high cost, financially or in terms of necessary, expertise, as to render them marginal to the discussion. The best example of a country pursuing subnet-based regulation of the Internet is China[63]. With the help of several United States companies, China has already built two major government operated intranets connected to the rest of the Internet through a limited number of regulated servers, The China Wide Web, a subnet that will connect all of China's major population centers and provide Chinese language content, is supposed to begin operation soon. It too will have controlled contacts with the internet[64].

1.5.3 Regulation via Software

Another form of content regulation discussed by Johnson and Post is the software barrier, which they predict "will likely to fail as well". But again, the evidence for this view seems slender. There are two loci where software regulation is most effective one at the router[65] level and the other at the end user level. At the router level, Internet regulation is typically accomplished through use of a firewall, or comprehensive system of network filtration and control, implemented typically at a gateway router. A major component of a firewall system is what is called a packet filtration router. Such a router can filter out packets coming from or going to

---

[63] Freedom of Expression and the Internet in china: A Human Rights Watch Backgrounder, available at http://www.hrw.org , visited on 14 Apr 2005
[64] ibid
[65] In packet-switched networks such as the Internet, a router is a device or, in some cases, software in a computer, that determines the next network point to which a packet should be forwarded toward its destination. The router is connected to at least two networks and decides which way to send each information packet based on its current understanding of the state of the networks it is connected to. A router is located at any gateway (where one network meets another), including each point-of-presence on the Internet. A router is often included as part of a network switch. This definition is from SearchNetworking.Definitions, available at
http://searchnetworking.techtarget.com/sDefinition/0,,sid7_gci212924,00.html , visited on 3 Nov 2005

specific IP addresses. This allows the owner of the firewall system to prevent inside users from accessing outside sites, or vice versa. Much of what is considered the "free" Internet at present is already privately regulated through the use of firewalls, typically by corporations. There does not seem to be any intrinsic reason why nation states will "fail" using similar technology. As a part of the subnet system discussed above, China is presently investing considerable energy in the development of a "digital Great Wall of China " for its intranets using firewall technology developed by or with the assistance of United States companies. Singapore also relies on firewall technology, especially proxy servers. At the end-user level, the state can rely on what is called "end-user filtering software" to filter out content. Recently there has been enormous development in the sophistication of end-user filtration systems. Most significantly, wide adoption of the PICS[66] protocol would disallow both sensitive and harmful content thorough content filtration, at least for the World Wide Web. Where every site is reliably PICS rated, private individuals using PICS compatible browsers can elect to receive undesirable content based on several content variables, such as violence, sex, and so forth. Theoretically, such screening can be done with complete accuracy. End user filtering software may also be used to facilitate state control over Internet content. For example, a state could require by law that all browsers made available in the country come equipped with filtration software. This regulation would be easier to avoid than router regulation, because the filtration program would be in the hands of end users. Furthermore, pirated browsers would likely to proliferate. Yet insofar as the bundled filtration software served to increase the costs of exit from the state's rule set, such regulation will be another means by which the state can effectively regulate cyberspace.

China and Singapore furnish the paradigm for effective cyberspace regulation. The point here is not that the regulation exercised by China and Singapore is perfect, of course it is not. What matters is that, by all accounts, these nations have been able to limit the activity of ordinary users. So far these users have accepted the restrictions, or at least have not considered them worth complaining about. It might be argued

---

[66] Abbreviation for Platform for Internet Content Selection

that China and Singapore are bizarre examples of Internet regulation, made uniquely possible only by a combination of limited Internet connections and a strong government. Or perhaps because so many Asian countries are planning to or already regulate the internet, this can be considered a regional quirk. Yet many of the descriptive claims for cyberspace sovereignty seem plausible only in the face of a highly decentralized network and a limited government. Such features are characteristic of Western liberal democracy in general, and American society in particular; in the world's nations they are absent. There is a reason, then, to question the arguments for cyberspace sovereignty inasmuch as they seem to make sense only in particular contexts[67].

1.5.4 Application of Common Law Principles for Internet Regulation

Common law principles can be effectively used to regulate certain conduct of netizens over the cyberspace. Common law doctrines like Nuisance[68], Trespass[69], Negligence and Strict liability can be applied to control cyberspace activities.

Application of property law, with its ancient roots, to something as recently evolved as the Internet raises questions about the use of such antiquated laws in cyberspace. In spite of its "virtual" nature, the Internet readily lends itself to parallels with real property. Like real property, Internet sites are "fixed" in a cyberspace location. They are identified by an address, have definable borders and are capable of being exclusively controlled. Courts have also recognized these similarities by applying property law to cyberspace in upholding a registrant's property right in an Internet

---

[67] Wu S ,Timothy, Cyberspace Sovereignty – The Internet and the International system, Harvard Journal of Law & Technology, Volume 10, Number 3 Summer 1997

[68] For example Nuisance doctrine can be used to restrict 'SPAM'
[69] California Supreme Court applied Trespass doctrine in Intel Corp V Hamidi (1 Cal.Rptr. 3d 32(2003), available at http://cyber.law.harvard.edu/openlaw/intelvhamidi/ , visited 3 Feb 2004; this judgment was widely criticized citing the reason that in cyberspace every transaction amounts to 'trespass' in the traditional sense;

domain name, enabling claims of conversion for web sites, and enabling owners of web sites to bring claims of trespass to prevent unauthorized access to their site[70].

Critics of the chattels theory fear that allowing web site owners to exert control over who can access a web site and the means by which they can access that web site will have "disastrous implications for basic types of behavior fundamental to the Internet." Since open access to information on the Web has been, and continues to be, the lifeblood of the Internet, some fear the application of antiquated notions of property and trespass may threaten the critical interests of cyberspace. One of the most cited fears is that trespass doctrine, if applied to cyberspace, threatens the legality of the search engines that make finding useful information in the vast repository of the Internet feasible. What this argument fails to take into account, however, is that Internet standards and technology have already ranted web site owners the type of power needed to control access to their web sites. The law of trespass simply affirms and gives a legal framework to these rights[71].

It is also possible to use law of nuisance to prevent unsolicited e-mails, which are popularly known as SPAM, which are flooding e-mail accounts of netizens thereby irritating and harassing them. Sometimes they are also causing the netizens to delete their legitimate e-mails. Law as of now provides for opt-out option only, principle of nuisance can be effectively used to keep the spammers at bay.

1.5.5 Private Regulation

Private entities like Yahoo!, AOL, Google etc will play an increasingly large role in regulating space by prescribing policies for netizens[72]. They can reject or admit members based on their own polices. They also perform censoring speech of their members. They are actually deciding what is good or bad for their members. The

---

[70] Fricth M David, Click Here For Lawsuit- Trespass To Chattels in Cyberspace, Journal of Technology Law and Policy, Vol.9, Issue1, June 2004, available at http://grove.ulf.edu/~techlaw/vol9/issue1/fritch.html at p 2, Visited on 10 Dec 2005
[71] ibid at p 5
[72] Nunziato C, Dawn, The Death of Public Forum in Cyberspace, George Washington University Law School, available at www.papers.ssrn.org , visited on 2 Jan 2005

point to be noted here is that they are not subjected to any of the checks and balances that we usually associate with democratic governance[73]. And the relationship between these private actors and netizens is of contractual in nature and human rights of netizens cannot enforced easily.

There is no remedy available to aggrieved netizen as violations of human rights can be enforced only against state action. As a matter of legal doctrine, the question of how to apply constitutional or legal norms to private entities implicates the so called state-action or act of state doctrine. The most important question needs to be answered is that whether public-private distinction can be maintained in cyberspace?[74]

1.6 Human Rights in Cyberspace

The Internet is a unique communications medium. Like no other medium before, it allows individuals to express their ideas and opinions directly to a world audience and easily to each other, while allowing access to many more ideas, opinions and information than previous media have allowed. Consequently, there is a vital connection between the Internet and human rights[75].

Through the Internet, citizens from the most repressive regimes are able to find information about matters concerning their own governments and their human rights records that no newspaper may dare print, while denouncing the conditions under which they live, for the world to hear. The Internet allows an intimate look at other countries, other people and other cultures that few before were ever able to attain.

---

[73] Radin Jane, Margaret and Wagner Polk, R, The Myth of Private Ordering: Rediscovering Legal Realism in cyberspace, Chicago-Kent Law Review, Vol.1, 1999
[74] Bellia L, Patricia, Berman Schieff Paul, and Post G David, Cyberlaw: Problems of Policy & Jurisprudence in the Information Age, Thomson/west, USA, 2003
[75] Center for Democracy & Technology, The internet and the Human Rights: An Overview, available at http://www.cdt.org/international/000105humanrights.shtml , visited on 29 Jun 2004

This power to give and receive information, so central to any conception of democracy, can be truly achieved on the Internet, as nowhere before[76].

Further, through the use of encryption technology, citizens can have instantaneous communications with individuals all over the world that are much more resistant to government and private surveillance[77].

On the Internet, citizens are not mere consumers of content but also creators of content. This fundamental shift in power has created a possibility for every individual to be a publisher. Consequently, the content on the Internet is as diverse as human thought. Individuals and communities have been using the new-found freedom online to link, interact and work collectively in this global work space[78].

The effect of access to and use of this global interactive medium has been to promote and defend civil and political rights worldwide. This unprecedented power, however, can be very threatening to repressive regimes. The experiences of communities in different countries so far indicates that few things could be more threatening to authoritarian regimes than access and use of a medium that knows no boundaries and is very hard to control. While traditional methods of censorship - embargoing newspapers and closing down presses - do not work on the Internet, the online censoring techniques that these regimes attempt can be just as destructive[79].

While the Internet is technologically resistant to government control, it is not immune from such control. Indeed, some countries have been quite sophisticated in exploiting the control and surveillance potential to great effect, at least in the short run. Just because the younger generation may know how to "hack" through proxy servers to avoid censorship does not mean that the youth are safe. These actions

---

[76] Balkin M, Jack, Digital Speech and Democratic Culture: A Theory of Freedom of Expression for the Information society, 79 N.Y.U.L Rev1 (2004)
[77] Park, John E, Protecting the core values of the First amendment in an Age of New Technologies: Scientific Expression Vs. National security, Virginia Journal of Law and Technology, Va.J.L & Tech.3 (Fall 1997), available at http://vjolt.student.virginia.edu , visited on 3 Apr 2005
[78] ibid
[79] Human Rights in the Information Society, available at http://rights.jinbo.net/english/into.html , visited on 6 Nov 2005.

should be understood in the technological context - that such hacking is probably obvious to government system administrators, and may make people vulnerable to being identified and prosecuted. Meanwhile, nations around the world are seeking to exploit the surveillance potential of this new medium, including by asserting control over the design and development of communications networks to maximize their surveillance capabilities.

Some of the human rights concerns in cyberspace are related to Civil and Political Rights such as Free Speech, Defamation, Privacy and Economic Rights like right to enjoy the benefits of scientific, literary, artistic work etc discovery and creation are examined in this research work.

(a) Freedom of Expression

The Universal Declaration of Human Rights (UDHR), International Covenant on Civil and Political Rights (ICCPR), the European Convention and other international human rights agreements enshrine the rights to freedom of expression and access to information. These core documents explicitly protect freedom of expression "regardless of frontiers," a phrase especially pertinent to the global Internet:

"Everyone has the right to freedom of opinion and expression; this right includes freedom to hold opinions without interference and to seek, receive and impart information and ideas through any media, and **regardless of frontiers**." As stated in Article 19, Universal Declaration of Human Rights.

"Everyone shall have the right to freedom of expression; this right shall include freedom to seek, receive, and impart information and ideas of all kinds, regardless of frontiers, either orally, in writing or in print, in the form of art, or through any other media of his choice." As provided under Article 19, International Covenant on Civil and Political Rights.

"Everyone has the right to freedom of expression. This right shall include freedom to hold opinions and to receive and impart information and ideas without interference by public authority and regardless of borders." As provided under Article 10, European Convention for the Protection of Human Rights and Fundamental Freedoms.

No matter what the means, government restrictions on speech or access to speech of others violate basic freedom of expression protections. In addition to direct government censorship of Internet communications, or privatized censorship, freedom of speech in the Internet is threatened by diverse factors.

Blocking, filtering, and labeling techniques can restrict freedom of expression and limit access to information. Government-mandated use of blocking, filtering, and label systems violates basic international human rights protections. Global rating or labeling systems squelch (crush down) the free flow of information. Efforts to force all Internet speech to be labeled or rated according to a single classification system distort the fundamental cultural diversity of the Internet and will lead to domination of one set of political or moral viewpoints. Diversity and user choice are essential: To the extent that individuals choose to employ filtering tools, it is vital that they have access to a wide variety of such tools[80].

"Self-regulatory" controls over Internet content, which have been promoted by some as an alternative to government regulation, ought not to place private ISPs in the role of police officers for the Internet. With regards to content, what is being suggested in the name of "self-regulation" is not that ISPs should as a group regulates their own behavior, but rather that they should regulate the speech of their customers. This is not true "self-regulation." The role of an Internet Service Provider is crucial for access to the Internet and because of the crucial role that they play. ISPs have been targeted by law enforcement agencies in many countries to act as content censors. While ISPs ought to provide law enforcement reasonable

---

[80] A Starting Point: Legal implications of Internet Filtering, A Publication of the OpenNet Initiative, available at ,http://www.opennetinitiative.org , visited 12 Feb 2005.

assistance in investigating criminal activity, confusing the role of private companies and police authorities risks substantial violation of individual civil liberties[81].

(b) Privacy

The UDHR, ICCPR, the European Convention and international human rights instruments enshrine the right to privacy. These core documents explicitly protect the privacy of correspondence and communication:

"No one shall be subjected to arbitrary interference with his privacy, family, home or **correspondence,** nor to attacks upon his honor and reputation. Everyone has the right to the protection of the law against such interference or attacks."[82]

"No one shall be subjected to arbitrary or unlawful interference with his privacy, family, home or correspondence, nor to unlawful attacks on his honour and reputation."[83]

"Everyone has the right to respect for his private and family life, his home and his correspondence."[84]

Privacy is becoming increasingly important for citizens in the information society. Electronic communications can be very easily intercepted by anyone who wants to. Sending an e-mail message is thus the equivalent of sending a postcard. In the human rights arena especially, many matters discussed among NGOs are extremely confidential. Names of witnesses to human rights violations, for example, need to be kept from those who would harm them. Repressive governments commonly use

---

[81] Sunstein R, Cass, The First Amendment in Cyberspace, The Yale Law Journal, Vol.104, N0.7, May 1995, available at http://www.jstor.org/ , visited on 9 Jun 2006
[82] Article 12, Universal Declaration of Human Rights

[83] Article 17, International Covenant on Civil and Political Rights

[84] Article 8, European Convention for the Protection of Human Rights and Fundamental Freedoms

their intelligence services to tap the phone communications of human rights groups and intercept their mail. It is very likely that they are also intercepting electronic mail[85].

(c) Anonymity, Harassment and defamation

Central to free expression and the protection of privacy is the right to express political beliefs without fear of retribution and to control the disclosure of personal identity. Protecting the right of anonymity is therefore an essential goal for the protection of personal freedoms in the online world.

The right of anonymity is recognized in law and accepted by custom. It has been an integral part of the growth and development of the Internet. Some governments are working to extend techniques for anonymity[86]. But at the same time anonymity protection should not be abused. Defamatory speech, threatening speech, hate speech or speech aimed at harassing cannot be tolerated and these can be grounds for imposing restriction on free speech.

But other efforts are underway to establish mandatory identification requirements and to limit the use of techniques that protect anonymity. For example, the G-8 recently considered a proposal to require caller identification for Internet users. Some local governments have also tried to adopt legislation that would prohibit access to the Internet without the disclosure of personal identity.

Governments should not require the identification of Internet users or restrict the ability to express political beliefs on the Internet anonymously. Efforts to develop new techniques to protect anonymity and identity should be encouraged. ISPs should not establish unnecessary identification requirements for customers and

---

[85] Human Rights in the Information society, Right to Privacy Vs. Government's Surveillance available at http://rights.jinbo.net/english/privacy.html, visited on 11 June 2005
[86] Spencer H, Michael, Anonymous Internet Communication and the First Amendment: A Crack in the Dam of National Sovereignty, Virginia Journal of Law and Technology, 3 Va.J.L & tech (Spring 1998), available at http://vjolt.student.virginia.edu , visited on 3 Mar 2005

should, wherever practicable, preserve the right of users to access the Internet anonymously.

(d) Economic Rights – Democratic rights alone will not be sufficient to realize the full potential of human beings. Economic rights like to right to work which involves physical labor and right to enjoy the benefits of scientific discovery and creativity which are derived from mental labor must also be suitably protected to protect and promote the human rights of individuals. In this regard UN Convention on the Economic, Social and Cultural Rights, 1966 plays a vital role in the development of economic rights of individuals. This convention imposes a responsibility on the signatories under Art.11 to make available the scientific knowledge and its application to all the members of the society. Hence States in order to fulfill their obligations under Art.11 have to recognize and protect the rights of creators and inventors as provided under Art.15 of the Convention which reads as follows;

Article 15 -

1. The States Parties to the present Covenant recognize the right of everyone:
(a) To take part in cultural life;

(b) To enjoy the benefits of scientific progress and its applications;

(c) To benefit from the protection of the moral and material interests resulting from any scientific, literary or artistic production of which he is the author.

2. The steps to be taken by the States Parties to the present Covenant to achieve the full realization of this right shall include those necessary for the conservation, the development and the diffusion of science and culture.

3. The States Parties to the present Covenant undertake to respect the freedom indispensable for scientific research and creative activity.

4. The States Parties to the present Covenant recognize the benefits to be derived from the encouragement and development of international contacts and co-operation in the scientific and cultural fields.

Commercialization of internet has affected the rights of copyright holders and also created problems for trademark owners. Business method patents have become a reality owing to the nature of the e-commerce business models.

Economic rights in the intellectual field provide for incentive to invent, incentive to disclose, incentive to commercialize and incentive to design around[87].

Human rights discourse in the IPR regime has added a new approach to that analysis of the content and scope of IPR's[88]. As an embodiment of expressional act, IPR has important human rights dimension. Internet assists in the promotion of learning and research and at the same time it might impact upon the rights of copyright holders. Copyright law's basic inclination to support liberty and is an expressional freedom rather than a tool of censorship. Internationalization of intellectual property law with the same purpose, rather than treating it as sheer object of trade is contemplated in human rights philosophy[89].

(e) **Jurisdiction** – It is not enough for the State to recognize the basic human rights but it should also provide appropriate mechanism for enforcing them through competent courts. To determine the jurisdiction of the courts is very difficult owing to the multi-jurisdictionality nature of the Internet[90]. Determination of jurisdiction for the enforcement of rights cyberspace entities is vital but needs different treatment in this new environment.

---

[87] Chisum S Donald, Nard Allen Craig, Schwatrz F Herbert,Newman Pauline, Kieff Scott F, Cases and Materials : Principles of Patent law, Foundation Press, New York, 1998
[88] Bhat P, Ishwara, Historical Evolution and Development of IPR,1 KLJ [2005] at p, 6 (Kare Law Journal, Issue 1, November, 2005)
[89] ibid at p 7
[90] See generally Yahoo! Inc V LA LIGUE CONTRE LE RACISME ET L'ANTISEMITISME, A French Association, No.01-17424, D.CNo.cV-00-21275-JF, decided by northern District Court of California;

1.7 Protecting Human Dignity in the Digital Age

New technology offers opportunities both to expand and to limit the freedom to communicate and the opportunity to protect private life. For example, new digital networks can provide a high level of security and privacy through the incorporation of such techniques as encryption. The Secure Socket Layer in Internet browser software enables the secure transfer of credit card numbers and reduces the risk that "sniffer" programs will capture credit card numbers. But encryption is not widely used for personal email. As a result it is relatively easy to capture private messages sent over the Internet[91].

New technology can also enable anonymous transactions over the Internet so that individuals can obtain access to information and purchase products without disclosing actual identity. Some object to online anonymity and say that it could be a cloak for criminal conduct. But the question could fairly be asked why individuals should be required to disclose identity when such requirements did not exist in traditional information environments, such as the print world of newspapers and books or the broadcast world or radio and television[92].

Similar questions arise with the protocols for electronic mail services. Strong encryption products could ensure that individuals could exchange private messages with little concern that third parties would gain access to private messages. But slight modifications in these protocols, though such methods as "key escrow" or "key recovery" could enable the routine interception of personal communications[93].

Filtering techniques incorporated in the architecture of the Internet also raise far reaching questions about the character and impact of the new communication services. These programs allow government and private enterprises to restrict access

---

[91] Rotenberg,, Marc, Protecting Human Dignity in Digital Age, Electronic Privacy Information Center, www.epic.org , available at
www.webworld.unesco.org/infoethics2000/documents/study_rotenberg.rtf , visited on 3 Oct 2005
[92] ibid
[93] ibid

to information that is otherwise available. Such methods could limit access to a wide range of important cultural, medical, and scientific information. Already these techniques have been used to limit access to public information[94].

Just as these new technologies are emerging that could significantly influence the future of human dignity in the digital age, technical organizations are playing an increasingly significant role in the policy world. Simultaneously, international organizations are playing an increasingly important role in shaping the policies for the Internet[95].

The quality of human person in cyberspace or in real space involves right to dignified life, personal liberty, Freedom of speech and expression, Freedom of Assembly and association, Freedom of business, trade and occupation, Freedom of religion, Cultural and educational rights and property rights[96]. Protecting and promoting these fundamental human rights in cyberspace is vital for the development of internet and related technologies.

1.7.1 Main Challenges

New technology has always presented opportunities and risks. Industrialization promoted productivity and increased the standard of living in many parts of the world. Industrialization also caused enormous damage to the physical environment. Information technology also presents opportunity and risk. But the main challenges to human dignity in the digital age are not in the nature of the technology itself but in the capacity of individuals acting through democratic institutions to respond effectively to these new challenges.

---

[94] ibid
[95] ibid
[96] Bhat P, Ishwara, Fundamental Rights: A study of Their Interrelationship, Eastern Law House Pvt Ltd, Kolkata, 2004

These new challenges include the commercialization of the Internet, the growth of law enforcement authority, and the globalization of decision making authority. There is also a critical need to understand the appropriate relationship between the two central interests of privacy and free expression.

1.7.2 The Commercialization of the Internet

Since the development of the World Wide Web in 1993, the character of the Internet has changed. The graphical interface has made it easier for many organizations to take advantage of global computer networks, to establish an online presence and to exchange information and ideas in the digital world. Educational institutions, cultural associations, scientific societies and others have all benefited from the dramatic growth of network communications. The web has also made possible the rapid development of new commercial applications that include both business to business services and business to consumer services[97].

Commercialization of the Internet also poses the threat that rights which would otherwise be protected in the political sphere will be turned over to the marketplace and individuals will be forced to pay for services that might otherwise be routinely provided. A critical example is the confidentiality of correspondence. By tradition, communication services have assured the privacy of personal correspondence and personal communication. But commercial forces have found that the records of communications and the transactions generated in the interactive environment are valuable for marketing purposes. Moreover, in the absence of legislation clearly establishing the privacy of new electronic communications, service providers may choose to offers communication services without assurance of confidentiality[98].

Citizens may then be required to purchase confidentiality for routine personal communication or to forgo privacy for commercial benefit. Two classes of Internet

---

[97] Kasky V, Nike 27 Cal.4th 939 (2002), available on www.findlaw.com , visited on Aug 12, 2005
[98] ibid

users may emerge: the "privacy haves" and the "privacy have-nots." Inherent in the provision of new communications services should be that confidentiality will be protected in law.

Commercialization of the Internet may pose a different challenge to freedom of expression. Here the concern is that market concentration and the consolidation of commercial power could transform the decentralized character of the Internet and reduce the number of voices and the opportunities for non-commercial speakers to participate in the Digital Age. It is therefore appropriate to ensure the balance between these two entities[99].

Next challenge is related to the consumption of digital content in cyberspace. The availability of new techniques to track the use of copyright works in the digital environment; Copyright Management Systems, digital Rights management etc will be used to track the interests of Internet users. Such systems should be developed so as to permit compensation of copyright holders without the compelled disclosure of the identity of Internet users. In this context, anonymity protects both privacy and free expression.

1.8 Hypotheses and Research Questions

For the first decade or so after the development of computer networks and related communications technologies, there was little need for policymakers to pay attention to activities taking place in cyberspace. Back then, the user community was, for the most part, a relatively homogenous group of researchers at universities and commercial laboratories who tended to use the networks to communicate the results of their work or work in progress and not to cause trouble. Once networking and other technologies evolved to the point that ordinary people could easily use the network, and once the National Science Foundation (NSF) lifted the earlier ban on

---

[99] Johnson E H, Bruce, California's "Creeping Commercial Speech": Kasky Decision Attacks Business Participation in public Debates, available at
http://library.findlaw.com/2002/Aug/6/132599.html , visited on 22 July 2005

commercial activities on the networks, policymakers came to realize that they would have to decide how to regulate this new medium of communication[100].

Keeping the above in mind the Hypothesis for the research work is formulated as follows;

" **Legal and Regulatory model for the protection , promotion and enforcement of human rights of cyberspace entities is possible only with the co-operation of sovereign nation-states, who should collaborate, and act together to decide on appropriate best practices, models and legislation to handle human right issues in cyberspace; and to strengthen the international legal system and establish international institutions to meet the challenges posed by new information and communication technologies for the national and international legal regimes"**

Following Research Questions have been raised in order to test the Hypothesis;

(a) **Freedom of Speech and Expression**: - Should the Online world continue to be a freewheeling, unregulated "market place of ideas" or things have gone out of control? If restrictions are appropriate, what steps should be taken? What is the standard of obscenity or indecency?

(b) **Anonymity & Harassment:** - What is the nature of threats posed by online flamers, cyber stalkers and online harassers? What steps might be taken to keep cyberspace safe and to prevent hate and hatreds?

(c) **Privacy**: - Why are electronic privacy rights so much weaker than analogous rights in other venues? Does the public care? Should the public care? How judiciary has responded to the threat of privacy?

---

[100] Samuelson, Pamela, Five Challenges for Regulating Global Information Society. This paper is based on a presentation given at a conference on Communications Regulation in the Global Information Society held at the University of Warwick in June of 1999.

(d) **Intellectual Property**: - How applicable are traditional copyright laws in an environment where reproduction and distribution of someone else's creations can occur with ease impunity? How right holder interest can be balanced with the rights of the public in digital communication environment? Do information technologies tilting the balance in favour of right holders?

(e) **Jurisdiction**: - With cyberspace existing beyond state lines and beyond international borders, what laws are applicable and in what context? And even if these questions are resolved, how can such laws are enforced? How human rights of cyberspace entities can be enforced?

1.9 Methodology

Doctrinal method has been employed to do the research work. Research involves analysis of case law, arranging, ordering and systematizing legal propositions and study of adjudicatory decisions of legal institutions.

Authoritative books on cyber law, national legislations, statutes of states, Government reports and international treaties were part of the primary source of research and internet, journals, articles, periodicals, Private Institutions reports were used as secondary sources of research.

A critical and analytical method was employed in the analysis of the RIGHTS of the entities involved keeping in view of the judicial decisions of US, European countries and Indian courts.

Internet was invented by the US Government initiative and US courts had the first opportunity to examine and determine the legal issues raised by internet technology. Hence most of the research work uses US court decisions and legislations for the purpose of analysis.

1.10 Significance of Research

The importance of the study lies in the fact that the existing regulatory norms are found to be inadequate to deal with new facts situations created by digital environment. This is clear from the Yahoo! France where freedom of speech and expression issues were involved and while dealing with this issue American and French courts have taken a diagonally opposite view. In addition to free speech issues, privacy, security and intellectual property rights have also become issues of concern for the legal systems. Human rights of the Netizens have to be placed at the higher level of legal norms so that these guaranteed rights in the real world remain intact , when they go 'online' in cyberspace. Legal restrictions that should be imposed on online defamers, harassers etc are also inadequate and there is an urgent need to deal with cyber crimes. The purpose of the study is to address theses kinds of problems to find out possible effective solutions and restricted to the examination of basic human rights.

The Information Technology Act 2000 of India has laid emphasis on e-commerce and has not addressed various other issues such as free speech, right to reputation, privacy, intellectual property rights, jurisdiction etc.

Conflicting judicial decisions of American courts and European courts over cyberspace activities have added to the difficulties of regulating cyberspace.

In this regard it is desirable to examine the existing legal frame work and develop regulatory norms from the global and national perspective. The purpose of the study is to identify the difficulties posed by these new technologies to law and to make an attempt to find out the effective legislative measures required to be adopted to regulate the cyberspace activities.

1.11 Structure of the Research work

There are seven chapters including the first introductory chapter. In the introductory **Chapter 1,** titled as **"The world of Cyberspace",** I have identified some important human rights issues which need to be protected and promoted in cyberspace for the effective utilization of internet technology. Basically research involves around Freedom of Expression extending to other collateral rights of right to privacy, right to reputation and copyright.

In this chapter relationship between law and technology has been highlighted. Technology has been an instrument of social change and internet technology is no exception to this rule. I have also discussed the historical events that led to the invention of internet. Some technical aspects of the internet are also covered. The major features of internet, anonymity and multijurisdictionality have been analyzed to understand the nature of internet. The impact of internet on society is illustrated. The debate that whether we should really need have a cyberlaw between Judge Frank Easterbrook and Larence Lessig is analyzed and an attempt has been made to answer the question. I have also discussed the kind of regulation that may be required to regulate the conduct of cyberspace entities and current thinking among the legal scholars regarding regulation and control. A hypothesis is formulated and research questions have been raised in this chapter. This chapter also includes methodology adopted for research and significance of research work.

Chapter 2, titled as **"Freedom Speech in Cyberspace",** discusses the fundamental human right, freedom of speech and expression in cyberspace and the extent of protection and promotion offered so far and the prohibition of obscene speech in the light of Communication Decency Act, 1996 of US. In this chapter I have discussed various justifications for free speech protection and its importance in a democratic society as a basic human right. The chapter also covers and highlights protection and promotion of free speech under international and national laws. Various case laws decided by Indian courts and US courts are discussed to understand the extent to which restrictions can be imposed on exercising freedom of speech and expression in India. The chapter also covers various channels that are available on the internet for expression. The highlight of the chapter is the right of adults to indecent material that is largely available on the internet. Invalidation of Sec.230 of CDA has upheld the right of the adults to porn like material. US congress attempt to stall the distribution of obscene material has taken beating by the decision of US Supreme Court in Reno V ACLU. I have also discussed the Miller test of US and Hecklin test of India, to analyze what constitutes obscene material. Various attempt made by the US Congress in protecting the interest of children and women against harmful material have also been analyzed.

Chapter 3, titled as **"Cyber Defamation, Anonymity and Hate Speech",** is an extension of chapter 2 and deals with anonymity, defamation and harassment in cyberspace and analyzes the basis on which restrictions are being imposed on free speech. No right is absolute. Free speech cannot used to harm the reputation of others. But there is a difficulty in drawing the line between harmful speech and the right speech. Over the internet one can be defamed by just clicking a button. The standards used to determine whether speech is harmful vary from country to country. Australian courts making an attempt punish the American defendant is an example in this regard. In this chapter I have focused on the application of traditional rules to online world and examined the difficulties in their application. Right to speak anonymously is another human right that has assumed greater significance with the advent of internet. This right is examined keeping in view with the current judicial trends in US.

Chapter 4, titled as **"Privacy in Cyberspace",** focuses on another important fundamental human right, right to privacy. Protection of privacy interest in cyberspace through existing legislations and judicial decisions and its adequacy is being examined here. American consumers have been actively participating in the commodification of personal data. The tussle between US and EU in sharing personal data is analyzed and safe harbor treaty between US and EU is highlighted. Treatment of informational privacy as human right by EU is the core idea discussed in this chapter. I have also discussed Fair Information Practices and focused on OECD guidelines for collection and dissemination of personal data. These Principles must be made part of the national law also. It is not the collection of the data that matters, it is the use and dissemination of personal data that might harm the interest of the cyberspace entities. Experience has shown that, through various consumer surveys conducted, consumers can be easily lured to disclose their personal data by offering small gifts by the marketing companies. Legislative attempts by US Congress in the form of Privacy Act have been discussed along with limitations of the Privacy Act. A balance needs to be maintained between marketer's right to collect personal data and the right to privacy of the individuals.

Chapter 5, titled as **"Intellectual Property Rights in Cyberspace",** is about protecting economic human rights of creators and innovators in cyberspace. Protection of intellectual property rights, particularly in the area of copyright is the major point of discussion in this chapter. Most blatantly violated human right in cyberspace is copyright. Majority of the cases that come to the courts are related to copyright violations. Copyright violations have indirectly impacted on trade names and domain names. Judicial decisions in leading cases like Napster, where P2P sharing held to be invalid, and MGM V Grokster are used to identify and analyze the difficulties faced by right holders in the new digital environment. Tilting of traditional balance by the Digital Rights Management System is also discussed. The effects of DMCA on consumers and right holders are also analyzed. Advent of commerce in cyberspace has resulted in granting patents to business methods, which are expressly barred in many countries.

Chapter 6, titled as **"Jurisdiction",** is concerned with the enforcement of human rights mentioned above. It deals with the problem of multijurisdictionality and an attempt has been to suggest the possible solutions to resolve the jurisdictional problems in this borderless medium of communication. Yahoo! France case and John Doe cases have raised lot of issues relating to international jurisdiction. The problem of jurisdiction actually provides an opportunity to create international agencies to take care of these issues. This again brings back the importance of international law in dealing with the human rights of cyberspace entities. If international law is, in some ways, at the vanishing point of law, the problem of jurisdiction created by the internet technology is bringing back the need and showing the necessity of having a body of international law by its global nature. Taking this point into account I have discussed and analyzed various solutions offered by different scholars which might act as guidelines for policy makers. It is pertinent to note here that promotion and protection of human rights in cyberspace would become meaningless if there is no mechanism to enforce them. Hence jurisdiction assumes greater significance in the study of cyberspace.

In the last chapter (**Chapter 7- Conclusion**), findings of the research have been highlighted. An attempt has been made to answer all the research questions raised in the first chapter. Some of the observation and recommendations based upon my study have been provided under the recommendations in this report.

Chapter 2

FREEDOM OF SPEECH IN CYBERSPACE

Governments of the Industrial World, you weary giants of flesh and steel, We come from cyberspace ....We are creating a world where anyone, anywhere may express his or her beliefs, no matter how singular, without fear of being coerced into silence or conformity.

John Perry Barlow[101]

2.1 Introduction

Freedom of Expression is one of the most universally recognized and prominent rights in all democratic legal systems. The right to impart and receive information has long been a cornerstone of human rights law, and of democratic theory[102]. On 26th August 1789, , the architects of the French Revolution issued the Declaration of the Rights of Man, which secured the right of citizens to communicate ideas and opinions freely, and which right has been retained virtually unchanged throughout the history of democracy. Almost exactly a month later, the United States, declared free speech to be fundamental to its nascent political structure by amending its recently adopted Constitution to protect that right explicitly[103]. Over a century and a half later, the United Nations' Universal Declaration of Human Rights (UDHR) recognized the right to free speech[104]. Similarly International Covenant on Civil and Political Rights (ICCPR) and European Convention on Human Rights have upheld the significance and importance of freedom of expression. Although the protection of freedom of expression was not given prominence in most western democracies fifty or even thirty years ago, recent developments indicate that most democracies

---

[101] John Perry Barlow is a retired Wyoming cattle rancher, a former lyricist for the Grateful Dead, and co-founder of the Electronic Frontier Foundation. Since May of 1998, he has been a Fellow at Harvard Law School's Berkman Center for Internet and Society.
[102] Brian W Esler, Human Rights in the Digital age, (ed.,Mathias Klang & Andrew Murray), Cavendish Publishing Ltd., US, 2005
[103] ibid
[104] Art.19, UDHR

have started developing protective freedom of expression jurisprudence in the past ten to twenty-five years[105].

2.2 Freedom of Speech and Expression – Justifications

Right to free speech as invaluable fundamental right of human beings can be justified on several grounds. The liberty to express one's self freely is important for a number of reasons[106], which help to shape development and application of law on freedom of expression[107]. The main free speech justifications are widely referred as the classical model. This model offers explanations regarding the core of free speech, the speech truly valued by society[108]. In this research work we have considered five justifications for the protection of free speech viz., freedom of conscience, personal identity and self-fulfillment, market place of ideas, democracy and self-governance, and right to self-expression which includes artistic and scholarly endeavor.

---

[105] See Fredick Schauer, Freedom of Expression of Adjudication in Europe and the United Sates: A case study in Comparative constitutional Architecture, in Europe and US constitutionalism, 53-56 Edited by George Nolte, Council of Europe Publishing 2005

[106] Supreme Court of India has provided certain insights as to the significance of Freedom of expression and the purpose it serves in society in Indian Express Newspapers (Bombay) Pvt. Ltd. and Ors. v. Union of India and Ors. MANU/SC/0340/1984. The Court observed that The freedom of expression has four broad social purposes to serve; (i) it helps an individual to attain self fulfillment, (ii) it assists in the discovery of truth, (iii) it strengthens the capacity of an individual in participating in decision-making and (iv) it provides a mechanism by which it would be possible to establish a reasonable balance between stability and social change. All members of the society should be able to form their own beliefs and communicate them freely to others. In sum, the fundamental principle involved here is the people's right to know. Freedom of speech and expression should, therefore, receive a generous support from all those who believe in the participation of people in the administration.

[107] Barendt .E, Freedom of Speech, Oxford-Clarendon Press, London,1987

[108] Carmi E Guy, Dignity-The Enemy from within: A theoretical and Comparative Analysis of Human Dignity as a Free Speech Justification, University of Pennsylvania Journal of Constitutional Law, Vol. 9, No. 4, 2007 , available at http://papers.ssrn.com/sol3/papers.cfm?abstract_id=896162 , visited on 14 May 2006

2.2.1 Freedom of conscience, Personal identity and Self-fulfillment

First, self-expression is a significant instrument of freedom of conscience, personal identity, and self-fulfillment. From the point of view of civil liberties, this is probably the most important justification which can be offered for free speech. The commitment to liberty lies mainly in the idea of individual autonomy, an ability to live a life according to choices consciously made between a reasonable range of options. The freedom to choose between values, to have fun through communication, to identify and be identified with particular values or ideas, and to live one's life according to one's choice, is the essence of liberty. Freedom of expression has an important role to play here. If one takes seriously one's choice of values, it will be important to be able to express them through words and actions alike. Such expression does not only serve the instrumental goal of persuading others or advancing understanding. It is also the means by which people acknowledge and start to put into effect their commitments to selected values and choices, thereby defining an important aspect of their personal identities. In all such cases expression has to be protected. Some expressions, verbal or written textual outpourings do not merit protection because they do not express any choice between values. For this reason, Edwin Baker has argued that, while the First amendment to the US Constitution 'bars certain governing nonverbal conduct, it does not bar controls on commercial speech including advertising[109]. The commercial speech is not substantially valuable as they are not expressions of life choices but are, at best, instrumentally useful ways of exercising commercial freedom, or informing potential purchasers about products. This would be a more powerful argument if the liberty model were the only theoretical framework for justifying protection for freedom of expression, but it is not[110]. There are others, which overlap with it in

---

[109] Baker C E, Human Liberty and Freedom of Speech, Oxford University Press, London, 1989 at p 73
[110] Feldman, David, Civil Liberties and Human Rights in England and Wales, 2nd Edition, Oxford University Press, UK, 2002, at 763

core areas, but also extend it to justify free speech on other grounds at the peripheries[111].

2.2.2 Discovery and Truth- Market place of ideas

The second justification can be drawn from the "discovery and truth" model suggested by John Stuart Mill[112] in his work "On Liberty". This model, also known as "market place of ideas" since it suggests that in a free market the exchange of ideas will enable the truth to be established[113]. Oliver Wendell Holmes and Louis Brandeis of US Supreme Court have justified free speech on this idea[114]. Freedom of expression enables people to contribute to debates about social and moral values. It is arguable that the best way to find the best or truest theory or model of anything is to permit the widest possible range of ideas to circulate[115]. The interplay of these ideas, challenging each other and allowing the strengths and weaknesses of each to be exposed , is more likely than any alternative strategy to lead to the best possible

---

[111] ibid at p763

[112] Mill, John Stuart. *On Liberty*. Vol. XXV, Part 2. The Harvard Classics. New York: P.F. Collier & Son, 1909–14; Bartleby.com, 2001, available at www.bartleby.com/25/2/. Visited 3 Nov 2003

[113] Adams V United Sates, 250 US 616, 630(1919) (Holmes J, dissenting) , available at http://www.realcampaignreform.org/decision/thomas.pdf, visited 4 Dec 2004 . In this case Holmes J, proposed the now-famous theory of market place of ideas : But when men have realized that time has upset many fighting faiths, they may come to believe even more than they believe the very foundations of their own conduct that the ultimate good desired is better reached by free trade in ideas—that the best test of truth is the power of the thought to get itself accepted in the competition of the market, and that truth is the only ground upon which their wishes safely can be carried out. That at any rate is the theory of our Constitution. It is an experiment, as all life is an experiment. . . . While that experiment is part of our system I think that we should be eternally vigilant against attempts to check the expression of opinions that we loathe and believe to be fraught with death, unless they so imminently threaten immediate interference with the lawful and pressing purposes of the law that an immediate check is required to save the country. He held that defendant could not constitutionally be convicted because – " nobody can suppose that the surreptitious publishing of silly leaflet by an unknown man, without more, would present any immediate danger that its opinion would hinder the success of the government arm....."

[114] Voon, Tania, Online Pornography in Australia: Lessons from the First Amendment – [2001] UNSWLJ 15

[115] Feldman, David, Civil Liberties and Human Rights in England and Wales, 2nd Edition, Oxford University Press, UK, 2002, at 764

conclusion[116]. This treats freedom of expression as an instrumental value, advancing other goods, that is, development of the true or good ideas, with a consequential benefit for the individual and society[117].

Stuart Mill argued on utilitarian grounds that there was a distinction in principle between facts and opinion. When dealing with opinions, all should be freely expressed, subject to any restrictions necessary to protect against identifiable harm. This wide freedom would benefit individuals by allowing them to choose between the widest possible range of opinions, where none could be definitively shown to be right or wrong, maximizing personal autonomy. It would also extend freedom of political choice, and bolster democratic process by encouraging rational debate which, it was confidently expected, would render it more likely that the best solution would be found for any problem[118]. Assertions of fact, on the other hand, could by definition be either true or false[119]. There would be good reason to allow free expression of truth, as this would lead to advances in knowledge and material improvements in society, but this does not justify permitting free expression of falsehoods. However, it is not always possible to say whether an assertion is true or false, and many benefits may flow from allowing statements of facts to be asserted so that they may be tested, even if they are ultimately found to be false[120]. This cannot in itself justify the publication of factual claims which are known to be false, but on a utilitarian rule analysis the benefits of general principle permitting freedom of expression are held to outweigh the disbenefits resulting from express opinions and facts, even if future, rather than to adopt a general rule which permits censorship and coercion in relation to expression.

This approach is sometimes linked with the notion of market place of ideas, in which the best win through the operation of market forces. The market place theory was influential in the USA, where it was developed by the Supreme Court to justify First amendment protection for unpopular speech, such as advocacy of racist

---

[116] ibid at p 764
[117] ibid at p 764
[118] ibid at p 765
[119] ibid at p 765
[120] This is particularly important in the physical sciences if one accepts Karl Popper's portrayal of scientific advance as occurring through the testing of factual hypotheses. See K.Popper, The Logic of Scientific Discovery , Hutchinson, London, 1959

theories by the Ku Klux Klan[121], but also to deny protection to those forms of expression- such as obscenity- which were regarded as offering nothing worthwhile to the market place of ides, and so having no redeeming social merit[122]. Obscenity was considered to be useful, it at all, only as a sex aid.[123] However, the fact that it adds nothing valuable to the market place of ideas does not necessarily mean that obscenity or any other form of expression ought not to be protected[124]. A privacy issue then arises , even if the material is of purely prurient interest and is resorted to as an aid to, let us say, masturbation, it is hard to see how the state can have a sufficient interest in its effects to justify making it unavailable for use by consenting adults[125].

The market-place-of-ideas model has implications for commercial speech. In a market economy, commercial speech, including advertising, may be useful in order to permit information about products and the relative merits of commercial competitors to be promulgated, facilitating informed choices by customers. This in a liberal society with a market economy, freedom of expression could be thought to support an important aspect of collective economic life[126]. This depends on the assumption the information will be presented to the markets, through advertising, in a way which enables potential customers to choose between products. That is, of course, highly questionable. We have seen very successful advertisements giving very little information about the products. Magazine and poster advertisements for cigarettes (TV advertisements banned in India) rely almost wholly on image, and purposely give no information (save the health warning required by law) about the qualities of the product. The same applies to most liquor advertisements. The

---

[121]Bradenburg v Ohio 395 US 444 (1969), available at
http://caselaw.lp.findlaw.com/scripts/getcase.pl?court=US&vol=395&invol=444, visited on 23 Sep 2004
[122] Roth V United Staes 354 US 476 (1957), available at
http://caselaw.lp.findlaw.com/scripts/getcase.pl?court=US&vol=354&invol=476 , visited 26 Nov 2004
[123] Supra Note 107
[124] Supra Note 109 at p 622

[125] ibid at p 766
[126] ibid at p 767

argument does not justify protection for all commercial speech, unless one takes the view that, on a utilitarian analysis, the social costs involved in vetting commercial speech would outweigh the benefits[127].

In reality this approach is not without its limitations. The free speech does not always produce truth, and protecting Nazi messages or pornography demands some justification other than truth discovery. Similarly, by itself, this justification does not explain clearly why statements of mere opinion that are neither true nor false should be protected[128].

2.2.3 Democracy and Self-governance

The third justification for free expression is that it allows the political discourse which is necessary in any country which aspires to be a democracy. This justification based on democracy[129] and self-governance is most closely identified with the work of Alexander Meiklejohn[130]. This approach reinforces the personal autonomy justification by mandating protection for the political expression of those who regard participating in politics as an aspect of their self-fulfillment as people and citizens. The power of this justification depends on the view which one adopts about the structural arrangements which democracy entails. A democratic rationale for freedom of expression makes perfect sense if applied to a society in which the operative model of democracy is one in which the people have the right to participate directly in day-to-day governmental decision making, or to have their

---

[127] ibid at p 767

[128] Wojceiech Sadurski, Freedom of Speech and its Limits, (1999) quoted by Tania Voon, Online Pornography in Australia:Lessons from the First Amendment – [2001] UNSWLJ 15

[129] Justifying the importance of Freedom of expression, Supreme Court of India in S. Rangarajan V. P. Jagjivan Ram and Ors. MANU/SC/0475/1989, observed that the democracy is a government by the people via open discussion. The democratic form of government itself demands its citizens an active and intelligent participation in the affairs of the community. The public discussion with people's participation is a basic feature and a rational process of democracy which distinguishes it from all other forms of government.

[130] See generally, Alexander Meiklejohn, Free Speech and its Relation to Self-Government, Harper& Brothers, US, 1948.

views considered in the choice of policies by government[131]. It works less well if the prevailing model for the way in which it has used power. The representative system, such as we have in India, would offer less support to free expression rights than a participatory system.

For any democratic process a measure of free speech coupled with right to information is sine qua non for its success. As the Privy Council observed in Hector V Attorney-General of Antigua and Barbuda[132]:

"In a free democratic society it is almost too obvious to need stating that those who hold office in government and who are responsible for public administration must always be open to criticism. Any attempt to stifle or fetter such criticism amounts to political censorship of the most insidious and objectionable kid..../ It is no less obvious that the very purpose of criticism leveled at those who have the conduct of public affairs by their political opponents is to undermine public confidence in their stewardship and to persuade the electorate that the opponents would make viewing a statutory provision which criminalizes statements likely to undermine public confidence in the conduct of public affairs with the utmost suspicion."[133]

Democratic theory, however, has been subject to its own ambiguities. The constitutional meaning of self-government has proved intensely controversial. It is of course generally agreed that democracy subsists in the people governing themselves, but historically there have been two competing accounts of the practice of self-determination, each with different implications for Freedom of speech and expression.

One account, associated with the work of Alexander Meiklejohn, views democracy as a process of "the voting of wise decisions."[134] The First Amendment is

---

[131] Supra Note 109 ; The problem lies with the definition of the term democracy. Even China calls itself as Republic of China but imposes huge burden on free speech. Recently Chinese Government ordered web search giant Google to censor certain category of information. In response to Chinese order Google's launched a new, self-censored search engine in China. This has been regarded as a "black day" for freedom of expression in China by leading international media watchdogs. See "Google move 'Black day for China'" available at BBC NEWS: available at http://news.bbc.co.uk/go/pr/fr/-2/hi/technology/4647398.stm ,visited on 25 July 2006
[132] [1990] 2 ALL ER 103
[133] [1990] 2 ALL ER at 106
[134] Post, Robert, Reconciling Theory and Doctrine in First Amendment Jurisprudence, California Law Review, Vol.89, January, 2001

understood to protect the communicative processes necessary to disseminate the information and ideas required for citizens to vote in a fully informed and intelligent way. Meiklejohn analogizes democracy to a town meeting; the state is imagined as a moderator, regulating and abridging speech "as the doing of the business under actual conditions may require."[135] For this reason "abusive" speech, or speech otherwise inconsistent with "responsible and regulated discussion," can and should be suppressed[136]. From the Meiklejohnian perspective, "the point of ultimate interest is not the words of the speakers, but the minds of the hearers," so that the First Amendment is seen as safeguarding collective processes of decision making rather than individual rights. Meiklejohn summarizes this assumption in a much quoted and influential aphorism: "What is essential is not that everyone shall speak, but that everything worth saying shall be said."[137]

The alternative account of democracy, which we can call the "participatory" theory, does not locate self-governance in mechanisms of decision making, but rather in the processes through which citizens come to identify a government as their own[138]. According to this theory, democracy requires that citizens experience their state as an example of authentic self-determination. How such an experience can be sustained presents something of a puzzle, because citizens can expect to disagree with many of the specific actions of their government[139]. The solution to this puzzle must be that citizens in a democracy experience their authorship of the state in ways that are anterior to the making of particular decisions. The participatory account postulates that it is a necessary precondition for this experience that a state be structured so as to subordinate its actions to public opinion, and that a state be constitutionally prohibited from preventing its citizens from participating in the communicative processes relevant to the formation of democratic public opinion.

If, following the usage of the Court, we term these communicative processes "public discourse," then the participatory approach views the function of the First

---

[135] ibid at p 22
[136] ibid at p 22
[137] ibid at p 23
[138] Post, Robert, Equality and Autonomy in First Amendment Jurisprudence, 95 Mich.L.Rev.1517,1523(1997)
[139] ibid p 1518

Amendment to be the safeguarding of public discourse from regulations that are inconsistent with democratic legitimacy. State restrictions on public discourse can be inconsistent with democratic legitimacy in two distinct ways. First, to the extent that the state cuts off particular citizens from participation in public discourse, it *pro tanto* negates its claim to democratic legitimacy with respect to such citizens[140]. Second, to the extent that the state regulates public discourse so as to reflect the values and priorities of some vision of collective identity, it preempts the very democratic process by which collective identity is to be determined.

Although both the Meiklejohnian and participatory perspectives share the common problem of specifying which communication is necessary for self-government and hence worthy of constitutional protection, they differ in at least two fundamental respects[141]. First, the Meiklejohnian approach interprets the First Amendment primarily as a shield against the "mutilation of the thinking process of the community," whereas the participatory approach understands the First Amendment instead as safeguarding the ability of individual citizens to participate in the formation of public opinion[142]. The Meiklejohnian theory thus stresses the quality of public debate, whereas the participatory perspective emphasizes the autonomy of individual citizens[143].

Second, the Meiklejohnian perspective imagines the state within the arena of public discourse as occupying the position of a neutral moderator, capable of saving public discourse from "mutilation" by distinguishing between relevant and irrelevant speech, abusive and non-abusive speech, high and low value speech, and so forth. It specifically repudiates the notion that public discourse is filled with "unregulated talkativeness." The participatory approach, in contrast, denies that there can be any possible neutral position within public discourse, because public discourse is precisely the site of political contention about the nature of collective identity, and it is only by reference to some vision of collective identity that speech can be categorized as relevant or irrelevant, abusive or not abusive, high or low value. The

---

[140] ibid
[141] ibid
[142] Supra Note 130
[143] ibid at p 26

participatory theory understands national identity to be endlessly controversial, so that national identity cannot without contradiction provide grounds for the censorship of public discourse itself[144].

In both of these respects the Meiklejohnian perspective is structurally quite analogous to the theory of the marketplace of ideas. Both theories focus primarily on maintaining the integrity of processes of collective thinking. The Meiklejohnian approach seeks to safeguard the dialogue necessary for voting wise decisions; the theory of the marketplace of ideas seeks to protect the dialogue necessary for advancing truth. Just as Holmes J, in his *Abrams* dissent stressed that in proposing the theory of the market-place of ideas he was "speaking only of expressions of opinion and exhortations,"[145] so contemporary

Meiklejohnians seek to distinguish "between cognitive and non-cognitive aspects of speech" and to award "less constitutional protection" to the latter. Both theories are keenly aware of the prerequisites for constructive thinking. Just as Dewey viewed "ridicule, abuse, and intimidation" as incompatible with rational discussion so also Meiklejohn viewed "abusive" speech as incompatible with a well ordered town meeting[146].

2.2.4 Right to self-expression

Fourthly, it has been suggested that it is good for people to be forced to respect each other's right to self-expression, especially if they disapprove of the way it is being exercised, because it helps to develop a capacity for tolerance[147]. This, it is said can be done most easily in the relatively harmless sphere of speech acts, making it more likely that people will extend the same attitude to other fields which are not as obviously harmless[148]. This controversially assumes both that speech is relatively harmless often, but not always, the case and that tolerance is one filed can and should be translated into tolerance of other activities. Alternatively, accepting that

---

[144] ibid
[145] ibid
[146] ibid
[147] Feldman, David, Civil Liberties and Human Rights in England and Wales, 2nd Edition, Oxford University Press, UK, 2002, at 766
[148] ibid

speech is sometimes dangerously harmful, it can be argued that allowing harmful speech stimulates opponents of racist or sexist speech to campaign in ways which ultimately overcome the harm and revolutionize the law and society[149].

Finally, freedom of expression facilitates artistic and scholarly endeavor of all sorts. This is not, perhaps, a separate head of justification. It is a specialized form of the first and second heads, and depends on accepting that art and scholarship are valuable in their own right[150].

These justifications draw mainly on three values: personal autonomy, which is served by maximizing the range of information and choice of opinions to which people have access; truth, which may be advanced by full information and open debate (this would be meaningful if conducted under conditions of fairness in which no one ideology is permitted to dominate or dictate the terms of the discussion) and democracy , which depends on some choice at least being available in the market-place of ideas, as well as drawing strength from the combination of personal autonomy of electors legislators in the political sphere and the hope that it will lead to the selection of the 'best' or 'most true' policies. For example, where a government proposes to introduce a law regulating commercial advertising, the autonomy of consumer choice favours free advertising, subject to any controls needed to ensure that people are not misled by false claims which advertisers might make for products[151]. Were there no constraints on freedom of expression, the difficulty would arise that one of the objects of upholding free expression- truth could be defeated if it were in a person's commercial interest to do so. There is an element, as the Committee on Obscenity and Film Censorship[152] noted, of bad expressive coinage driving out of the good, and it is important to regulate expression to limit the extent to which this can happen.

While theorists disagree regarding which identifiable values ought to be given precedence over other, the 'truth' and 'democratic' arguments are generally

---

[149] ibid
[150] ibid at 767
[151] ibid
[152] Report of the Committee on Obscenity and Film Censorship (Chairman: Prof Bernard Williams), Cmnd.7772 (London :HMSO, 1979)

perceived as the most powerful free speech justifications, especially in the United States[153].

2.3 The Nature of Free Speech in International and National Law

The right to freedom of expression is protected by all the major international human rights instruments. In Art.19 of the UN Universal Declaration of Human Rights (UDHR) and Art.10[154] of the European Convention on Human Rights (ECHR), it is sated to include rights to hold opinions and to receive and impart information and ideas. The International Covenant on Civil and Political rights (ICCPR) , Art.19[155],

---

[153] Lee Bollinger, The Tolerant Society, Oxford University Press, USA, 1988 at 41-42; Bollinger provides a critique of the major theories of freedom of expression, finding these theories persuasive but inadequate. Supporting his argument with references to the case laws and many other examples, as well as a careful analysis of the primary literature on free speech, he contends that the real value of toleration of extremist speech lies in the extraordinary self-control toward antisocial behavior that it elicits: society is strengthened by the exercise of tolerance.
[154] Art.10 of ECHR provides as follows;

(1).Everyone has the right to freedom of expression. this right shall include freedom to hold opinions and to receive and impart information and ideas without interference by public authority and regardless of frontiers. This article shall not prevent States from requiring the licensing of broadcasting, television or cinema enterprises.

(2).The exercise of these freedoms, since it carries with it duties and responsibilities, may be subject to such formalities, conditions, restrictions or penalties as are prescribed by law and are necessary in a democratic society, in the interests of national security, territorial integrity or public safety, for the prevention of disorder or crime, for the protection of health or morals, for the protection of the reputation or the rights of others, for preventing the disclosure of information received in confidence, or for maintaining the authority and impartiality of the judiciary.

[155] Art.19 of ICCPR provides as follows;

(1). Everyone shall have the right to hold opinions without interference.

(2). Everyone shall have the right to freedom of expression; this right shall include freedom to seek, receive and impart information and ideas of all kinds, regardless of frontiers, either orally, in writing or in print, in the form of art, or through any other media of his choice.

(3). The exercise of the rights provided for in paragraph 2 of this article carries with it special duties and responsibilities. It may therefore be subject to certain restrictions, but these shall only be such as are provided by law and are necessary:

(a) For respect of the rights or reputations of others;

separates the right to hold opinions in Art.19(1) from freedom of expression in Art.19(2), but includes in the latter the right to seek, as well as receive and impart, information and ideas. The ICCPR and the ECHR recognize that the exercise of these freedoms carries with it special responsibilities, and so may be subjected to restriction for specified purpose. The ECHR contains the most extensive grounds for restricting the freedom, which apply to the right to hold opinions as well as to the other elements in freedom of expression. The blanket authority to license to broadcasting, television, and cinema enterprises under ECHR Art.10 (1) does not depend on there being a justification for restricting the freedom under Art.10 (2). By contrast, ICCPR Art.19 requires any licensing regime has to be justified by reference to the permitted grounds of restrictions set out in Art.19(3). Neither the ICCPR nor the ECHR permits licensing regimes to be imposed on the dissemination of printed material, which may be restricted only in accordance with ECHR Art.10(2). Art.19 of the ICCPR does not permit any restrictions of the freedom to hold opinions without interference, guaranteed by Art.19 (1).

In India Freedom of speech and expression is guaranteed under Art.19(1)(a) of the Constitution of India. ICCPR binds India in international law and right to free speech is recognized through   Protection of Human Rights Act, 1993 apart from Constitutional guarantee. The Act defines human rights under Sec.2 (d) - "human rights" means the rights relating to life, liberty, equality and dignity of the individual guaranteed by the Constitution or embodied in the International Covenants and enforceable by courts in India. India being a signatory to ICCPR, abridgment of free speech can be easily enforced in India.

The protection of free speech in India is somewhat similar to the protection offered to it in US. But if we look into the various Indian court decisions another different

---

(b) For the protection of national security or of public order (ordre public), or of public health or morals.

view seems to be plausible. In Express Newspapers Pvt.Ltd., V Union of India[156], Bhgwati J, observed that – " .. the fundamental right to the freedom of speech and expression enshrined in our Constitution is based on the First amendment of the Constitution of the United States and it would be therefore legitimate and proper to refer to those decisions of the US Supreme Court to appreciate the true nature, scope and extent of this right in spite of the warning administered by this Court against use of American and other cases".[157]

But as to this opinion of Bhagwathi J, H.M. Seervai[158] begs to differ. He submits that the provisions of the two Constitutions as to freedom of speech are essentially different, the difference being accentuated by provisions in our Constitution for preventive detention which have no counterpart in the US Constitution. The First amendment enacts an absolute prohibition, so that a heavy burden lies on anyone transgressing it to justify such transgression[159]. Again, since the first amendment contains no exception, it is not surprising that exceptions have had to be evolved by judicial decisions which have limited the scope of such exceptions with increasing stringency. The position in India is different[160]. The right to freedom of speech and expression and the limitation on that right, are contained in Art.19 (1) (a) read with sub-Art. (2). Laws which fall under sub-Art(2) are expressly permitted by our Constitution and the problem in India is to determine whether an impugned law falls within the Art.19(2), and that is essentially problem of construction. No doubt Art.19 (2) of the Constitution authorizes the imposition of 'reasonable restrictions' and in the end, the question of reasonableness is a question for Court to decide. However, a law made in respect of the matters referred to in Art.19(2) must prima facie be presumed to be constitutionally valid and due weight must be given to the legislative judgement on the question of reasonableness , though that judgment is subject to judicial review. It is difficult, if not impossible, to read into the words 'reasonable restrictions' the test of 'clear and present danger' evolved by the US

---

[156] (1959) SCR 12
[157] As per H.M.Seervai, such warning (not to follow US Precednts) was given by the Supreme Court in trav-Cochin V Bombay Co, Ltd., and Bombay v R M D Chamarbaguwalla
[158] Seervai H.M, Constitutional Law of India, 4th Edition, N.M.Tripathi Pvt Ltd., 1991
[159] ibid
[160] ibid

Supreme Court in dealing with the freedom of speech and the press. He also draws our attention to difference between First amendment and Art.19 (1)(a) noted by Douglas J in Kingsley Corp V Regents of the University of New York[161]. In holding that all pre-censorship of cinema films was constitutionally void, Douglas J, said – " if we had a provision in our Constitution for reasonable regulation of the press such as India has included in hers there would be room for argument that censorship in the interest of morality would be permissible."[162]

In US, the right to free speech is guaranteed in absolute terms. But Courts have invented a doctrine called 'Police Power of the State' to prevent the abuse of First amendment right. In various cases US courts have held that State can exercise Police Power, only when State can show the compelling state interest factor. This is quite similar to the ground specified in Art.19 (2) of the Indian Constitution.

It is very difficult to accept the views of H.M.Seervai, in the light of new technological developments. Indian Judiciary has very limited knowledge and experience in applying traditional principles and doctrines of law to new technological environment. Indian courts have been relying excessively on American courts decisions for settling legal matters including free speech issues, which not only poses challenges as rights issue but also has created jurisdictional issues. Internet was introduced by Americans and hence they had the first opportunity of determining legal issues. It is good for the Indian courts to a take a leaf out of the American experience when dealing with the problems created by new media communication technologies. Canada and Australia have largely followed the precedents set by American courts.

2.4 Restrictions on Freedom of Speech

The freedoms enumerated in Art.19 (1) of the Indian Constitution are those great and basic rights which are recognized as the natural rights inherent in the status of a

---

[161] 360 US 684 (1959), available at http://supreme.justia.com/us/360/684/case.html , visited on 12 Jan 2004
[162] Supra Note 158

citizen[163]. But none of these freedoms including freedom of speech and expression is an absolute or uncontrolled, for each is liable to be curtailed by laws made or to be made by the State to the extent mentioned in clauses (2) to (6) of Art.19. Clauses (2) to (6) of the Art.19 recognize the right of the State to make laws putting reasonable restrictions in the interest of general public, the sovereignty and integrity of India, security of the state, public order, decency or morality or in relation to contempt of court , defamation or incitement to an offence. The principles on which the power of the State to impose restriction is based is that all individual rights of a person are held subject to such reasonable limitations and regulations as may be necessary or expedient for the protection of the general welfare[164]. In the words of Das, J., "social interest in individual liberty may be well have to be subordinated to other greater social interest[165]. Indeed there has to be a balance between individual rights guaranteed under Art.19(1) and the exigencies of the state which is the custodian of the interests of the general public, public order, decency or morality and of the other public interests which may compendiously be described as social welfare"[166]. The restrictions that may be imposed on the exercise of free speech right must be reasonable. It may be emphasized that the requirement that a restriction should be reasonable is of great constitutional significance, for it acts as a limitation on the power of the legislature, and consequently, widens the scope of judicial review of laws restraining the exercise of freedoms guaranteed by Art.19[167]. The determination by the legislature of what constitutes a reasonable restriction is not final or conclusive; it is subject to supervision of courts[168].

Sovereignty and integrity of India is one of the grounds on which free speech can be restricted. The object is to enable the Government to combat cries for secession and the like. Security of State means 'the absence of serious and aggravated forms of

---

[163] Sate of WB V Subodh Gopal Bose AIR 1954 SC 92
[164] Shukla V N, Constitution of India (edited by Mahendra P.Singh), Eastern Book Company, Lucknow, 1994 , at p 101
[165] A.K.Goplan V State of Madras AIR 1950 SC 27
[166] Hari KHemu Gawali V Dy.Commissioner of Police, AIR 1956 SC 559
[167] Shukla V N, Constitution of India (edited by Mahendra P.Singh), Eastern Book Company, Lucknow, 1994 , at p 102

[168] Chintaman Rao V State of M.P AIR 1951 SC 118

public disorder, as distinguished from ordinary breaches of public safety or public order which may not involve any danger to the State itself. Thus, security of the State is endangered by crimes of violence intended to overthrow the government, levying of war and rebellion against government, external aggression or war but not by minor breaches of public order or tranquility, such as unlawful assembly, riot, promoting enmity between classes etc[169]. But incitement of violent crimes like murder which is an offence against public order may also undermines the security of the State[170]. But the advocacy of revolutionary socialism as a panacea for present day evils cannot be restricted under the ground of 'security of state' unless the use of violence is suggested. The object of restricting freedom of speech and expression on the ground of 'friendly relations with foreign States' is to prevent libels against foreign State in the interests of maintaining friendly relations with them.

Another ground on which State can restrict free speech is Public Order. The concept of public order is different from the concept of 'law and order' and of security of the State'. They refer to three concentric circles. Law and order represents the largest circle, within which is the next circle representing public order and the smallest circle represents security of the State[171]. Hence an activity which affects law and order may necessarily affect public order and an activity which may be prejudicial to public order may not necessarily affect security of the State[172]. In the interest of public order, the State may impose restrictions on the incitement

(i) to withhold services by public employees or persons engaged in any employment which is essential for securing the public safety or for maintaining services essential for the life of the community[173]

(ii) for committing breach of discipline amongst employees[174]

(iii) of feelings of enmity or hatred between different sections of the community[175]

---

[169] Romesh Thappar V State of Madras AIR 1950 SC 124
[170] State of Bihar V Shailabala Devi AIR 1952 SC 329
[171] Ram Manhoar Lohia V state of Bihar AIR 1966 SC 740
[172] Ibid
[173] Dalbir Singh V State of Punjab AIR 1962 SC 1106
[174] ibid
[175] Virendra V State of Punjab AIR 1957 SC 896

(iv) of the use of loudspeakers likely to cause a public nuisance or to affect the health of the inmates of residential premises, hospitals and the like[176]

(v) for insulting the religious feelings of any class of citizens with deliberate and malicious intention under Sec.295A of Indian Penal Code (IPC) and Sec.99 of Criminal Procedure Code (Cr.PC)[177]

On the other hand criticism of government policies[178], criticism of or defamatory slogan against a Minister[179], scurrilous attacks upon a judge[180], exhibition of which , though it depicted scenes of violence, was capable of creating a message of peace and co-existence[181] have been held by the courts cannot be restricted or penalized in the interests of public order.

The ground of decency or morality has been engrafted for the purpose of restricting speeches and publications which tend to undermine public morals[182]. Decency or morality is not confined to sexual morality alone. Decency indicates that the action must be in conformity with the current standards of behaviour or propriety[183]. The question whether an utterance is likely to undermine decency or morality is to be determined with reference to the probable effects it may have upon the audience to which it is addressed[184]. The age, culture[185] and the like of the audience thus becomes a material question. But the use of mere abusive language, which has no suggestion of obscenity to the persons in whose presence they are uttered, would not come under this ground[186] and so would the use of expletives in a nude scene of rape to advance the message intended by the film by arousing a sense of revulsion against the perpetrators and pity for the victim[187].

---

[176] Rajani Kant verma V State of Bihar AIR 1958 All 360
[177] State of Rajasthan V Chawla G AIR 1959 SC 544
[178] Jawali V K V State of Mysore AIR 1966 SC 1387
[179] Ram Nandan V State of UP AIR 1956 All 101
[180] Sodhi Shamsher Singh V State of Pepsu AIR 1954 SC 276
[181] Ramesh Chotalal Dalal V Union of India AIR 1988 SC 775
[182] Ranjit D Udeshi V State of Maharashtra AIR 1965 SC 881
[183] Ramesh Yeshwant Prabhoo V Prabhakar Kashinath Kunte AIR 1996 SC 1113
[184] Ranjit D Udeshi V State of Maharashtra AIR 1965 SC 881
[185] Rajani Kant verma V State of Bihar AIR 1958 All 360
[186] Kartar Singh V State of Punjab AIR 1956 SC 541
[187] Bobby Art International V Om Pal Singh AIR 1996 SC 1846

2.4.1 Blocking Internet Blogs – Public Interest as a ground for restriction

One of the recent controversy as to the control and regulation of free speech is related to the use of blogs by Indian netizens. Block out of blogs and websites were ordered by Central Government in public interest in the month of July, 2006. Millions of domestic internet users could not access some of the world's most popular blogs like geocities.com, blogspot.com and typepad.com, as the government ordered a blackout of around 18 sites for publishing content that was 'anti-national' and 'against public interest'[188]. Blogging[189], particularly on fanatic and religious websites, had surged soon after the Mumbai bomb blasts on July 11. Over 25% of India's 38 million internet users are active bloggers. Currently, there are over 120 million bloggers worldwide and multiplying at the rate of about 10 million per month. The number is expected to cross 160 million in 2006[190].ISPs are believed to have been asked to block sites like bloodspot.com, hinduhumanrights.org, hinduunity.org and clickatell.com, besides frontline blogs like the Google owned blogspot.com[191]. However, Government soon withdrawn its order owing public outcry. There is no provision in the IT Act as it stands now for the government to impose such a ban on the publication of websites or blogs. But government can always use provisions of Art.19(2) to restrict speech on Internet or any other media. The problem of exercising control over cyberspace is that it is multi-jurisdictional and not easily amenable to jurisdiction of Indian courts.

In the exercise of one's right of freedom of speech and expression, nobody can be allowed to interfere with the due course of justice or to lower the prestige or

---

[188] Financial Express, Blogs, websites go blank, Tuesday , July 18, 2006 available at
http://www.financialexpress.com/fe_full_story.php?content_id=134366 , visited on 4 Nov 2005
[189] A weblog (usually shortened to blog, but occasionally spelled web log) is a web-based publication consisting primarily of periodic articles (normally in reverse chronological order). Although most early weblogs were manually updated, tools to automate the maintenance of such sites made them accessible to a much larger population, and the use of some sort of browser-based software is now a typical aspect of "blogging".;available at www.en.wikipedia.orgwiki/Blogging , visited on 23 Nov 2003
See generally, Sullenger Wes , Silencing the Blogoshpere : A First Amendment Caution to Legislators considering Using Blogs to Communicate directly with constitutents , 13 RICH.J.L & TECH. 15 (2007), available at http://law.richmond.edu/jolt/v13i4/article15.pdf , visited on 25 Jan 25, 2007.
[190] ibid
[191] ibid

authority of the Court[192]. But the contempt jurisdiction should not be used by judges to uphold their own dignity. In the free market place of ideas, criticism about the judicial system or the Judges should be welcomed, so long as criticisms do not impair or hamper the administration of justice[193]. Restriction on the ground of defamation protects the right of a person to his reputation. Just as every person possesses the freedom of speech and expression, every person also possesses a right to his reputation which is regarded as property. Hence, nobody can so use his freedom of speech or expression as to injure another's reputation. Laws penalizing defamation do not, therefore, constitute infringement of the freedom of speech[194]. The last ground on which free speech can be restricted under Art.19 (2) is incitement to an offence. This ground will permit legislation not only to punish or prevent incitement to commit serious offences like murder which led to breach of public border, but also to commit any offence[195]. Hence, it is not permissible to instigate another to do any act which is prohibited and penalized by any law. But mere instigation not to pay a tax may not necessarily constitute incitement to an offence[196]. US courts follow time, place and manner principle to restrict free speech. In India, the laws and judicial decisions governing freedom of press[197] are equally applicable to publications or writings in cyberspace. Hence, any restriction that is directly imposed upon the right to publish[198], to disseminate information or to circulate[199] constitutes a restriction upon the freedom of press in the real world as well as virtual world. The right to publish includes the right to publish not only its own views but also those of its correspondents.[200] This right protects the right of

---

[192] Namboodripad E.M.Sankaran V Narayan Nambiar AIR 1970 SC 2015
[193] Duda P N V Shivashankar P AIR 1988 SC 1208
[194] Dupthary C K V Gupta O P AIR 1971 SC 1132
[195] Sankoth Singh V Delhi Administration AIR 1973 SC 1901
[196] Kedar Nath Singh V State of Bihar AIR 1962 SC 995
[197] Under Indian Constitution there is no separate guarantee of freedom of the press. It is implicit in the freedom of expression which is conferred on all citizens. However, this freedom cannot be claimed by person who is not a citizen of India. On the other hand, First Amendment of US Constitution expressly guarantees freedom of press. It reads as follows – "Congress shall make no law respecting an establishment of religion, or prohibiting the free exercise thereof; or abridging the **freedom of speech, or of the press**; or the right of the people peaceably to assemble, and to petition the Government for a redress of grievances."
[198] Express Newspaper Ltd., V Union of India AIR 1958 SC 578
[199] ibid
[200] Sakal Papers (p) Ltd., V Union of India AIR 1962 SC 305

ISP's to publish the views of their subscribers. To require a newspaper to reduce its space for advertisements would directly affect its circulation since it would be bound to raise its price[201]. In cyberspace price of hosting may not raise by reducing website size but it definitely affects the revenue earned by the website through websites. Also traditional law recognizes right to reply[202] as a part of freedom of speech. As a result of these entities which are providing blogging or website hosting facilities must also allow the aggrieved person to post his reply on appropriate forum.

2.4.2 Free Speech – American Jurisprudence

In US, Content based governmental restrictions on speech are unconstitutional unless they advance a "compelling state interest." To this principle, there are six exceptions:

1. Speech that is likely to lead to imminent lawless action may be prohibited[203].
2. Fighting words -- i.e., words so insulting that people are likely to fight back mabe prohibited[204].
3. Obscenity -- i.e., erotic expression, grossly or patently offensive to an average person that lacks serious artistic or social value may be prohibited[205].
4. Child pornography may be banned whether or not it is legally obscene and whether or not it has serious artistic or social value, because it induces people to engage in lewd displays, and the creation of it threatens the welfare of children[206].
5. Defamatory statements may be prohibited. (In other words, the making of such statements may constitutionally give rise to civil liability.) However, if the target of the defamation is a "public figure," she must prove that the defendant acted with

---

[201] ibid
[202] Manubahi Shah V L.I.C AIR 1981 Guj 15
[203] Fed.Election Commission V Colo.Republican Fed. Campaign Comm, 533 U.S.431, 465 (20010; available on www.findlaw.com website, visited on 10 Dec 2005
[204] Chaplinsky V New York, 340 U.S.315 568, 571-74 (1942) available on www.findlaw.com website, visited on 20 Dec 2005
[205] Miller V California, 413 U.S. 15, 36-37 (1973), available on www.findlaw.com , visited on 20 Dec 2005
[206] Ginsberg v New York, 390 U.S. 629, 635-43(1968), also in New York V Feber, 458 U.S. 747, 754-58 (1968) , available on www.findlaw.com website, visited on 20 Dec 2005

"malice." If the target is not a "public figure" but the statement involved a matter of "public concern," the plaintiff must prove that the defendant acted with negligence concerning its falsity[207].

6. Commercial Speech may be banned only if it is misleading, pertains to illegal products, or directly advances a substantial state interest with a degree of suppression no greater than is reasonably necessary[208].

2.5 Free Speech Protection in cyberspace

Institutions[209] that are required to uphold Freedom of Speech and Expression generally must uphold these rights in cyberspace as well. For higher education, this means, for example, the public colleges and Universities have limited ability to filter incoming or outgoing web pages or Usenet newsgroups based on content. The question, whether cyberspace a public forum was raised in Loving V Boren[210]. The United States District Court for the Western District of Oklahoma addressed this issue. After an elected representative complained that material available in news groups stored on the public university's server violated state law, the university blocked access to some groups. A professor said this violated his free speech rights and filed suit. The court held that the computer systems of public institutions are not inherently public forums and that such institutions could limit servers to officially approved material[211]. This decision would not prevent a public or a private institution from creating a public forum, either intentionally or unintentionally.

---

[207] Dun & Bradstreet V Greenmoss Builders, 472 U.S. 749 , 763 (1985), available on www.findlaw.com website, visited on 22 Dec 2005
[208] Fla.Bar V Went for IT, Inc 515 U.S. 618, 623-24, 635 (1995) available on www.findlaw.com website, visited on 25 Dec 2005
[209] All those institutions, instrumentalities, authorities etc who would be regarded as 'State' within the meaning of Art.12 of Indian Constitution.
[210] Loving v. Boren_, 956 F. Supp. 953 (W.D. Okla. 1997) available at http://caselaw.lp.findlaw.com/cgi-bin/getcase.pl?court=10th&navby=case&no=976086 , visited on 25 Dec 2005
[211] ibid

2.5.1 Channels of Free Speech in Cyberspace and Media Freedom

In order to exercise the free speech right one has to find a medium. Undoubtedly, the first was communication through gestures before the human race invented speech. For many centuries, speech became the second mode of communication. The third mode of communication was writing. Writing brought in a series of written laws. The invention of telephone revolutionized the communication media. Then the revolutionary media, the broadcasting media appeared in the form of Radio. After radio the dream of seeing pictures and hearing sound from distance places was realized through Television. Radio and Television are regarded as push technologies as they provide one way communication. Aspiration and desire of common man to own his own printing press and publish his views and opinions became a reality when internet was opened to the public in 1993[212].

The medium of mass communication is vital to promote freedom to receive and impart information and ideas. Mass media includes Press, Radio, Television, Internet, Satellite, Cable broadcasting etc. There is an obvious relationship between free media and freedom of speech. It is therefore important on a number of grounds. Some of them are;

   (a) As a tool of self-expression it is a significant instrument of personal autonomy[213];

   (b) As a channel of communication it helps to allow the political discourse which is necessary in any country which aspires to democracy[214];

   (c) It helps to provide one of the essential conditions of scholarship , making possible the exchange and evaluation of theories, explanations and discoveries[215];

---

[212] See generally Castells , Manuel, The Rise of the Network Society, 2nd edition, Blackwell Publishers, USA, 2000

[213] Feldman, David, Civil Liberties and Human Rights in England and Wales, 2nd Edition, Oxford University Press, UK, 2002, at p 802

[214] ibid at p 802

[215] ibid at p 803

(d) It helps to promulgate a society's cultural values and where they are in flux, facilitates the debate about them, advancing development and survival of civilization[216];

(e) Free media can contribute to the implementation of both consumer choice and public policy by providing channels for communicating commercial information and governmental advice or information[217].

It is pertinent note here that while highlighting the difficulty of regulating the media and controlling the transmission of information across the border, the committee on Telecommunication of UK observed that -

"Many people brought up in a world in which there were only a few broadcasting channels feel bewildered by the explosion of choice. The boundaries of industries are blurring: telecommunication companies want to become broadcasters, while broadcasters are increasingly moving into e-commerce, and Internet Service Providers are offering television channels."[218]

This makes it impossible for any country to control the media of communication. The growth of communication across frontiers by satellite, telephone lines, and the Internet has necessitated an international approach to regulation and a framework for these increasingly convergent industries that combines different ingredients[219].

The earliest dated printed book known as the "Diamond Sutra", printed in China in 868 CE. However, it is suspected that book printing may have occurred long before this date. In 1041, movable clay type was first invented in China. Johannes Gutenberg invented the printing press with replaceable wooden or metal letters in 1436[220]. The Gutenberg press with its wooden and later metal movable type printing brought down the price of printed materials and made such materials available for the masses. It remained the standard until the 20th century. During the centuries,

---

[216] ibid
[217] ibid
[218] Department of Trade and Industry and Department of Culture, Media and Sport, A New Future for Telecommunications, available at http://www.culture.gov.uk/PDF/CM5010.PDF , visited 2 Jan 2006
[219] ibid
[220] Bellis, Mary, Johannes Gutenberg and the Printing Press, available at http://inventors.about.com/library/inventors/blJohannesGutenberg.htm , visited on 23 Sep 2006

many newer printing technologies were developed based on Gutenberg's printing machine e.g. offset printing[221]. The press has developed a special meaning and a particular significance over and above that attaching to freedom of speech. The invention of printing press vastly increased the capacity of books and pamphlets-especially political ones- to reach people of all sorts. This made it a powerful medium of instruction, but also opposition to the established order[222].

Reactions to government's overuse of powers to control the press varied. In India judiciary has clearly recognized through various judicial decisions the freedom of press to be implicit in freedom of speech and expression guaranteed under Art.19 (1)(a)[223]. There was civil disobedience against the government's arbitrary control over the press in England. The courts and Parliament have slowly come to recognize that there is a special public interest in press freedom and legislative steps have been taken to protect it.

Even though printing press provided an opportunity to express and communicate freely, owning a printing press remained a distant reality owing to cost factor and the lack of printing skills.

On March 10, 1876, in Boston, Massachusetts, Alexander Graham Bell invented the telephone. Thomas Watson fashioned the device itself; a crude thing made of a wooden stand, a funnel, a cup of acid, and some copper wire. But these simple parts and the equally simple first telephone call -"Mr. Watson, come here, I want you!"- belie a complicated past. From that day onwards the man has been empowered with new medium of communication which has come to a stage of mobile phones and fancy wireless handsets[224].

---

[221] ibid
[222] Feldman, David, Civil Liberties and Human Rights in England and Wales, 2nd Edition, Oxford University Press, UK, 2002, at p 807

[223] Romesh Thappar V State of Madras AIR 1950 SC 124
[224] Tom Farley's Telephone History Series, available at
http://www.privateline.com/TelephoneHistory/History1.htm, visited on 25 Sep 2006

The invention of radio by Guglielmo Marconi in 1896 heralded the new era for music, drama and talk. But the broadcasting media remained largely as a push technology and listeners are held as captive audience by this media[225].

Work on Electronic television, based on the cathode ray tube done independently in 1907 by English inventor A.A. Campbell-Swinton and Russian scientist Boris Rosing. During the same period, American Charles Jenkins and Scotsman John Baird followed the mechanical model while Philo Farnsworth, working independently in San Francisco, and Russian émigré Vladimir Zworkin, working for Westinghouse and later RCA, advanced the electronic model[226]. Television also remained in the category of broadcasting and was not of much use to common man for expressing his views.

The world of cyberspace is a true democracy[227]. The influence of the netizens is not measured by wealth or position, but how well he writes and reason. Internet supports different kinds of communication- text, audio, video and so on. The perfect market place of idea is one where all ideas, not just the popular or well funded ones, are accessible to all. ICT have dramatically reduced the cost of distributing speech and therefore, the new media order these technologies bring will be much more

---

[225] History of American Broadcasting, available at http://members.aol.com/jeff560/jeff.html , visited on 29 Sep 2005
[226] Federal Communication Commission, Vision Period, 1880's through 1920's, available at, http://www.fcc.gov/omd/history/tv/1880-1929.html , visited on 20 Mar 2006
[227] Balkin , Jack, Digital Speech and Democratic Culture: A theory of Freedom of Expression for the Information Society, 79 N.Y.L. Rev 1 (2004) available at www.papers.ssrn.com . In this essay, Professor Balkin argues that digital technologies alter the social conditions of speech and therefore should change the focus of free speech theory, from a Meiklejohnian or republican concern with protecting democratic process and democratic deliberation, to a larger concern with protecting and promoting a democratic culture. A democratic culture is a culture in which individuals have a fair opportunity to participate in the forms of meaning-making that constitute them as individuals. Democratic culture is about individual liberty as well as collective self-governance; it concerns each individual's ability to participate in the production and distribution of culture. Balkin argues that Meiklejohn and his followers were influenced by the social conditions of speech produced by the rise of mass media in the twentieth century, in which only a relative few could broadcast to large numbers of people. Republican or progressivist theories of free speech also tend to downplay the importance of nonpolitical expression, popular culture, and individual liberty. The limitations of this approach have become increasingly apparent in the age of the Internet

democratic and diverse than the environment we saw earlier to this[228]. Cheap speech will mean that far more speakers, rich and poor, popular and not, banal and avant-garde will be able to make their work available to all[229]. The internet communication, however, has turned out to be the great equalizer. Suddenly anyone can become a publisher, reporter, or editorialist. What is more, each of us has as good a chance of being heard as anyone else in the electronic community. The new internet based forums for debate and information exchange are witnessing perhaps the greatest exercise of freedom of expression that the world has ever seen[230].

The special feature of the internet speech is that the community content creation. The community content creation is just opposite to the traditional model of collaborative content creation[231]. Instead of a team, it relies on the individual, it depends on propagation and instead of an assured cycle time, its key differentiator is the spontaneous nature of propagation over the internet[232]. While collaborative content creation is limited by the size of available team, and its skill sets, community content creation relies on the availability of thousands, spread across time zones and over inaccessible geographies, with arrange of talent and capabilities that an organized team can never match. Because of its very nature, community content displays all characteristics of mob at work. More often than not, it is disruptive of the established order[233]. Lacking in an established leadership and hierarchy, its effectiveness on a given issue is difficult to predict, once community, depending on the way speaker wants to see it, gets galvanized, seemingly no force

---

[228] Godwin, Mike, Cyber Rights- Defending Free Speech in the Digital age, 1st Edition, Times Books, New York, 1998 at p 21
[229] ibid at p 22
[230] ibid at p 23
[231] Collaborative content creation depends on team work. Take the example of publishing articles in a weekly magazine. One of the writer in the team writes an article that is checked by a senior in the team. The article then moves to the copy desk where it is checked for language and reliability, before it moves to the design department. From there, it traverses back for proof reading and checking before finally going to the printing department from where it is sent to the press. This is a chain of collaborative activities that takes up some cycle time from the creation of content to the time it reaches readers.
[232] Binesh Kutty, Krishna Kumar, Rinku Tyagi, Sujay V Sharma and Varun Dubey, Will Technology Kill the News Paper?, PC Quest, Cybermedia Publications, November, 2005
[233] ibid

on earth can match or stop its impact[234]. So, of millions of community content initiatives, only few reach mass proportions and ones that do reach mass movement proportions do so rather quickly[235].

2.5.2 Community Content Creation Tools in Cyberspace

Some of the content creation tools that may be used in cyberspace are;

(a) Bulletin Board Systems (BBS) – it is one of the oldest community content creation tool, whose origin can be traced back to pre-internet days. This is one of the most moderated community content initiatives. It lets people post their opinions about a topic and string together opinions posted under the same thread. Since these forums are created by some other entity, there is some amount of moderation of the content posted.

(b) Wiki – Wiki[236] is where individuals from across the globe collaborate to create, edit and update content on a page. The traditional method of creating the page, laying it out and subsequently updating it on the server is given the go by. It allows us to edit or add content posted by someone else on the same page as it was originally posted. Wiki's are traditionally used to collate knowledge as in www.wikipedia.org. The practice of using a wiki site as a personal website is known as wikisquatting.

(c) Weblogs- These are popularly known as blogs. Originally these were online diaries maintained by individuals. Soon they evolved into online commentary, and what has made them a raging success is ease with which one can create a blog on a site such as blogspot.com and the ability to hyperlink to other blogs and sites easily. Blogs have give rise to Moblogs (blogs updated over the mobile phone), Plogs (Picture blogs) Vlogs(Video blogs) and Splogs[237] (spam blogs).

---

[234] ibid
[235] ibid
[236] The word wiki is derived from the Hawaian word 'wki wki' which means 'rapid'.
[237] Also known as SPLOGGING. It is an art of creating fake blogs in an effort to drive up search engine ranking on websites and get more hits.

(d) Social Networks- These networks are more like online clubs. They allow people to come together and find each other and form groups based on commonality of interests. There are social networking sites that cater to almost every need, from business networking to friendship to dating and marriage[238].

(e) Podcasts – These are audio and video files of contemporary thought made available online. The word has its origin in iPod + broadcast, with practice originally being to create and download these files to an iPod. They are not as amenable to hyper linking as with text[239].

2.6 Content Regulation- Hicklin Speech – Sexually Explicit Material

Pornography is a curious example of an issue which has grown very quickly from a state of insignificance to become a major social issue at least in some parts of the world. From the very beginning in the early 1960s of what has been termed the 'modern pornography wave', there has been controversy over nearly all aspects of the topic: definition, amounts and contents of material, uses and users, economy and, most importantly, effects[240].

Erotic art is probably as old as art itself. Sexual themes appear in the artistic creations of all times and cultures. The first erotic paintings, sculptures and writings were probably

produced   by the first painters, sculptors and writers in the early youth of humanity, and

every milestone in the arts usually saw new developments in the field of erotica[241].

The real development and distribution of pornographic pictures started with the invention of printing press[242]. The next giant step towards mass media production,

---

[238] Wikipedia, Online Free Encyclopedia, available at http://en.wikipedia.org/wiki/Social_networks , vsisited 2 Mar 2006
[239] Definition as given in Wikipedia, Online Free encyclopedia, available at http://en.wikipedia.org/wiki/Podcast , visited 2 Mar 2006
[240] Berl Kutchinsky, Pornography, Sex Crime,And Public Policy, available at http://www.aic.gov.au/publications/proceedings/14/kutchinsky.pdf visited on 13 June 2005.

[241] ibid

the invention of the photographic process in 1832, had very similar consequences. Forty years later, in 1874, 130,000 'obscene' photographs and 5,000 slides were seized by police in a raid on two houses in London owned by photographer Henry Hayler. By this time, pornography was beginning to broaden its appeal beyond the narrow literate class that had been its primary audience[243].

When Edison invented the moving pictures, the pornographic potential of this new media was, of course, too obvious to be overlooked, and very soon a prosperous, underground production of 'blue movies' began, particularly in South America. In fact, Edison himself produced an erotic motion picture as early as in 1886; called *The Kiss*. It created a public scandal, and was a tremendous success. The film was not pornographic, of course, but heralded a new era in the erotic industry which has now, in very recent years, reached another stage with the video tape, cable and satellite television productions of pornography[244].

So, erotic art has a long history, and even if we restrict ourselves to speaking about commercial pornography, that is, a commodity depicting explicit nudity and sexual behaviour, produced and sold with the sole purpose of creating sexual arousal, this product has an age of more than 300 years. The starting point seems to be the appearance in about 1650 of *La Puttana Errante The Wandering Whore*. Although this was not the first book to describe the life of a prostitute in intimate detail hence the word *pornographos* (there is a classic Greek and renaissance Italian tradition of 'writing about prostitutes'). This book was the first which skipped the social, philosophical, satirical, and artistic aspects in order to concentrate on the only thing that mattered: the titillation of the reader[245].

---

[242] This is apart from stone carvings on Temples which may be regarded as indecent rather than obscene. For example, Johann Gutenberg developed the art of printing around 1448, and one of the very first books to appear in print was *Il Decamerone*, Boccacio's erotic masterpiece. Suppression of freedom of the press — a phenomenon which is a significant part of the history of eroticism — followed immediately after. In 1497, sections of the *Decameron* were thrown into Savonarola's 'bonfire of the vanities' in Florence.

[243] Berl , Kutchinsky, Pornography, Sex Crime, And Public Policy, available at http://www.aic.gov.au/publications/proceedings/14/kutchinsky.pdf , , Visited on 13 Jan 2003
[244] ibid
[245] ibid

In the eighteenth and nineteenth centuries, Europe experienced a 'porno wave' which as far as the number of different publications were concerned, can match the present times. Alfred Rose (alias Rolf S. Reade) listed more than 5,000 English, French, German, Italian and Spanish titles in his *Register Librorum Eroticorum* in London in 1936[246].

Nevertheless, there are certain unique features about the pornography situation which has developed during the last twenty-five years and is now prevailing in most countries of the Western world, Japan and some other developed countries in Asia, and is now quickly developing in the former communist countries of Central and Eastern Europe. One important feature is that pornography has become easily available to people in general, while earlier it was mostly restricted to the economic and intellectual upper class. Another feature is that, to a large extent, pornography at least in some forms, has become morally and socially acceptable and in a few countries even legal, which has not been the case for about 200 years[247].

An important factor in this development is that new technologies have made possible the mass production of colour magazines, films and videos of high technical quality at a very low cost. Another, and perhaps the most important factor, has been the emergence of a more liberalised view of sexual behaviour, which has exonerated the naked body and the sexual act from earlier indictments of sinfulness. This new sexual liberalism, the so-called 'sexual revolution', has been influential in several different ways. It has awakened and strengthened a latent need for erotica among many people. It has also made possible the economic exploitation of this new attitude. And it has paved the way for a more lenient enforcement and eventual abolition of existing bans[248].

In most countries, the emergence of pornography as an everyday commodity has stirred relatively little controversy although at times great public interest. This is true of Denmark, which was the first country to legalise pornography, and most other continental European countries. In other countries, such as Norway, Great Britain, the United States, Canada and Australia, pornography has continued to be

---

[246] ibid
[247] ibid
[248] ibid

an issue of sometimes considerable controversy, giving rise to heated debate, mass demonstrations, violent actions, citizens' associations and rallies, criminal prosecutions as well as civil law suits, legislative initiatives, and numerous conferences and commission reports[249].

Expression of a sort which might contravene accepted standards of social morality is potentially subject to restrictions of three types in law. First, there are various statutory and common law offences for which people may be prosecuted. Secondly, there are provisions restricting access to material, and requiring outlets selling the material to be licensed and regulated. Thirdly, there are provisions allowing seizure and forefeiture of immoral goods in certain circumstances, without the need for anyone to be shown to have committed any offence.

There are various statutory provisions in India which regulate pornography. Secs 292[250], 292-A[251] and 293[252] of Indian Penal Code, 1860 and Sec.67[253] of

---

[249]ibid

[250] **Sale ,etc., or obscene books, etc.**- [(1)] For the purpose of sub-section (2), a book, pamphlet, paper, writing drawing, panting , representation, figure or any other object, shall be deemed to be obscene if it is lascivious or appeals to the prurient interest or if its effect, or (where it comprises two or more distinct items) the effect of any one of its items, is , if taken as a whole , such as to ten to deprave and corrupt person , who are likely, having regard to all relevant circumstances, to read, see or hear the matter contained or embodied in it].
[(2)] Whoever-
(a)   sells, less to hire, distributes, publicly exhibits or in any manner puts into circulation, or for purpose of sale, hire, distribution, public exhibition or circulation, makes , produces or has in his possession any obscene book, pamphlet, paper , drawing, painting, representation or figure or any other obscene object whatsoever, or
(b)   imports, exports or conveys any obscene object for any of the purpose aforesaid, or knowing or having reason to believe that such as to tend to deprave and corrupt person, who are likely , having regard to all relevant circumstance, to read, see or hear the matter contained or emboldened in it].
(c)   takes part in or receives profits from any business in the course of which he knows or has reason to believe that any such obscene   objects are for any of the purposes aforesaid, made , produced, purched , kept, imported, exported, conveyed, , publicly exhibited or in any manner put into circulation, or
(d)   advertises or makes known by any means whatsoever that any person is engaged or is ready to engage in any which is an offence under this section, or that any such obscene object can be procured from or through any person, oroffers or attempts to do any act which is an offence under this section, shall be punished [on first conviction with imprisonment or either description for a term which may extend to two years, and with fine which may extend to two thousand rupees, and ,in the event of a second or subsequent conviction, with imprisonment of either description for a term which may extend to five years, and also with fine which may extend to five thousand rupees].
    [Exception . – This section does not extend to-
        (a) any book, pamphlet, paper, writing , drawing, painting, representation or figure-
            the publication of which is proved to be justified as being for the public good on
            the ground that such book, pamphlet, paper, writing , drawing, painting,

84

representation or figure is in the interest of science, literature, act of learning or other objects of general concern, or

(ii)   which is kept or used bona fide for religious purposes;

(b) any representation sculptured, engraved, painted or otherwise represented on or in-any ancient monument within the meaning of the Ancient Monuments and Archaeological Sites and Remains Act, 1958 (24 of 1958), or

(ii)   any temple , or an any car used for the conveyance of idols, or kept or used for any religious purpose.]]

[251] **Printing, etc., of grossly indecent or scurrilous matter or matter intended for blackmail**.-

Whoever.-

(a)   print or causes to be printed in any newspaper, periodical or circular, or exhibits or causes to be exhibited , to public view or distributes or cause to be distributed or in any manner puts into circulation any picture or any printed or written document which is grossly indecent, or in scurrilous or intended for blackmail; or

(b)   sells or lets for hire, or for purpose of sale or hire makes , produces or has in his possession any picture or any printed or written document which is grossly indecent or is scurrilous or intended for blackmail; or

(c)   conveys any picture or any printed or written document which is grossly indecent or is scurrilous or intended for blackmail knowing or having reason to believe that such picture or document will be printed, sold, let for hire distributed or publicly exhibited or in any manner put into circulation; or

(d)   takes part in, or receives profits from, any business in the course of which he knows or has reason to believe that any such newspaper , periodical, circular, picture or other printed or written document is printed, exhibited, distributed, circulated, sold, let for hire, made, produced, kept, conveyed or purchased; or

(e)   advertises or makes known by any means whatsoever that any person is engaged or is ready to engage in any Act which is an offence under this section, or that any such newspaper , periodical , circular , picture or other printed or written document which is grossly indecent or is scurrilous or intended for blackmail , can be procured from or through any person; or

(f)   offers or attempts to do any act which is an offence under this section *[shall be punished with imprisonment of either description for a term which may extend to two years, or with fine, or with both] :

Provided that for a second or any subsequent offence under this section , he shall be punished with imprisonment of either description for a term which shall not be less than six months *[and not more than two years].

Explanation I .- For the purposes of this section , the word scurrilous shall be deemed to include any matter which is likely to be injurious to morality or is calculated to injure any person:

Provided that it is not scurrilous to express in good faith anything whatever respecting the conduct of-

(i)   a public servant in the discharge of his public functions or respecting or respecting his character so far as his character appears in that conduct and no further; or

(ii)   any person touching any public question, and respecting his character, so far as his character appears in that conduct and no further.

Explanation II.- In deciding whether any person has committed an offence under this section, the court shall have regard inter alia, to the following considerations-

(a)   The general character of the person charged, and where relevant the nature of his business;

(b)   the general character and dominant effect of the matter alleged to be grossly indecent or scurrilous or intended for blackmail;

Information Technology Act, 2000 (IT Act). The essence of all these provisions is that they prohibit and penalize dealing with pornographic material. Indian courts have been following the test laid down by Privy Council in R V Hicklin to determine whether the material under consideration is obscene or not?. In that case Cockburn J, laid down the test of obscenity which has been widely accepted as the correct exposition of the law. According to him the test of obscenity is this, whether the tendency of the matter charged as obscenity is to deprave and corrupt those whose minds are open to such immoral influence and into whose hands a publication of this sort may fall? It is quite certain that it would suggest to the minds of the young of either sex, or even to persons of more advanced year, thoughts of most impure and lubricious character[254].

The Supreme Court has accepted this test in Ranjit D.Udeshi V State[255]. The appellant who was one of the four partners of a firm owning a book stall was convicted along with other partners under Sec.292 of IPC by the magistrate for keeping a banned book named 'Lady Chatterly's Lover' in his stall for sale. The High Court and the Supreme Court maintained his conviction. The Supreme Court observed that treatment of sex in such a way as to appeal to the carnal side or as to have a tendency towards that is obscene, and it must be seen as to whether such a matter is likely to deprave and corrupt those whose minds are open to such influences and into whose hands such material is likely to fall. Obscenity which is

---

(c)   any evidence offered or called by or on behalf of the accused person as to his intention in committing any of the acts specified in this section

[252] **Sale, etc., of obscene objects to young person.-** Whoever sells, lets to hire, distributes, exhibits or circulates to any person under the age of twenty years any such do , shall be punished [2][on first conviction with imprisonment or either description for a term which may extend to there years and with fine which may extend to two thousand rupees ,and, in the event of a second or subsequent conviction, with imprisonment of either description for a term which may extend to seven years, and also with fine which may extend to five thousand rupees].]
[253] **Publishing of information which is obscene in electronic form:** Whoever publishes or transmits or causes to be published in the electronic form, any material which is lascivious or appeals to the prurient interest or if its effect is such as to tend to deprave and corrupt persons who are likely, having regard to all relevant circumstances, to read, see or hear the matter contained or embodied in it, shall be punished on first conviction with imprisonment of either description for a term which may extend to five years and with fine which may extend to one lakh rupees and in the event of a second or subsequent conviction with imprisonment of either description for a term which may extend to ten years and also with fine which may extend to two lakh rupees.
[254] Bhattacharya T, Indian Penal Code, Central Law Agency,3d Edition, Allahabad, 2001
[255] AIR 1965 SC 881

offensive to modesty or decency cannot be protected on the ground of the constitutional protection of freedom of speech and expression guaranteed under Art.19 (1)(a) as this freedom is subject to reasonable restrictions in the interest of public order, decency or morality[256].

Commenting on the continued application and its relevancy in the contemporary era on Hicklin test of obscenity Stable J, observed that – "because that is a test laid down in 1868, that does not mean that what you have to consider is, supposing this book had been published in 1868 and the publishers had been prosecuted in 1868, whether the Court or a jury, nearly a century ago, would have reached the conclusion that the book was an obscene book. Your tasks are open to such immoral influences and into whose hands the book may fall in this year, or last year when it was published in this country, or next year or the year after that".[257]

The test of obscenity in England is laid down in Sec.1 of the Obscene Publications Act, 1959. This section states that, for the purpose of this Act an article shall be deemed to obscene if its effect is, if taken as a whole , such as to tend to deprave and corrupt persons who are likely , having regard to all relevant circumstances, to read it. This Act has been supplemented by the Obscene Publications Act, 1964 and amended by the Criminal Law Act, 1977. Discussing the scope and ambit of the obscene Publication Act Cross and Jones states that an article is deemed to be obscene if its effect or the effect of any one of its items, is, taken as a whole, such as to tend to deprave and corrupt persons who are likely, having regard to all the circumstances to read, see or hear the matter contained in it. Though a novel may be considered as a whole, a magazine must be considered item by item and, if any one of the items is obscene, the accused is guilty. A novelist who writes a complete novel and who cannot cut out particular passages without destroying the theme of the novel is entitled to have his work judged as a whole, but a magazine publisher who has a far wider discretion as to what he will and will not insert by way of items is to be judged under Act on what we call the item to item basis.

---

[256] AIR 1970 SC 1390
[257] R V Reiter (1954), 1 All ER 741

In US, the test of obscenity is laid down in Miller V California[258]. The basic guidelines for the jury under the Miller test are:

(a) Whether 'the average person, applying contemporary community standards' would find that the work, taken as a whole, appeals to the prurient interest[259];

(b) Whether the work depicts or describes, in a patently offensive way, sexual conduct specifically defined by the applicable state law[260]; and

(c) Whether the work, taken as a whole, lacks serious literary, artistic, political, or scientific value[261].

Rejecting as unworkable the "utterly without redeeming social value" prong, the Court restricted the permissible scope of regulations to works that depict or describe sexual conduct and such works include "patently offensive representations or descriptions of ultimate sexual acts, normal or perverted, actual or simulated" and patently offensive representations or descriptions of masturbation, excretory functions, and lewd exhibition of the genitals." The first two prongs of the Miller test use contemporary community standards to determine subjectively whether or not a work as a whole appeals to a prurient interest in sex and describes sexual conduct in a patently offensive way. The third prong examines serious literary, artistic, political, or scientific value according to the reasonable person standard. Because the definitions of patent offensiveness and prurient appeal are dependent upon a jury's determination, outcomes may vary. Nevertheless, in Miller case the Court rejected the requirement of a national community standard, and subsequently determined that the Constitution did not mandate a statewide standard either[262]. For the internet world where pornographic material seems to be the darling of majority net users, Miller test appears to be appropriate to determine whether a particular

---

[258] Miller V. California, 413 U.S. 15 (1973) available at http://laws.findlaw.com/us/413/15.html, visited 20 Jan 2003

[259] ibid
[260] ibid
[261] ibid
[262] Burke D Debra, Thinking Outside the Box: Child Pornography, Obscenity and the Constitutionl, Virginia Journal of Law & Technology, Vol.8, No.11, Fall 2003

article is obscene or not as the standards for judging obscenity vary from country to country.

2.6.1 Why Pornography is bad?

Sexual expression which might contravene accepted standards of social morality is potentially subject to restrictions of three types in India and England. First, there are various statutory and common law offences for which people may be prosecuted. Secondly, there are provisions restricting access to material, and requiring outlets selling the material to be licensed and regulated. Thirdly, there are provisions allowing seizure and forfeiture of immoral goods in certain circumstances, without the need for anyone to be shown to have committed any offence. The law is in a confused state. It has developed over the centuries since the invention of printing press. The confused state of law have different purposes. In particular, there is difference between the law on obscene publications and the law on indecency[263].

The term pornography includes obscenity and indecency. Law prohibits obscenity and some sort of protection is given to indecent speech. The definition of 'obscenity' has been controversial and varies from country to country. In England and India, obscenity is criminalized to protect those who come to it willingly against moral harm- depravity and corruption- which the obscene article is held to threaten. In US courts follow guidelines given in Miller V California[264] to determine obscenity of object.

It is not clear whether the objective of the law is, or should be, to put a stop to pornography and, if so why; to prevent pornography from falling into the wrong hands; to maintain standards of morality, and if, so whose; to stop people from being upset by public displays; or to achieve some combination of those objects[265]. Were it acceptable to criminalize or contain all conduct or expression which the

---

[263] See generally, Mullin I Dorothy, The First Amendment and the Web: The internet Porn Panic and Restricting Indecency in Cyberspace, available at http://www.library.uscb.edu/untangle/mullin.html, visited on 25 May 2006
[264] Supra Note 258, 413 US 15 (1973)
[265] Feldman, David, Civil Liberties and Human Rights in England and Wales, 2nd Edition, Oxford University Press, UK, 2002, at p 807

dominant members of society found offensive or immoral, it would seriously restrict the range of discussion of ethical and political issues, since many expressions of opinion will be found offensive by those who disagree with the opinion or with the way in which it is expressed[266].

The view of the liberal theory is that tolerating offensive conduct and speech is one of the prices to be paid for a reasonably free and open society. Alternatively, free speech can be regarded as a forum for debate, in which societies develop their intellectual attitudes. A bias in favour of toleration can be best be developed and systematized in cases concerning relatively innocuous forms of offensiveness and, once established , can then be applied and extended in relation to other, potentially more upsetting, offences. In a pluralist society there is unlikely to be agreement about moral standards and in a liberal society it is a commonplace assumption that choice between moral values is primarily a matter of individuals.

One of the widely discussed thought about why pornography is bad is based on the articulation made by John Stuart Mill's in his work On Liberty about the harm principle[267]. There is considerable variation between people's views of what constitutes harm for the purpose of prohibiting pornography. For some people, impressed by the wide range of interferences with rights which would become permissible if harm is given an extended meaning, desirable to restrict it to harm which is objectively verifiable according to established scientific criteria. They therefore look for physical or psychological harm which constitutes a condition or syndrome recognized by competent medical or social opinion[268]. On this basis, the Williams committee[269] took the view in 1979 that burden of establishing harm lay on those who seek to justify interference with liberty of expression, and those people had failed to discharge the burden of showing a causative link between reading or watching pornography and committing criminal or anti-social acts. However, there is growing evidence that people who commit crimes of violence ,

[266] ibid
[267] Mill, John Stuart, On liberty, vol.XXV, Part2, The Harvard Classics, P.F. Collier & Sons, 1909, New York; Bartleby.com, 2001, at p 25, available at www.bartleby.com/25/2/ , visited on 3 Nov 2003
[268] ibid
[269] Coldham, Simon, Report of the Committee on Obscenity and Film Censorship , Chaired by Bernard Williams, The Modern Law Review, Vol. 43, No. 3 (May, 1980), pp. 306-318

especially sexual violence, are likely to have been influenced by pornographic or violent books, magazines, pictures and films, even if there is as yet limited evidence as to the likelihood of exposure to that material causing people to go on to commit such offences[270].

On the other hand, some contend that rather than material harm one should take account of moral social or ideological harm for preventing pornography. This is less easy to establish on objective criteria than the former kind of harm. It is more impressionistic and allows people to propose interferences with liberty on the strength of assertions of social or moral harm which can not be scientifically tested.

2.6.2 Feminist Theory of Obscenity – Women & Pornography

Generally, the notion of restricting sexually offensive material is problematic, for two reasons. First, the standard of offensiveness can be criticized as being unacceptably indeterminate standard for the law governing the availability of public expression. The implications of this is liberal in a traditional sense: any interference with freedom must be aimed at meeting a pressing social need and should be circumscribed in sufficiently clear terms to enable people to know what the law is, and plan their activities accordingly. Secondly, restricting, but not banning, offensive matter can be seen as based on a misconception about the type and significance of the harm which pornography works. Feminist theorists have argued that pornography causes a kind of social harm distinct both from any damage it does to the shared values of the community. Instead, they suggest that all pornographic representations harm all women. The harm is done by degrading women, presenting them as dominated by men in context in which such domination is thought to be regarded as natural and even enjoyable. Women may be entirely dehumanized in pornography, becoming merely recipients of treatment by men. MacKinnon and Andrea Dworkin argue that sexual explicitness in the representation of this sort of relationship, combined with sexual arousal in the viewer or reader, cause or

---

[270] Feldman, David, Civil Liberties and Human Rights in England and Wales, 2nd Edition, Oxford University Press, UK, 2002, at p 924

reinforce attitudes of men towards women, and of women towards themselves which tend to encourage male domination in all areas of life[271]. Pornography is seen as form of discrimination against women disempowering them and tending to silence them politically and it merits banning as such. But in reality, there are many varieties, reflecting many different types of sexual activity[272]. It is only possible to argue convincingly that all pornography is violence against women if one imposes a definition which artificially limits pornography to material which represents sadistic heterosexual or lesbian activity. Other types of pornography may represent violence against entities other than women such as dogs, pigs, children, men etc , but it is it objectionable because it reflects violent and dominating attitudes in the relationships between the parties, or because it may be in some way harmful, or because it is revolting? . To insist upon the equation P=V (where P is pornography and V is violence against women) wrongly treats pornography as one indivisible phenomenon[273].

Contrary to the above feminist argument the importance of sexual expression is stressed by Justice Brennan in Roth V US in the following words – "The protection of sex e.g., in art, literature and scientific works is not itself sufficient reason to deny material the constitutional protection of freedom of speech and press. Sex, a great and mysterious motive force in human life, has indisputably been a subject of absorbing interest to mankind through the ages; it is one of the vital problems of human interest and public concern."[274]

Finally, Leonore Tiefer[275], Psychologist and Sex Therapist , argues that "Women are more in danger from the repression of sexually explicit materials than from their free expression."

---

[271] ibid at p 927
[272] ibid at p 928
[273] See Freedman On Lloyd's, Introduction to Jurisprudence, 6th Edition, Sweet & Maxwell International Students Edition, London, 1996 at p 255-565
[274] Roth V. United States, 354 U.S. 476 (1957), available at http://caselaw.lp.findlaw.com/cgi-bin/getcase.pl?court=us&vol=354&invol=476 , visited on 24 Nov 2003

[275] The X-Rated Hoax: A tale of harridans, charlatans & poppycock, available at http://libertus.net/censor/xrhoax6.html , visited on 10 Dec 2003

The moral basis of society is important, but it is probably impossible to establish which moral standards are basic to the survival of any society and which are merely peripheral. It would be unsafe to allow indiscriminate criminalization of all immoral conduct or expression, both because of the uncertain scope of the morality in a pluralist society and because the resulting interference with freedom would be likely to cause social and economic stagnation. At the same time, people sometimes suffer offence which is of such a type, and so intense, as to be experienced subjectively as a form of harm which may be as wounding as physical harm. When this happens, it is understandable that there are demands for the cause to be repressed by law. These demands are ultimately political demands, rather than moral or legal ones, and have to be addressed by members of society in the context of a debate about the type of society in which they wish to live[276].

2.6.3 Child Pornography

Child Pornography is a major abuse of Child's legal right[277]. The damage which sex abuse can do to a child is extremely grave. If, in addition, the abuse has been captured via a pornographic image, the original abuse is both compounded and magnified. Historically child pornography tended to be found mainly in paper based photographic forms, magazines, on videos and in drawings. In many countries these forms still predominate. However, the arrival of the Internet, linked with other technological advances, has introduced an enormous step change both in the volume and the nature of available child pornography. The Internet not only acts as a mechanism for making, displaying, trading and distributing child pornography, it

---

[276] Feldman, David, Civil Liberties and Human Rights in England and Wales, 2nd Edition, Oxford University Press, UK, 2002, at p 925

[277] Article 34 of the UN Convention on the Rights of the Child (CRC) provides that:
States Parties undertake to protect the child from all forms of sexual exploitation and sexual abuse. For these purposes, States Parties shall in particular take all appropriate national, bilateral and multilateral measures to prevent: The inducement or coercion of a child to engage in any unlawful sexual activity; The exploitative use of children in prostitution or other unlawful sexual practises; The exploitative use of children in pornographic performances and materials;

also acts as a vehicle for child pornographers to make contact with and ensnare new victims[278].

The idea of protecting children from sexual exploitation is relatively modern. As late as the 1880s in the United States, the age of consent for girls was just 10 years. In 1977, only two states had legislation specifically outlawing the use of children in obscene material[279].

The first US federal law concerning child pornography, Sexual Exploitation of Children Act was passed in 1978. This Act prohibited the manufacture and commercial distribution of obscene material involving minors under the age of 16. In 1982, the US Supreme Court held that child pornography is not protected by Firs amendment. Further, child pornography has to be separated from obscenity laws and has to be judged on a different standard[280].

Child Protection Act, 1984 raised the age of minor covered by child pornography legislation to 18 and distinction between child pornography and obscenity codified.

In United States V Dost[281], the court expanded the definition of child pornography to include sexually suggestive depictions of a lascivious nature.

The first law that specifically referred to computers and child pornography were passed in 1988 as Child Protection and Obscenity Enforcement Act. Under the provisions of the Act it is illegal to use a computer to depict or advertise child pornography. In applying the provisions of this enactment the court ruled that private possession of child pornography illegal.

Definition of child pornography expanded to include virtual images of children and images that appear to be of a minor under Child Pornography Protection Act[282].

---

[278] Child Pornography, Theme Paper,2nd World Congress against Commercial Sexual Exploitation of Children, Yokohoma, Japan, 2001 , available at
http://www.csecworldcongress.org/en/yokohama/Background/Theme_papers.htm , visited 4 Jul 2004
[279] Child Pornography on the Internet, Community Oriented Policing Services, US Department of Justices, available at http://www.cops.usdoj.gov/mime/open.pdf?Item=1729 , visited on 3 Nov 2004
[280] New York v. Ferber, 458 U.S. 747 (1982) , available at http://laws.findlaw.com/us/458/747.html , visited on 3 Jan 2005
[281] United States V Dost, 636 F. Supp. 828 (S.D. Cal. 1986), available at www.findlaw.com , visited on 4 Feb 2005
[282] Child Pornography on the Internet, Community Oriented Policing Services, US Department of Justices, available at http://www.cops.usdoj.gov/mime/open.pdf?Item=1729, visited on 3 Oct 2005

Child Protector and sexual Predator Punishment Act imposes an obligation on ISP to report known incidents of child pornography to authorities[283].

2.7 Online 'Porn Panic'- Hailing Adults Right to Porn

Pornography, particularly child pornography[284] poses a direct threat to the online users per se. The utilization of cyberspace for the distribution of child pornography is an area of great concern. The practice arguably less prevalent now than it was before international law enforcement officials began to focus on it, but digital images of persons under the age of eighteen engaging in sexually explicit conduct continue to be exchanged via e-mail, Usenet, IRC and file-sharing software[285]. Posting is often to tantamount to distributing, because internet technology typically enables users to copy these pictures easily by clicking on the images and saving it to their hard drives. Usenet has been particularly troubling in this regard. Usenet groups are often filled with nude and suggestive images of young people who are clearly under eighteen. It is generally believed that the mergence of cyberspace has resulted in the widespread and, indeed unprecedented availability of child pornography worldwide[286].

The highly publicized case of US V Thomas[287] is seen by many as a watershed event in the development of cyberlaw. Working out of their Northern California home, the Thomases (husband & wife) operated a highly profitable Bulletin Board System (BBS). Through this system, online customers who registered and paid a

---

[283] ibid

[284] The term 'child pornography' implies conventional pornography with child subjects and includes nay representation whatever means, of any child engaged in real or simulated explicit sexual activities or any representation of the sexual parts of a child for primarily sexual purposes as well as the sue of child to create such representation; as defined by International Centre for Missing & Exploited Children in Child Pornography: Model legislation & Global Review, 2006,available at www.icmec.org , visited on 12 June 2006

[285] Biegel, Stuart, "Beyond our Control – Confronting the limits of our Legal System in the Age of Cyberspace", IT Press, London, 2003
[286] ibid
[287] US V Thomas 74 F.3d 701 (6th Cir. 1996) (upholding conviction of California system administrators for distribution of obscene materials in Tennessee), *cert. den.*, 519 U.S. 820 (1996) available at
http://caselaw.lp.findlaw.com/cgibin/getcase.pl?court=US&navby=case&vol=000&invol=03-218 , visited on 3 Oct 2004

membership fee were able to access sexually explicit pictures via computer. Responding to a complaint from a person in Tennessee, an undercover postal inspector signed on to the system and downloaded sexually explicit Graphic Interchange Format (GIF) files and based primarily on that evidence , the Thomases were indicted in the US District court for the Western District of Tennessee and convicted under a variety of federal obscenity statutes which prohibited " knowingly using and causing to be used a facility and means of interstate commerce - a combined computer/telephone system- for the purpose of transporting obscene computer generated materials in interstate commerce". The US Court of Appeals for the Sixth Circuit upheld the conviction and the US Supreme Court declined to hear the case. The most central and the most controversial aspect of the Thomas decision was its treatment of the Jurisdiction and community standards. Thomas case fired the debate of distribution of pornography over the cyberspace.

The credit of making first legislation to regulate online pornography went to US, when it enacted Communication Decency Act in 1996 (CDA). The enactment of CDA has renewed and extended the debate on pornography in the wake of rapidly changing technology. The perceived proliferation of sexually explicit messages across computer networks has reignited discussion of adults right of access to sexual messages versus the possible contribution of such exposure to antisocial attitudes or behaviour (e.g., discrimination against women, sexual assault). Moreover, the easy point and click nature of many online media, including the WWW, has given rise to the additional concern about the availability of sexually rented materials to an audience of children and adolescents. Media attention to a study conducted by Marty Rimm in 1995 proclaiming widespread and especially deviant pornography on the information superhighway has particularly fuelled these concerns[288]. The report of Marty Rimm is now seriously discredited[289].

---

[288] Mullin Imrich, Doothy, The First Amendment and the Web: The internet Porn Panic and Restricting Indecency in Cyberspace in cyberspace, available at
http://www.library.uscb.edu/untangle/mullin.html , visited on 23 Jun 2004
[289] In a report published in the Georgetown Law Journal (a non-peer-reviewed legal journal), Marty Rimm (1995) examined the download patterns of images from a number of private, self- proclaimed "adult"
BBSs (i.e., BBSs that require payment and proof of age before subscribing). He also examined the number of image postings to a small subset of Usenet newsgroups. Despite his examination of only a

The relationship between technology and distribution of pornographic material can be traced back to 1995 California legislation which made selling/distribution of porn material through machine as an offence. More precisely, the statute made it a crime to sell 'harmful matter.'[290] Free speech activists challenged this statute under the First and Fourteenth Amendments. They claimed that statute is too broad and blocks the distribution of porn through vending machines. The essence of the statute was that it requires porn can be sold only by humans. Lawrence Lessig argues that by requiring that porn can be sold by people, the statute had created two sorts of

---

limited portion of computer network activity, Rimm made a number of alarming assertions about online pornography in general that researchers (especially Hoffman, Novak and Godwin, 1995) have since challenged as unsupported, misleading, or outright misrepresentations of his data.

One now famous statement about the prevalence of computer pornography is Rimm's conclusion that "83.5% of all images posted on the Usenet are pornographic". This proportion of Internet pornography could not appear credible to anyone familiar with the Internet. The percentage actually refers to numbers of images posted to a narrow subset of 32 Usenet newsgroups called "alt.binaries." Specifically, Rimm found that 83.5% of the images posted to 32 "alt.binaries" newsgroups were posted to the 17 of those newsgroups that Rimm labeled "pornographic" . However, even this is likely an inflation, given that Rimm does not disclose how he counted "images" (many image files consist of multiple posts), he does not discuss how he determined which newsgroups were in fact "pornographic" (in a separate table of the forty most accessed newsgroups, he labelled "alt.binaries.pictures.supermodels" as pornographic), and he does not examine whether all the images posted to those groups were actually even sexually explicit. Both Hoffman and Novak and Post maintain that the 83.5% figure is grossly misleading. Using Rimm's own figures, they point out that the part of the Internet that involves Usenet newsgroups represents only 11.5% of total Internet traffic, and of that, only about 3% (by message count) is associated with newsgroups containing pornographic imagery. Thus, they conclude that less than onehalf of 1% (3% of 11.5%) of messages on the Internet is associated with newsgroups that contain pornography (and many of the messages in these "pornographic" newsgroups are text files that may not even be sexually explicit). Although we do not have such data about sexual explicitness in the remaining 88.5% of the non-Usenet Internet traffic (e.g., world wide web use), it is fair to say that only a small percentage of pornographic imagery, relative to non-pornographic content, occurs in the Usenet newsgroups. Nevertheless, the misrepresented 83.5% is what Rimm listed in his summary of findings (and what *Time* publicized).

Interestingly, the 83.5% figure itself comes from the small part of Rimm's study that deals with readership statistics of selected Usenet newsgroups. Most of Rimm's data concerns download patterns on selected private "adult" BBSs. Nevertheless, even with this data, Rimm obscures important methodological procedures: he does not make explicit how his sample of adult BBSs was chosen to be "representative", he confuses the actual numbers of image descriptors that were examined (917, 410 versus 292,114, among others), and he professes both "reliability" and "validity" for his categorizing procedure without providing any data for support . See Ethics of Maty Rimm, available at http://w2.eff.org/Misc/Publications/Declan_McCullagh/www/rimm/rimm.html , visited on 26 Nov 2004

[290] California Penal Code S313.1(c)(2) and (h), it was aimed at protecting the children from harmful material.

constraints, both of which apply to adults as well as kids[291]. One, he says, the constraints of Norms. The norms frown or better, sneer on porn consumers and hence consumers prefer to purchase porn anonymously as machines cannot sneer[292]. Therefore California Statute abridges the constitutionally protected speech, right to read. Second constraint identified by Lessig is cash. Porn distributed in machines costs less money. Perhaps not much less, but for the poor, marginal differences are more than marginally significant. By eliminating this form of distribution, California was effectively eliminating a particular kind of porn — namely, poor-persons'-porn. And so again, with respect to these people, the law effectively "abridges" access to constitutionally protected speech[293]. But the Supreme Court of US refused to accept these arguments and upheld the validity of the statute by denying certiorari[294].

There is a special irony in the Court's denial of certiorari that very week. The week of March 17th, 1997 was an important week for technologies that distribute speech anonymously. On Wednesday of that week, the Court heard arguments on the Communications Decency Act[295] of 1996 (CDA) — Congress's own attempt (failed) to limit the anonymous distribution of porn. Of course there are big differences between the two laws. But there are similarities as well: both deals with technologies that (in their present state) can't easily discriminate in the distribution of porn to kids. And both create incentives to modify these technologies to enable them to discriminate on the basis of age.

And both create incentives to modify these technologies to enable them to discriminate on the basis of age[296]. Yet while the Court let stand the decision in California case (Crawford), it struck down the CDA in *Reno v. ACLU*[297].

---

[291] Lessig, Lawrence, What Things Regulate Speech:CDA2.0 Vs Filtering, Berkman Center for Internet & Society, available at http://cyber.law.harvard.edu/publications, visited on Apr 2004
[292] ibid
[293] ibid
[294] Crawford v Lungren 96 F.3d 280 (1996), available at www.findlaw.com , visited on 4 Nov 2004
[295] Telecommunications Act of 1996, Pub. L 104-104, Title V, 110 Stat. 56, 133-43 (Communications Decency Act).

[296] Lessig, Lawrence, What Things Regulate Speech:CDA2.0 Vs Filtering, Berkman Center for Internet & Society, available at http://cyber.law.harvard.edu/publications
[297] 521 US 844

In Reno, provisions of the CDA were challenged by various free speech organizations led by ACLU. Plaintiffs focused their challenge on two provisions of section 502 of the CDA which amend 47 U.S.C. Secs.223 (a) and 223(d).

Section 223(a)(1)(B) provides in part that any person in interstate or foreign communications who, "by means of a telecommunications device," "knowingly . . . makes, creates, or solicits" and "initiates the transmission" of "any comment, request, suggestion, proposal, image or other communication which is obscene or indecent, knowing that the recipient of the communication is under 18 years of age," "shall be criminally fined or imprisoned."[298]

Section 223(d)(1) ("the patently offensive provision"), makes it a crime to use an "interactive computer service to "send" or "display in a manner available" to a person under age 18, "any comment, request, suggestion, proposal, image, or other communication that, in context, depicts or describes, in terms patently offensive as measured by contemporary community standards, sexual or excretory activities or organs, regardless of whether the user of such service placed the call or initiated the communication."[299]

Plaintiffs also challenge on the same grounds the provisions in Sec. 223(a)(2) and Sec. 223(d)(2), which make it a crime for anyone to "knowingly permit any telecommunications facility under [his or her] control to be used for any activity prohibited" in Secs. 223(a)(1)(B) and 223(d)(1). The challenged provisions impose a punishment of a fine, up to two years imprisonment, or both for each offense. Plaintiffs make clear that they do not quarrel with the statute to the extent that it covers obscenity or child pornography, which were already proscribed before the CDA's adoption[300].

In defense Government argued that CDA was not constitutionally overbroad and cited "safe harbor" defenses in new Sec. 223 (e) which provides as follows;

---

[298] As discussed in the judgment by Sloviter, Chief Judge, United States Court of Appeals for the Third Circuit; Buckwalter and Dalzell, Judges, United States District Court for the Eastern District of Pennsylvania in ACLU v Reno, available at
http://supreme.usatoday.findlaw.com/supreme_court/decisions/lower_court/98-5591.html , visited on 3 Nov 2003

[299] ibid
[300] See 18 U.S.C. Secs. 1464-65 (criminalizing obscene material)

In addition to any other defenses available by law[301]

(1) No person shall be held to have violated subsection (a) or (d) of this section solely for providing access or connection to or from a facility, system, or network not under that person's control, including transmission, downloading, intermediate storage, access software, or other related capabilities that are incidental to providing such access or

connection that does not include the creation of the content of the communication.

(2) The defenses provided by paragraph (1) of this subsection shall not be applicable to a person who is a conspirator with an entity actively involved in the creation or knowing distribution of communications that violate this section, or who knowingly advertises the availability of such communications.

(3) The defenses provided in paragraph (1) of this subsection shall not be applicable to a person who provides access or connection to a facility, system, or network engaged in the violation of this section that is owned or controlled by such person.

(4) No employer shall be held liable under this section for the actions of an employee or agent unless the employee's or agent's conduct is within the scope of his or her employment or agency and the employer (A) having knowledge of such conduct, authorizes or ratifies such conduct, or (B) recklessly disregards such conduct.

(5) It is a defense to a prosecution under subsection (a)(1)(B) or (d) of this section, or under subsection (a)(2) of this section with respect to the use of a facility for an activity under subsection (a)(1)(B) that a person --

(A) has taken, in good faith, reasonable, effective, and appropriate actions under the circumstances to restrict or prevent access by minors to a communication specified in such subsections, which may involve any appropriate measures to restrict minors from such communications, including any method which is feasible under available technology; or

(B) has restricted access to such communication by requiring use of a verified credit card, debit account, adult access code, or adult personal identification number.

---

[301] 47 U.S.C Sec.223(e)

(6) the Federal Communications Commission may describe measures which are reasonable, effective, and appropriate to restrict access to prohibited communications under subsection (d) of this section. Nothing in this section authorizes the Commission to enforce, or is intended to provide the Commission with the authority to approve, sanction, or permit, the use of such measures. The Commission shall have no enforcement authority over the failure to utilize such measures.

The District court found that the CDA places an unacceptably heavy burden on protected speech, and held that the defenses do not constitute the sort of 'narrow tailoring' that will save an otherwise patently invalid unconstitutional provision. In Sable Communication, the court remarked that the speech restriction at issue in that case amounted to 'burning the house to roast the pig'[302]. The CDA casting a far darker shadow over free speech threatens to torch a large segment of the internet community[303].

2.7.1 The Child Online Protection Act of 1998

Following the CDA defeat, the members of the Congress went back to the drawing board, attempting to craft a second statue that would serve to protect children from obscene and pornographic material in cyberspace. Labeled as "Son of CDA" or "CDA II" by many commentators, this Statute – the Child Online Protection Act (COPA)- was passed and signed into law by President Clinton in 1998.

The congressional team that worked on the COPA knew that the court in Reno V ACLU had identified three basic structural flaws in the provisions of the Communication Decency Act that were ultimately struck down. They are

(a) the prohibitions were too broad

(b) key terms were vague and undefined

(c) the steps potential defendants might take to avoid prosecution and conviction may not have been technologically feasible at the time

---

[302] Sable Communications of Cal.Inc V FCC, 492 US 115 (1989), available at http://laws.findlaw.com/us/492/115.html, visited 3 Nov 2004
[303] ibid

Congress sought to respond to the ruling by crafting much narrower statute aimed at commercial activity directed toward young people. It only addressed the World Wide Web (WWW) and only prohibited material harmful to minors. Under the terms of the Act, both civil and criminal penalties were mandated for persons who "knowingly and with knowledge of the character of the material, in interstate or foreign commerce by means of WWW, make any communication for commercial purposes that is available to any minor and that includes any material that is harmful to minors[304].

By using the term 'harmful to minors' and defining it precisely, Congress hoped to avoid the problems that had arisen in Reno I (Reno V ACLU) because of such vague and indeterminate terms as indecent. Under the COPA, a minor was defined as a person under the age of seventeen and material that is harmful to minors was defined as:

Any communication, picture, image, graphic image file, article, recording, writing, or other matter of any kind that is obscene or that

(a) the average person, applying contemporary community standards, would find, taking the material as a whole and with respect to minors, is designed to appeal to, or is designed to pander to, the prurient interest;

(b)depicts, describes, or represents in a manner patently offensive with respect to minors, an actual or simulated sexual act or sexual contact, an actual or simulated normal or perverted sexual act, or a lewd exhibition of the genitals or post pubescent female breast ; and

(c) taken as a whole , lacks serious literary , artisitic, political or scientific value for minors

It is important to note that other statutes prohibiting material that is harmful to minors are on the books at the state level, and a similar prohibition focusing entirely

---

[304] Burke D Debra, Thinking outside the Box: Child Pornography, obscenity and the Constitution, Virginia Journal of Law and Technology, Vol.8, N0.11, Fall 2003, available at www.vjolt.net , visited on 12 Apr 2005

on the offline world had already been deemed constitutional in a 1968 US Supreme Court decision[305].

Given the apparent precision of the COPA and the fact that it appeared to target commercial pornographers, there was much less concern in the online community that these prohibitions might actually have negative impact on day-to-day activities of the average online user. Indeed, compared to the outcry that greeted the passage of the CDA, the reaction to the COPA was relatively muted. And the coalition of plaintiffs assembled by the ACLU to challenge the Act was significantly smaller than the coalition that had challenged the CDA.

In ACLU V Reno II, plaintiff challenged the provisions of COPA and asserted that the legislation " threatens to turn....the internet... into a child proof medium whose level of discourse would be reduced to that suitable for a sandbox". Further, they asserted that the implementation of the Act would unconstitutionally burden the speech of adults. Analyzing the Act under traditional First amendment principles, the trial court determined that any assessment of burden placed on protected speech by COPA must " take into consideration the unique factors that affect communication in the new and technology laden medium of the Web." In particular, the court found that "the nature of the Web and the Internet is such that Web site operators and content providers cannot know who is accessing their sites, or from where, or how old the users are, unless they take affirmative steps to gather information from the user and the user is willing to give them truthful responses." Thus, Web site owners and content providers who think they may be displaying material harmful to minors must construct barriers to the material that adults must cross as well[306].

The trial court agreed with the plaintiffs that "the implementation of credit card or adult verification screens in front of material that is harmful to minors may deter users accessing such materials and that the loss of users of such material may affect the website owner's ability to provide such communications". The US Government

---

[305] See Ginsberg v New York 390 US 629, available at,
http://caselaw.lp.findlaw.com/scripts/getcase.pl?court=US&vol=390&invol=629, visited on 4 Feb 2003
[306] ACLU V Reno II 31 E.Supp.2d 473, available at , http://epic.org/free_speech/copa/ , visited on 1 Jan 2003 (Ashcroft V ACLU)

had argued that the statute targeted only commercial pornographers, but the court agreed with the plaintiffs that many respectable sites be implicated as well.[307] Indeed, the trial court questioned whether the statute could "efficaciously meet its goal" at all, given that minors could still gain access to material harmful to minors via overseas sites, noncommercial sites and online protocols other than HTTP (Hyper Text Transport Protocol). Moreover, minors could legitimately possess a credit or debit card and access material harmful to minors despite the existence of screening mechanisms. Echoing the US Supreme Court's conclusion in Reno I, the court declared that a more effective and less restrictive means to shield minors from harmful materials is to rely upon filtering and blocking technology. Judge Reed succinctly explained the limitations of COPA. He wrote "There is nothing in the text of COPA that limits its applicability to so-called commercial pornographers only". The court reasoned that because COPA (i) imposed liability on someone whose communication includes any material that is harmful to minors (ii) defined a communication for commercial purposes very broadly and (iii) expressly indicated that it is neither necessary that the person make a profit from the communication nor that such communications be the person's sole or principal business or source of income, the prohibitions could apply to a very wide range of Web sites that contain some potentially harmful to minors.

Not only the trial court rule for the plaintiffs, but the decision was upheld by the third Circuit courts of Appeals in the summer of 2000. Central to the appellate court's reasoning was the determination that key differences exist between the WWW and other forms of communication. In a language reflecting the view that cyberspace is at times unique enough to merit significantly different legal approaches and conclusions the court of appeals declared:

"Each medium of expression must be assessed for First Amendment purposes by standards suited to it, for each may present its own problems. In considering the unique factors that affect communication in the new and technology laden medium of the Web, we are convinced that there are crucial differences between a 'brick and

---

[307] ibid

mortar' outlet and the online Web that dramatically affect a First Amendment analysis."

But US Supreme Court has refused to accept the ruling of Reno II by Third Circuit Court, holding that COPA's reliance on community standards to identify material that is harmful to minors does not , in itself , render the statute substantially overbroad[308]. The Court however, expressed no view about other issues raised in the Third Circuit, including (i) whether COPA suffers from substantial over breadth for reasons other than its use of community standards[309]; (ii) whether COPA is unconstitutionally vague or (3) whether COPA survives strict scrutiny.

From the above discussion it is clear that censorship and filtering of internet is prevailing and the government's efforts to regulate the fundamental human right like freedom of speech is being adversely affected.

2.8 Regulation of Sexually Explicit Material in Cyberspace- Analysis

Sexually explicit material on the internet includes text, pictures, and chat and extends from the modesty titillating to the hardest core. These files are created, named, and posted in the same manner as material that is not sexually explicit, and may be accessed either deliberately or unintentionally during the course of imprecise search. Once a provider posts its content on the internet, it cannot prevent that content from entering any community. Some of the communications over the internet that originates in foreign countries is also sexually explicit[310]. Though such material is widely available, users seldom encounter such content accidentally. A document's title or a description of the document will usually appear before the document itself and in many cases the user will receive detailed information about a site's content before by warning he or she need take the step to access the document.

---

[308] Ashcroft V ACLU, 122S.Ct.1700, 1713 (2002), available at www.laws.findlaw.com , visited on 14 Sep 2004
[309] Harper John A, Traditional Free Speech Law: Does it Apply on the Internet", Computer Law Review and Technology Journal, Vol.VI, 2002
[310] Justice Stevens in Reno v ACLU 521 US 844 , available at http://www.law.cornell.edu/supct/html/historics/USSC_CR_0521_0844_ZS.html, visited on 1 Jan 2003

Almost all sexually explicit images are preceded by warnings as to the content[311]. For that reason, the 'odds are slim' that a user would enter a sexually explicit site by accident. Unlike communications received by radio or television, the receipt of information on the internet requires a series of affirmative steps more deliberate and directed than merely turning a dial. A child requires some sophistication and some ability to read to retrieve material and thereby to use the internet unattended[312].

Systems like, filtering software, have been developed to help parents control the harmful material that may be available on a home computer with internet access. A system may either limit a computer's access to an approved list of sources that have been identified as containing no adult material, it may block designated inappropriate sites, or it may attempt to block messages containing identifiable objectionable features. Although parental control software currently can screen for certain suggestive words or for known sexually explicit sites, it cannot screen for sexually explicit images[313].

Justice Stevens seems to be transferring the burden of protecting the children from harmful material to their parents. To explain the extent of regulation of speech in cyberspace Lawrence Lessig divides free speech law into three classes[314]. One class is speech that everyone has the right to. Over this class, the state's power is quite slight or minimal: The state may effect reasonable time, place, and manner restrictions, but no more. The paradigm is political speech, but in effect it includes any speech not described in the next two classes. A second class is speech that no one has the right to. The model here is obscene speech, or more strongly, child pornography. Here the state's power is practically unlimited[315]. With child porn at least, the state can ban the production, distribution, and consumption of such speech; and with obscene speech, the state can for example ban production and distribution. The third class is speeches that people over the age of seventeen have a

---

[311] ibid
[312] ibid
[313] ibid
[314] Lessig, Lawrence, Code and Other Laws of Cyberspace, Basic Books, New York,1999 at p 92-94
[315] Lessig cites the decision of the court in Roth V United States, 354 U.S. 476 (1957), available at http://laws.findlaw.com/us/354/476.html , visited on 4 Dec 2005

right to, while people under seventeen do not. This is sometimes, and unhelpfully called, "indecent" speech, but that moniker is plainly too broad. A more precise description would be speech that is "obscene as to children" even though not obscene as to adults. The category is obscenity, with the status of the relevant community determined by age rather than geography[316].

According to Lessig it is the class II regulations that increase the regulability of cyberspace. By reducing the burden of regulations generally, class II regulations make other regulations easier and hence more regulation possible. At this stage he seeks to answer two questions[317]. The first one is, is such regulations permissible? And the second, if it is permissible, how should it be evaluated? For the first question his answer is yes. There is no constitutional right to an unregulable space or in cyberspace designed to facilitate otherwise legitimate regulations are plainly permissible. In constitutional terms, class II regulations are regulations of the necessary and proper clause regulations that make it easier to carry other regulations into effect, implied in a grant of legislative power even if not expressly granted[318]. This view of Lessig is very difficult to accept. Cyberpsace being a borderless medium, it is almost impossible for any country to regulate all alone including US and regulating the cyberspace or real space without legislative power is even worse. Lessig's answer to the second question is even more evasive as he suggests cyberspace could be extraordinarily regulable space with proper architecture and behaviour.

If we take necessary clues regarding regulation of pornography over the cyberspace from US courts, three times in the past several years, critics of pornography on the Internet have sought through federal legislations, to prevent children from gaining access to it. The first of these described above, was the Communication Decency Act of 1996 (CDA) which criminalized the 'knowing' transmission over the Internet of 'obscene or indecent messages to any recipient under18 years of age. The CDA was widely criticized by civil libertarians and soon succumbed to a constitutional

---

[316] Lessig, Lawrence, What Things Regulate Speech:CDA2.0 Vs Filtering, Berkman Center for Internet & Society, available at http://cyber.law.harvard.edu/publications, visited on 2 Feb 2005
[317] ibid
[318] ibid

challenge. US Supreme Court holding that it violated First Amendment provided the following reasons;

(i) because it restricted speech on the basis of its content, it could not be justified as a "time, place, and manner" regulation;

(ii) its references to "indecent" and "patently offensive" messages were unconstitutionally vague;

(iii) its supposed objectives could all be achieved through regulations less restrictive of speech;

(iv) it failed to exempt from its prohibitions sexually explicit material with scientific, educational, or other redeeming social value.

Two aspects of the Court's ruling are likely to have considerable impact on future constitutional decisions in this area. First, the Court rejected the Government's effort to analogize the Internet to traditional broadcast media (especially television), which the Court had previously held could be regulated more strictly than other media. Unlike TV, the Court reasoned, the Internet has not historically been subject to extensive regulation, is not characterized by a limited spectrum of available frequencies, and is not "invasive." Consequently, the Internet enjoys full First Amendment protection. Second, the Court encouraged the development of technologies that would enable parents to block their children's access to Internet sites offering kinds of material that the parents deemed offensive[319].

To overcome the deficiencies pointed out by the Supreme Court in Reno V ACLU, Congress enacted another legislation aimed protecting children, Children Online Protection Act, 1998 (COPA) which provided obliged commercial Web operators to restrict access to material considered "harmful to minors" which was, in turn, defined as any communication, picture, image, graphic image file, article, recording, writing or other matter of any kind that is obscene or that meets three requirements:

(1) "The average person, applying contemporary community standards, would find, taking the material as a whole and with respect to minors, is designed to appeal to, or is designed to pander to, the prurient interest."

---

[319] Fisher William , Benkler Yochai , Brackley Rebecca and Ma Sarah , Freedom of Expression on the Internet, Internet Law Program, Berkman Center for Internet and Society, available at http://cyber.law.harvard.edu/ilaw/mexico_2006_module_4_freedom , visited on 2 Jan 2006

(2) The material "depicts, describes, or represents, in a manner patently offensive with respect to minors, an actual or simulated sexual act or sexual conduct, an actual or simulated normal or perverted sexual act or a lewd exhibition of the genitals or post-pubescent female breast."

(3) The material, "taken as a whole, lacks serious literary, artistic, political, or scientific value for minors."

Once again, civil libertarians and online publishers challenged the statute on the grounds that it was unduly burdensome and would excessively chill online speech. The case was decided by the Supreme Court in May 2002[320]. Both of the lower courts found that Congress had exceeded its constitutional authority. In the judgment of the Third Circuit Court of Appeals, the critical defect of COPA was its reliance upon the criterion of "contemporary community standards" to determine what kinds of speech are permitted on the Internet[321].

Because material posted on the Web is accessible by all Internet users worldwide, and because current technology does not permit a Web publisher to restrict access to its site based on the geographic locale of a each particular Internet user, COPA essentially requires that every Web publisher subject to the statute abide by the most restrictive and conservative state's community standard in order to avoid criminal liability[322].

The net result was to impose burdens on permissible expression more severe than can be tolerated by the Constitution. The court acknowledged that its ruling did not leave much room for constitutionally valid restrictions on Internet pornography:

"We are forced to recognize that, at present, due to technological limitations, there may be no other means by which harmful material on the Web may be constitutionally restricted, although, in light of rapidly developing technological

---

[320] Ashcroft V ACLU 542 U.S. 656 (2004) available at http://www.law.cornell.edu/supct/html/03-218.ZS.html , visited on 2 Jan, 2006
[321] ibid
[322] Supra Note 219

advances, what may now be impossible to regulate constitutionally may, in the not-too-distant future, become feasible."[323]

One of the arguments made by those who had opposed the CDA was that there was no need for such expansive regulation, because technology provided filters that would allow parents to control what their children would see. The children would thus be protected, but adults could access whatever they wanted to see. Very few voices were raised at the time concerned that the censorial effects of filters were as bad in many cases as some form of direct regulation.

The congress again   mad e an attempt to curb child pornography by enacting children Internet Protection Act   (CIPA) in 2000,   which required schools and libraries that receive federal funding (either grants or "e-rate" subsidies) to install Internet filtering equipment on library computers that can be used by children.

Again CIPA was opposed by many libertarians. Opponents claimed that it suffers from all the constitutional infirmities of the CDA and COPA. In addition, it reinforces one form of the "digital divide" - by subjecting poor children, who lack home computers and must rely upon public libraries for access to the Internet, to restrictions that more wealthy children can avoid. However, the Supreme Court disagreed in a complex ruling, and upheld CIPA in United States v. American Library Association[324].

The CDA, COPA, and CIPA have one thing in common: they all involve overt governmental action and thus are subject to challenge under the First Amendment. Some observers of the Internet argue that more dangerous than these obvious legislative initiatives are the efforts by private Internet Service Providers to install filters on their systems that screen out kinds of content that the ISPs believe their subscribers would find offensive. Because policies of this sort are neither mandated nor encouraged by the government, they would not, under conventional constitutional principles, constitute "state action" -- and thus would not be

---

[323] Supra Note 219
[324] United States v. American Library Association. 123 S.Ct. 2297 (2003)., available at www.findlaw.com , visited on 23 Sep 2005

vulnerable to constitutional scrutiny. Such a result, argues Larry Lessig, would be pernicious; to avoid it, we need to revise our understanding of the "state action" doctrine[325].

2.9 Conclusion

Internet offers a great platform for self-expression. It promotes democratic values and gives us an opportunity to express and share our views and opinions with others. As John Stuart Mill calls 'Market place of idea for discovering truth' is greatly fulfilled by this new revolutionary media.

Pornography has been the central issue that is making legislators to impose restrictions on free speech in cyberspace. Several attempts made by the US government to bring in some control over the netizens free speech so far have not been successful. Free speech being a basic human right the policy of the government has to be promoting and protecting it rather than restricting it. Protection offered to free speech by American courts is the highest in the world.

Panics about the corruptive influences of new media technology are not new. Every major technological innovation, from the telephone to the radio to motion pictures to television, has seen an outpouring of public and political concern about its potential for facilitating societal decay, particularly regarding influences on children. Furthermore, fears about changing sexual morals or deviant sexual behavior have accompanied most of these technological outcries. Therefore, recent uproar about sexually explicit images, stories, and discussion available via computer networks, what Mike Godwin of the Electronic Frontier Foundation has called "the great Internet sex panic of 1995" is not surprising. Nevertheless, this panic is important because its influence on government attempts at regulation and public use

---

[325] Fisher William, Benkler Yochai, Brackley Rebecca & Sarah Ma, Freedom of Expression on the Internet, Internet Law Program, Berkman Center for Internet & Society, available at http://cyber.law.harvard.edu/ilaw/mexico_2006_module_4_freedom , visited on 6 Dec 2006.

of computer networks pose potentially dangerous restrictions on online communication behavior[326].

Policy makers and researchers that attempt to treat the sexual content of all of these media as mere "cybersex" or "cyberporn" may ultimately encourage regulatory efforts based on inaccurate assumptions about the pervasiveness, intrusiveness, or social effects of very different content. For example, most political and public concern about sex-related materials has centered on pornographic visual imagery, despite evidence that it is only a small part of online sexual content. Unfortunately, where social science might have served to illuminate the public about online imagery, conflating findings and misrepresented data in Marty Rimm's study of download patterns of images from private "adult" BBSs and readership data for a small subset of Usenet newsgroups unfortunately has only served to cloud the debate.

Everyone agrees that children interests have to be protected but at the same we should not make an attempt to harm the free speech interest of adults. Drawing a line between 'harmful material to children' and adults right to such kind of material is a very difficult one and appropriate policies have to be evolved through consensus among net users to achieve this otherwise total governmental regulations becomes inevitable.

---

[326] Mullin Imrich Dorothy, The First Amendment and the Web: The Internet Porn Panic and Restricting Indecency in Cyberspace, available at http://www.library.ucsb.edu/untangle/mullin4.html , visited on 25 May 2006

Chapter 3

CYBER DEFAMATION, ANONYMITY AND HATE SPEECH

The Internet presents new opportunities and challenges. With its information filled Web sites, it offers great platform for everyone to express and to reach more people than ever - opinion molders, the media, law enforcement, educators, students, parents and the general public - around the world and at the same time it has become breeding ground for defamation, hate, harassment, anti-Semitism, bigotry and extremism (emphasis added)

www.adl.org[327]

3.1 Introduction

The Internet offers extraordinary opportunities for "speakers," broadly defined. Political candidates, cultural critics, corporate gadflies - anyone who wants to express an opinion about anything - can make their thoughts available to a world-wide audience far more easily than has ever been possible before. A large and growing group of Internet participants have seized that opportunity[328].

Some observers find the resultant outpouring of speech exhilarating. They see in it nothing less than the revival of democracy and the restoration of community. Other observers find the amount and, above all, the kind of speech that the Internet has stimulated offensive or frightening. Pornography, hate speech, defamation, lurid threats -- these flourish alongside debates over the future of the political parties and exchanges of views concerning almost any matter. This phenomenon has provoked various efforts to limit the kind of speech in which one may engage on the Internet or to develop systems to "filter out" the more offensive material[329].

---

[327] Anti-defamation League, www.adl.org ; the object of the league is to stop, by appeals to reason and conscience and if necessary, by appeals to law and ultimate purpose is to secure justice and fair treatment to all citizens alike and to put an end forever to unjust and unfair discrimination against and ridicule any sect or body of citizen

[328] Fisher William, Benckler Yochai, Brackely Rebacca and Ma Shara, Freedom of Expression on the Internet, Berkmen Center for Internet and Society, available at
http://cyber.law.harvard.edu/ilaw/mexico_2006_module_4_freedom , visited on 2 Feb 2005.

[329] ibid

3.2 The Nature of Defamation

The origins of the law relating to defamation, of which libel and slander are the twin components, date back as far as King Alfred the Great who, in the ninth century , decreed that slanderers should have their tongues cut out. Although over the years the penalties imposed upon those who transgress this branch of the civil law have become financial rather than physical, the principles have remained virtually unchanged[330]. The legal rationale was expressed with great clarity by Justice Potter Stewart of the American Supreme Court in 1966 – "The right of a man to the protection of his own reputation from unjustified invasion and wrongful hurt reflects no more than our basic concept of the essential dignity and worth of every human being, a concept at the root of any decent system of liberty"[331]

What is defamatory? There is no single, comprehensive definition recognized by law. The classic formula devised by Baron Parke in an 1840 case is that a defamatory statement is one which injures someone's reputation by exposing him to hatred, contempt or ridicule'. By the 1920s courts recognized that the definition was too narrow. It was after all, easy to damage a man's reputation, say in his business dealings, by statements which would provoke neither hatred, contempt or ridicule. Lord Aitken set out an alternative test in 1924: "…would the words tend to lower the plaintiff in the estimation of reasonable people generally"[332].

As society and its morals adapt with the passage of time so also the proper standard to be applied in judging what amounts to defamation. It is after all geared to the thinking of reasonable man or right thinking member of society. Thus, what may have been clearly defamatory fifty years ago might not now be regarded as such. Nowhere is this demonstrated better than society's attitudes on sexual matters[333]. To say in 1920 that a young lady spent her vacation in a Paris hotel with her boyfriend

---

[330] Crone, Tom, "Law and the Media- An everyday guide for Professionals ", 3rd Edition, Focal Press, London, 1995, at p 220
[331] Franklin A Marc, Rabin L Robert and Green D Michael, Tort Law and Alternatives : Cases and Materials, 8th Edition, Foundation Press, US, 2006
[332] ibid
[333] Glannon W Joseph, ; 2nd edition, Aspen Publishers, US,2000

would certainly have reflected discredit upon her but it is by no means certain that the average person today think any worse of her for it[334].

The wrong of defamation is of two kinds namely, libel and slander. In libel the defamatory statement is made in some permanent and visible form, such as writing, printing, pictures or effigies. In slander it is made in spoken words or in some other transitory form, whether visible or audible, such as gestures or inarticulate but significant sounds[335].

Defamation laws differ widely. Thus, for example, English law imposes liability regardless of whether the publisher of a statement knew or ought to have known it was defamatory[336] whereas under Finnish law a distinction is made between intentional and negligent defamation[337]. Under US law a statement referring to a public figure will only be defamatory if malice can be proved on the part of the maker of the statement[338]. Whether a defendant has an obligation to identify anonymous statements which it has made available is also a policy question to which national statements which it has made available is also a policy question to which national laws may give different answers. These national differences make it difficult for an internet publisher to assess in advance whether material is likely to give rise to liability.

3.2.1 Right against Defamation - A Human Right

Right to reputation or right against defamation is recognized as a basic human rights in international as well as national legal instruments. Art.12 of the Universal declaration of Human rights seeks to protect the reputation of individuals from arbitrary attack on reputation and reads as follows;

---

[334] Crone, Tom, "Law and the Media- An everyday guide for Professionals ", 3rd Edition, Focal Press, London, 1995, at p 222

[335] ibid

[336] E Hulton and Co V Jones [1910] AC 20 cited by Chris Reed in Internet Law- Text and Materials, 2nd Edition, universal Publishing Co.,2004

[337] Finnish Penal code

[338] New York times Co V Sullivan 376 uS 254 (1964), available at www.findlaw.com , visited on 5 Feb 2005

"No one shall be subjected to arbitrary interference with his privacy, family, home or correspondence, **nor to attacks upon his honour and reputation**. Everyone has the right to the protection of the law against such interference or attacks."[339]

Art.10 of the European Convention on Human Rights also recognizes right to reputation as basic human right by way of imposing restriction on freedom of speech and expression[340].

3.3 Defamation in Cyberspace

Like obscene expression defamation stands out as an example of behaviour that has remained widespread in an online environment that many believe to be too free. While some continue to insist that this freedom is a breath of fresh air, others argue that all democracies have their limits and bemoan the apparent disappearance of these limits in the online world, where rampant violations of copyright, obscenity and defamation laws is not only tolerated but often encouraged[341]. At the heart of the matter in the defamation context is the often unrestrained dissemination of unsubstantiated allegations in cyberspace. Such activity not only includes defamatory statements by ordinary citizens, but also encompasses irresponsible and legally questionable remarks by a variety of persons and groups whose status

---

[339] Art.17 of International Covenant on Civil and Political Rights reiterates what is stated in UDHR-No one shall be subjected to arbitrary or unlawful interference with his privacy, family, home or correspondence, nor to unlawful attacks on his honour and reputation.

[340] Article 10 (1) - Everyone has the right to freedom of expression. this right shall include freedom to hold opinions and to receive and impart information and ideas without interference by public authority and regardless of frontiers. This article shall not prevent States from requiring the licensing of broadcasting, television or cinema enterprises. (2)The exercise of these freedoms, since it carries with it duties and responsibilities, may be subject to such formalities, conditions, restrictions or penalties as are prescribed by law and are necessary in a democratic society, in the interests of national security, territorial integrity or public safety, for the prevention of disorder or crime, for the protection of health or morals, for the **protection of the reputation or the rights of others**, for preventing the disclosure of information received in confidence, or for maintaining the authority and impartiality of the judiciary.

[341] Biegel, Stuart, Beyond our Control – Confronting the limits of our Legal System in the Age of Cyberspace, MIT Press, London, 2003 at p 82

enables them to attract large audience to their web sites[342]. Allegations that are true at the time they are made cannot generally be defamatory under the law. But the online world on any given day is filled with absolute lies regarding persons, groups, and companies. Some of the worst allegations in recent years were reserved for former President Clinton himself, with many of the accusers taking advantage of the technology to remain anonymous even as they spread rumor and innuendo across the globe[343].

In the early 1990s, online moderators often enforced a certain level of civility and ethical on bulletin boards, discussion forums and mailing lists. By the latter part of the decade, however, most of these moderators disappeared. The freewheeling nature of the current public discourse is seen as a right by the great majority of netizens[344]. But some are beginning to wonder about the possible negative consequences of such unrestrained openness as a large percentage of the population migrates to the online world.

Laws regarding defamation specifically and freedom of expression in general can vary tremendously from country to country, leading to some very difficult controversies in the areas of jurisdiction and enforcement. In the US, the issue has arisen within the context of several trials addressing the liability of ISPs and content provides for defamatory acts, particularly as the courts attempt to interpret the provisions in the Telecommunication Act of 1996 that insulates service providers from liability in particular situations[345].

It has been clearly established that libel law will apply in case of broadcasting in respect of any statements made over it. In the case of e-mail and the content of internet and WWW, it seems beyond question that there is a sufficient degree of recording to ensure that the law of libel will apply. Some doubt, perhaps, remains

---

[342] ibid

[343] ibid at p 83

[344] Zittrain Jonathan, The Rise and Fall of Sysdom , Harvard Journal Law and technology 10 (1997):495

[345] Sec.230 of Telecommunication Act, 1996 states:"No provider or user of an interactive computer service shall be treated as the publisher or speaker of any information provided by another information content provider." The term information content provider is defined as 'any person or entity that is responsible , in whole or in part, for the creation or development of information provided through the internet or any other interactive computer service'.

concerning the status of services such as chat rooms, where the atmosphere at least is closer to a conversational forum and where no permanent record is maintained[346]. In cases of slander a defence is available, commonly referred as 'vulgar abuse'. The essence of the defence is that words, albeit defamatory in content, were neither intended as such nor would be so regarded by anyone listening to the exchange. Such a defence might seem appropriate in relation to the many postings to internet newsgroups, where the concept of the 'flame war' is well established. Anyone perusing computer newsgroup will be aware that forthright expression is often the order of the day and that 'flame wars', in which discussion is reduced to a level of personal abuse, are not uncommon[347]. Although the existence of a culture encouraging robust and blunt debate cannot affect the determination whether a message is defamatory, there may be an element of consent on the part of those participating in such fora. With newsgroups, although there would seem no doubt that postings are written and the range of dissemination is comparable than that associated with the written word, the attitudes and practices coupled with the speed of communication are perhaps more akin to the spoken word[348].

3.4 Liability of Internet Service Providers

Internet Service Providers (ISP) play vital role in connecting the user to cyberspace. They are intermediary between the user and the Internet.

In its physical world sense, publishing is seen as a positive activity, that is, a publisher would have had to do something such as arranging for the printing of a work, sending out copies, selling copies etc. to perform his role as a publisher[349]. This is in line with definition of publication as the communication of statement to at least one person other than the claimant[350]. In many cases, however, the process hereby a user access information held by an intermediary does not require any

---

[346] Lloyd , Ian, Legal Aspects of the Information Society,Butterworths,London,2000
[347] ibid at p 214
[348] ibid at p 216
[349] See definition of publication in the Oxford advanced Learner's Dictionary, 7th edition; 'The action of making publicly known; public notification or pronouncement; promulgation'
[350] Halsbury's Laws of England, vol.28, 4th Edition, Butterworths, London, Libel and slander, para 60

positive action on the intermediary's part. If the transaction is analyzed at the level of the human or legal persons involved, it appears that the user pulls the information from the intermediary's server, so that the intermediary plays an entirely passive role. Viewed at the software and hardware level, though, it might be argued that the information is in fact pushed out by the software running on the defendant's computer. The process actually carried out as follows;

(i)   the user or the user's software issues a request to the intermediary's computer system[351];

(ii)   software has been set up by the intermediary which automatically responds to such a request with no human intervention[352];

(iii)   that software transmits the information requested from the intermediary's system to the user[353].

From one perspective, the user is controlling the software running on the intermediary's system and is thus responsible for the transmission. From a different perspective, the transmission is undertaken by software which is in the possession of and under the overall control of the intermediary, making him responsible for the transmission. This second approach was adopted by the UK courts in Godfrey V Demon Internet Ltd[354]., where the defendant ISP was sued for a defamatory statement carried in a news group hosted on its server. Defendant argued that it could not be a publisher, as it merely played a passive role by providing infrastructure necessary for the posters of messages to make their views known. This contention was rejected by the court, stating that because the defendant chose to receive and store the newsgroup and had the power to delete messages from it, hence it was at common law a publisher.

---

[351] Reed, Chris, Internet Law- Text and Materials, 2nd Edition, Universal Publishingco.,New Delhi, 2004 at 114
[352] ibid at p 114
[353] ibid at p 114
[354] [1999] 4 All ER 342

3.4.1 Case Law Development – Conflicting decisions

Two US district court decisions that came to very different conclusions in cases with very similar fact patterns brought the issue of online defamation to the forefront by the mid 1990s.Both cases focused not on the liability of persons who originally made the libelous statements, but on the liability of commercial online services for defamatory conduct in moderated bulletin board discussions. The disputes were litigated under the legal principle that "one who repeats or otherwise republishes defamatory matter is subject to liability as if he had originally published it".

In the first case, Cubby V Compuserve Inc.,[355] the commercial online service provider was absolved of any responsibility for the defamatory comments posted in an online newsletter called 'Rumorville[356]'. The newsletter, which appeared on Compuserve's Journalism Forum, had been moderated by an independent company under contract with the online service. The court found that posts to the forum were uploaded instantly, and that Compuserve had no more ability to monitor and control the transmission of the defamatory material than a public library, bookstore or news stand.

---

[355] Cubby V Compuserve 776 F.Supp. 135 Oct. 29, 1991 Case No. 90 Civ. 6571 (PKL) available at http://www.bitlaw.com/source/cases/copyright/cubby.html , visited 5 Feb 2005

[356] In 1990, plaintiffs Cubby, Inc. ("Cubby") and Robert Blanchard ("Blanchard") (collectively, "plaintiffs") developed Skuttlebut, a computer database designed to publish and distribute electronically news and gossip in the television news and radio industries. Plaintiffs intended to compete with Rumorville; subscribers gained access to Skuttlebut through their personal computers after completing subscription agreements with plaintiffs.

Plaintiffs claim that, on separate occasions in April 1990, Rumorville published false and defamatory statements relating to Skuttlebut and Blanchard, and that CompuServe carried these statements as part of the Journalism Forum. The allegedly defamatory remarks included a suggestion that individuals at Skuttlebut gained access to information first published by Rumorville "through some back door"; a statement that Blanchard was "bounced" from his previous employer, WABC; and a description of Skuttlebut as a "new start-up scam."

Plaintiffs have asserted claims against CompuServe and Fitzpatrick under New York law for libel of Blanchard, business disparagement of Skuttlebut, and unfair competition as to Skuttlebut, based largely upon the allegedly defamatory statements contained in Rumorville. CompuServe has moved, pursuant to Fed.R.Civ.P. 56, for summary judgment on all claims against it. CompuServe does not dispute, solely for the purposes of this motion, that the statements relating to Skuttlebut and Blanchard were defamatory; rather, it argued that it acted as a distributor, and not a publisher, of the statements, and cannot be held liable for the statements because it did not know and had no reason to know of the statements. Plaintiffs oppose CompuServe's motion for summary judgment, claiming that genuine issues of material fact exist and that little in the way of discovery has been undertaken thus far.

Four years later, however, in the case of Stratton Oakmont V Prodigy[357], the commercial online service was held responsible for defamatory comments posted on its bulletin board. At issue in this case are statements about Plaintiffs made by an unidentified bulletin board user or "poster" on PRODIGY's "Money Talk" computer bulletin board on October 23rd and 25th of 1994[358]. Following issues were raised before the court;

(i) that PRODIGY was a "publisher" of statements concerning Plaintiffs on its "Money Talk" computer bulletin board for the purposes of Plaintiffs' libel claims[359]; and,

(ii) that Charles Epstein, the Board Leader of PRODIGY's "Money Talk" computer bulletin board, acted as PRODIGY's agent for the purposes of the acts and omissions alleged in the complaint[360].

By way of background, it is undisputed that PRODIGY's computer network has at least two million subscribers who communicate with each other and with the general subscriber population on PRODIGY's bulletin boards. "Money Talk" the board on which the aforementioned statements appeared, in allegedly the leading and most widely read financial computer bulletin board in the United States, where members can post statements regarding stocks, investments and other financial matters. PRODIGY contracts with bulletin Board Leaders, who, among other things, participate in board discussions and undertake promotional efforts to encourage usage and increase users. The Board Leader for "Money Talk" at the time the alleged libelous statements were posted was Charles Epstein[361].

---

[357] 1995 N.Y. Misc. LEXIS 229, 1995 WL 323710, 23 Media L. Rep. 1794 (N.Y. Sup. Ct. May 24, 1995), available at www.findlaw.com , visited 10 Feb 2005
[358] These statements included the following:
(a) STRATTON OAKMONTH, INC. ("STRATTON"), a securities investment banking firm, and DANIEL PORUSH, STRATTON's president, committed criminal and fraudulent acts in connection with the initial public offering of stock of Solomon-Page Ltd.,
(b) the Solomon-Page offering was a "major criminal fraud" and "100% criminal fraud";
(c) PORUSH was "seen to be proven criminal"; and,
(d) STRATTON was a "cult of brokers who either lie for a living or get fired."
[359] 1995 N.Y. Misc. LEXIS 229, 1995 WL 323710, 23 Media L. Rep. 1794 (N.Y. Sup. Ct. May 24, 1995), available at www.findlaw.com , visited on 10 Feb 2005
[360] ibid
[361] ibid

PRODIGY commenced operations in 1990. Plaintiffs base their claims that PRODIGY is a publisher in large measure on PRODIGY's stated policy, starting in 1990, that it was a family oriented computer network. In various national newspaper articles written by Geoffrey Moore, PRODIGY's Director of Market Programs and Communications, PRODIGY held itself out as an online service that exercised editorial control over the content of messages posted on its computer bulletin boards, thereby expressly differentiating itself from its competitors and expressly likening itself to a newspaper. In one article PRODIGY stated:

"We make no apology for pursuing a value system that reflects the culture of the millions of American families we aspire to serve. Certainly no responsible newspaper does less when it carries the type of advertising it published, the letters it prints, the degree of nudity and unsupported gossip its editors tolerate.[362]"

Plaintiffs characterize the aforementioned articles by PRODIGY as admissions and argued that, together with certain documentation and deposition testimony, these articles establish Plaintiffs' prima facie case. In opposition, PRODIGY insisted that its policies have changed and evolved since 1990 and that the latest article on the subject, dated February, 1993, did not reflect PRODIGY's policies in October, 1994, when the allegedly libelous statements were posted. Although the eighteen month lapse of time between the last article and the aforementioned statements is not insignificant, and the Court was wary of interpreting statements and admissions out of context, these considerations go solely to the weight of this evidence.

Plaintiffs further relied upon the following additional evidence in support of their claim that PRODIGY is a publisher:

(A) promulgation of "content guidelines" in which, inter alia, users are requested to refrain from posting notes that are "insulting" and are advised that "notes that harass other members or are deemed to be in bad taste or grossly repugnant to community standards, or are deemed harmful to maintaining a harmonious online community, will be removed when brought to PRODIGY's attention"; the Guidelines all

---

[362] ibid

expressly state that although "Prodigy is committed to open debate and discussion on the bulletin boards, . . . this doesn't mean that 'anything goes'"[363];

(B) use of a software screening program which automatically prescreens all bulletin board postings for offensive language[364];

(C) the use of Board Leaders such as Epstein whose duties include enforcement of the Guidelines, according to Jennifer Ambrozek, the Manager of PRODIGY's bulletin boards and the person at Prodigy responsible for supervising the Board Leaders[365], and

(D) testimony by Epstein as to a tool for Board Leaders known as an "emergency delete function" pursuant to which a Board Leader could remove a note and send a previously prepared message of explanation "ranging from solicitation, bad advice, insulting, wrong topic, off topic, bad taste, etcetera."

The court by referring to Cubby Inc. v. CompuServe Inc[366] and Auvil v CBS 60 Minutes[367] determined that the evidence established a prime facie case that PRODIGY exercised sufficient editorial control over its computer bulletin boards to render it a publisher with the same responsibilities as a newspaper.

The key distinction between CompuServe and PRODIGY is two fold. First, PRODIGY held itself out to the public and its members as controlling the content of its computer bulletin boards. Second, PRODIGY implemented this control through its automatic software screening program, and the Guidelines which Board Leaders are required to enforce. By actively utilizing technology and manpower to delete notes from its computer bulletin boards on the basis of offensiveness and "bad taste", for example, PRODIGY is clearly making decisions as to content, and such

---

[363] ibid
[364] ibid
[365] ibid
[366] 776 F. Supp. 135, 139 (S.D.N.Y. 1991), available at www.findlaw.com , visited on 10 Feb 2005
[367] 800 F. Supp. 928, 932 (E.D. Wash. 1992 available at www.findlaw.com , visited on 21 Feb 2005

decisions constitute editorial control. That such control is not complete and is enforced both as early as the notes arrive and as late as a complaint is made, does not minimize or eviscerate the simple fact that PRODIGY has uniquely arrogated to itself the role of determining what is proper for its members to post and read on its bulletin boards. Based on above reasons the court held that it was compelled to conclude that for the purposes of Plaintiffs' claims in the action, PRODIGY is a publisher rather than a distributor[368].

An interesting comparison may be found in Auvil v. CBS 60 Minutes[369] where apple growers sued a television network and local affiliates because of an allegedly defamatory investigative report generated by the network and broadcast by the affiliates. The record established that the affiliates exercised no editorial control over the broadcast although they had the power to do so by virtue of their contract with CBS, they had the opportunity to do so by virtue of a three hour hiatus for the west coast differential, they had the technical capability to do so, and they in fact had occasionally censored network programming in the past, albeit never in connection with "60 Minutes". The court found that:

It is argued that these features, coupled with the power to censor, triggered the duty to censor. That is a leap which the Court is not prepared to join in. further it held that plaintiffs' construction would force the creation of full time editorial boards at local stations throughout the country which possess sufficient knowledge, legal acumen and access to experts to continually monitor incoming transmissions and exercise on-the-spot discretionary calls or face $75 million dollar lawsuits at every turn and that is not realistic. More than merely unrealistic in economic terms, it is difficult to imagine a scenario more chilling on the media's right of expression and the public's right to know.

Consequently, the court dismissed all claims against the affiliates on the basis of "conduit liability", which could not be established therein absent fault, which was not shown.

---

[368] 1995 N.Y. Misc. LEXIS 229, 1995 WL 323710, 23 Media L. Rep. 1794 (N.Y. Sup. Ct. May 24, 1995) available at www.findlaw.com , visited on 10 Feb 2005
[369] Supra Note 367

In contrast, here PRODIGY has virtually created an editorial staff of Board Leaders who have the ability to continually monitor incoming transmissions and in fact do spend time censoring notes. Indeed, it could be said that PRODIGY's current system of automatic scanning, Guidelines and Board Leaders may have a chilling effect on freedom of communication in Cyberspace, and it appears that this chilling effect is exactly what PRODIGY wants, but for the legal liability that attaches to such censorship.

Congress enacted Communication Decency Act (Sec. 230) to remove the disincentives to self-regulation created by the PRODIGY decision. Under that court's holding, computer service providers who regulated the dissemination of offensive material on their services risked subjecting themselves to liability, because such regulation cast the service provider in the role of a publisher. Fearing that the specter of liability would therefore deter service providers from blocking and screening offensive material, Congress enacted Sec. 230's and provided broad immunity "to remove disincentives for the development and utilization of blocking and filtering technologies that empower parents to restrict their children's access to objectionable or inappropriate online material." In line with this purpose, Sec.230 forbids the imposition of publisher liability on a service provider for the exercise of its editorial and self-regulatory functions[370].

3.4.2 ISP Distributor or Publisher? Immunity under CDA

Whether services rendered by an ISP in relation to digital content constitutes distribution of content or publication of content ? This distinction was brought out before the Federal 4th Circuit court for the first time in Zeran.

In Zeran v. America Online Inc[371]., Plaintiff filed a suit against America Online, Inc. ("AOL"), arguing that AOL unreasonably delayed in removing defamatory

---

[370] Supra Note 367,1995 N.Y. Misc. LEXIS 229, 1995 WL 323710, 23 Media L. Rep. 1794 (N.Y. Sup. Ct. May 24, 1995)
[371] 129 F.3d 327 (4th Cir. 1997), available at www.findlaw.com , visited on 14 Feb 2005

messages posted by an unidentified third party, refused to post retractions of those messages, and failed to screen for similar postings thereafter. The plaintiff argued that immunity under Sec.230 is not available to the defendant as it only protects publisher and not distributor. According to plaintiff, publishing and distributing are different and defendant is liable for alleged defamatory statements[372]. But the court refused to accept the contention and held that "the terms "publisher" and "distributor" derive their legal significance from the context of defamation law. Although plaintiff attempts to artfully plead his claims as ones of negligence, they are indistinguishable from a garden variety defamation action. Because the publication of a statement is a necessary element in a defamation action, only one who publishes can be subject to this form of tort liability. Publication does not only describe the choice by an author to include certain information. In addition, both the negligent communication of a defamatory statement and the failure to remove such a statement when first communicated by another party each alleged by plaintiff here under a negligence label constitute publication. In fact, every repetition of a defamatory statement is considered a publication."[373] Hence we can see court has applied the traditional defamation law to decide the case and the immunity granted by Sec.230 to service providers had saved the defendant.

Again in Blumenthal v. Drudge[374], the court found that CDA immunizes interactive computer service providers from liability for statements made even by third parties under contract with and promoted by the service. So far the liability of the original internet publisher, if known, has not been seriously questioned in court. But Mike Godwin, an attorney with Electronic Frontier Foundation has suggested the nature of the internet might render libel law obsolete[375].

PRODIGY alarmed many commentators and arguably provided the primary impetus for the CDA's safe harbor provisions. What would the Internet look like today were

---

[372] Zeran v. America Online Inc., 129 F.3d 327 (4th Cir. 1997), available at http://laws.lp.findlaw.com/4th/971523P.html , visited 16 Feb 2005
[373] ibid
[374] Blumenthal v. Drudge[374], 992 F. Supp. 44 (D.D.C. 1998), available at www.findlaw.com , visited 3 Mar 2005
[375] Godwin Mike, Libel Law: Let it Dies, wired News, Mar 1996, http://www.wired.com/wired/archive/4.03/letitdie_pr.html , visited 12 Mar 2005

if decision in PRODIGY, rather than the CDA, the standard for determining liability for defamation? There may be several answers to this, but life of the ISPs would have been made miserable through litigation. But the court in Blumenthal sounds less than fully pleased with the effect of the CDA on defamation law. Apart from the CDA and the   self-help, yet another reason has arisen why online speech is less likely to give rise to defamation claims than offline speech: courts are more willing to regard Internet speech as expressing mere rhetoric or opinion[376].

Recent judicial decisions have differing interpretation on immunity provided to ISP under Sec.230 of CDA. Two important decisions given by the courts, the U.S. District Court for the Northern District of Illinois, and the Supreme Court of California, have issued opinions examining the contours of the immunity provided under the Communications Decency Act at 47 U.S.C. 230. That section provides, among other things, that "no provider or user of any interactive computer service shall be treated as the publisher or speaker of any information provided by another information content provider." Although both cases were defense victories, the two courts gave different treatment to Section 230 in their reading of the statute and in their interpretation of the leading case on point[377].

On November 14, 2006, the Northern District of Illinois issued its decision in the case of CLC v. Craigslist [No. 06-657]. In that case, a Chicago based nonprofit organization had filed suit against Craigslist, asserting that the popular site should be held liable under the Fair Housing Act for the publication of certain discriminatory online advertisements for apartment rentals[378].

In a 28 page decision, the court held that Craigslist could not be liable for any discriminatory postings, because to impose such liability "would be to treat

---

[376] Global Telemedia International v. Doe 1 aka BUSTEDAGAIN40, 132 F. Supp.2d 1261, 1267-1270 (C.D. Cal. 2001); court explaining that chat room messages lacked "the formality and polish typically found in documents in which a reader would expect to find facts."
[377] Tsesis, Alexander, Prohibiting Incitement on the Internet, Virginia Journal of Law and Technology, 7 Va.J.L & Tech.5 (2002), available at http://www.vjolt.net , visited on 4 Apr 2005
[378] ibid,

Craigslist as if it were the publisher of third party content, and the plain language of Section 230(c) forecloses the cause of action."[379]

But in the process of arriving at that conclusion, Judge St. Eve gave a thorough rundown of Section 230 immunity, taking a close and critical look at what the court called the "fountainhead" of Section 230 immunity, the Fourth Circuit's decision in Zeran v. America Online, 129 F.3d 327 (4th Cir. 1997)[380].

Despite the wide acceptance that the case has enjoyed over the past decade, Judge St. Eve "respectfully declined to follow Zeran's lead." She identified three problems with its holding. First, Zeran overstated the plain language of the statute when it held that Section 230 creates a federal immunity to any cause of action that would make service providers liable for information originating with third party users of the service. Secondly, the court found Zeran's holding to be internally inconsistent. Third, the court noted that application of the statute would be problematic, inasmuch as the policy of encouraging providers of online computer services to police for objectionable content is at odds with the immunity that would attach to providers that choose to do nothing to filter objectionable content[381].

In the end, Judge St. Eve's observations about Zeran were merely dicta, as the court ultimately held that Craigslist was entitled to the publisher immunity provided under Section 230. What's more, the court aptly observed that plaintiffs in cases against interactive computer services attempting to hold them liable for content provided by others will still have tough time[382].

---

[379] Brown, Evan, InternetCases.com, available at
www.internetcases.com/archives/2006/11/index.html , visited on 2 Feb 2005
[380] Supra Note 372
[381] Brown, Evan, InternetCases.com, available at
www.internetcases.com/archives/2006/11/index.html , visited on 2 Feb 2005

[382] ibid

In a much anticipated ruling, the California Supreme Court handed down its decision on November 20, 2006 in the case of Barrett v. Rosenthal[383]. In this case, the state Supreme Court overturned the Court of Appeal, and, in contrast to the court in the Craigslist case, heartily endorsed the Zeran holding. So we can conclude that the court's decision, interpretation and construction of the term 'publisher' is sound.

At issue in the Barret case was whether the defendant Rosenthal could be liable for defamatory content contained in an article written by another party, which she posted to a message board. The court examined whether, given the circumstances, Rosenthal should be considered a "user" of an interactive computer service as provided for in Section 230(c) and thus subject to immunity. The court answered that question in the affirmative[384].

The heavy endorsement of Zeran came in rejecting the Court of Appeal's distinction between distributor and publisher liability. The Court of Appeal (as had the plaintiff in Zeran), reasoned that Section 230 might not foreclose liability for one in Rosenthal's position as a distributor of defamatory content. But the Supreme Court held that the distinction was one without a difference in the modern online publishing context, and that "distributor" is encompassed within "publisher" as the term is used in Section 230.

3.5 Corporate Cybersmear and Employer's Liability

An unfortunate byproduct of the explosive growth of the internet is the rapid rise of "cybersmearing"- the anonymous or pseudonymous defamation on the internet of individuals, companies and company executives[385]. The challenge here is that maintaing the balance between employee right to free speech and employer's right

---

[383] Barrett V Rosenthal , Ct.App. 1/2 A096451, Almeda County Super. Ct. 833021-5, available at www.eff.org/legal/cases/Barrett_v_Rosenthal/ruling.pdf , visited on 10 May 2005
[384] ibid
[385] Roger M Rosen; Charles B Rosenberg ,Suing anonymous defendants for Internet defamation Computer and Internet Lawyer; Feb 2002; 19, 2;

to productivity and efficiency. Media and entertainment companies use websites to distribute content throughout the world. Sometimes, a company publishes matter online that offends a person or a rival company. This can happen by accident, perhaps due to lack of understanding of concerns or sensitivities in a foreign country[386].

The internet has created an unprecedented way for dissatisfied customers to criticize companies they believe have wronged them or that engage in practices with which they disagree. In the past, customers had few outlets through which they could express their dissatisfaction passing out leaflets is time consuming and reaches a rather limited audience, and getting the mainstream media interested in any particular issue is often quite difficult. But the internet has provided critics with the world's largest soapbox, by allowing anyone with only limited technical skills to create a website for the entire world to see, a forum where every critical opinion can be expressed[387]. Many disgruntled employees of companies are posting information online that defames the management and divulges proprietary information anonymously.

Cybersmearing[388] does what it says on the tin. It is the smearing of an individual or company online. Cybersmearing can take a number of different forms including websites, message boards, e-mail and auctions.

Now let us take a scenario to consider the harms of cybersmear. Interested in what potential investors think about his company, a corporate CEO goes on line to check the online message boards devoted to the organization. What he finds appalls him: dozens of comments, posted under a variety of pseudonyms, some describing the company as being on the verge of bankruptcy, and others accusing the CEO of various types of misconduct, including "groping all the women who work with him" and embezzling corporate funds" "to feed his filthy drug habit". Still other messages

---

[386] Goel Madhu, Internet Defamation: Where Must a Defedant Defend?, Intellectual Property Law Journal: Nov 2005;17
[387] Isenberg, Doug, The Giga Law-Guide to Internet Law, Random House Trade Paperback Edition, Newyork, 2000 at p 134
[388] Cybersmearing means harming the reputation of an individual or company online.

disclose a highly confidential marketing approach the company is planning to implement in a few weeks, describing it as a 'ridiculous concept' opposed by key managers, including those posting the message. Angry and appalled, the CEO calls his lawyer, wanting to know what can be done to unmask, silence and punish the employees who posted the message[389].

Over the past few years, dozens of employers have been faced with comparable situations. Such "cybersmear" rise a host of difficult legal and strategic issues. How can an employer determine whether the person who posted a message is an employee? Do employees have a right of speech and expression to criticize their employee anonymously? What risks does an employee face in trying to silence such online critics? What sort of claims can be filed? What can an employee do in advance to make it easier to stop online attacks by employees?

The most difficult part in the cases of cybersmearing is to identify the anonymous defendant. In this regard it is pertinent note here that how courts would view such situations[390]. In 1999, the US District was called upon to determine a question relating to online free speech in Columbia Insurance v. SeesCandy.com[391]. The question was whether right to speak anonymously exists in cyberspace? . In this case the plaintiff sued for the infringement of its trademark "Seescandy.com". Unfortunately for the plaintiff, however, it was difficult to identify the particular individuals who had registered that name. The court noted that although plaintiffs are generally prohibited from conducting discovery until after the defendant has been served with the lawsuit, exceptions are occasionally made to allow the plaintiff 'to learn the identifying facts necessary to permit service on the defendant.' The court held that -"With the rise of the Internet individuals have acquired the ability to commit certain tortious acts, such as defamation, copyright infringement, and

---

[389] Isenberg, Doug, The Giga Law-Guide to Internet Law, Random HouseTrade Paperback Edition, Newyork, 2000 at p 135

[390] ibid at p 137
[391] Cited in Isenberg, Doug, The Giga Law-Guide to Internet Law, Random House Trade Paperback Edition, New York, 2000

trademark infringement, entirely online. The tortfeasor can act pseudonymously or anonymously and may give fictitious or incomplete identifying information. Parties who have been injured by these acts are likely to find themselves chasing the tortfeasor from ISP to ISP, with little or no hope of actually discovering the identity of the tortfeasor."[392]

Further the court observed that "In such cases the traditional reluctance for permitting filings against John Doe defendants or fictitious names and the traditional enforcement of strict compliance with service requirements should be tempered by the need to provide injured parties with a forum in which they may seek redress for grievances."[393]

Hence, it is quite clear that employer can seek the help of ISP to identify the anonymous netizen so that he may initiate legal action for defamatory postings.

As more and more companies make use of e-mails as a method of communication between staff, there will be increasing exposure of communication on the basis of vicarious liability in respect of the use of misuse made of the communications network. In 1997 the Norwich Union insurance company reached a settlement in a libel action brought by a health insurance company, Western Provident Association. Under the terms of agreement, Norwich Union agreed to pay huge sum in damages and costs in respect of libelous messages concerning the association's financial stability which had been contained in e-mail message exchanged between members of Norwich Union's staff[394]. The fact that a settlement was reached prior to trial means that the case is of no value as a legal precedent. The lesson for those engaging in e-mail discussions is obvious: that although communications may be approached as form of conversation, everything is recorded almost without limit of time and can be retrieved at a later date. A similar example of this phenomenon can be seen in the discovery of internal Microsoft e-mails during the legal investigations

---

[392] Isenberg, Doug, The Giga Law-Guide to Internet Law, Random House Trade Paperback Edition, New York, 2000 at p 233
[393] ibid
[394] Lloyd , Ian, "Legal Aspects of the Information Society",Butterworths,London,2000 at p 217

into their commercial practices[395]. One significant factor limiting the extent of liability for defamatory communications made by employees may be that the vicarious liability applies only in respect of acts committed in the course of employment. In the Norwich Union case, the communications were clearly work related but it is unlikely that an employer would be held liable in the event, for example, that employee used e-mail facilities to exchange defamatory comments on subjects unconnected with work. To minimize the risks of liability, it would be advisable for employers to indicate clearly in contracts of employment or staff handbooks what uses may or may not be made of electronic communications[396].

Faced with concern at their potential liabilities for misuse of electronic communications, it is common place for employers to monitor use of the facilities. In the US a number of actions have been reported of corporations being sued for millions of dollars by employees alleging that fellow workers have been engaging in some form of electronic harassment involving the posting of abusive or offensive messages. It has been suggested that – "Lawyers are bracing themselves for a wave of litigation as people catch on to the fact that they can redress grievances- and possibly become very rich- by producing e-mail evidence of prejudice based on gender, sexual preference, race, nationality or age. Proving cases that depend on spoken jests and casual remarks has always presented its difficulties in court. The beauty of e-mail is that plaintiffs have to do is retrieve it from their company's computer system and then print it out. Plenty of material is certain to be available in a country where 80 per cent of organization use e-mail.[397]   Faced with such exposure, employers may well be tempted to use packages to monitor e-mail communication in the workplace[398]. In the case of Halfford V UK[399] , the European Court of Human Rights held that the convention's requirements relating to

---

[395] See generally Volokh, Eugene, Freedom of Speech, Cyberspace and Harassment Law, 2001 Stan.Tech.Rev 3, available at http://stlr.stanford.edu/STLR/Articles/01_STLR_3 or www.papers.ssrn.com , visited on 2 Sep 2004 ; in this article author brings out the ramification of e-mail during the controversy of Clinton-Lewinsky scandal.
[396] Lloyd , Ian, Legal Aspects of the Information Society,Butterworths,London,2000 at p 218

[397] ibid
[398] ibid
[399] Cited from Lloyd , Ian, "Legal Aspects of the Information Society",Butterworths,London,2000

protection of privacy had been breached where telephone calls made from work premises by a senior police officer had been bugged on the authority of her chief constable. Argument on behalf of the UK Government to the effect that the telephones in question belonged to the employer did not save the government[400]. It would appear that any monitoring of e-mail might be challenged on this basis, although it is not clear whether the giving of notice to employees that phone calls or e-mail messages might be monitored would remove their reasonable expectation of privacy in their communications. We will have to wait and see how the doctrine of reasonable expectation of privacy applies in these situations.

3.6 Suing Anonymous Defendants for Internet Defamation

Anonymity promotes honesty. However, if the protection extended to anonymous speech is abused it would cause irreparable loss to the victim especially in the context of employer-employee relationship. An employer contemplating suing an anonymous poster must decide what causes of action are possible, figure out where such a suit may be brought, determine how it can persuade a court to permit discovery aimed at identifying the anonymous defendant, and prepare to defend what may be strenuous efforts to prevent such discovery from going forward[401].

Employers that sue those who post inappropriate messages can choose from the variety of possible claims. Most suits against anonymous message posters have involved claims of defamation. Such a claim requires proof that the defendant made s false statement about the plaintiff, that the statement was published, that the statement was defamatory (that is, it injured the plaintiffs reputation in the eyes of the community, caused others to avoid associating or dealing with the plaintiff, or subjected to ridicule or contempt), and that the plaintiff was actually damaged by the defendant's publication of the statement[402].

---

[400] ibid
[401] Lidsky B, Lyrissa, Silencing John Doe: Defamation & Discourse in Cyberspace, Duke Law Journal, Vol.49, No.4, Feb 2000
[402] Burns A James & Rosenman Zavis K M , Battling the Unknown: online cybersmears by anonymous employees, Employee Relations Law, Vol.28, Number 2, Autumn 2002

Numerous employers require employees to sign non-disclosure agreements promising never to divulge any confidential and proprietary information of the employer, including trade secrets. If a posted message contains such information, and the employer believes its author signed such an agreement, the employer may sue the poster for breach of contract. In Immunomedics Inc., V Doe[403], for example, someone describing herself as a "worried employee" of the plaintiff company posted a message saying that the company had run out of stock for particular products in Europe, threatening its sales. Although the statements were true, the company argued their disclosure violated the confidentiality of the agreement. After Yahoo! Notified the poster about the subpoena it had received from the company, she moved to quash the subpoena, acting through counsel to preserve her anonymity. In a decision upheld on appeal, the court denied the motion to quash, based in large part on the non-disclosure agreement[404].

3.7 John Doe Concept

John Doe is a name assigned to anonymous speaker in the online world. The John Doe concept is popular in the US where victims of cyberstalking or defamation file lawsuits against "John Does". John Doe has become a popular defamation defendant as corporations and their officers bring defamation suits for statements made about them in Internet discussion fora. These new suits are not even arguably about recovering money damages but instead are brought for symbolic reasons some worthy, some not so worthy or even to threaten the anonymous speaker with a legal suit. If the only consequence of these suits were that Internet users were held accountable for their speech, the suits would be an unalloyed good. However, these suits threaten to suppress legitimate criticism along with intentional and reckless

---

[403] 342 N.J. Super. 160 (App. Div. 2001), available at http://cyber.law.harvard.edu/stjohns/anon-net.html , visited on 12 Sep 2005
[404] ibid

falsehoods, and existing First Amendment law doctrines are not responsive to the threat these suits pose to Internet discourse[405].

What is unique about these new Internet suits is the threat they pose to the new realm of discourse that has sprung up on the Internet. The promise of the Internet is empowerment: it empowers ordinary individuals with limited financial resources to "publish" their views on matters of public concern[406]. The Internet is therefore a powerful tool for equalizing imbalances of power by giving voice to the disenfranchised and by allowing more democratic participation in public discourse. In other words, the Internet allows ordinary John Does to participate as never before in public discourse, and hence, to shape public policy[407]. Yet, suits like the hypothetical John Doe suit discussed above threaten to reestablish existing hierarchies of power, as powerful corporate Goliaths sue their critics for speaking their minds. Defendants like John Doe typically lack the resources necessary to defend against a defamation action, much less the resources to satisfy a judgment. Thus, these Internet defamation actions threaten not only to deter the individual who is sued from speaking out, but also to encourage undue self-censorship among the other John Does who frequent Internet discussion fora[408].

In India the Delhi High Court has admitted a petition introducing for the first time in Indian jurisprudence the equivalent of the American concept of `John Doe' in information technology related litigation. Earlier to this Indian courts never entertained a suit where defendant is unnamed[409].

---

[405] Lidsky Barnett Lyrissa, Silencing John Doe: Defamation & Discourse in Cyberspace, Duke Law Journal, Vol.49, No.4, Feb 2000
[406] ibid
[407] ibid
[408] ibid
[409] Business Line International Edition, Indian `John Doe' sued, Date:29/03/2006, available at http://www.thehindubusinessline.com/2006/03/29/stories/2006032903190100.htm , visited on 1 Apr 2006.

3.7.1 Standards for Protecting Anonymous Internet Speech

Even though there is no hard and fast rule to say to what extent anonymous speakers are protected in cyberspace and could be unmasked for their views or expressions under the John Doe concept, American courts have been using three pronged test to give fair treatment to John Does.

Two of these were formulated by Supreme Court of Delaware in Doe v Cahill[410] an dthe third one was in Mobilira inc V Doe[411] by the Arizona court. They are

(1) that the anonymous party sought to be unmask be given notice of the proceedings[412]

(2) that the party seeking the identity of the anonymous party put forth sufficient facts to survive a motion for summary judgement[413]

(3) balancing of relative interest of the parties.[414]

3.8 Threatening Speech

When speech does qualify as a   threatening speech? Or when does a communication over the Internet inflict or threaten to inflict sufficient damage on its recipient that it ceases to be protected by the Free speech doctrine and properly gives rise to criminal sanctions?

Threatening expressions are not new in the virtual world and they are same as in the physical world. The US moralistic stance against any limits on fighting words, except which are content neutral and control only imminently harmful acts obsequiously protects free speech more than any other constitutional rights. When speech intentionally threatens the autonomy of identifiable individuals or groups, especially those groups in less favorable social positions, some limitations must be

---

[410] A.2d —, 2005 WL 2455266 (Del., October 5, 2005), available at
http://www.internetcases.com/library/cases/2005-10-05-doe_v_cahill.pdf , visited 10 Nov 2006
[411] P.3d —, 2007 WL 4167007 (Ariz. App. November 27, 2007), available at http://intercases.com, visited on 27 Nov 2007
[412] Supra Note 410
[413] ibid
[414] Supra Note 411

placed on its expression. The new information transmission technologies should not become unbridled forums for fascist and terrorist indoctrination[415].

Two popular cases illustrate the effect of threatening speech over the internet. The first was popularly known as the "Jake Baker" case[416]. In 1994 and 1995, Abraham Jacob Alkhabaz, also known as Jake Baker, was an undergraduate student at the University of Michigan. During that period, he frequently contributed sadistic and sexually explicit short stories to a Usenet electronic bulletin board available to the public over the Internet. In one such story, he described in detail how he and a companion tortured, sexually abused, and killed a young woman, who was given the name of one of Baker's classmates[417].

Baker's stories came to the attention of another Internet user, who assumed the name of Arthur Gonda. Baker and Gonda then exchanged many email messages, sharing their sadistic fantasies and discussing the methods by which they might kidnap and torture a woman in Baker's dormitory. When these stories and email exchanges came to light, Baker was indicted for violation of 18 U.S.C. 875(c), which provides as follows:

> Whoever transmits in interstate or foreign commerce any communication containing any threat to kidnap any person or any threat to injure the person of another, shall be fined under this title or imprisoned not more than five years, or both[418].

US Federal courts have traditionally construed this provision narrowly, lest it penalize expression shielded by the First Amendment. Specifically, the courts have required that a defendant's statement, in order to trigger criminal sanctions,

---

[415] Burch Edgar, Censoring Hate Speech in Cyberspace: A New Debate in a New America, North Carolina Journal of Law & Technology, Vol.3, Issue 1: Fall 2001
[416] U.S. v. Jake Baker, 890 F. Supp. 1375 (E.D. Mich. 1995) available at http://ic.net/~sberaha/baker.html , visited on 13 Sep 2005
[417] Fisher William, Benckler Yochai, Brackely Rebacca and Ma Shara, Freedom of Expression on the Internet, Berkman Center for Internet and Society, available at http://cyber.law.harvard.edu/ilaw/mexico_2006_module_4_freedom , visited on 2 Feb 2005.

[418] 18 U.S.C 875(c) (Title 18 deals with crimes and criminal procedure)

constitute a "true threat" as distinguished from, for example, inadvertent statements, hyperbole, innocuous talk, or political commentary[419].

Baker moved to quash the indictment on the ground that his statements on the Internet did not constitute "true threats." The District Court agreed, ruling that the class of women supposedly threatened was not identified in Baker's exchanges with Gonda with the degree of specificity required by the First Amendment and that, although Baker had expressed offensive desires, "it was not constitutionally permissible to infer an intention to act on a desire from a simple expression of desire." The District Judge's concluding remarks concerning the character of threatening speech on the Internet bear emphasis:

> Baker's words were transmitted by means of the Internet, a relatively new communications medium that is itself currently the subject of much media attention. The Internet makes it possible with unprecedented ease to achieve worldwide distribution of material, like Baker's story, posted to its public areas. When used in such a fashion, the Internet may be likened to a newspaper with unlimited distribution and no locatable printing press and with no supervising editorial control. But Baker's e-mail messages, on which the superseding indictment is based, were not publicly published but privately sent to Gonda. While new technology such as the Internet may complicate analysis and may sometimes require new or modified laws, it does not in this instance qualitatively change the analysis under the statute or under the First Amendment. Whatever Baker's faults, and he is to be faulted, he did not violate 18 U.S.C. § 875(c)[420].

---

[419] U.S. v. Jake Baker, 890 F. Supp. 1375 (E.D. Mich. 1995) available at http://ic.net/~sberaha/baker.html , visited on 13 Sep 2005

[420] ibid

Two of the three judges on the panel that heard the appeal agreed. In their view, a violation of Sec. 875(c) requires a demonstration, first, that a reasonable person would interpret the communication in question as serious expression of an intention to inflict bodily harm and, second, that a reasonable person would perceive the communications as being conveyed "to effect some change or achieve some goal through intimidation." Baker's speech failed, in their judgment, to rise to this level[421].

Judge Krupansky, the third member of the panel, dissented. In a sharply worded opinion, he denounced the majority for compelling the prosecution to meet a standard higher that Congress intended or than the First Amendment required. In his view, "the pertinent inquiry is whether a jury could find that a reasonable recipient of the communication would objectively tend to believe that the speaker was serious about his stated intention." A reasonable jury, he argued, could conclude that Baker's speech met this standard especially in light of the fact that the woman named in the short story had, upon learning of it, experienced a "shattering traumatic reaction that resulted in recommended psychological counseling."[422]

The second case related to threatening speech on Internet is popularly known as the "Nuremberg files". In 1995, the American Coalition of Life Activists (ACLA), an anti-abortion group that advocates the use of force in their efforts to curtail abortions, created a poster featuring what the ACLA described as the "Dirty Dozen," a group of doctors who performed abortions. The posters offered "a $ 5,000 reward for information leading to arrest, conviction and revocation of license to practice medicine" of the doctors in question, and listed their home addresses and, in some instances, their phone numbers. Versions of the poster were distributed at anti-abortion rallies and later on television. In 1996, an expanded list of abortion providers, now dubbed the "Nuremberg files," was posted on the Internet with the assistance of an anti-abortion activist named Neil Horsley. The Internet version of the list designated doctors and clinic workers who had been attacked by anti-

---

[421] ibid
[422] ibid

abortion terrorists in two ways: the names of people who had been murdered were crossed out; the names of people who had been wounded were printed in grey[423].

The doctors named and described on the list feared for their lives. In particular, some testified that they feared that, by publicizing their addresses and descriptions, the ACLA had increased the ease with which terrorists could locate and attack them and that, by publicizing the names of doctors who had already been killed, the ACLA was encouraging those attacks.

Some of the doctors sought recourse in the courts. They sued the ACLA, twelve individual anti-abortion activists and an affiliated organization, contending that their actions violated the federal Freedom of Access to Clinic Entrances Act of 1994 (FACE), 18 U.S.C. Sec.248, and the Racketeer Influenced and Corrupt Organizations Act (RICO), 18 U.S.C. Sec.1962. In an effort to avoid a First-Amendment challenge to the suit, the trial judge instructed the jury that defendants could be liable only if their statements were "true threats." The jury, concluding that the ACLA had indeed made such true threats, awarded the plaintiffs $107 million in actual and punitive damages. The trial court then enjoined the defendants from making or distributing the posters, the webpage or anything similar[424]. However, this judgment was overruled by Court of Appeals for the Ninth Circuit[425].

---

[423] American Coalition of Life Activists v. Planned Parenthood, 123 S. Ct. 2637 (2003), available at www.findlaw.com, visited on 14 Feb 2006

[424] ibid

[425] In March 2001, a panel of the Court of Appeals for the Ninth Circuit overturned the verdict, ruling that it violated the First Amendment. Judge Kozinski began his opinion by likening the anti-abortion movement to other "political movements in American history," such as the Patriots in the American Revolution, abolitionism, the labor movement, the anti-war movement in the 1960s, the animal-rights movement, and the environmental movement. All, he argued, have had their "violent fringes," which have lent to the language of their non-violent members "a tinge of menace." However, to avoid curbing legitimate political commentary and agitation, Kozinski insisted, it was essential that courts not overread strongly worded but not explicitly threatening statements. Specifically, he held that:

 Defendants can only be held liable if they "authorized, ratified, or directly threatened" violence. If defendants threatened to commit violent acts, by working alone or with others, then their statements could properly support the verdict. But if

Over a year later, however, in May 2002, the full court of the Court of Appeals for the Ninth Circuit reversed and vacated the panel decision, and reinstated the trial court's determination. The Court of Appeals was very closely divided, with six judges favoring a finding that the Nuremberg Files site did not merit protection, and five judges holding that it did. The majority defined what constitutes threatening speech as follows;

"A threat is an expression of an intention to inflict evil, injury, or damage on another. Alleged threats should be considered in light of their entire factual context, including the surrounding events and reaction of the listeners. Moreover, the fact that a threat is subtle does not make it less of a threat. A true threat, that is one where a reasonable person would foresee that the listener will believe he will be subjected to physical violence upon his person, is unprotected by the first amendment. It is not necessary that the defendant intends to, or be able to carry out

---

their statements merely encouraged unrelated terrorists, then their words are protected by the First Amendment.

In the course of his opinion, Kozinski offered the following reflections on the fact that the defendants' speech had occurred in public discourse -- including the Internet:

In considering whether context could import a violent meaning to ACLA's non-violent statements, we deem it highly significant that all the statements were made in the context of public discourse, not in direct personal communications. Although the First Amendment does not protect all forms of public speech, such as statements inciting violence or an imminent panic, the public nature of the speech bears heavily upon whether it could be interpreted as a threat. As we held in McCalden v. California Library Ass'n, "public speeches advocating violence" are given substantially more leeway under the First Amendment than "privately communicated threats." There are two reasons for this distinction: First, what may be hyperbole in a public speech may be understood (and intended) as a threat if communicated directly to the person threatened, whether face-to-face, by telephone or by letter. In targeting the recipient personally, the speaker leaves no doubt that he is sending the recipient a message of some sort. In contrast, typical political statements at rallies or through the media are far more diffuse in their focus because they are generally intended, at least in part, to shore up political support for the speaker's position. Second, and more importantly, speech made through the normal channels of group communication, and concerning matters of public policy, is given the maximum level of protection by the Free Speech Clause because it lies at the core of the First Amendment.

his threat; the only intent requirement for a true threat is that the defendants intentionally or knowingly communicate the threat."[426]

The threatening speech made in public is entitled to heightened constitutional protection as it is communicated publicly rather than privately. Threats are unprotected by the First Amendment however communicated. Therefore, we can say that "threat of force" a statement which, in the entire context and under all the circumstances, a reasonable person would foresee would be interpreted by those to whom the statement is communicated as a serious expression of intent to inflict bodily harm upon that person. So defined, a threatening statement is unprotected under the Free speech doctrine in cyberspace.

3.9 Hate Speech

While Internet is a marvelous medium for education, communication, entertainment and commerce, the Internet has a dark side. Hate groups have emerged from the back alleys of the past to post their hateful ideas online, in full view of everyone, where they can hide behind their anonymity while spewing their hatred for a potential audience of thousands, if not millions. The Internet is a relatively cheap and highly effective way for hate groups as diverse as the National Alliance[427] and the Ku Klux Klan[428], as well as anti-Semites, right-wing extremists, militia groups and others to propagate their hateful ideas[429].

What's more, it's becoming a powerful recruitment tool for these groups. Where the activities of hate groups once were limited by geographical boundaries, the Internet

---

[426] American Coalition of Life Activists v. Planned Parenthood, 123 S. Ct. 2637 (2003), available at www.findlaw.com, visited on 14 Feb 2006

[427] Pro-white activists
[428] Ku Klux Klan (KKK) is the name of several past and present organizations in the United States that have advocated white supremacy, anti-Semitism, anti-Catholicism, racism, homophobia, anti-Communism and nativism. These organizations have often used terrorism, violence, and acts of intimidation, such as cross burning and lynching, to oppress African Americans and other social or ethnic groups; available at http://en.wikipedia.org/wiki/Ku_Klux_Klan, visited 10 Nov 2006
[429] Wolf, Chritopher, Racists, Bigots and the Law on the Internet, Anti-Defamation league, available at http://www.adl.org/internet , visited on 2 May 2005.

allows even the smallest fringe group to spread hate and freely recruit members online by tapping into the worldwide audience that the Web provides. Technology also offers such groups the ability to post messages in chat rooms and communicate like never before[430].

Hate speech is not, like pornography, something that is obvious at first sight. Hate speech combines in a volatile cocktail two separate speech crimes, incitement to violence and fraud. It is insidious, devious. While one can say, at least for adults, that they can choose to click on to or not to click on to pornography, one cannot say the same for hate speech. Those susceptible to the messages of hate mongers are those with little appreciation of the danger of the messages[431].

Hate is pervasive on the Internet and it takes many forms. According to Anti-defamation League (ADL), organization which fights against hate speech in the online world, hate groups have become increasingly sophisticated in their approach and many hate sites are being specifically designed to ensnare children[432]. Dozens of hate groups have established 'clubs' on servers like Yhaoo! Etc. Even tough online companies are making all out effort eliminate hate groups. But hate groups are enjoying protection under US First amendment. Hate speech and the many varied forums available on the Internet for the exchange of information have opened up a new set of legal quandaries. Many of the thorniest issues surrounding the hate speech ultimately will be decided in the courts[433].

3.9.1   Hate Speech and the Law

American courts have been trying to protect the free speech interest even at the cost of hate speech. Significant First Amendment jurisprudence began in the early twentieth century, when Justice Oliver Wendell Holmes wrote a series of influential

---

[430] ibid

[431] Matas, Dvaid, Countering Hate on the Internet: Recommendations for Actions, available at http://www.media-awareness.ca ,visited on 10 May 2005.

[432] Anti-Defamation League Report on 'Poisoning the Web: Hatred Online', available at http://www.adl.org/internet , visited 2 May 2005.

[433] ibid

opinions. The first of these, Schenck v. United States[434], arose from constitutional issues surrounding the Espionage Act of 1917. Schenck was convicted and sentenced to six months in jail for printing and circulating pamphlets stating that forced conscription during World War I was a form of involuntary servitude, prohibited by the Thirteenth Amendment. Holmes held that Schenck intended to influence men to refuse to participate in the draft. In upholding Schenck's conviction, Holmes formulated the still influential "clear and present danger" test:

"The question in every case is whether the words used are used in such circumstances and are of such a nature as to create a clear and present danger that they will bring about the substantive evils that Congress has a right to prevent. It is a question of proximity and degree."[435]

Clearly present danger is analogous to someone "falsely shouting fire in a theater and causing a panic." Holmes J, clarified the doctrine against inflammatory speech in a dissent to a later decision, Abrams v. United States[436]. Abrams was a member of an anarchist group, which drafted a pamphlet opposing President Woodrow Wilson's policy of sending troops to oppose the communist victory in Russia. Five members of the anarchist group were sentenced to twenty years in prison for printing the leaflet[437].

In his dissent, opposing Abrams' conviction, Holmes J, asserted that, "It is only the present danger of immediate evil or intent to bring it about that warrants Congress in setting a limit to the expression of opinion where private rights are not concerned." For Holmes, the crucial factor was that while Abrams supported the sovereignty of the Russian government, he did not advocate overthrowing the U.S. government. Abrams was only prosecuted and convicted because he advocated communism, not because his words posed an immediate danger to the safety of the United States.

---

[434] Schenck v. U.S. , 249 U.S. 47 (1919), available at http://laws.findlaw.com/us/249/47.html , visited on 23 Sep 2005
[435] ibid
[436] Abrams v. U S , 250 U.S. 616 (1919), available at http://laws.findlaw.com/us/250/616.html , visited on 23 Sep 23, 2005

[437] ibid

Holmes J, dissent, then, represents his opposition to suppressing controversial political ideas.

Based on the distinction between words expressing abstract ideas and those fomenting violence, the Court further clarified its position in Chaplinsky v. New Hampshire[438]. In determining whether it is reasonably foreseeable that words will provoke a violent reaction, the Court evaluated how they would affect an "ordinary citizen." These sorts of utterances are "fighting words" with "no essential part of any exposition of ideas, and are of such slight social value as a step to truth that any benefit that may be derived from them is clearly outweighed by the social interest in order and morality."[439]

The Supreme Court's next pronouncement on the subject of incitement came in 1969. Brandenburg v. Ohio[440] established the principle on which courts continue to rely. The Brandenburg Court enunciated the current rule for determining whether a statute, which was aimed at limiting incitement, infringes on individuals' First Amendment rights. At issue was a film showing a speech in which the defendant, the leader of an Ohio Ku Klux Klan chapter, asserted that revenge might be taken against the United States government if it "continues to suppress the white race." Reversing the defendant's conviction, the Court held that the First Amendment guarantee of free speech prohibits the government from proscribing the "advocacy of the use of force or of law violation except where such advocacy is directed to inciting or producing imminent lawless action and is likely to incite or produce such action." Further, the Court declared the Ohio statute unconstitutional because it did

---

[438] Chaplinsky v. State Of New Hampshire, 315 U.S. 568 (1942), http://laws.findlaw.com/us/315/568.html , visited on 1 3 Jan 2006
[439] ibid

[440] Brandenburg v. Ohio, 395 U.S. 444 (1969) , available at http://laws.findlaw.com/us/395/444.html , visited on 12 Jan 2006

not distinguish between persons calling for the immediate use of violence and those teaching an abstract doctrine about the use of force[441].

Racist diatribe is not a progressive form of political discourse. Hate crimes and terrorist acts are not committed in a social vacuum. There is a close, and virtually necessary, connection between advocacy, preparation, coordination, infrastructure development, training, indoctrination, desensitization, discrimination, singular violent acts, and systematic oppression. Angry words, spoken in the heat of the moment, may result in violence, but the entrenchment of out-group hatred in an entire culture takes time and has far more impact than spontaneous aggression. On the other hand, the imminent threat of harm perspective insists that only fighting words that resemble the verbal taunting immediately preceding an unplanned riot are dangerous enough to justify legal intervention. The realities of how essential bias speech is to the popularization of nefarious social movements evinces that this view is too narrow[442].

Hostile expressions do not contribute to the free flow of ideas. They do not test the legitimacy of democratic institutions because their very aim is to exclude out-groups from participating in policy debates. Just as with other anti-discrimination laws, such as those prohibiting exclusionary employment practice and housing discrimination, the prohibition of virulent animus would improve race relations and diminish arbitrary hate. Organizations purposefully using new technologies to disseminate hatred, intent on hurting identifiable groups, can broaden their audience and substantially increase the likelihood of causing their desired end. For instance, given enough time and repetition, flashy Web sites advocating the piousness of committing suicide bombings may enkindle aggression against the targeted group.

---

[441] ibid
[442] Tsesis, Alexander, Prohibiting Incitement on the Internet, Virginia Journal of Law and Technology, 7Va.J.L.&Tech.5, Summer 2002 available at http://www.vjolt.net, visited on 14 May 2005

This is particularly true when the electronic transmissions are part of a concerted campaign to de-legitimize the aspirations of a hated group[443].

3.9.2 Content Neutral Standard – R.A.V v St.Paul

Next stage of legal development in relation to hate speech started with Supreme Court hurdle against enacting a statute prohibiting hate speech on the Internet is the content neutral standard for fighting words established by Justice Scalia's majority opinion in R.A.V. v. St. Paul[444]. The concurrences to that case are so significantly different from the majority opinion that knowing their conclusions is   essential to understanding the current state of the prevailing law.

The case arose when Juveniles set fire to a cross on a black family's lawn. They were charged with violating a   St. Paul ordinance[445] which made it a misdemeanor to publicly   or privately   display any   symbols known to "arouse anger, alarm or resentment … on the basis of race, color, creed, religion or gender." Scalia J, found that law an unconstitutional "content discrimination." His view was that the ordinance violated the First Amendment because it prohibited the enumerated forms of inciteful speech, but tolerated un-enumerated forms, such as those directed against persons' political affiliation. The Court recognized that the City had a compelling interest in protecting the human rights of the "members of groups that have historically been subjected to discrimination."[446] While St. Paul could have adopted a blanket prohibition against all fighting words, the court found it

---

[443] Kathleen E. Mahoney, Hate Speech: Affirmation or Contradiction of Freedom of Expression, 1996 U. ILL. L. REV. 789, 801; Steven H. Shiffrin, Racist Speech, Outsider Jurisprudence, and the Meaning of America, 80 CORNELL L. REV. 43, 80 (1994).

[444] R.A.V. v. ST. PAUL, 505 U.S. 377 (1992), available at http://laws.findlaw.com/us/505/377.html , visited on 10 Dec 2005

[445] St. Paul, Minnesota., Legis. Code 292.02 (1990), which provides: "Whoever places on public or private property a symbol, object, appellation, characterization or graffiti, including, but not limited to, a burning cross or Nazi swastika, which one knows or has reasonable grounds to know arouses anger, alarm or resentment in others on the basis of race, color, creed, religion or gender commits disorderly conduct and shall be guilty of a misdemeanor."

[446] Supra Note 444

unconstitutional that legislators adopted laws intended only to prohibit some inflammatory messages[447].

All three concurrences complained that Justice Scalia had significantly departed from precedent, which had long permitted some content specific limitations on speech. Justice Blackmun J, wrote that it was irreconcilable to hold that the state "cannot regulate speech that causes great harm unless it also regulates speech that does not." Blackmun J, thought R.A.V. to be so significant a departure from traditional protections on speech that it would be an anomalous opinion that would "not significantly alter First Amendment jurisprudence." Unlike Scalia J, Blackmun J found that no First Amendment principles were jeopardized by a law preventing "hoodlums from driving minorities out of their homes by burning crosses on their lawns." To the contrary, Blackmun J regarded it a "great harm" to prohibit St. Paul from penalizing racist fighting words because it "so prejudices their community." Justice Blackmun's concurrence makes clear that he was not averse to hate speech laws; he nevertheless found the language of the St. Paul ordinance constitutionally overbroad[448].

Justice Scalia's opinion dismisses the numerous instances in which the Supreme Court found restrictions on constitutional speech. Content based restrictions have been found constitutional in cases which dealt with operating adult theaters, threatening the President, electioneering within 100 feet of a polling place on election day, using trade names, burning draft cards, and distributing obscene materials. This list indicates that constitutionally permissible content specific restrictions involve both political and non-political expressions. Electioneering is a form of dialogue about the merits of various political candidates. Draft card burning also pertains to political statements, speaking against government involvement in

---

[447] ibid
[448] Fisher William, Benckler Yochai, Brackely Rebacca and Ma Shara, Freedom of Expression on the Internet, Berkmen Center for Internet and Society, available at http://cyber.law.harvard.edu/ilaw/mexico_2006_module_4_freedom , visited on 2 Feb 2005.

military action or affirming the validity of pacifism. Speech which is not political, such as practicing medicine without a license, is also subject to regulations[449].

Justice Scalia's holding in R.A.V. case is incongruous with the numerous cases in which narrowly tailored and content specific speech laws were found to be a legitimate use of governmental power. The majority turned a blind eye to St. Paul's compelling reasons for focusing its attention to rooting out hate speech. The opinion manifests a lack of empathy for minority sensibilities about the threat hate speech poses to their communities. Even though the Court recognized that St. Paul had a compelling interest in passing the ordinance, it nevertheless held to a novel opinion, unsubstantiated by any socio-historical analysis, about the regulation of content specific speech[450].

Free speech is one of the fundamental rights protected under the Constitution of US (India), but conflicts sometimes arise between persons wanting to express themselves and the people affected by their speech. In the R.A.V. case majority did not balance bigots' rights to express their views against the rights of vulnerable minorities to be free from the substantial risks hate groups pose through their content specific indoctrination and recruitment. For instance, absent is any reflection on the symbolic meaning of cross burnings. That symbol, after all is not only expressive, but also motivational. Cultural symbolism delimits people's parameters of thought and influences their attitudes, behaviors, and reactions. Cross burnings are meant to demean and increase support networks for persons with supremacist ideologies. To comprehend the public meaning of a given symbol, it is important to consider what it represents. Such an evaluation must reflect on the object and the context within which it appears. Social history is part of the context of racist expressions they are used to interlink speakers and audiences through a racist past, a concurrent racist network, and mutually intolerant plans. With the broad, and international reach of the Internet, the threat of galvanization and massive acts of

---

[449] ibid
[450] ibid

oppression is greater than ever before because it can facilitate the creation of a concerted effort to undermine human rights. Bias motivated crimes might, in fact, be perpetrated in states other than those from which the message was sent[451].

3.9.3 Hate Speech – International Perspective

The Internet enables hate groups to transmit their messages internationally; therefore, to determine the plausibility of regulating hate speech on this medium we must evaluate international human rights instruments on hate speech.

Several international conventions also affirm that the substantial threat to targets of hate speech outweighs the burden imposed on orators. For instance the Convention on the Prevention and Punishment of the Crime of Genocide requires contracting parties to punish "direct and public incitement to commit genocide."[452]

The European Convention on the Protection of Human Rights and Fundamental Freedoms not only commits twenty-three party states to protecting the rights to free expression and opinion but also acknowledges other civil rights: "The exercise of these freedoms … may be subject to such formalities, conditions, restrictions or penalties as are prescribed by law and are necessary in a democratic society, in the interests of … public safety, for the prevention of disorder or crime, for the protection of health or morals, for the protection of the reputation or rights of others.."[453]

These conventions are further strengthened by the U.N. Convention on the Elimination of All Forms of Racial Discrimination[454] which commits governments to actions against hate speech:

It requires States Parties to condemn all propaganda and all organizations which are based on ideas or theories of superiority of one race or group of persons of one

---

[451] ibid

[452] Art.3 , Convention on the Prevention and Punishment of the Crime of Genocide, available at http://www.unhchr.ch/html/menu3/b/p_genoci.htm , visited on 3 Sep 2005

[453] Art. 10 of European Convention on Human Rights, available at http://www.hri.org/docs/ECHR50.html , visited on 4 Sep 2005

[454] Office of the High Commissioner for Human Rights, convention available at http://www.unhchr.ch/html/menu3/b/d_icerd.htm , visited on 3 Nov 2005

colour or ethnic origin, or which attempt to justify or promote racial hatred and discrimination in any form, and undertake to adopt immediate and positive measures designed to eradicate all incitement to, or acts of, such discrimination, and to this end, with due regard to the principles embodied in the Universal Declaration of Human Rights and the rights expressly set forth in Article 5 of this Convention, inter alia:

(a) Shall declare an offence punishable by law all dissemination of ideas based on racial superiority or hatred, incitement to racial discrimination, as well as all acts of violence or incitement to such acts against any race or group of other persons of another colour or ethnic origin, and also the provision of any assistance to racist activities, including the financing thereof;

(b) Shall declare illegal and prohibit organizations, and also organized and all other propaganda activities, which promote and incite racial discrimination, and shall recognize participation in such organizations or activities as an offence punishable by law;

(c) Shall not permit public authorities or public institutions, national or local, to promote or incite racial discrimination.

A look at the laws of Western democracies and European Union makes it clear that the United States is following anomalous pure speech jurisprudence. A variety of governments understand that the intentional spread of bias against insular groups is detrimental to society[455]. Democracies generally recognize that preserving human rights supersedes a bigot's desire to spread instigatory vitriol. Representative government is only weakened by an unrestricted freedom on speech which comes at the expense of out group security. Speech that is purposefully, recklessly, or knowingly designed to suppress out group enjoyment of a country's privileges and immunities is antagonistic to social contract ideals. Surveying the history of racism in the United States, from Native American dislocation, to slavery, to Japanese internment, makes clear that here, as in other democracies; intolerance and

---

[455] Tsesis, Alexander, Prohibiting Incitement on the Internet, Virginia Journal of Law and Technology, 7Va.J.L.&Tech.5, Summer 2002 available at http://www.vjolt.net, visited on 1 4 May 2005.

persecution can exist in spite of a constitutional commitment to fairness and equality. Enacting narrowly tailored laws against hate speech can prevent socially regressive forces from establishing effective movements[456].

3.10 Conclusion

Cyber defamation and hate speech on the Internet is a growing problem. Many commentators , points out that the ways in which the Supreme Court has deployed the First Amendment to limit the application of the tort of defamation are founded on the assumption that most defamation suits will be brought against relatively powerful institutions (e.g., newspapers, television stations). The Internet, by enabling relatively poor and powerless persons to broadcast to the world their opinions of powerful institutions (e.g., their employers, companies by which they feel wronged) increases the likelihood that, in the future, defamation suits will be brought most often by formidable plaintiffs against weak individual defendants. If we believe that "the Internet is . . . a powerful tool for equalizing imbalances of power by giving voice to the disenfranchised and by allowing more democratic participation in public discourse," we should not be worried by this development. We should be able to suggest that it may be necessary, in this altered climate, to reconsider the shape of the constitutional limitations on defamation.

Combating online extremism presents enormous technological and legal difficulties, and as noted earlier, the few examples provided here are only the tip of the iceberg. Even if it were electronically feasible to keep sites off the Internet, the international nature of the medium makes legal regulation virtually impossible.

As a result, governments, corporations and people of goodwill continue to look for alternative ways to address the problem.

---

[456] ibid at p 313

153

Chapter 4

PRIVACY IN CYBERSPACE

Information privacy is a social goal, not a technological one. To achieve information privacy goals will require social innovations, including the formation of new norms and perhaps new legal rules to establish boundary lines between acceptable and unacceptable uses of personal data.

Pamela Samuelson[457]

4.1 Introduction

Information and Communication Technologies (ICT) have fulfilled Justice Brandeis' 1928 prophesy in his landmark dissent in Olmstead v. United States[458]. Our private lives are now exposed by electronic retrieval and publication of personal information. While Justice Brandeis was primarily concerned about governmental intrusion into private lives, his prophesy and his description of the right to privacy as "the right to be let alone-the most comprehensive of rights and the right most valued by civilized men" should apply equally to such intrusion by non-governmental entities. ICT provides both an economical and efficient means of

---

[457] Pamela Samuelson, Privacy as Intellectual Property?, 52 STAN. L. REV. 1125, 1169 (2000).

[458] A famous legal article titled "The Right to Privacy" written by Samuel Warren and Louis Brandeis and published by the Harvard Law Review in 1890. In this article authors had shown concern for privacy more than a century ago about how new technologies could affect privacy. They wrote: " recent inventions and business methods call attention to the next step which must be taken for the protection of the person, and for securing to the individual what Judge Cooley calls the right 'to be let alone'. Instantaneous photographs and newspaper enterprise have invaded the sacred precincts of private and domestic life; and numerous mechanical devices threaten to make good the prediction that 'what is whispered in the closet shall be proclaimed from the house-tops'. For years there has been a feeling that the law must afford some remedy for the unauthorized circulation of portraits of private persons; and the evil of the invasion of privacy by the newspapers, long keenly felt, has been but recently discussed by an able writer. The alleged facts of a somewhat notorious case brought before an inferior tribunal in New York a few months ago, directly involved the consideration of the right of circulating portraits; and the question whether our law will recognize and protect the right to privacy in this and in other respects must soon come before our courts for consideration." The article Right to Privacy by the authors is available at http://freedomlaw.com/Brandeis.htm , visited 1 4 May 2005.
The case, Olmstead V U.S. 227 US 438 (1928), with Justice Brandies dissenting, available at http://caselaw.lp.findlaw.com/cgi-bin/getcase.pl?court=us&vol=277&invol=438 , visited on 14 May 2005

finding needed information. Yet, as increasing amounts of personal information are collected and revealed electronically, there is growing concern over the resulting loss of privacy[459].

Uses of new technologies raise policy issues that are often defined in terms of invasion of privacy. Supporting this contention, one commentator, Patricia Mell, notes that the use of computers to manage information has considerably blurred the demarcation between public and private realms[460]. Unfortunately, this blurring of the realms of privacy by the influx of technological advances only adds to the problem we are now striving to address. This contention also supports a similar, and ever present condition, which Arthur Miller noted in 1971, by stating that, "it is essential to expose the ways computer technology is magnifying the threat to informational privacy - a threat that we have faced in some form ever since man began to take notes about himself and his neighbors[461] and which have also been supported by the 1978 and 1993 Louis Harris poll"[462]. Yet, another legal scholar, Henry Perritt observes "in the long run, adoption of information technologies will blur the boundaries between citizen and agency and between agency and court. Blurring of these boundaries may necessitate rethinking the definitions of some of the basic events that define the administrative process, public participation, and judicial review."[463]

Noted constitutional scholar Lawrence Tribe recommends, that "policy makers look not at what technology makes possible, but at the core values the Constitution enshrines."[464] Principles, such as those that underlie privacy, must be "invariable ...

---

[459] Susan E. Gindin, Lost And Found In Cyberspace: Informational Privacy in the Age of the Internet, available at http://www.info-law.com/lost.html , visited 20 May 2005

[460] Priscilla M. Regan, Privacy, Technology And Public Policy, University of North Carolina Press (September 1995) at p 2 .
[461] Miller Arthur,, The Assault On Privacy, Signet publications. New York,1971 at p 23
[462] ibid
[463] Henry H. Perritt Jr., The Electronic Agency and the Traditional Paradigms of Administrative Law, 44 ADMIN. L. REV. 79, 80 (1992).
[464] Tribe Laurence, The Constitution in Cyberspace: Law and Liberty Beyond the Electronic Frontier, Keynote address at the First Conference on Computers, Freedom and Privacy (Boston, March 1991) available at http://www.swissnet.ai.mit.edu/6095/ articles/tribe-constitution.txt, visited 13 Sep 2005

despite accidents of technology."[465] Thus, an irony now presents itself: the very technology that simplifies our lives simultaneously complicates our legal analysis of this most fundamental of concepts.

The Internet offers many benefits. Web sites provide a vast world of information, entertainment, and shopping at our fingertips. Electronic mail, instant messaging, and chat rooms enable us to communicate with friends, family, and strangers in ways we never dreamed of a decade ago.

The Internet has become an indispensable tool for data retrieval, communication, and business transactions. Companies increasingly look to the Internet to attract potential clients and customers and to stay in contact with current clients and customers. But with the ease in collecting and processing information on the Internet and the depth and richness of the data available, there exists the danger that Internet business transactions can render a party's information susceptible to interception, misappropriation, or other loss. The Internet exposes companies to the danger that third parties may access private, confidential client data, resulting in potential liability to the companies. The privacy and security concerns generated by the Internet increase the importance of a company's privacy policy[466].

The Constitution of India does not contain a provision granting a general right to privacy. But 'Right to Privacy' has been recognized by the Indian Judiciary as implicit in Art. 21 and Art.19 (1) (a) of the Constitution in many cases. Right to privacy has many dimensions and the most likely aspect of privacy that would be affected in cyberspace is informational privacy. There are currently no laws in India requiring websites to disclose how the information they gather about visitors is used, and online businesses are largely free to use data obtained on their websites without oversight by the consumer. In India, consumers have no statutory right to control the dissemination of their personal information to others by third parties.

---

[465] ibid
[466] Wendy S Meyer, Insurance Coverage for Potential Liability Arising from Internet Privacy Issues, journal of Corporation Law, Winter 2003

4.2 Aspects of Privacy

Privacy is a basic human right recognized all over the world and in cyberspace it is the most flagrantly violated right of the individual.

People enjoy having private spaces, and want to keep them. Key aspects include the following:

- Privacy is the interest that individuals have in sustaining a 'personal space', free from interference by other people and organizations[467];
- Privacy has multiple dimensions, including privacy of the physical person, privacy of personal behaviour, privacy of communications, and privacy of personal data. The last two are commonly bundled together as 'information privacy'[468];
- Individuals claim that data about themselves should not be automatically available to other individuals and organizations, and that, even where data is possessed by another party, the individual must be able to exercise a substantial degree of control over that data and its use[469]; and
- Dataveillance or intellectual privacy is the systematic use of personal data systems in the investigation or monitoring of the actions or communications of one or more persons[470];

4.2.1 Privacy under International Law

Universal Declaration of Human Rights defines Right to Privacy under Art.12 as follows;

---

[467] Clarke , Roger, Information Privacy On the Internet Cyberspace Invades Personal Space , http://www.anu.edu.au/people/Roger.Clarke/DV/IPrivacy.html

[468] ibid
[469] ibid
[470] ibid

157

"No one shall be subjected to arbitrary interference with his privacy, family, home or **correspondence**, nor to attacks upon his honour and reputation. Everyone has the right to the protection of the law against such interference or attacks."

Art.17 of he International Covenant on Civil and Political Rights (ICCPR) and European Convention for the Protection of Human Rights and Fundamental Freedoms (Art 8) are expressed similarly, and an extensive jurisprudence has developed in Europe interpreting Art 8 of the Convention. The European Court has measured member countries laws and procedures against Art 8's guarantees, and often found them wanting (for example, the United Kingdom's)[471].

The lack of any constitutional recognition of the right to privacy has led to a similar patchwork in the judicial response to privacy issues. The Supreme Court of India in several cases has held that Right to privacy is implicit in Art.21 of the Constitution which guarantees right to life and personal liberty[472].

The right to privacy as it has been developed in these cases reflects the values of a 19th century liberal democracy whose primary concern was to protect the individual from inappropriate interference from the state. The nature of communications networks now makes the need to protect against potential invasion of personal autonomy by private interests or individuals, equally pressing. The common law has been slow to develop tort remedies for invasion of personal privacy. There is little existing legal framework to help the courts determine new questions of privacy that arise from communications networks, such as: the limits to be placed on employer surveillance and data-tracking of employees; the determination of ownership of

---

[471] Cronin P Kevin & Weikers N Ronald, Data Security and Privacy Law:Combating Cyberthreats,Thomson –West, US, 2004

[472] In Kharak Singh V State of UP (AIR 1963 SC 1295), domiciliary visit by the police without the authority of a law , was held to be violative of Art.21 , assuming that a right of privacy was a fundamental right derived from the freedom of movement guaranteed by Art.19(1)(d) as well as personal liberty guaranteed by Art.21. Also in People's Union for Civil Liberties V Union of India (AIR 1997 SC 568) it was held that telephone tapping infringes right to privacy, if not resorted to by just, fair and reasonable procedure. Again in 'X' v 'Hospital Z' Supreme Court held that right to privacy is an essential component of the right to life but is not absolute and may be restricted for prevention of crime, disorder or protection of health or morals or protection of rights and freedom of others.

electronic mail messages created by employees while at the workplace; and the potential electronic intrusion of telemarketers into Indian homes.

4.3 Commodification, Privacy and Free Alienability

Personal information is an important currency in the new millennium. The monetary value of data is large and still growing and corporates are moving quickly to profit from this[473]. Companies view this information as a corporate asset and have invested heavily in software that facilitates the collection of consumer information. Moreover, a strong conception of personal data as a commodity is merging in the United States and individual Americans are already participating in the commodification of their personal data[474].Commodification of personal data falls into four broad categories (1) lists of those who are willing to commodify their personal data (2) lists of those who wish to receive tailored ads and the particular interests of those persons (3) lists of transactional activities such as purchases that follow, the release of commodified personal data and (4) privacy metadata which comprises information about one's privacy preferences[475].

Metadata are a relatively common phenomenon in the information age and is capable of creating privacy metadata. Metadata are information about information; they are, for example, found in the popular text-processing software like Microsoft Word, which permits association of rich metadata with documents[476]. Metadata in Word can include the author's name and initials; the names of previous document authors; the name of the author's company or organization ; the name of the one's computer ; the name of the network server or hard disk where the document was

---

[473] Jennifer Sullivan & Christopher Jones, How Much Is Your Playlist worth? Wired News, Nov 3, 1999, available at http://www.wired.com/news/technology/1.32258-0.html, visited 4 Nov 2005
[474] Schwartz M Paul, Property, Privacy and Personal Data, Harvard Law Review, Vol117:2055, May 2004, at p 2057
[475] Lessig , Lawrence, Code and Other Laws of Cyberspace, Basic Books, New York, 1999 at p 142-63
[476] See Microsoft Corp, OFF: How To minimize Metadata in Microsoft Office Document (Microsoft Knowledge Base article No.223,396) available at http://support.microsoft.com/default.aspx?scid=kb;en-us;223396, visited 10 Apr 2005

saved; document revisions; hidden text or cells; and personalized editing comments[477]. All these metadata can be associated with a single document.

The personal data market will increasingly include privacy metadata and this metadata will in turn be commodified and contribute to additional privacy invasions. Already in the offline world and in no small irony, direct marketers generate and sell lists of people who have expressed interest in protecting their privacy[478]. Analogous to these marketing lists of those who wish to protect their privacy, privacy metadata can include information concerning an interest in not receiving certain kinds of solicitations or not receiving telemarketing calls at certain times. These meatadata will be highly marketable[479].

Personal data inalienability is any restriction on the transferability, ownership or use of data. In the context of these new technologies, inalienability relates to restrictions on the exchange of personal data, even restrictions contrary to individual's wishes. In other words, even if someone wants to engage in data trade, society may wish to limit her ability to do so. A principle of free alienability for personal information would mean, in contrast, that an individual has a right to do what he wants with his data. Alienability is yet to emerge as a policy issue for adware[480] and spyware[481] because the makers of these products generally offer inadequate notice of their data practices. It would be difficult for adware and spyware companies to make an argument for free choice to trade personal data in the absence of sufficient notice of data collection and processing practices. Informed consent to adware and spyware

---

[477] ibid
[478] For battle over privacy metadata in the context of traditional telephony see US West Inc., V FCC 182 F.3d 1224, 1228 (10th circuit, 1999), available at
http://www.kscourts.org/CA10/cases/1999/03/98-9501.htm , visted on Nov 5, 2005
[479] Schwartz M Paul, Property, Privacy and Personal Data, Harvard Law Review, Vol117:2055, May 2004, at p 2070

[480] Spyware and adware are controversial applications of networked computing. Smart Computing Magazine defines spyware as a program that "installs itself without your permission, runs without your permission and uses your computer without your permission. Adware is something but not always, delivered as part of spyware; the definitional line between the two depends on whether the computer user receives adequate notice of the program installation. See Tracy Baker, Here's Looking at you, Kid: How to Avoid Spyware, SMART COMPUTING, Sept.2003 at 68
[481] Developments in the Law-The Law of Cyberspace, The Harvard Law Association, Vol 12:1574,1999

would require notice of such practices, without it, there is no free choice to trade data[482].

4.4 The Lack of Privacy in Cyberspace

In cyberspace, as in today's real world, there seems to be confusion in regard to what privacy is and what it is not. One scholar, Ruth Granson highlights recent efforts to fully comprehend privacy: "the concept of privacy is a central one in most discussions of modern Western life, yet only recently have there been serious efforts to analyze just what is meant by *privacy*." Over the years, the conception of the nature and extent of privacy has been severely bent out of shape. The definitions and concepts of privacy are as varied as those in the legal and academic circles who explore privacy. Another scholar, Judith DeCew, examines the diversity of privacy conceptions: "the idea of privacy which is employed by various legal scholars, is not always the same. Privacy may refer to the separation of spheres of activity, limits on governmental authority, forbidden knowledge and experience, limited access, and ideas of group membership consequently privacy is commonly taken to incorporate different clusters of interest."[483]

At one time, privacy implied that individuals could be secluded, but that has radically changed. Logistical barriers created by geography once protected a person. This too, though, has radically changed. The geographical wall of protection, which incidentally was not created by our legal system, has been removed by the development of the Internet, and more recently, by the World Wide Web. The loss of these once formidable barriers has not been accounted for in the scholarship available today[484].For today, "effective protection of personal data and privacy is developing into an essential precondition for social acceptance of the new digital networks and services." Privacy can no longer be assumed, even in the security of

---

[482] Schwartz M Paul, Property, Privacy and Personal Data, Harvard Law Review, Vol117:2055, May 2004, at p 2065

[483] Robert A. Reilly, Conceptual Foundations of Privacy: Looking Backward Before Stepping Forward, 6 RICH. J.L. & TECH. 6 (Fall 1999), available at
http://www.richmond.edu/jolt/v6i2/article1.html, visited 22 May 2005
[484] ibid

one's own home. Instead, privacy is a condition that is much easier to violate, and thus, is much more difficult to establish and protect[485].

The way in which we continue to view privacy has not significantly changed across time, and in some cases, change has been actively resisted. Yet somehow, privacy has evolved from a small single function business into a complex conglomerate. A basic paradigm shift in the way we conceptualize privacy is in order. For at this instance, "privacy" should be viewed as a foundational concept in the same manner that life, liberty, and the pursuit of happiness are foundational concepts in our society. In order to begin to accomplish this paradigm shift, it is first necessary to revisit the cultural evolution of "privacy" so that we can fully analyze the ramifications and impact of emerging technologies[486].

4.5 Electronic Invasion of Privacy

An individual's privacy may be invaded electronically in several ways: first, by the significant amount of personal information which is available in online databases; second, by the transactional information collected as the individual participates in online activities which specifically identifies the individual; and third, by the massive computerized databases which are maintained by governments and non-governmental entities, that may be subject to security breaches[487].

Many people expect that their online activities are anonymous. They are not. It is possible to record virtually all online activities, including which newsgroups or files subscriber accesses, which web sites are visited and reading of e-mails. This information can be collected by a subscriber's own ISP and by web site operators[488].

"Online communications" are communications over telephone, cable networks, or wireless systems using computers. Examples of online communications include

---

[485] ibid
[486] Cronin P Kevin & Weikers N Ronald, Data Security and Privacy Law: Combating Cyberthreats, Thomson-West, New York, 2004 at 1-49
[487] ibid at p 2-7
[488] Privacy Rights In cyberspace, http://www.privacyrights.org/fs/fs18-cyb.htm

connecting to the Internet through an Internet Service Provider (ISP) such as America Online or Earthlink, or accessing the Internet from a public library or community computer center. Mobile access to the Internet is increasing via hand held Personal Digital Assistants (PDAs), pagers, and other devices[489].

The Internet raises some unique privacy concerns. Information sent over this vast global network may pass through dozens of different computer systems on the way to its destination. Each of these systems is operated by its own administrator and may be capable of capturing and storing online communications. Furthermore, online activities can potentially be monitored by Internet Service Provider (ISP) and by web sites that we visit[490].

The informational consequences of activities in cyberspace result from the generation, storage, and transmission of personal data in three areas: (1) personal computers; (2) Internet Service Providers ("ISPs") (3) Web sites, and (4) Spyware. Visitors to cyberspace sometimes believe that they will be fully able to choose among anonymity, semi-anonymity, and complete disclosure of identity and preferences. Yet, in each of the three areas, finely granulated personal data are created—often in unexpected ways. Moreover, most people are unable to control, and are often in ignorance of, the complex processes by which their personal data are created, combined, and sold[491].

4.5.1 Personal Computers

When tied to a network, an individual's personal computer makes access to the Internet available at her desk[492]. For some people, this machine may be no more than a necessary evil; they imagine the computer to be a glorified typewriter. For

---

[489] Privacy Rights Clearinghouse / UCAN ,June 1995. Revised   August 2003 available at http://www.privacyrights.org/fs/fs18-cyb.htm, visited on 23 Jun 2005

[490] ibid

[491] Paul M. Schwartz, Privacy and Democracy in Cyberspace, Vanderbilt Law Review, Vol. 52:1609

[492] Reno V ACLU, 521 U.S. at 844-49; Nathan J. Muller, Desktop Encyclopedia Of Telecommunications, 3rd Edition, McGrawhill, New York,1998, at p 168-70 .

others, it is an evocative object, perhaps even a kind of friend with whom one can have an intense relationship[493].The computer is not always a silent and loyal friend, but sometimes, the recorder and betrayer of Monica Lewinsky's confidences. A personal computer records and reveals its users' confidences in a number of ways[494].

First, information deleted from a personal computer is generally easily recoverable, whether from the machine's hard drive or elsewhere. Our own digital experiences provide examples of how computer files may be deleted, but not destroyed. Deletion removes data from the hard disk drive's directory of files and marks the disk space where the file is still stored as available for reuse[495].In time, another file may be written over this area, but in the period before deleted data are overwritten, anyone with access to the computer can locate and restore the deleted file with relatively simple commands found in many software utility programs[496]. Even if files have been written over, or, more drastically, "wiped" by programs that hash over the designated disk space, software utility programs are sometimes capable of recovering the underlying data from the computer[497]. Moreover, deleted files can be found not only on a personal computer's hard drive but also on another personal computer or elsewhere in a networked system[498].

As these examples show, a personal computer can betray confidences by failing to destroy files that its users sought to remove by use of a "delete" button. This

---

[493] *See* Reno v. ACLU, 521 U.S. 844, 868-73 (1997) (describing some of the myriad forms on online behavior);

[494] Volokh, Eugene, Freedom of Speech, Cyberspace and Harassment Law, 2001 Stan.Tech.Rev 3, available at http://stlr.stanford.edu/STLR/Articles/01_STLR_3 or www.papers.ssrn.com , visited on 2 Sep 2004 ; in this article author brings out the ramification of e-mail during the controversy of Clinton-Lewinsky scandal highlighting how technology can be used to violate privacy;

[495] Ron, White," How Computers Work " 4th ed., Random House Publications, New York, 1999 at p 78-79

[496] ibid at p 81

[497] David S., Bennahum, *Daemon Seed: Old email never dies*, WIRED, May 1999, at p 100, 102

[498] Jerry ,Adler, When E-Mail Bites Back, NEWSWEEK, Nov. 23, 1998, at p 45 (noting that in its investigation of Microsoft, the Justice Department has obtained an estimated 3.3 *million* Microsoft documents, including megabytes of e-mail messages dating from the early 1990s and is using them to contradict Gate's own videotaped testimony in the most significant antitrust case of the decade".

machine causes a further problem for privacy, however, through its storage of information about Internet activities. Computers' Web browsers, such as Netscape Navigator or Microsoft Internet Explorer, contain software protocols that create files about Web sites that have been visited. Anyone with physical access to a computer can access these data in a matter of seconds either by looking at drop down files on the browser's location bar or by accessing the "History" menu item found on both Netscape Navigator or Microsoft Internet Explorer. Even more significantly, remote access to these files is possible from the Internet by exploiting security flaws in Web browsers[499].

Cyberspace behavior also results in the recording of data in computer cache files. In order to increase the computer's speed of access to information, these special memory subsystems duplicate frequently used data values, such as Web pages frequently visited[500].Cache files exist on a computer's hard drive and, more temporarily, in its random access memory ("RAM")[501].From the Web, it is possible to access cache files through "JavaScripts" and "Java applets" that permit the remote uploading of these files[502].These terms refer to programming languages for writing Web applications; both allow routines to be executed on an individual's personal computer remotely from the Web[503].

4.5.2 Cookies

When we "surf" the web, many web sites deposit data about our visit, called "cookies," on our hard drive so that when we return to that site, the cookie data will reveal that we have been there before. The web site might offer us products or advertisements tailored to our interests, based on the contents of the cookie data.

---

[499] Bryan, Pfaffenberger , "Protect Your Privacy on the Internet", John Wiley & Sons, Bk&CD-Rom edition , USA, 1997 at p 85
[500] Microsoft Press Computer Dictionary, 3d ed. 1997 , at p 382
[501] ibid at , p 73
[502] ibid, at p 82
[503] Bryan Pfaffenberger , "Protect Your Privacy on the Internet", John Wiley & Sons, Bk&CD-Rom edition , USA, 1997, at 120-40

Most cookies are used only by the web site that placed it on our computer. But some, called third-party cookies, communicate data about us to an advertising clearinghouse which in turn shares that data with other online marketers. Our web browser and some software products enable us to detect and delete cookies, including third-party cookies[504].

A personal computer linked to the Internet can reveal confidences by their acceptance of "cookies," also known as "persistent client-side hypertext transfer protocol files."[505] These terms refer to identification tags and other blocks of data that a Web site sends to and stores on the hard drive of the computer of anyone who visits it[506].When an individual returns to this same site at a later date, her browser automatically sends a copy of the cookie back to the Web site; the data identify her as a previous visitor and allow the site to match her to details regarding her prior visit[507]. As the Microsoft Computing Dictionary explains, "cookies are used to identify users, to instruct the server to send a customized version of the requested Web page, to submit account information for the user, and for other administrative purposes." This definition is, however, misleadingly soothing: cookies are a ready source of detailed information about personal online habits[508].

To begin with, anyone who sits at another's computer or has remote access to it through an internal network can examine the machine's cookies to gain the names of the Web sites that placed these blocks of data[509]. In addition, access to the cookies placed on one's computer is available from the Internet. Cookies are

---

[504] Privacy Rights In cyberspace, http://www.privacyrights.org/fs/fs18-cyb.html , visited on 23 Aug 2005

[505] Microsoft Dictionary, supra note 500, at 119. Somewhat confusingly, the disks found inside a standard floppy disk case or a zip drive are also called "cookies."

[506] See Persistent Cookie FAQ ,visited Sept. 2, 2003, http://www.cookiecentral.com/-faq.htm, visited on 2 Nov 2005

[507] See ibid

[508] Paul M. Schwartz, Privacy and Democracy in Cyberspace, Vanderbilt Law Review, Vol. 52:1609 at p 1624

[509] See MICROSOFT DICTIONARY, supra note 500, at p 92 (providing a definition of "clickstream" data);

designed to report back exclusively to the Web site that placed them and to reveal only a particular identification number assigned by that site on previous visits. Nevertheless, access to cookies from the Internet can turn this numerical tag and information associated with it into "personal information." Once Web sites identify a specific visitor, they can match her to their rich stores of "clickstream data," which is information about the precise path a user takes while browsing at a Web site, including how long she spent at any part of a site[510]. Such finely grained information exists because, after all, a person only "moves" about cyberspace by means of a series of digital commands that her computer sends to HTTP (Hyper Text Transport Protocol) servers[511].A Web site's collection of the names and addresses of its visitors is one way that this linkage takes place. One way that this linkage takes place is by a Web site's collection of the names and addresses of its visitors, which often occurs through different kinds of registration requirements or through participation in a sweepstake at the site[512].Disclosure is not generally made, however, regarding the consequences of registration or participation in these sweepstakes. In addition, some browsers can be set to provide one's name and home address, thereby furnishing another means for the site that set the cookie to identify a specific computer user[513].As for technical limitations aimed at restricting the reading of a cookie to the Web site that set it, these can be made ineffectual. At the simplest level, nothing forbids the company that set a cookie from using it to gather personal data and then selling this information to third parties or sharing it with an affiliate[514].In addition, under the right circumstances, a third party can gain

---

[510] ibid

[511] Knag, Jerry , Information Privacy in Cyberspace Transactions, 50 STAN. L. REV. 1193, 1198 (1998) (explaining that in cyberspace, "you are invisibly stamped with a bar code").

[512] Bryan Pfaffenberger ,Protect Your Privacy on the Internet, John Wiley & Sons, Bk&CD-Rom edition , USA, 1997, at 59-60

[513] See Netscape, Cookies and Privacy Frequently Asked Questions , available at http://www.home.netscape.com/products/security/resources/faq.cookies.html (explaining that "cookies can be used to store any information that the user volunteers"), visited 2 Sep 2003

[514] As an example, Microsoft purchased Hotmail, a free Internet e-mail service, to gain access to Hotmail's existing customer base of 9.5 million subscribers. See Microsoft Finds Free Email for MSN , available at http://www.wired.com/news/news/business/story/-9450.html . Since Microsoft's purchase of this company at the end of 1997, Hotmail has grown to 28 million accounts. Polly

information from a cookie without recourse to the company that set it. Because most cookies are placed in the same disk files, third parties on the Web can use malicious code to upload the contents of an entire cookies file. Moreover, a series of different software "bugs" permit the overriding of restrictions set on the sharing of cookies[515]. Finally, a recent news story reported that some existing cookie files are accidentally being transmitted to Web sites other than the ones that set them[516]. In some cases, these transmitted data include identification information, including PINs (Personal Identity Numbers), used at the site that set the cookies. The current best explanation for this software problem is that computer crashes or other hardware problems "corrupted" the cookie files.[517]

4.5.3 DoubleClick Shock and Cookies

Use of cookies to gather user's information and its legal implications was first considered by courts in Doubleclick case. In a class action lawsuit against DoubleClick[518], a number of plaintiffs complained the internet advertising company's use of cookies to track web surfers violated the Electronic Communiation Privacy Act (ECPA). The Court dismisses claims advanced by the plaintiff class under the Electronic Communications Privacy Act, the Computer Fraud and Abuse Act, and the Wiretap Act arising out of Doubleclick's use and placement of "cookies" on plaintiffs' computers. Doubleclick uses such "cookies" to gather information about the users' use of Doubleclick client web sites. Because

Sprenger, Hotel Hotmail, available at http://www. wired.com/-news/news/business/story/18617.html , visited on 23 Oct 2005

[515] See Cookie Exploit, available at ,http://www.cookiecentral.com/bug/-index.shtml , visited 3 Sep 2005

[516] See What's in them Cookies? Web Site is Finding Out, PRIVACY TIMES, Feb. 15, 1999, at p 1
[517] ibid
[518] DoubleClick, a Delaware corporation, is the largest provider of Internet advertising products and services in the world. Its Internet-based advertising network of over 11,000 Web publishers has enabled DoubleClick to become the market leader in delivering online advertising. DoubleClick specializes in collecting, compiling and analyzing information about Internet users through proprietary technologies and techniques, and using it to target online advertising. DoubleClick has placed billions of advertisements on its clients' behalf and its services reach the majority of Internet users in the United States

Doubleclick's clients consented to such information gathering, the court held that Doubleclick's activities did not run afoul of either the Electronic Communications Privacy Act or the Wiretap Act. The court also dismissed the claims plaintiffs advanced under the Computer Fraud and Abuse Act because any damages caused by Doubleclick's activities did not meet the threshold required by the Computer Fraud and Abuse Act[519].

The information gathered by Doubleclick falls into three categories, described by the court as GET, POST and GIF. Typically a user accesses a Doubleclick client web site in response to a query to a search engine. Doubleclick will gather information contained in this query string, known as GET information (get me information about ....). Doubleclick will also gather information about a user that he POSTs to a Doubleclick web site in response to a query by the site, such as a request for that user's name and e-mail address. Lastly, Doubleclick will use a GIF tag to track the users' movements thru the client web site, such as the pages in the site the user visited. Doubleclick will gather this information as well[520].

Doubleclick uses this information to select the advertising the user will see when he visits a Doubleclick client web site. The user will send a command seeking access to a web site. The command will go to the servers housing that web site, which will deliver the site's contents, minus advertising, to the user. The user will also receive a link that instructs the user's computer to send a communication automatically to Doubleclick's servers. This will cause the user's computer to send a communication to Doubleclick's servers, which communication provides the number of the cookie Doubleclick has placed on the user's computer. Doubleclick uses this information to identify the user and determine the appropriate advertising that should be presented to him. Doubleclick then causes that advertising to appear on the web site the user sought by sending it to his computer. In addition, Doubleclick will update the users' profile with information of the type noted above that is gathered during this

---

[519] In Re DoubleClick, Inc. Privacy Litigation, 154 F.Supp.2d 497 (S.D.N.Y. 2001) available at http://www.nysd.uscourts.gov/courtweb/pdf/D02NYSC/01-03797.PDF , visited on 2 Nov 2005
[520] ibid at p 7

particular web site query. Users can prevent Doubleclick from obtaining this information by visiting Doubleclick's web site and requesting an opt-out cookie, or by configuring their browsers so as to prevent any cookies from being placed on their computers[521].

The plaintiffs contended that this conduct violated the Electronic Communications Privacy Act, 18 U.S.C. Section 2701[522] . ("ECPA"), the Wiretap Act, 18 U.S.C. Section 2510[523], and the Computer Fraud and Abuse Act, 18 U.S.C. Section 1030[524], ("CFAA"), plaintiffs commenced this class action suit. Plaintiffs also asserted a number of state law claims, including invasion of privacy and trespass.

Doubleclick argued that its conduct was exempt from the ECPA because it was authorized by its clients, to whom plaintiffs' communications were directed. The court agreed, and dismissed plaintiffs' ECPA claims. The court found that the facility through which the electronic information services at issue (communications between plaintiffs and the Doubleclick client web sites) was provided was the

---

[521] ibid at p 8

[522] It is a violation of the ECPA to "access without authorization a facility through which an electronic information service is provided ... and thereby obtain[] ... access to a wire or electronic communication while it is in electronic storage in such system ...". The statute contains an express exception, however, exempting from its coverage "conduct authorized ... (2) by a user of that service with respect to a communication of or intended for that user." 18 U.S.C. 2701(c)(2).

[523] This section states that "Any person who intentionally intercepts ... [an] electronic communication" violates the Wiretap Act. However, the statute contains an express exception for one who intercepts such a communication "where one of the parties to the communication has given prior consent to such interception unless such communication is intercepted for the purpose of committing any criminal or tortuous act ...".

[524] It is a violation of the Act to "intentionally access a computer without authorization ... and thereby obtain ... information from any protected computer ...". However, the statute sets a damage threshold that must be met before a claim for damages can be pursued. Under the statute, 18 U.S.C. Section 1030(g), "any person who suffers damage or loss by reason of a violation of this section may maintain a civil action ... to obtain compensatory damages and injunctive relief or other equitable relief. Damages for violations involving damage as defined in section (e)(8)(A) are limited to economic damages ...". Under section 18 U.S.C. section 1030(e)(8), damage is defined as "any impairment to the integrity or availability of data, a program, a system or information that - (a) causes loss aggregating at least $5000 in value during any 1-year period to one or more individuals; (b) impairs medical care; (c) causes physical injury; (d) threatens public health or safety."

service by which plaintiffs were provided access to the Internet from their home or other PCs. The court further found that Doubleclick's client web sites were authorized users of those services. Lastly, the court found that each of the communications as to which Doubleclick gather information were communications addressed to its clients web sites (either seeking access to that web site (a GET), or a portion thereof (a GIF) or responding to a query on that web site (a POST)[525]. As Doubleclick's clients authorized Doubleclick to access that information, the gathering in question was exempt from the ECPA. It should be noted that Doubleclick does not gather information from the users' computer, or any information other than that derived from the users' use of a Doubleclick client web site. The court further held that accessing "cookie" identification numbers fell outside the ambit of the statute, because the statute only covered communications in "electronic storage", which relates only to communications "temporarily stored" or "for a limited time." "The cookies long term residence on plaintiffs' hard drives place them outside of Section 2510(17)'s definition of 'electronic storage' and hence the protection under exception clause"[526]

The court found that Doubleclick had intercepted electronic communications between plaintiffs and Doubleclick's clients. However, the court further held that Doubleclick's client web sites had consented to such interception. Thus, Doubleclick's acts were exempt from the Wiretap Act provided the interception was not for the purpose of committing a criminal or tortuous act[527].

Lastly, the court held that plaintiffs could not establish a claim against Doubleclick for violating the CFAA because they could not establish the requisite damage there under. Plaintiffs argued that this damage threshold did not apply because it was inapplicable to a "loss" caused by Doubleclick's actions. As noted above, the statute creates a cause of action in any individual "who suffers damage or loss by reason of

---

[525] In Re DoubleClick, Inc. Privacy Litigation, 154 F.Supp.2d 497 (S.D.N.Y. 2001) available at http://www.nysd.uscourts.gov/courtweb/pdf/D02NYSC/01-03797.PDF at p 25, visited on 2 Nov 2005
[526] ibid at p 45
[527] ibid at p 56

a violation ...". While the court conceded there was "ambiguous" and "inconsistent" language in the statute, it held that the Legislative history and existing case law indicated that whatever type of injury a plaintiff sustained, be it damage or loss, had to meet the statutory minimum[528].

The implications of Doubleclick case is that if user consents to the collection of personal information by a cyberspace entity, then he cannot complain. However, there is an obligation on the part of the collector to adhere to accepted principles of data collection or as outlined in OECD guidelines for personal data collection.

4.5.4 Internet Service Providers (ISP)

Access to the Internet generally requires an individual to utilize an ISP, which is the entity that supplies Internet connectivity. ISPs can take roughly two forms. First, commercial entities, such as American Online ("AOL"), provide access to the internet for a monthly fee. Second, other entities, such as employers or schools, supply Internet access, often without a fee; these bodies either function directly as an ISP or outsource this task to another company[529].

ISPs obtain access to detailed and sometimes highly sensitive information about their customers' behavior on the Internet. ISPs can combine these data with profiling information, which their clients share with them, as well as with information purchased from direct marketing companies[530]. Many outside entities, both governmental and commercial, are increasingly seeking access to these rich databases of personal information[531].

ISPs are in an advantageous position to tie together the information that exists about anyone who surfs the Web. First, the ISP has highly accurate data about the identity of anyone who uses its services. This information is within its grasp because the ISP generally collects the client's name, address, phone number, and credit card number

---

[528] ibid at p 59
[529] See Lawrence Lessig, The Path of Cyberlaw, 104 YALE L.J.1743, 1748-49 (1995) (noting how a systems operator at a university can monitor activities of students and faculty on the Internet).
[530] See Edward C. Baig et al., Privacy, BUS. WK., Apr. 5, 1999, at 84 ("Personal details are acquiring enormous financial value. They are the new currency of the digital economy.").
[531] ibid

at the time it assigns an account[532]. Second, the ISP has detailed information about the Internet behavior of each of its customers. Through its role as an entrance ramp to the Internet, the ISP gains access to clickstream data and other kinds of detailed information about personal online habits[533]. It can easily take these scattered bits of cyberspace data, pieces of which at times enjoy different degrees of practical obscurity, and make them into "personal information" by linking them to the identity of its customers[534].

The question whether ISPs should disclose the identity of its subscribers without warrant was considered by US court in Timoty McVeigh v. Cohen[535]. AOL was involved in this case which was the chief provider of Internet access in the United States with over nineteen million subscribers[536]. In 1996, AOL surrendered subscriber information about Timothy McVeigh, one of its customers, to the United States Navy, which believed that these data gave it grounds to court martial him. The contested investigation had started because McVeigh, a highly decorated enlisted man assigned to a nuclear submarine, had sent an e-mail to a crew member's wife, who was a volunteer for a charity[537].AOL provides its subscribers with up to five different e-mail names, or "aliases," per account; McVeigh used his AOL account to join in a charity drive, but inadvertently sent his communication under his e-mail name "boysrch."[538] Through an option available to AOL subscribers, the crew member's wife searched through the "member profile directory" to locate additional information about the sender of this e-mail[539].Although this profile did not include his full name, address, or phone number, it specified that "boysrch" was an AOL subscriber named Tim, who lived

---

[532] Kang, Jerry , Information Privacy in Cyberspace Transactions, 50 STAN. L. REV. 1193, 1198 (1998) at p 1233
[533] ibid at p 1234
[534] ibid at p 1234
[535] 983 F. Supp. 215 (D.D.C. 1998) (finding ECPA bars government from obtaining a user's private information from an online service provider absent a warrant, subpoena, or court order) available at http://www.tomwbell.com/NetLaw/Ch05/McVeigh.html , visited on 23 Dec 2005

[536] ibid
[537] ibid
[538] ibid
[539] ibid

in Honolulu, worked in the military, and identified his marital status as "gay."[540] At this moment, the ISP's role became critical. Once McVeigh's e-mail and the directory information were brought to the Navy's attention, a military investigator promptly contacted AOL[541]. Without identifying himself as representing the government, the investigator explained that he wished to find out the identity of "boysrch". Despite its established policy otherwise, AOL promptly turned over subscriber data that linked McVeigh to this specific account[542].

The court held that the action of AOL illegal under the Electronic Communications Privacy Act of 1996 ("ECPA"). The ECPA, enacted by Congress to address privacy concerns on the Internet, allows the government to obtain information from an online service provider, as the Navy did in this instance from AOL,but only if (required to satisfy two conditions) viz.,

 a) it obtains a warrant issued under the Federal Rules of Criminal Procedure or state equivalent; or

b) it gives prior notice to the online subscriber and then issues a subpoena or receives a court order authorizing disclosure of the information in question[543].

Further the court observed that "…….In these days of "big brother," where through technology and otherwise the privacy interests of individuals from all walks of life are being ignored or marginalized, it is imperative that statues explicitly protecting these rights be strictly observed. Certainly, the public has an inherent interest in the preservation of privacy rights as advanced by Plaintiff in this case. With literally the entire world on the world wide web, enforcement of the ECPA is of great concern to those who bare the most personal information about their lives in private accounts through the Internet."[544]

This clearly demonstrates that right to privacy is limited by statutory provisions. Had the Navy department obtained warrant before taking the information from AOL, the action of the department could have been valid under ECPA and plaintiff

---

[540] ibid
[541] ibid
[542] ibid
[543] See 18 U.S.C. § 2703 (b)(A)-(B), (c)(1)(B).
[544] Supra Note 535

might have been left with the only option of questioning reasonableness of the order.

What is pertinent to note here that the court could not have protected the privacy of a private individual under ECPA enjoyed by Mcveigh, Navy officer because of the congressional mandate "Don't Ask, Don't Tell, Don't Pursue"[545]. The problem with the ECPA is that it permits ISPs to disclose subscriber information to entities other than the government and in cyberspace most of the entities are non-governmental.

This is clearly demonstrated by a Michigan court in Jessup-Morgan v. AOL, Inc[546]. In this the court held that ECPA does not regulate disclosure to private individual of identity of a subscriber of an electronic communication service. In this case AOL disclosed the private information of plaintiff subscriber who was facing the charge of offensive posting after being served with subpoena.

This disclosure fits in with a pattern of behavior on AOL's part; it has sold different kinds of subscriber information to third parties, such as direct marketers, and even proposed sale of home phone numbers before a storm of protest forced it to change this plan[547].

4.5.5 Web Bugs

A web bug is a graphic in a web site or an "enhanced" e-mail message that enables a third party to monitor who is reading the page or message. The graphic may be a standard size image that is easily seen, or it may be a nearly invisible one pixel graphic. E-mail messages that include graphic displays like web sites are known as enhanced messages, also called stylized or HTML e-mail. The web bug can confirm when the message or web page is viewed and record the IP address of the viewer.

---

[545] In McVeigh, Judge sporkin observed "at this point in history, our society should not be deprived of the many accomplishments provided by people who happen to be gay.The Don't Tell, don't Ask . Don't Pursue was a bow to society's growing recognition of this fact.
[546] 20 F. Supp. 2d 1105 (E.D. Mich. 1998) available at
http://www.tomwbell.com/NetLaw/Ch05/Jessup-Morgan.html, visited on 26 Dec 2005
[547] Seth Schiesel, American Online Backs Off Plan to Give Out Phone Numbers, N.Y. TIMES ON THE WEB 1-3 (July 25, 1997) http://www.nytimes.com/library/cyber/week/-072597aol.htm

The IP address is a multi-digit number that uniquely identifies a computer or other hardware device (such as a printer) attached to the Internet[548].

According to a recent survey by the Federal Trade Commission ("FTC"), up to eighty-five percent of Web sites collect personal information from consumers[549]. A widespread capture, sharing, and commercialization of personal data take place on this part of the Internet. Web sites collect personal data through cookies, registration forms, and sweepstakes that require surrendering e-mail addresses and other information[550]. Other invasions of privacy relating to Web sites involve archives of comments made on the "Usenet" or to "list servs"; the deceptive promises that Web sites sometimes make about privacy practices; and, finally, an increase by Web sites of the availability of information about behavior both in cyberspace and in Real Space[551]. These additional problem areas will now be examined in turn. Participation on the "Usenet" or in a "list serv" has significant informational consequences. The Usenet allows participants to post communications into a database that others can access; list servs are listings of names and e-mail addresses that are grouped under a single name[552]. Although sending messages to these areas feels like an ephemeral activity, an individual may be creating a permanent record of her opinions. Transcripts of contributions to both the Usenet and list servs are sometimes collected and archived, often without disclosure to participants and without restrictions on further use[553]. One such catalogue of these comments, "www.deja.com," provides four different archives, including one for "adult" messages.

---

[548] Privacy Rights In cyberspace, available at ,http://www.privacyrights.org/fs/fs18-cyb.html , visited 12 Jan 2005

[549] See FTC, PRIVACY ONLINE: A REPORT TO CONGRESS 7-14 (June 1998) ,available at http://www.ftc.gov/os/1999/07/SFAtestimony.htm , visited on 23 Sep 2005

[550] ibid at p 88-89

[551] ibid at p 141-146

[552] Microsoft Press Computer Dictionary, 3 ed, 1997, at p 286

[553] See, e.g., Deja.com , available at , http://www.deja.com , visited don 3 Sep 2005

The FTC's enforcement action in 1998 against the GeoCities company provides a further illustration of weak privacy practices at Web sites[554]. GeoCities markets itself as a "virtual community"; it organizes its members' home pages into forty different areas, termed "neighborhoods." In these areas, members can post a personal Web page, receive e-mail, and participate in chat rooms[555].Non-members can also visit many areas of GeoCities. According to the FTC, GeoCities engaged in two kinds of deceptive practices in connection with its collection and use of personal information[556]. First, although GeoCities promised a limited use of the data it collected, it in fact sold, rented, and otherwise disclosed this information to third parties who used it for purposes well beyond those for which individuals had given permission[557]. Second, GeoCities promised that it would be responsible for maintenance of the data collected from children in the "Enchanted Forest" part of its Web site[558]. Instead, it turned such personal information over to third parties, whom it had dubbed "community leaders."[559] Finally FTC settled the issues with Geocities[560]. Through the enactment of the Children's Online Privacy Protection Act in 1998, however, Congress has created strong pressure to end at least some deceptive practices regarding the collection and use of children's personal data on the Internet. Yet, adults on the Web are unprotected by this law.

---

[554] *See* GeoCities, File No. 9823015 (Fed. Trade Comm. 1998) (agreement containing consent order). The Geo-Cities Consent Order can also be found at http://www.ftc.gov/os/1998/-9808/geo-ord.htm , visited on 3 Sep 2005

[555] ibid
[556] For a discussion, *see* FTC, Analysis of Proposed Consent Order to Aid Public Comment , available at http:www.ftc.gov/os/1998/9808/9823015.-ana.htm, visited on 3 Sep 2005. The GeoCities Web site was available at http://www.geocities.com, but now part of Yahoo., visited on 23 Sep 2005

[557] ibid
[558] ibid
[559] ibid
[560] Despite the adverse publicity, GeoCities continued to grow, and just five months after the settlement and at the peak of the internet boom, Yahoo agreed to buy the company in a stock deal reported to be worth $3.6 billion. The deal was completed in May 1999 and today GeoCities is a fully integrated part of Yahoo's diverse offerings of web services.

4.5.6 Spyware and Adware

Any software that covertly gathers user information through the user's Internet connection without his or her knowledge, usually for advertising purposes is known as spyware. Spyware applications are typically bundled as a hidden component of freeware or shareware programs that can be downloaded from the Internet; however, it should be noted that the majority of shareware[561] and freeware[562] applications do not come with Spyware[563]. Once installed, the Spyware monitors user activity on the Internet and transmits that information in the background to someone else. Spyware can also gather information about e-mail addresses and even passwords and credit card numbers[564].

Spyware programs usually collect information from a user's computer – personal information, such as a name or an email address and send it back to their host server[565].

Some Spyware programs collect information using "keystroke loggers[566]," which capture information about the user's computer activities, including cookies and time spent on certain sites. Some capture all keystrokes users make; others are more

---

[561] Software distributed freely, but with certain conditions applying to it. Either the software is released on a trial basis only, and must be registered after a certain period of time, or in other cases no support can be offered with the software without registering it. In some cases direct payment to the author is required, Legend Communications, available at www.legend.co.uk/resources/gloss.html , visited 20 Jan 2006

[562] Software which is distributed free by the author. Although it is available for free, the author retains the copyright, which means that it cannot be altered or sold. Introduction to Internet Research, available at valencia.cc.fl.us/lrcwest/lis2004/glossary.htm, visited 20 Jan 2006

[563] Tribal Justice Information system, available at www.tjiss.net/glossary_s.html , visited on 20 Jun 2006

[564] See http://www.webopedia.com/TERM/s/spyware.html , visited 20 Sep 2005

[565] A recent study found that the average computer houses 28 items of monitoring software, unbeknown to the user.(Source: Internet Service Provider Earthlink and Webroot Software)

[566] Keystroke logging (often called keylogging) is a diagnostic used in software development that captures the user's keystrokes. It can be useful to determine sources of error in computer systems and is sometimes used to measure employee productivity on certain clerical tasks. Such systems are also highly useful for law enforcement and espionage—for instance, providing a means to obtain passwords or encryption keys and thus bypassing other security measures. However, keyloggers are widely available on the internet and can be used by anyone for the same purposes, available at http://en.wikipedia.org/wiki/Keylogger, visited on 2 Sep 2005

focused, recording Web sites visited, passwords, emails, credit card numbers, and so on. Most keyloggers are invisible and save recorded keystrokes into a log file that is transmitted periodically back to the host server. Some can even record both sides of instant messaging chat conversations (for example, MSN® Messenger and Yahoo!® Messenger)[567].

Although similar, adware is distinguished from spyware by the fact that, when downloading adware, the user is first given an opportunity to agree to its being placed on his or her computer. The explanation of an adware program and what it will do is often buried in a long, complex End-User License Agreement (EULA) that many users simply scroll through and accept without reading completely. In practice, adware acts as spyware. Both may trigger the display of pop-up or banner advertisements, and both may gather and transmit information from the user's computer[568].

Spyware is fast-becoming the biggest PC annoyance these days, degrading system performance, tracking our computing habits, popping up annoying advertisements, and even stealing our important personal information. Detecting and removing spyware can be difficult, since it occurs in so many different forms[569].

4.5.7 Marketing uses and SPAM

Records of browsing patterns are a potentially valuable source of revenue for online services and commercial web site operators. Direct marketers can use such data to develop targeted lists of online users with similar likes and behaviors. Such data can also lead to unsolicited e-mail, known as "spam". Additionally, browsing data may prove embarrassing for users who have accessed sensitive or controversial materials online.

---

[567] ibid
[568] eLearners.com, available at http://www.elearners.com/resources/advertising-glossary.asp, visited on 20 Jan 2006
[569] Crystal Blackshear, Tiffany Carlisle, Kara Cook, And Sean Faulkner The Dangers Of Adware And Spywarelaw And The Internet, Fall 2004, available at http://gsulaw.gsu.edu/lawand/papers/fa04/blackshear_carlisle_cook_faulkner/ , visited at 20 Jan 2006

In US spam is regulated through the CAN-SPAM Act of 2003 (Controlling the Assault of Non-Solicited Pornography and Marketing Act). This enactment establishes requirements for those who send commercial email, spells out penalties for spammers and companies whose products are advertised in spam if they violate the law, and gives consumers the right to ask e-mailers to stop spamming them.

The law, which became effective January 1, 2004, covers email whose primary purpose is advertising or promoting a commercial product or service, including content on a Web site. A "transactional or relationship message" email that facilitates an agreed-upon transaction or updates a customer in an existing business relationship may not contain false or misleading routing information, but otherwise is exempt from most provisions of the CAN-SPAM Act.

The Federal Trade Commission (FTC), US consumer protection agency, is authorized to enforce the CAN-SPAM Act. CAN-SPAM also gives the Department of Justice (DOJ) the authority to enforce its criminal sanctions. Other federal and state agencies can enforce the law against organizations under their jurisdiction, and companies that provide Internet access may sue violators, as well[570].

4.6 Privacy policies and web seals

Many Governments urge commercial web site operators to spell out their information collection practices in privacy policies posted on their web sites. Most commercial web sites now post policies about their information collection practices. But most of these policies provide for "opt-out" option , which is cumbersome and inconvenient for net users.

Website privacy policies are a recent phenomenon, having come into existence in the late 1990s. The universal feature of website privacy policies is that they are accessible as a link from the home page of many websites. Many sites also have links to the privacy policy from areas within the site, such as from internal pages

---

[570] Facts for Business, available at http://www.ftc.gov/bcp/conline/pubs/buspubs/canspam.shtm , visited on 3 Sep 2005

that request customer data. Privacy policies range from a half-page to ten pages in length. In terms of their apparent intent and rhetorical structure, privacy policies are hybrid documents that reflect both public relations and legal concerns. On the one hand, privacy policies often have a chatty and disarming tone that clearly seems motivated by an attempt to create an air of closeness and intimacy between the site and its users. On the other hand, privacy policies are becoming more legalistic in tone[571]. Privacy policies typically begin with some warm and fuzzy language about the online entity's respect for its users' privacy. Typical in this regard are statements such as, "At 1-800-flowers.com, we recognize and respect the importance of maintaining the privacy of our customers and members."[572] Some of the more scrupulous sites explicitly acknowledge the privacy rights of users in their opening remarks. Wal-Mart's privacy policy states, "We believe that you have a right to know, before shopping at Walmart.com or at any other time, exactly what information we might collect from you, why we collect it and how we use it."[573] Nike's privacy policy begins, "Nike is committed to respecting the privacy rights of all visitors to our web site."[574]

In the opening statements of their privacy policies, some sites are explicit in stating that their goal is to create a relationship of confidence and trust with consumers. The Walt Disney privacy policy begins, "The Walt Disney Internet Group is committed to helping you make the most of your free time on the Internet within a trusted environment . . . . We hope that this disclosure will help increase your confidence in our sites and enhance your experience on the Internet."[575] The introduction to the

---

[571] Hetcher, Steven ,Changing The Social Meaning Of Privacy In Cyberspace, Harvard Journal of Law & Technology Volume 15, Number 1 Fall 2001
[572] 1-800-flowers.com Privacy statement, *at* http://www.1800flowers.com/flowers/security/index.asp, visited on 11 Oct. 2004
[573] Walmart.com Security & Privacy, *at* http://www.walmart.com/cservice/ca_securityprivacy.gsp , visited on 11 Oct. 2004. Wal-Mart has an exemplary privacy policy. Sites of old economy firms like Wal-Mart are of particular interest, as they demonstrate the penetration of the growing ethos of Internet privacy beyond the now outdated notion of the dot.com economy. The Internet was never a marketplace but rather a technology platform.
[574] Niketown.com Privacy Policy, available *at* http://niketown.nike.com/info/privacy.jhtml, visited on 11 Oct 2004
[575] Disney.com Privacy Policy, *at* http://disney.go.com/legal/privacy_policy.html , visited on 11 Oct 2003

Wal-Mart privacy policy states that, "The security of your personal information is very important to us. . . . We value your trust very highly, and will work to protect the security and privacy of any personal information you provide to us and will only use it as we have described in our Privacy Policy."[576] Sears.com states, "We value the trust you place in Sears, Roebuck and Co . . . . We want to ensure that you understand what information we gather about you, how we use it, and the safeguards we have in place in order to protect it."[577]

Some sites make it apparent that they judge the moral relationship between website and consumer to be a two-way street. The first paragraph of the MadonnaFanClub.com privacy policy states that the site "always respects the privacy of Fan Club members and visitors to our website."[578] The last paragraph of the short document states that, "All information contained on this site is copyrighted. Your cooperation in respecting these copyrights is appreciated."[579] Here, a core normative principle is at play. Because the site holds itself out as respectful, it is appropriate by the lights of the ordinary moral principle of reciprocity to ask for respect in return. Privacy policies that are more legalistic in tone would be unlikely to make the same request for reciprocal treatment.

On the whole, however, privacy policies are increasingly employing more overtly legalistic formulations[580]. For example, Weather.com states, "This statement and the policies outlined here are not intended to and do not give you any contractual or other legal rights."[581] Toyota's privacy policy in part reads, "Toyota does not assume

---

[576] Walmart.com Security and Privacy, available *at*
http://www.walmart.com/cservice/ca_securityprivacy.gsp , visited on 11 Oct 2004
[577] Sears, Roebuck and Co. World Wide Web Site Customer Information and Privacy Policy, available at http://www.sears.com , visited on 2 Oct 2004.
[578] Madonna Fan Club Privacy Statement, available at
http://www.madonnafanclub.com/privacy.html , visited on 11 Oct 2004.
[579] See Eric, Roston, How to Opt Out of Database Sharing; Who's Got Your Number?, TIME, July 2, 2001, at 46.
[580] See Eric ,Roston, How to Opt Out of Database Sharing; Who's Got Your Number? TIME, July 2, 2001, at 46.
[581] Weather.com Privacy Statement, available *at*
http://www.weather.com/common/home/privacy.html , visited on 3 Jul 2004

any responsibility for the accuracy, completeness or authenticity of any information contained on this site. This site and all information and materials contained herein, is provided to you "as is" without warranty of any kind."[582]Toyota further states, "Toyota shall not be responsible for any harm that you or any person may suffer as a result of a breach of confidentiality in respect to your use of this site or any information you transmitted to this site."[583] Toyota's harsh legalistic tone illustrates the tension between a privacy policy crafted as a document meant to create trust in users and a legal document meant to protect the company against potential liability. The use of more legalistic language is perhaps not surprising, given that privacy policies are starting to play a role in lawsuits[584]. If privacy related lawsuits become more prevalent, privacy policies may become even more legalistic.

In the past few years, most websites have begun to address privacy concerns to one extent or another[585]. There are a number of common practices that websites are beginning to adopt. To some extent, these practices track the fair information practice principles that are being promoted by the privacy entrepreneurs. The FTC has noted that it is not possible to specify in detail how the privacy principles should be implemented, as the meaning of the principles will vary depending on the particular activities of the site in question[586]. Several surveys conducted to understand the privacy policies indicate how complex and varied the personal data practices of websites are becoming[587].

---

[582] Toyota Privacy Policy, available at http://www.toyota.com/html/privacy/index.html ,visited on 11 Oct 2003

[583] ibid

[584] See Judnick v. DoubleClick, No. CU-421 (Main Cty. Sup. Ct., filed Jan. 27,2000)

[585] See Federal Trade Commission, Privacy Online: Fair Information Practices in the Electronic Marketplace, A Federal Trade Commission Report to Congress 10 (May 2000), available at http://www.ftc.gov/reports/privacy2000/privacy2000.pdf (discussing the Commission's survey findings, which demonstrate continued improvement with eighty-eight percent of websites in the random sample posting at least one privacy disclosure), visited on 2 Nov 2005

[586] See Federal Trade Commission, Privacy Online: A Report to Congress (June 1998), available at http://www.ftc.gov/reports/privacy3/toc.htm , visited 2 Nov 2005

[587] See Federal Trade Commission, Fair Information Practices in the Electronic Marketplace, available at http://www.ftc.gov/reports/privacy2000/privacy2000.pdf , visited on 7 Nov 2005

Privacy seals signify that a company respectfully uses the personal information we provide. Privacy seals are the most difficult to obtain, as they require the company to undergo an extensive certification process that exposes internal data collection and usage processes. A privacy seal is the only type of seal that probes what happens behind the scenes. Seal programs also offer ongoing monitoring, and one can file a complaint with the issuing authority if you feel there has been misconduct[588]. Examples include TRUSTe, BBB Online Privacy, and ESRB Privacy.

4.6.1 The Platform for Privacy Preference (P3P)

Predictably, many people complain that websites' privacy policies are difficult to understand, sometimes because they are vague and other times because they are full of legalese. Partially as result of this complaint, the World Wide Consortium (W3C) has developed something called the Platform for privacy Preference, commonly known as P3P, a technological approach to interpreting and applying privacy policies. As sated by the W3C :

"At most basic level, P3P is standardized set of multiple questions, covering all the major aspects of a Web site's privacy policies. Taken together, they present a clear snapshot of how a site handles personal information about its users. P3P enabled websites make this information available in a standard, machine readable format. P3P enabled browsers can read this snapshot automatically and compare it to the consumer's own set of privacy preferences. P3P enhances user control by putting privacy polices where users can find them, in a form users can understand, and most importantly , enables users to act on what they see."[589] Any website may choose to implement P3P, but no law requires any website to do so.

---

[588] How Do You Make Sense of Web-Based Seals? , available at
http://www.truste.org/articles/seals_comparison.php , visited on 20 Jan 2005

[589] Platform for Privacy Preferences (P3P), available at www.w3c.org/p3p , visited on 20 Sep 2005

In theory, P3P should help consumers protect their privacy online. In practice, however, the impact of P3P is unclear. Although, by early 2002, six of the top ten websites had adopted P3P, and the other four websites were considering it[590], the technology has not yet been widely implemented and it is not certain that consumers really understand it. In one article criticizing Microsoft's adoption of P3P in version 6 of the internet browser, two lawyers said that the technology is expensive to implement and maintain; lacks enforcement and security; confuses consumers; and could create unclear legal consequences, such as if the P3P technology cannot accurately convey a subtle distinction in a website's privacy policy[591].

Ultimately, until the acceptability of P3P becomes better known, consumers and businesses should not ignore it. In particular, consumers should understand the limits of P3P, how their web browsers interpret it, and how to respond to the messages P3P can provide. And businesses should pay particular attention to whether consumers are demanding that the site they visit implement P3P. If this privacy technology takes off, drafting a P3P complaint privacy policy could become very important for a website's success[592].

4.7 Workplace monitoring

Employee empowerment with information technology is not without problems. Individuals who access the Internet from work should know that employers are increasingly monitoring the Internet sites that an employee visits. Legal requirement in such cases is that employer must communicate privacy policies of the organization clearly to employees. However, "expectation of privacy by employees" in certain situations limits the employer's right to surveillance.

Irrespective of the nature of the company, all companies are feeling the impact of the technological revolution. The most obvious example is the increased use of e-

---

[590] Gigalaw, available at http://www.gigalaw.com/articles/2002-all/carnor-2002-04-all.html , visited on 20 Sep 2005
[591] Gigalaw, available at http://www.gigalaw.com/articles/2002-all/harvey-2002-04-all.html, visited 20 Sep 2005
[592] Isenberg, Doug, "The Giga Law- Guide to Internet Law- The One-Stop Legal Resource for Conducting Business Online", Random House Trade Paperback Edition, New York, 2000

mail and the internet at more traditional, 'old economy' companies. This increased use of technology has resulted in a new wave of sexual harassment and racial hatred claims. Particularly, e-mail messages are now providing the evidentiary basis for aggrieved employees who claim discrimination, harassment or retaliation[593].

In Smyth v. The Pillsbury Company[594], the court found that an employee who transmitted inappropriate and unprofessional messages over the company's e-mail system could not have had a reasonable expectation of privacy. Once an employee disseminated the communication over the network provided by the employer, the message was no longer private. The court flatly declared that no "reasonable expectation" of privacy could exist in e-mail communications voluntarily made by an employee[595].

In the case of Strauss v. Microsoft Corp[596]., it was found that off-color comments made through email were admissible in a sex discrimination case. In this case, Karen Strauss, a former assistant editor of the Microsoft Systems Journal sued that Microsoft discriminatorily denied her promotion to technical editor and terminated her in retaliation for her complaints regarding that promotion. In support of her allegations, Strauss offered evidence of sexiest remarks and e-mail messages allegedly referred to another female employee as the "Spandex Queen" and included his offer to a temporary receptionist that he would pay her $500 if he could call her "Sweet Georgia Brown". The supervisor also allegedly proclaimed himself 'president of the Amateur Gynecology Club'[597].

Some of the most damaging evidence offered by Strauss came in the form of mass e-mail messages distributed throughout the workplace by coworkers. One such message contained a satirical essay titled "Alice in UNIX Land." Still another

---

[593] Isenberg, Doug, "The GigaLaw- Guide to Internet Law", Random House Paperbacks, New York, 2002 at 299
[594] 914 F. Supp. 97, E.D. (Penn. 1996), available at http://www.fidnalaw.com , visited 22 Sep 2005
[595] ibid
[596] 1995 US Dist. Lexis 7433 (1995), Strauss v. Microsoft Corp., 856 F. Supp. 821, 825 (S.D.N.Y. 1994), available at http://www.findlaw.com , visited on 24 Nov 2005
[597] ibid

e-mail, forwarded by her supervisor included a parody of a play titled "A Girl's Guide to Condoms." In total, Strauss proffered four e-mail messages gathered from Microsoft's own network. Although the e-mail messages and remarks were unrelated to the promotion and termination decisions at issue, the court found that the evidence was relevant and admissible. As a result, Strauss arguably possessed the added ammunition to support her allegations of gender discrimination[598].

Microsoft case illustrates the potential damages presented by the informal use of e-mail in the workplace. Although inappropriate e-mail messages typically form the basis of harassment suits, they also serve as powerful evidence in support of discrimination and retaliation suits[599].

Recently an administrative law judge in New York has found that surfing the Web at work is equivalent to reading a newspaper or talking on the phone. The judge recommended the lightest possible punishment for a city worker accused of disregarding warnings to stay off the Internet[600]. This again clearly shows the fluid state of law in relation to protection of privacy in cyberspace.

4.8 Law Enforcement Access

In order for law enforcement officials to gain access to subscriber transactional records, authorities usually must obtain a court order demonstrating that the records are relevant to an ongoing criminal investigation.

Some of the legislation used by US authorities for the enforcement which impact on privacy over the cyberspace area as follows;

---

[598] ibid
[599] Isenberg, Doug, "The GigaLaw- Guide to Internet Law", Random House Paperbacks, New York, 2002 at p 302

[600]Silicon Valley, http://www.siliconvalley.com/mld/siliconvalley/news/editorial/14417425.htm, visited on 24 Apr 2006

(a) <u>Fair Credit Reporting Act, 1970</u>[601] (FCRA)- This Act places limits on the use of consumer reports, that is, "information by consumer reporting agency bearing on a consumer's credit worthiness, credit standing, credit capacity, character, general reputation, personal characteristics or mode of living" where the information is for, among other things, credit , insurance, or employment purposes. Businesses creating, distributing or using consumer reports must comply with FCRA.

(b) <u>Electronic Communications Privacy Act, 1986</u>[602] (ECPA)- The ECPA has been used , with varying success, in a number of internet related cases. The law became effective many years before the rise of the internet as a popular communications medium, but it is probably the one preexisting law that has the greatest applicability to online privacy today. In general, the ECPA governs the interception of "wire, oral or electronic communications." Although ECPA does not refer to the internet, a number of lawyers believe the Act's reference to 'electronic communications' applies to certain online activities. The ECPA defines 'electronic communications' as "any transfer of signs, signals, writing, sounds, data or intelligence of any nature transmitted in whole or in part by a wire, radio, electromagnetic, photo electronic or photo optical system that affects interstate or foreign commerce".

---

[601] The Fair Credit Reporting Act (FCRA) is an American federal law (codified at 15 U.S.C. § 1681 et seq.) that regulates the collection, dissemination, and use of consumer credit information. It, along with the Fair Debt Collection Practices Act (FDCPA), forms the base of consumer credit rights in the United States.

[602] The Electronic Communications Privacy Act of 1986 (ECPA Pub. L. 99-508, Oct. 21, 1986, 100 Stat. 1848, 18 U.S.C. § 2510) was enacted by the U.S. Congress to extend government restrictions on wire taps from telephone calls to include transmissions of electronic data by computer

(c) <u>Health Insurance Portability and Accountability Act, 1996</u><u>603</u> (HIPPA) – Along with financial information, health care information is probably the most strongly protected and personal data that exists. Therefore, it's no surprise that the US Congress has passed laws that specifically protect certain health related information, HIPPA in 1996. As per the provisions of the Act, health providers are required to give clear written explanations of their privacy practices; the Act limits the disclosure of health information for non-health related purposes; compels the appointment of privacy officer; and sets civil and criminal penalties for violating privacy[604].

(d) <u>Gramm-Leach-Bliley, 1999</u><u>605</u> (GLB)- This law limits the instances in which financial institutions may disclose nonpublic personal information about a consumer to nonaffiliated third parties and requires then to disclose privacy polices to all of its customers.

4.9 Privacy Regulation

In 1970 the German state of Hesse enacted the first data protection statute; Sweden followed in 1973 with the first national statute. Today, Austria, Belgium, the Czeh Republic, Denmark, Finland, France, Germany, Hungary, Iceland, Ireland, Italy,

---

[603] The Health Insurance Portability and Accountability Act (HIPAA) was enacted by the U.S. Congress in 1996.According to the Centers for Medicare and Medicaid Services' (CMS) website, Title I of HIPAA protects health insurance coverage for workers and their families when they change or lose their jobs. Title II of HIPAA, the Administrative Simplification (AS) provisions, requires the establishment of national standards for electronic health care transactions and national identifiers for providers, health insurance plans, and employers. The AS provisions also address the security and privacy of health data. The standards are meant to improve the efficiency and effectiveness of the nation's health care system by encouraging the widespread use of electronic data interchange in the US health care system.

[604] Health and Human Services, available at
http://www.hhs.gov/news/press/2001pres/01fsprivacy.html, visited on 23 Sep 2005
[605] The Gramm-Leach-Bliley Act, also known as the *Gramm-Leach-Bliley Financial Services Modernization Act*, Pub. L. No. 106-102, 113 Stat. 1338 (November 12, 1999), is an Act of the United States Congress which repealed the Glass-Steagall Act, opening up competition among banks, securities companies and insurance companies. The Glass-Steagall Act prohibited a bank from offering investment, commercial banking, and insurance services. The Gramm-Leach-Bliley Act (*GLBA*) allowed commercial and investment banks to consolidate.

Luxembourg, the Netherlands, Norway, Portugal, Spain, Switzerland and the United Kingdom have broad privacy or data protection statutes.

These omnibus laws are often supplemented by other laws and regulations that apply to specific types of processing activities for specific subject matter. United States has broad category of legislations for the purpose of individual data protection.

European data protection laws are notable generally for four features: typically they apply to both public and private sectors; they apply to a wide range of activities, including data collection, storage, use, and dissemination; they impose affirmative obligations (often including registration with national authorities) on anyone wishing to engage any of these activities; and they have few, if any, sectoral limitations they apply without regard to the subject of data.

4.10 Children's Online Privacy

Although privacy on the internet is a 'hot-button' topic in general, children's privacy is certainly the hottest. As children are less able to appreciate the ramifications of disclosing personal information, they may become victims of child predators and molesters when they go online. The US Federal Trade Commission (FTC) has reported, "An investigation by the FBI and the Justice Department revealed that Chat rooms and Bulletin boards are quickly becoming the most common resources used by predators for identifying and contacting children."[606]

Children's Online Privacy Protection Act (COPPA) was enacted by US Congress in 1998 to regulate and control the website operators collection or maintenance of personal information about children who are under thirteen. In general COPPA requires that operators of websites directed to children and operators who knowingly collect personal information from children do the following;

---

[606] Federal Trade Commission, available at http://www.ftc.gov/os/1999/9910/64fr59888.htm , visited on 26 Jan 2006

(a) provide parents notice of their information practices[607]

(b) obtain prior verifiable parental consent for the collection, use and/or disclosure of personal information from children with certain limited exceptions for the collection of online contact information such as e-mail addresses etc[608];

(c) provide a parent, upon request, with means to review the personal information collected from his child[609];

(d) provide a parent with the opportunity to prevent the further use of personal information that has already been collected , or the future collection of personal information about that child[610];

(e) limit collection of personal information for a child's online participation in a game, prize offer other activity to information that is reasonably necessary[611] ; and

(f) establish and maintain reasonable procedures to protect the confidentiality , security and integrity of the personal information collected[612].

But accomplishing these goals is not an easy task. Indeed, after the FTC issued the Children's Online Privacy Protection Rules, many websites that had collected information from children simply decided that the law was either too complicated or too costly and they simply stopped collecting personal information from children altogether[613]. SurfMonkey , a community site for children, reporetedly spent $50,000 to $100,000 to comply with the law's numerous legal requirements[614].

No doubt laws required for protecting privacy of individuals, but the tendency of human beings is to ignore laws which are difficult to comply even with honest

---

[607] Children's Online Privacy Protection Act of 1998 ,Title Xiii-Children's Online Privacy Protection, Sec. 1303. Regulation Of Unfair and Deceptive Acts And Practices In Connection With The Collection And Use Of Personal Information from and About Children on the Internet.

[608] ibid Sec.1303
[609] ibid Sec.1303
[610] ibid Sec.1303
[611] ibid Sec.1303
[612] ibid Sec.1303
[613] GigaLaw, available at http://www.gigalaw.com/2000/articles/isenberg-2000-07a.html , visited on 29 Dec 2005
[614] See Surf Monkey website, available at http://www.surfmonkey.com/, visited on 3 Sep 2005

attempt to obey them. COPPA is the only internet specific privacy law in US, but it is very controversial and it can be complicated. But ignoring COPPA can be painful and costly.

4.11 EC Directive on Data Protection and Safe Harbor Treaty

In July 1990 the commission of European Community published a draft Council Directive on the Protection of individuals with regard to the Processing of Personal Data and on the free movement of such data. The Directive requires EU member states to enact laws governing the processing of personal data. The Directive defines 'processing' broadly as "any operation or set of operations", whether or not automated, including but not limited to "collection, recording, organization, storage, adaptation or alteration, retrieval or otherwise making available, alignment or combination, blocking, erasure or destruction". "Personal data" are defined equally broadly as "any information relating to an identified or identifiable natural person". This would include not only textual information but also photographs, audiovisual images, and sound recordings of an identified or identifiable person[615].

In Europe, privacy is viewed as a "human rights" issue and in the United States, it is more often seen as a matter for contractual negotiation. US privacy advocates will, on occasion, engage in some amount of cost/benefit analysis when arguing for certain data restrictions. In contrast, European advocates argue that the preservation of privacy must be seen as sacrosanct and cannot be bent to serve commercial ends[616].

There have been obvious differences in US and European privacy approaches for decades, they took on a more serious when the European Union adopted its "Data Protection Directive". The Directive requires that the purpose of data collection and

---

[615] Fred H. Cate ,Privacy in the Information Age (1997), available at
http://brookings.nap.edu/books/0815713169/html/14.html , visited on 20 Nov 2005

[616] ibid at p 33

the manner in which the data are to be used must be disclosed clearly to data subjects, especially , any secondary uses for direct marketing purposes must be spelled out. In addition, data subjects must be allowed to inspect and correct data about them. The Directive demands that Member states "take necessary measures to ensure that data subjects are aware of the existence of their right to object to secondary data uses". Further, it requires that a firm discontinue using a consumer's data for secondary purposes once a "justified objection" is received[617].

Discussion between the European Union and the US in relation to transboundary movement of personal data was finalized in July 2000 and an agreement was drawn known as "Safe Harbor" agreement. Under this agreement US firms wishing to handle personal data regarding European citizens must register with the US Department of Commerce, must agree to adhere to principles that are largely consistent with the more demanding approach and must provide an annual certification to the US department of Commerce[618].

4.12 OECD Guidelines on the Protection of Personal Data Protection

The OECD (Organization for Economic Co-operation and Development) Guidelines on the Protection of Privacy and Transborder Flows of Personal data was adopted on 23 September 1980, and represent international consensus on general guidance concerning the collection and management of personal information. By setting out core principles, the guidelines play a major role in assisting governments, business and consumer representatives in their efforts to protect privacy and personal data, and in obviating unnecessary restrictions to transborder data flows, both on and off line.

The preamble of OECD Guidelines on the Protection of Privacy and Transborder Flows of Personal Data (OECD Guidelines) states that the development of

---

[617] ibid at p 35
[618] ibid at p 41

automatic data processing, which enables vast quantities of data to be transmitted within seconds across national frontiers, and indeed across continents, has made it necessary to consider privacy protection in relation to personal data. Privacy protection laws are required to prevent what are considered to be violations of fundamental human rights, such as the unlawful storage of personal data, the storage of inaccurate personal data, or the abuse or unauthorised disclosure of such data[619].

Part two of the OECD Guidelines outlines principles of data collection applicable to all member countries of OECD. These principles which are regarded as Fair Information Practices (FIPP) and enforced by FTC are as follows:

(a) <u>Collection Limitation Principle</u> - There should be limits to the collection of personal data and any such data should be obtained by lawful and fair means and, where appropriate, with the knowledge or consent of the data subject[620].

The provision of notice of a website's personal-data-related activities is the first of the fair practice principles. The principle of notice is a second order principle that supports each of the other principles[621]. It is only when a user has knowledge of the data related activities of a website that the user can make informed decisions about how to interact with the site regarding each of the other privacy principles[622]. At first glance, notice might seem like a straightforward requirement with which to comply. A site simply writes down a description of its data related practices and creates a link to this text. For some sites with simple and minimal data related practices, the provision of straightforward notice is possible. For example, the "Official Madonna Fan Club" site's privacy policy, when printed out, is only half a

---

[619] OECD Guidelines on the Protection of Privacy and Transborder Flows of Personal Data, available at http://www.oecd.org/document/18/0,2340,en_2649_34255_1815186_1_1_1_1,00.html

[620] ibid , principle no. 1

[621] Hetcher ,Steven, Changing the Social Meaning of Privacy in Cyberspace, Harvard Journal of Law & Technology Volume 15, Number 1 Fall 2001 at p 129

[622] ibid at p 31

page long and contains three short paragraphs[623]. The site is able to state in a straightforward manner, "We do not sell, rent or trade your personal information with others."[624] This site uses personal data in order to process commercial transactions, such as merchandise sales and membership dues. The site claims not to use cookies or other passive means of data gathering[625].Notice becomes difficult to provide, however, when a site has complex data related practices. The first layer of complexity is introduced by means of the manner in which data is collected. Users of course understand that data is being collected from them when this data is explicitly provided by them. More opaque is data collection by means of cookies and other means of so called passive tracking of user online activities. Many sites provide definitions of arcane terms such as "cookies" and "IPO addresses," and offer explanations of their importance for privacy purposes[626]. For many sites, how the personal data is gathered is the determining factor in whether the data becomes "personally identifiable information" or "personal information," as compared to "anonymous information." The information that people explicitly volunteer to the website such as name, address, social security number, age, etc. is personally identifiable in the sense that it can be traced back to particular individuals. By contrast, websites collect information through the use of cookies on such activities as the users' visitation to various sites. Sites typically state that this information is

---

[623] Madonna Fan Club Privacy Statement, available *at* http://www.madonnafanclub.com/privacy.html , visited 11 Oct 2003.

[624] ibid
[625] Weather.com Privacy Statement, available *at* http://www.weather.com/common/home/privacy.html visited on 3 July 2005.

[626] See, for example, Motorola Privacy Practices, *at* http://www.motorola.com/content/0,1037,3,00.html visited 11 Oct 2005."When you come into our site, our server attaches a small text file to your hard drive — a cookie. Your unique cookie tells us that it is you whenever you re-enter our site, so we can recall where you've previously been on our site, and what if anything, you have in your shopping cart."); Hallmark.com Privacy Policy, *available at* http://www.hallmark.com , visited 11Oct 2005) ("An IP [Internet Protocol] address is a number that is assigned to your computer when you are using your browser on the Internet. The servers that serve our web site automatically identify your computer by its IP address. We do log IP addresses, but the addresses are not linked to individual customer accounts nor are they used in any other way to personally identify our customers."

not personally identifiable[627].In other words, though the sites keep records of cookie generated information, they claim not to keep track of which personally identifiable person is attached to this information. Perhaps the most significant challenge to adequate notice arises regarding the relationships that sites have with third parties. Privacy advocates and consumers are especially concerned about the fact that personal data may be transferred to these third parties[628].Privacy policies refer to these entities as, "trustworthy third parties," "reputable third-parties,"[629] etc. The main challenge to giving effective notice is the complexity and diversity of the relationships that sites have with these third parties. The difficult issue is determining how much description is necessary in order to provide adequate notice. Some sites are moving in the direction of providing fuller descriptions of their relationships with third parties. This means, however, that their privacy policies are becoming increasingly long and complex and difficult to understand.

(b) Data Quality Principle-   Personal data should be relevant to the purposes for which they are to be used, and, to the extent necessary for those purposes, should be accurate, complete and kept up-to-date[630].

The intuitive idea is that users should have some say when it comes to the use of their personal information by websites. Some sites, however, treat choice in the narrowest sense so as to mean simple consent or assent. Toyota writes, "By using this site, you signify your assent to the Toyota Online Privacy Policy. If you do not

---

[627] The Kinkos.com privacy policy states, "Also, Kinkos uses a reputable third party to collect and accumulate other anonymous data that helps us understand and analyze the Internet experience of our visitors. . . . This information may be stored in a cookie on your computer's hard drive. However, none of this information is personally identifiable and we only share this information in the aggregate, reflecting overall web site or Internet usage trends." Kinko's Security and Privacy Policy, available *at* http://www.kinkos.com/ privacy.html, visited 11 Oct 2005.

[628] Hetcher Steven, Changing the Social Meaning of Privacy in Cyberspace, Harvard Journal of Law & Technology Volume 15, Number 1 Fall 2001 at p179

[629] Nokia.com Privacy Policy, available at http://www.nokia.com/privacy.html visited 12 Oct 2005.

[630] [630] OECD Guidelines on the Protection of Privacy and Transborder Flows of Personal Data, available at http://www.oecd.org/document/18/0,2340,en_2649_34255_1815186_1_1_1_1,00.html , principle no.2

agree to this policy, please do not use this site."[631] Under the heading of, "Your Consent" on its site, Nike simply states, "By using our web site, you consent to our privacy policy."[632]

Many sites, however, do offer users choices other than the option of leaving. The most common choice made available to users is whether they want to have their personal data stored with, and used, by, the site. Many sites give the user the option of removing their personal data from the site. For example, Kinkos.com states, "You can easily change any of the information you have been asked to provide by Kinko's. You can also permanently remove your information from the Kinko's database."[633]

As already mentioned, websites offer two types of consent, which are widely referred to as opt-in and opt-out. With opt-out, the user must take some positive step in order to stop what would otherwise be a default process whereby user data would be available for use by the website[634]. Typically, the user cannot simply opt-out without consequence. Sites often condition access to the site or to some portion of the site on the provision of data by consumers. Thus, opting out of the provision of data entails opting out of receiving some or all of the site's services[635]. Other sites, however, simply allow consumers to opt-out of at least some of the site's collection practices without adversely affecting the consumers' abilities to benefit from the site[636].Until recently, it has been very uncommon for websites to provide opt-in as a choice to users. A small but growing number of sites are now offering users the

---

[631] Toyota Privacy Policy, available *at* http://www.toyota.com/html/privacy/index.html, visited 12 Oct 2005

[632] Niketown.com Privacy Policy, available *at* http://niketown.nike.com/info/privacy.jhtml , visited 12 Oct. 11, 2005

[633] Kinko's Security and Privacy Policy, available at www.kinko.com , visited 2 Jan 2003

[634] Motorola Privacy Practices, *at* http://www.motorola.com/content/0,1037,3,00.html visited on 12 Oct 2003 ("You also have choices with respect to cookies. By modifying your browser preferences, you have the choice to accept all cookies, to be notified when a cookie is set, or to reject all cookies. If you choose to reject all cookies you will be unable to use those services or engage in activities that require registration in order to participate.")

[635] ibid

[636] *See* jcrew.com (permitting customers to refuse cookies and decline to receive promotional emails and catalogs without limiting the customer's shopping experience).

choice to opt-in to some or all of the site's data practices. With opt-in, personal data will not be collected or used unless the user provides his explicit permission. In particular, sites that deal with more sensitive data are beginning to offer opt-in for this data[637].

(c) <u>Purpose Specification Principle and Use Limitation Principle</u> - The purposes for which personal data are collected should be specified not later than at the time of data collection and the subsequent use limited to the fulfillment of those purposes or such others as are not incompatible with those purposes and as are specified on each occasion of change of purpose.

Use Limitation Principle provides that personal data should not be disclosed, made available or otherwise used for purposes other than those specified in accordance with the Purpose Specification Principle except for (i) with the consent of the data subject; or (ii) by the authority of law.

(d) <u>Access/Participation Principle</u>- This principle prescribes that websites provide users with access to their personal data stored with the website. It is often discussed in conjunction with the principle of allowing consumers to contest data stored at the site that they deem to be incorrect. It is getting increasingly common for sites to allow users to access their data. For example, microsoft.com states, "If you ever want to review or update your profile, simply visit the Profile Center and edit your personal information. We'll ask you to disclose your Microsoft Passport (e-mail address and password) so that only you can access your profile."[638] Despite opportunities for access, fewer sites offer the ability to contest data. One that does is

---

[637] Davidson, Paul, Capitol Hill Support Brews for Internet Privacy Laws, USA TODAY, July 12, 2001, at 3B (noting that there is consensus building for requiring opt-in for more sensitive data, such as financial and medical).

[638] *See* Microsoft.com Statement of Privacy, available at http://www.microsoft.com/info/privacy.htm visited 23 Feb 2004.

nokia.com, which states, "Nokia will on its own initiative, or at your request, replenish, rectify or erase any incomplete, inaccurate or outdated personal data."[639]

(e) Integrity/Security Principle - A solid minority of sites now address the issue of security in their privacy policies. Under the heading of "Security" in its privacy policy, Sun Microsystems unhelpfully states merely that, "We intend to take reasonable and appropriate steps to protect the Personal Information that you share with us from unauthorized access or disclosure."[640]Many sites employ Secure Socket Layer[641] ("SSL") technology to protect the security of credit card information as it is transmitted to the site[642].With SSL, the website's server scrambles the data as it travels from the user's computer to the website. It is much less common, however, for sites to make remarks in their privacy policies regarding the security of the user's data as it resides on the site's server. This latter form of security is more important than protecting the data while in transit, as most significant breaches of website security have involved hackers gaining access to

---

[639] Nokia.com Privacy Policy, available at http://www.nokia.com/privacy.html visited 23 Feb 2004.

[640] Sun Online Privacy Policy, at http://www.sun.com/privacy , visited on 3 Oct 2005

[641] SSL (Secure Socket Layer) is a protocol for encrypting and decrypting data sent across direct internet connections. When a client makes an SSL connection with a server, all data sent to and from that server is encoded with a complex mathematical algorithm that makes it extremely difficult to decode anything that is intercepted. The following is a step by step illustration of how SSL works. **Step 1**. The client makes the initial connection with the server and requests that an SSL connection be made. **Step 2**. If the server is properly configured, the server will send to the client its certificate and public key. **Step 3**. The client uses that public key to encrypt a session key and sends the session key to the server. If the server asks for the client's certificate in Step 2, the client must send it at this point. **Step 4**. If the server is set up to receive certificates, it compares the certificate it received with those listed in its trusted authorities database and either accepts or rejects the connection. If the connection is rejected, a fail message is sent to the client. If the connection is accepted, or if the server is not set up to receive certificates, it decodes the session key from the client with its own private key and sends a success message back to the client, thereby opening a secure data channel. WSFTP.server, User's Guide, available at http://www.ipswitch.com/support/ws_ftp-server/guide/v5/ch10_sslconfiga2.html , visited on 3 Nov 2005

[642] Motorola Privacy Practices, available at http:/ /www.motorola.com , visited on 6 Nov 2005 ("You also have choices with respect to cookies. By modifying your browser preferences, you have the choice to accept all cookies, to be notified when a cookie is set, or to reject all cookies. If you choose to reject all cookies you will be unable to use those services or engage in activities that require registration in order to participate."

199

databases in storage on a firm's website[643].Increasingly, websites are addressing the issue of the security of data stored by the site. Some sites are limiting the number of employees with access to personally identifiable data as well as employing security systems to protect the data from external intruders[644].

(f) Enforcement/Redress – Next principle is that of enforcement/redress. According to this principle, the user should be provided with some means of enforcing the above principles or of receiving redress in cases of injury due to a failure to provide protective practices that instantiate the Fair information practices. Websites have done very little to promote this norm[645].

(g) Stopping Data Transfers to Third Parties- It is important to note that the fair information practice principles do not prohibit data transfers by websites to third parties. The first two principles, notice/awareness and choice/consent, are essentially an informed consent requirement. They do not prescribe a particular substantive set of privacy protections but rather stipulate that whatever data related practices a website engages in, the site should receive the informed consent of its users as to these practices (with failure to opt-out counting as a form of consent). The latter three fair information practices provide more substantive requirements of access, security and enforcement. None of these principles, however, prohibits data transfers to third parties. Nevertheless, a small number of sites do promise that they will not sell or trade data to third parties. For example, Wal-Mart states that, "We never sell or rent your personal information to any third parties under any

---

[643] Jeffrey Kluger, Extortion on the Internet; A daring hacker tries to blackmail an e-tailer — and sparks new worries about credit-card cybertheft, TIME, Jan. 24, 2000, at 56

[644] For example, MTV's website, MTV.com, states, "We have taken steps to ensure that personally identifiable information collected is secure, including limiting the number of people who have physical access to its database servers, as well as electronic security systems and password protections which guard against unauthorized access." MTV.com Terms of Use & Privacy Policy, available at http://www.mtv.com/sitewide/mtvinfo/terms.jhtml#privacy , visited on 24 Feb 2005

[645] For example see barnesandnoble.com ("We're so certain that our online ordering systems are secure that we back it up with a guarantee. In the unlikely event that you are subject to fraudulent charges....we will cover the entire liability for you, up to $50, as long as the unauthorized use of your credit card resulted through no fault of your own from purchases made from Barnes & Noble.com while using our secure server.") visited on 3 Mar 2005

circumstances."[646]For sites with complex data activities — even sites with no intention to sell or trade data to third parties — it will be difficult to promise to make no data transfers whatsoever. The reason is that simple corporate efficiency may require outsourcing various data related activities necessary to a firm's own internal usage of the data. Some firms are making a serious effort to protect the integrity of user data despite these third party transfers. Wal-Mart, for example, promises to only transfer data for specific purposes and then under contract[647]. This achieves a similar function to a complete prohibition on data transfers. Hallmark.com treats information in the site's Address book as highly confidential and states that the information will not be disclosed to third parties[648].

4.13 Digital Rights Management (DRM) and Privacy

Digital Rights Management refers to the technologies and processes that are applied to digital content to describe and identify it and to apply and enforce usage rules in a secure manner. The primary purpose of DRM is to control the access, use, distribution and disclosure of digital content online and thereby protect the interests of copyright holders in the online environment. Digital Rights Management systems are also referred to as Electronic Rights Management Systems (ERMS), Rights Management Information Systems (RMIs) and Copyright Management Systems (CMS).

The impetus for DRM is to be found in increases in telecommunications bandwidth, especially to the home, and the concomitant increases in digital file transfer and copying over the internet. Abetting the affects of bandwidth are advances in compression algorithms which improve transmission times and facilitate the storage of high-fidelity content. Duplication of content has thus become easy, cheap, and

---

[646] Walmart.com Security & Privacy, available *at*
http://www.walmart.com/cservice/ca_securityprivacy.gsp, visited on 25 Mar 2005

[647] ibid
[648] Hallmark.com Privacy Policy, available at http://www.hallmark.com , visited on 22 Mar 2005

perfect. Acquisition of duplicated content has become nearly instantaneous, and free. No wonder copyright holders are looking for ways to protect their franchise. Content creation is typically expensive; its reproduction in the digital environment is not. At the same time, digital technology has presented an unprecedented opportunity to engage in communication and creative speech. Indeed the very characteristics leading copyright holders to the shoals of piracy suggest the possibility of a paradise of practically cost free delivery of content. This "paradise" is profoundly threatening to existing business models. More germane is the balancing act between internet threat and promise that DRM policy must perform. The delivery and consumption of digital content depends on satisfaction of both copyright holders and end users. Each has different concerns, ranging from piracy to privacy. Copyright policy can ignore neither[649].

In order to manage and protect the interest of the copyright holders, it is essential to have adequate identification and description pertaining to content available (i.e., metadata). Such "metadata" needs, however, to be persistently associated with the content itself so that various applications including anti-piracy services can have access to the metadata. In the analog world such association between content and its metadata can be achieved by printing an identifier onto the data carrier containing the content (e.g., by printing a bar code onto a CD cover or an ISBN onto one page in a book). This approach fails in the digital world, however, because there are no physical carriers to carry the identifiers. Hence a technology is needed that allows obtaining the metadata from looking at the content itself[650].

Some of the technologies used for Digital Rights Management are;

(1) **Fingerprinting**: Fingerprinting technologies can be used to identify content by the process depicted in the diagram below. Fingerprinting, or "content-based

---

[649] Owens, Richards and Akalu Rajen, Legal Policy and Digital Rights Management, available at http://www.cippic.ca/en/faqs-resources/digital-rights-management , visited on 4 Dec 2005
[650] WIPO, Standing Committee On Copyright And Related Rights, Tenth Session Geneva, November 3 To 5, 2003, available at www.wipo.org , visited on 4 Dec 2005

identification technologies" function by extracting the characteristics of a file and storing them in a database. When the technology is presented with an unknown file, the characteristics of that file are calculated and matched against those stored in the database, in an attempt to find a match. If a match is found, the system will return the appropriate metadata from the fingerprint database[651].

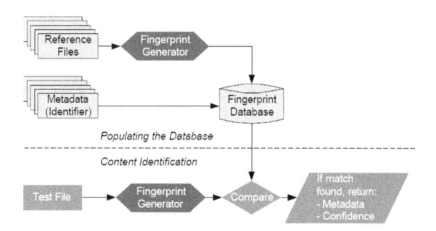

Source: WIPO, Standing Committee on Copyright and Related Rights, 10th Session, Geneva November, 3 to 5, 2003 document no. SCCR10/2

Fingerprints, while highly effective with certain content types, are less equipped to aid the unique identification of other content types, depending on the "detail" they provide.

Hence fingerprints are suitable for audio, video and audio-visual content as well as photographs but less for computer graphics or text.

---

[651] WIPO, Standing Committee On Copyright And Related Rights, Tenth Session
Geneva, November 3 To 5, 2003

(2) **Watermarking:** Watermarking is also often cited when discussing copyright protection technologies. A watermark is "(imperceptibly) embedded information." This information (often a file or IP identifier) can, though imperceptible is to normal consumers be extracted by special software. This "watermarking detector" can, when applied to content that is suspected to be pirated, check if the content bears the watermark and thereby prove or disprove the suspicion. Typically, all files that are to be distributed are watermarked before they are allowed into the content chain[652]. A functional flow diagram of this is shown in the diagram below.

Source: WIPO, Standing Committee on Copyright and Related Rights, 10th Session, Geneva November, 3 to 5, 2003 document no. SCCR10/2

Similar to fingerprinting, watermarks cannot be used with all content types. Small graphic elements such as logos or text are not able to carry watermarks because of a general limitation on the amount of data that can be embedded into the content. All watermark systems known today are susceptible to being removed without substantially affecting the quality of the content itself which may lead to the situation that, when a watermarking system has been broken, the originally governed content may become uncontrollable[653].

(3) **Digital Signature**: Digital Signatures akin to hand written signatures can be used to regulate the access to digital content. It is important to see that information

---

[652] ibid
[653] ibid

associated with content (e.g., IDs and rights expressions) can be trusted. Such functionality can be achieved when the party adding the metadata

(a) digitally signs the metadata and

(b) is known to be authorized to add the metadata.

A digital signature provides information about the origin of a piece of information and knowledge about whether the information has been altered or not and also non-repudiation of transactions[654].

In India under Information Technology Act, 2000 (IT Act) a digital signature can be used to authenticate an electronic record. It Act being technology specific requires asymmetric technology to used for generation of digital signatures.

4.13.1 Implications of DRM on Privacy

The future of online privacy is increasingly linked to the future of online copyright enforcement. In their push to control the proliferation of unauthorized copies, copyright owners and their technology partners are building into the technologies of Digital Rights Management (DRM) a range of capabilities that implicate the privacy interests of users.

The potential consequences of DRM for user privacy warrant far greater attention from policymakers and systems designers than they have yet received[655].

DRM initiatives may be viewed as a series of concentric levels of control, each penetrating more deeply into the user's home electronic and computing environment. At the first level, DRM systems impose direct restrictions on what individuals can do in the privacy of their own homes with copies of works they have paid for. At the next level of control, DRM systems report back to the copyright owner on the activities of individual users. Such reporting may occur as part of a pay-per-use arrangement for access to the work or independent of payment terms;

---

[654] ibid

[655] Choen E Julie, DRM and Privacy, Berkley Law and Technology Journal, Vo.18, 2003, at 45-49

for example, the system might be designed to report attempts to make unauthorized copies or determine which other software programs a user is running in conjunction with the DRM protected program[656].

The capabilities of DRM systems implicate two different types of privacy interests in the circumstances of intellectual consumption. Direct functionality restrictions intrude on the seclusion, or "private space," that long-established social practice reserves to the individual or family, while forcing changes in a set of behaviors within that space[657] . In so doing, they shift the baseline conditions of user autonomy to determine the circumstances of the use and enjoyment of intellectual goods. Information supplied by DRM technologies can be used to build a dossier about the user's informational preferences and patterns of use. This information in turn can be sold to data aggregators or obtained by the government and used for a variety of purposes.

US privacy laws protecting computers and electronic communications also are unhelpful in the context of DRM. The RealNetworks and Netscape products are now the subject of class actions alleging, respectively, violations of the Computer Fraud and Abuse Act (CFAA) and the Electronic Communications Privacy Act (ECPA). However, neither statute was designed to address this sort of overreaching. The CFAA prohibits only unauthorized access to computer systems, or access that exceeds the scope of authority. The ECPA's prohibitions against interception of electronic communications do not extend to interception that is consensual or that is undertaken by one of the parties to the communication. Thus, it is difficult to see how either statute would prohibit implementation of DRM functions that have been disclosed and purportedly agreed upon.

The questions that law and policymakers must confront, then, are whether the privacy invasions caused by DRM restrictions should be legally cognizable and, if

---

[656] Cohen J, Copyright and Jurisprudence of self-help, Bekely Law and Technology Journal, vol.13,1998, at 1089-1143
[657] Burk D and Cohen J, Fair Use infrastructure for rights management systems, Harvard Law and Technology Journal, vol.15, 2001, at p 41-83

so, whether they may legitimately be imposed under contract[658], regardless of their invasiveness. There are good reasons to conclude that the scope of privacy in intellectual consumption is a matter of considerable public policy importance and that the law should provide at least some inalienable privacy protection for users of intellectual goods.

If we look at the provisions of Digital Millennium Copyright Act (DMCA), DRM seems to affect the fair use practices. Circumvention of digital content amounts to offence under DMCA. DRM technologies give more protection to copyright holders. Because of this, copyright holders can now determine whether their work should be allowed for fair use practices. This obviously tilts the balance of copyright protection in favour of copyright holder. Hence traditional copyright balance of copyright law may be disturbed.

4.14 Do Consumers really care for Privacy?

Consumer surveys overwhelmingly express concern about Internet Privacy. In a June 2005, report by Jupiter Research , 70% of online consumers said they were worried about online privacy. In another survey 93% of e-commerce users said it was very important that sites discloses their privacy practices. But what do these surveys really prove? Consumers may tell survey takers they fear for their privacy, but their behavoiur belies it. People don't read privacy policies, for example. In a survey taken last year (2004) by the Privacy leadership Initiative, a group of corporate and trade association executives, only 3% of consumers read privacy policies carefully, and 64% only glanced at or never read privacy policies[659].

---

[658] Copyright owners and other information providers argue that this baseline distribution of rights and limitations may be altered by contract, or "license," the terms of which users are free to accept or reject. If this is right, then there is no reason the range of enforceable contractual restrictions could not include restrictions that diminish user privacy. But such a position is far too simplistic. See generally, Julie E.Choen, DRM and Privacy, Communications of the ACM, April 2003/Vo.46 N0.4

[659] Goldman , Eric, The Privacy Hoax, Forbes, 10/14/2002, vol.170 Issue 8, P42

Most of the online marketers know, people will 'sell' their personal data incredibly cheaply. As internet Pundit Esther Dyson has said[660] : "You do a survey, and consumers say they are very concerned about their privacy. Then you offer them a discount on a book, and they will tell you everything." Indeed, a recent Jupiter report said that 82% of the respondents would give personal information to new shopping sites to enter a $100 sweepstakes[661].

4.15 Conclusion

Technology has again brought us to a critical juncture. We must now look at what technology has made possible, rather than simply at the legal principles that underlie these advances. We tend to misapply legal metaphors due to a lack of conceptual understanding of privacy itself, as well as of modern day technology. A number of critical issues must be addressed in order to move technology and society forward in tandem. Understanding the foundational concept of privacy is paramount in such a paradigm shift[662].

Technology is merely another variable to add to the equation, and should not be viewed as an insurmountable stumbling block. Just as Warren and Brandeis advocated change in the paradigm surrounding privacy in their 1890 law journal article, today we should also reassess "our metaphors, customs, and rules" to account for that which can intrude on our basic right to be let alone and not intruded upon. And, in this day in digital age, our right to have our personal data kept private must be ensured. We must accomplish this from a paradigm that has already been developed, by revisiting the conceptual foundations of privacy in light of cyberspace[663].

---

[660] ibid
[661] Sweepstakes (called prize draws in Great Britain) promotion where prizes are given away for free. They are different from a lottery or contest by requiring no purchase to enter.
[662] Robert A. Reilly, *Conceptual Foundations of Privacy: Looking Backward Before Stepping Forward*, 6 RICH. J.L. & TECH. 6 (Fall 1999) , available at http://www.richmond.edu/jolt/v6i2/article1.html, visited on 23 Sep 2005
[663] ibid

To resolve privacy issues, we must first ask what kind of human interaction we want to develop on the information highway. In other words, whether the values of individual autonomy, cultural inclusiveness and knowledge sharing will determine the environment of electronic communications, or whether the building of the information highway will be driven by the market needs of large vested interests. Privacy rights must reflect the assumptions we as a society make about personal autonomy and the need to control our own lives. Only when this debate is open to all who will likely to be affected by the changing technology, will governments be able to formulate the appropriate rules for Cyberspace.

Even though consumers let out their personal data easily, it still remains the responsibility of the State concerned to protect the interests of its netizens. Beyond the shortcomings of statutory law, courts have failed to enforce promises made by companies that collect data in cyberspace.

European model of data protection seems to be the appropriate model for Indian conditions for the protection of privacy over cyberspace. Taking a clue from developed countries in protecting netizens privacy, Indian Parliament must take steps to enact a legislation to protect the privacy of netizens.

Chapter 5

INTELLECTUAL PROPERTY RIGHTS IN CYBERSPACE

"If nature has made any one thing less susceptible than all others of exclusive property, it is the action of the thinking power called an idea, which an individual may exclusively possess as long as he keeps it to himself; but the moment it is divulged, it forces itself into the possession of everyone, and the receiver cannot dispossess himself of it. Its peculiar character, too, is that no one possesses the less, because every other possesses the whole of it. He, who receives an idea from me, receives instruction himself without lessening mine; as he who lights his taper at mine, receives light without darkening me. That ideas should freely spread from one to another over the globe, for the moral and mutual instruction of man, and improvement of his condition, seems to have been peculiarly and benevolently designed by nature, when she made them, like fire, expansible over all space, without lessening their density at any point, and like the air in which we breathe, move, and have our physical being, incapable of confinement or exclusive appropriation. Inventions then cannot, in nature, be a subject of property."

Thomas Jefferson

(Third President of US, 1801-1809)

5.1 Introduction

Thomas Jefferson view of invention or creation cannot be a subject matter of property was rarely acknowledged in the civilized world and US Constitution itself made a provision to empower the inventors and creators by conferring exclusive rights on them[664].Intellectual Property (IP) can be loosely defined as creations of human mind[665]. The impetus for the development of intellectual property law, at its inception, was to ensure that sufficient incentives exist to lead to innovation and the creation of new and original works and products. The physical world has been relatively successful at erecting barriers to prevent acts that would limit this

---

[664] Art.1 Sec.8 of US Constitution states that "Congress has power ....To promote the Progress of Science and useful Arts, by securing for limited Times to Authors and Inventors the exclusive Right to their respective Writings and Discoveries;"
[665] See definition given by WTO, available at http://www.wto.org, visited 2 Feb 2004

innovation, in the form of copyright, trademark and patent regulations. This enabled Intellectual Property Rights (IPR) owners to use or disclose their creations without fear of loss of control over their use, thus helping their dissemination. It is generally assumed that IPR help encourage creative and inventive activity and make for orderly marketing of proprietary goods and services[666]. But with the advent of internet, copying has become so simple and easy that rampant violation of intellectual property is taking place affecting the rights of IPR owners.

When intellectual property laws were first drafted, computer technology did not exist. At that time, it was not foreseen that it would be necessary to protect information stored by digital means, nor was it foreseen that information would become such a sought after commodity[667]. The Internet, Software, Business methods for e-commerce applications & electronic databases are relatively new territories where innovators have created an environment in which information exists in plentiful quantities and available to many people.

Human rights and intellectual property, two bodies of law that were once strangers, are now becoming increasingly intimate bedfellows. For decades the two subjects developed in virtual isolation from each other. But in the last few years, an explosion of international standard setting activities that beginning to map previously uncharted intersections between intellectual property law on the one hand and human rights law on the other[668].

Human rights concerns have been asserted in a number of contexts as counterweights to the expansion of intellectual property rights. Human rights issues are relevant in a range of issues that intersect with intellectual property protection, including: freedom of expression; public health; education and literacy; privacy;

---

[666] Watal Jayashree, Intellectual Property Rights in the WTO and Developing Countries, Oxford University Press, New Delhi, 2001 at p 1
[667] The Hindu, Technical know-how essential to check cyber crime, available at http://www.thehindu.com/2005/02/06/stories/2005020603910300.htm, visited on 17 May 2005
[668] Professor Laurence Helfer, Human Rights and Intellectual Property: Conflict or Coexistence? s Research Paper No. 2003-27 and Program in Law and Public Affairs Princeton University, available at http://ssrn.com/abstract=459120, visited on 25 Sep 2005

agriculture; technology transfer; rights of indigenous peoples. At the same time, creators of intellectual property are asserting human rights bases for the protection and expansion of intellectual property rights[669].

International Covenant on Economic, Social and Cultural Rights (ICESCR) and UDHR[670] guarantees everyone the right to benefit from the protection of the moral and material interests resulting from any scientific, literary or artistic production of which he is the author[671]. With the advent of Information Communication Technologies (ICTs), the relationship between human rights and intellectual property assumes greater significance as the traditional balance between intellectual property holders and users is slightly imbalanced in favour of users.

What distinguishes digital media[672] from conventional media are six characteristics that will make it difficult for existing categories of intellectual property law to adjust to the protection of works in digital form. They are[673]:

1) the ease with which works in digital form can be replicated,

2) the ease with which they can be transmitted,

3) the ease with which they can be modified and manipulated,

4) the equivalence of works in digital form,

5) the compactness of works in digital form, and

6) the capacity they have for creating new methods of searching digital space and linking works together.

---

[669] ibid

[670] Art.27(2), Universal Declaration of Human Rights

[671] Art.15(1)(c), International Covenant on Economic, Social and Cultural Rights

[672] "digital media," means intellectual products made available in digital/electronic form, whether operational in computers or other machines capable of "reading" works in digital form.

[673] Samuelson ,Pamela, "Digital Media and Changing Face of Intellectual Property Law", available at http://www.law.berkeley.edu/faculty/profiles/facultyPubsPDF.php?facID=346&publD=152 , visited on 2 Oct, 2005

5.2 Philosophy of Intellectual Property

The theory of intellectual property has not, until recently, attracted much philosophical interest or been the subject of deep controversy. Utilitarian theorists generally endorsed the creation of intellectual property rights as an appropriate means to foster innovation, subject to the caveat that such rights are limited in duration so as to balance the social welfare loss of monopoly exploitation. Non-utilitarian theorists emphasized creators' moral rights to control their work. With the increasing importance of intellectual property in society and the development of particular new technologies, most notably digital technology and the decoding of genetic structure, the theory of intellectual property has attracted huge interest. Economists and policy analysts have greatly enriched our understanding of the complex relationship between intellectual property protection and innovation and diffusion of technological advances. Non-utilitarian theories of intellectual property have proliferated in recent years, as philosophers and legal scholars have applied traditional and novel philosophical perspectives to the realm of intellectual property[674].

5.2.1 Locke's Theorem: Labour + Nature = Property[675]

For Locke, property was a foundation for an elaborate vision that opposed an absolute and irresponsible monarchy. Locke's theory[676] of property is itself subject to slightly different interpretations. One interpretation is that society rewards labor with property purely on the instrumental grounds that we must provide rewards to

---

[674] See generally for theories of Intellectual property, Chisum S Donald et., al , Cases and Materials-Principles of Patent Law, Foundation Press, New York, 1998
[675] Expression suggested by Peter Drahos in his Book'a Philosophy Of Intellectual Property', Applied Legal Philosophy Series, Dartmouth, 1996,

[676] Although Locke was concerned with the notion of property and paid scant attention to intellectual property, his general theory has been of such overwhelming importance that it is an appropriate starting point for any of us for the analysis of modern theories of property and intellectual property.

get labor. In contrast, a normative interpretation of this labor theory says that labor should be rewarded[677].

Locke describes a state of nature in which goods are held in common through a grant from God[678]. God grants this bounty to humanity for its enjoyment but these goods cannot be enjoyed in their natural state. The individual must convert these goods into private property by exerting labor upon them. This labor adds value to the goods, if in no other way than by allowing them to be enjoyed by a human being[679].

Locke proposes that in this primitive state there are enough unclaimed goods so that everyone can appropriate the objects of his labors without infringing upon goods that have been appropriated by someone else. The nature also imposes a limitation on human capacities on how much each individual may appropriate through labor[680].

A society that believes ideas come to people as manna (something of value a person receives unexpectedly) from heaven must look somewhere other than Locke to justify the establishment of intellectual property. The labor theory of property does not work if one subscribes to a pure "eureka" theory of ideas. Therefore, the initial question might be framed in two different ways. First, one would want to determine if society believes that the production of ideas requires labor. Second, one might want to know whether or not, regardless of society's beliefs, the production of ideas actually does require labor. This second question is the metaphysical one; in its shadow, society's belief may appear superficial. It is not. We are concerned with a

---

[677] Hughes ,Justin, The Philosophy of Intellectual Property, 77 Geo. L.J. 287 (1988), available at http://www.law.harvard.edu/faculty/tfisher/music/Hughes1988.html , visited 3 Feb 2005

[678] Loke, John , Two Treatise of Government (edt by Macpherson), Hackett Publishing,US, 1980
[679] ibid

[680] Hughes ,Justin, The Philosophy of Intellectual Property, 77 Geo. L.J. 287 (1988), available at http://www.law.harvard.edu/faculty/tfisher/music/Hughes1988.html , visited 3 Feb 2005

justification of intellectual property, and social attitudes -"understandings" as Justice Stewart said may be the only place to start[681].

Some writers begin with the assumption that ideas always or usually are the product of labor. For example, Professor Douglas Baird assumes that although one cannot physically possess or occupy ideas, property in ideas is justified because people "have the right to enjoy the fruits of their labor, even when the labors are intellectual." He believes the great weakness in this justification is that others also need free access to our ideas. In Lockean terms, this is an "enough and as good" problem. Baird, however, never considers the prospect that idea making may not involve labor[682].

One commentator has observed that this concept of labor is more likely the product of experience than logical rigor:

> Comparing labor and property is complicated by an equivocation about the idea of labor, which is dominated by the metaphor of sweat on the brow. Hence it is that the least imaginative work counts most securely as labor. The squires and merchants of the seventeenth century were far from idle men, but administration and entrepreneurship do not so obviously qualify for the title of labor as the felling of trees and the planting of corn[683].

We can justify propertizing ideas under Locke's approach with three propositions: first, that the production of ideas requires a person's labor; second, that these ideas are appropriated from a "common" which is not significantly devalued by the idea's removal; and third, that ideas can be made property without breaching the non-waste condition[684]. Many people implicitly accept these propositions. Indeed, the

---

[681] ibid
[682] ibid
[683] ibid
[684] According to Locke this condition prohibits the accumulation of so much property that some is destroyed without being used. Limited by this condition, Locke suggests that even after the primitive state there sometimes can be enough and as good left in the common to give those without property the opportunity to gain it. Spain and America, he says, illustrate the continuing applicability of this justification of property.

Lockean explanation of intellectual property has immediate, intuitive appeal: it seems as though people do work to produce ideas and that the value of these ideas - especially since there is no physical component -depends solely upon the individual's mental "work."[685]

5.2.2 Utilitarian/Economic Theories of Intellectual Property

Not surprisingly, the principal philosophical theory applied to the protection of utilitarian works - that is, technological inventions - has been utilitarianism. The social value of utilitarian works lies principally if not exclusively in their ability to perform tasks or satisfy desires more effectively or at lower costs. It is logical, therefore, that society would seek to protect such works within a governance regime that itself is based upon utilitarian precepts. Furthermore inventions, new processes, machines, manufactures, or compositions of matter – unlike artistic or literary expression do not generally implicate personal interests of the creator[686].

The United States Constitution expressly conditions the grant of power to Congress to create patent and copyright laws upon a utilitarian foundation under Art.1 Sec(8): 'to Promote the Progress of Science and useful Arts'.

Economic theory, a particular instantiation of utilitarianism, has provided the principal framework for analyzing intellectual property. In addition, the utilitarian perspective has relevance to other forms of intellectual property. Trade secret law often protects utilitarian works. Trademark law is principally concerned with ensuring that consumers are not misled in the marketplace and hence is particularly amenable to economic analysis. Even copyright law, which implicates a broader array of personal interests of the creator than patent law, may benefit from the

---

[685] Hughes,Justin, The Philosophy of Intellectual Property, 77 Geo. L.J. 287 (1988), available at http://www.law.harvard.edu/faculty/tfisher/music/Hughes1988.html , visited 3 Feb 2005

[686] Peter S. Menell, Professor of Law and Co-Director,Berkeley Center for Law and Technology University of California at Berkeley, Intellectual Property: General Theories at p 23, available at http://www.dklevine.com/archive/ittheory.pdf, visited 23 Dec 2005

application of the utilitarian framework to the extent that society seeks the production and diffusion of literary and artistic works.

The utilitarian framework has been particularly central to the development of copyright law in the United States. The Congressional Committee reporting on the 1909 Copyright Act stated: 'the enactment of copyright legislation by Congress under the terms of the

Constitution is not based upon any natural right that the author has in his writings, ... but upon the ground that the welfare of the public will be served ... by securing to authors for limited periods the exclusive rights to their writings[687].

5.2.3 Personhood Theory

The personhood justification for property derives from Kant's Philosophy of Law and Hegel's Philosophy of Right and has been elaborated in modern legal discourse in the work of Radin[688].The premise underlying the personhood perspective is that to achieve proper development an individual needs some control over resources in the external environment. The necessary assurances of control take the form of property rights[689]. The personhood justification for property emphasizes the extent to which property is personal as opposed to fungible: the justification is strongest where an object or idea is closely intertwined with an individual's personal identity and weakest where the 'thing' is valued by the individual at its market worth[690].

Netanel[691] traces the rich heritage of Continental copyright law and its moral rights tradition to the personality theory developed by Kant and Hegel, pointing out nuances distinguishing the various strains within the theory. For example, Kant viewed literary work as part of the author's person and hence is not alienable.

---

[687] ibid
[688] Radin, Margaret J. 'Market Inalienability', **100** Harvard Law Review, 1987, at p1849-1937.

[689] ibid
[690] ibid
[691] Netanel, Neil W. 'Copyright and a Democratic Civil Society', **106** Yale Law Journal, 1996 ,283-287.

Hegel, by contrast, distinguished between mental ability as an inalienable part of the self, but not the act of expression. Netanel presents a multifaceted argument for alienability restrictions upon copyright interests[692].

Personhood theory has been particularly central to the emerging debate, brought to the fore by advances in biotechnology, over property rights in body parts, cell lines and other body products[693].

5.2.4 Libertarian Theories

Palmer[694] constructs a libertarian argument against intellectual property rights by critiquing the dominant philosophical perspectives used to justify intellectual property protection. Coming from a different intellectual tradition, but reaching a similar conclusion, Barlow[695] argues that intellectual property rights threaten to undermine free exchange of ideas over the Internet and enable corporate interests to exercise substantial control over cultural and political expression. Netanel[696] suggests that these concerns can be addressed better through reworking rather than discarding copyright law. More generally, Waldron[697] points out that autonomy as ideal cuts both for and against intellectual property rights. Authors may claim that the integrity of their self-expression requires that they control the use and adaptation of their works. Social commentators may argue, however, that they are denied the

---

[692] ibid

[693] Munzer, Stephen R., 'An Uneasy Case Against Property Rights in Body Parts', 11 Social Philosophy and Policy, 1994, at p259-286.

[694] Palmer, Tom G. 'Are Patents and Copyrights Morally Justified? The Philosophy of Property Rights and Ideal Objects', 13 Harvard Journal of Law and Public Policy, 1990, at p 817-865.

[695] Barlow, John Perry (1994), 'The Framework for Economy of Ideas: Rethinking Patents and Copyrights in the Digital Age', 1994 WIRED, 83-97

[696] Netanel, Neil W. , 'Copyright and a Democratic Civil Society', 106 Yale Law Journal, 1996 at p 365-385.

[697] Waldron, Jeremy , 'From Authors to Copiers: Individual Rights and Social Values in Intellectual Property', 68 Chicago-Kent Law Review, 1993, 841-887.

ability to express themselves if they cannot parody the works of others or for fair use purposes.

5.2.5 Democratic Theories

Copyright law promotes political expression by encouraging expression, but it also potentially inhibits dissemination of works by prohibiting, subject to some limitations, the copying of expression. In its early history, copyright was used by the English Crown to regulate the press (and censor seditious expression) through bestowing selective royal grants of privilege[698] . Although copyright no longer functions directly to censor political expression, it nonetheless has the potential to inhibit the free flow of information. Goldstein discusses how the principles of copyright law - including the idea-expression dichotomy, the fair use doctrine and a misuse doctrine - harmonize this body of law with constitutional protections of freedom of speech and the press[699]. Coombe[700] offers a post-modernist critique of intellectual property law, arguing that the expanding domain of intellectual property protection limits the ability of individuals to express themselves. Netanel (1996) suggests that copyright plays an increasingly important role in modern democratic societies because of the ease with which expression can be disseminated through the use of digital technology. He argues that exisiting theories of intellectual property rights may undermine larger democratic principles and articulates a new model for the interpretation of copyright in the digital age which seeks to promote a democratic civil society[701].

---

[698] Goldstein, Paul , 'Copyright and the First Amendment', **70** *Columbia Law Review*, 1970 983-1057

[699] ibid

[700] Coombe, Rosemary J. 'Objects of Property and Subjects of Politics: Intellectual Property Laws and Democratic Dialogue', **69** Texas Law Review, 1991, 1853-1880.

[701] Netanel, Neil W. 'Copyright and a Democratic Civil Society', **106** *Yale Law Journal*, 1996 283-287.

5.2.6 Radical/Socialist Theories

A radical critique of some basic assumptions underlying intellectual property - most notably, the romantic concepts of 'the author' and 'the inventor' – has developed in recent years, building upon the work of deconstructists in the field of literary criticism. These scholars suggest that the concept of authorship and inventorship is so malleable, contingent and 'socially constructed' that we should be wary about identifying a creative work too closely with a particular person or entity[702].

According to this view, all creations are the product of communal forces to some extent. Dividing the stream of intellectual discourse into discrete units, each owned by and closely associated with a particular author or inventor, is therefore an incoherent exercise subject more to the political force of asserted authors' or inventors' groups than to recognition of inherent claims of natural right, personhood, or other justifications.

5.2.7 Relevance of Theories – Future of IPR

Intellectual property is rarely justified on one theory, although patents' grounding in utilitarianism comes to the closest. Consensus about philosophical perspective, however, has not produced consensus about what that perspective prescribes. Economic theorists have produced multiple plausible models for which empirical distillation will remain elusive and unlikely to be of much general predictive value due to the heterogeneity of inventive activity, the diversity of research environments, the complexity of technological diffusion, the richness and changing nature of real world institutions and the obvious measurement problems in conducting empirical research of this type[703].

---

[702] Aoki, Keith (1993-1994), 'Authors, Inventors and Trademark Owners: Private Intellectual Property
and the Public Domain (parts 1 and 2)', **18** *Columbia - VLA Journal of Law and the Arts*, 197-267.

[703] Peter S. Menell, Professor of Law and Co-Director, Berkeley Center for Law and Technology

As technology advances, the system continues to evolve, sometimes by new legislation, more often by the stretching and bending of existing rules. New technology commercialized in the past two decades, most notably the advent and diffusion of digital technology and new advances in the life sciences, portend deepening interest in the intellectual property system and scrutiny, reconsideration and re-conceptualization of the theories justifying intellectual property. Even within the existing theories of intellectual property, these technologies pose significant analytical challenges as a result of the ways in which they change key factors on which existing institutional rules and structures are based - for example, the nature of personal and liberty interests of creators and users, network dimensions, transaction costs etc. As intellectual property and technology have gained importance over the past two decades, the philosophical debates have melded with broader social and political discourse bearing upon the very foundation of modern society. One can expect that intellectual property will continue to press these frontiers as the information age progresses.

5.3 Impact of the Internet on Intellectual Property

The internet has driven many changes in the intellectual property community. As a data and resource access tool, it has expanded the reach of every user localized, regional resources, to true global information access.

Today the largest segment of business-to-consumer e-commerce involves intangible products that can be delivered directly over the network to the consumer's computer[704]. While these intangible products, by their very nature, are difficult to measure, an increasing amount of the content that is being offered is subject to

---

University of California at Berkeley, Intellectual Property: General Theories at p 163, available at http://www.dklevine.com/archive/ittheory.pdf, visited 23 Dec 2005

[704] OECD (1999), The Economic and Social impacts of e-commerce: Preliminary Findings and Research Agenda, available at http://www.oecd.org/subject/e_commerce/summary.htm

intellectual property rights[705]. This commerce in intangible products raises a number of issues for intellectual property in addition to those that would arise in respect of physical goods. There is a growing need to adopt technological measures in protecting the rights of intellectual property owners. In addition to this, questions of the scope of rights and how existing law applies , jurisdiction, applicable law, validity of contract and enforcement have become more complex and needs to be addressed in an appropriate way.

Some of the positive impacts of internet on intellectual property community are

(a) It has increased affordable access to intellectual property resources globally[706];

(b) It has enhanced the ability of patent prior art search[707];

(c) It has increased business , political and society awareness of the growing importance of all types of intellectual property[708];

(d) It has shortened the data access time, that is, days or weeks have been shortened to minutes or hours[709];

(e) There has been a geometric increase in the amount of accessible data and collections relative to intellectual property[710];

(f) It has provided access to an expanding number of web-based software and intellectual property management tools[711];

(g) It has provided a path for developing countries to catch up with world developments with regard to intellectual property data access , management etc[712];

---

[705] William Daley, WIPO Conference on Electronic Commerce and Intellectual Property , Sep 1999, available at http://ecommerce.wipo.int/conference/papers/daley.html , visited 10 Dec 2005
[706] Ryder, Rodney, Intellectual Property and the Internet, LexisNexis, New Delhi, 2002, at p 13

[707] ibid
[708] ibid
[709] ibid
[710] ibid
[711] ibid
[712] ibid

Notwithstanding the positive impact the internet has had on the intellectual property community, it has simultaneously created an alarming list of shortcomings. Although we can accept the benefits with complacency, we can not allow detrimental impacts to continue unchecked. Some of the negative impacts of the internet on intellectual property community are

(a) It has exacerbated the 'poor patent quality' and provided means to discover invalidating art. This negatively impacts share holder value, intellectual property value and the overall economy[713];

(b) Further, it has increased demands on patent office examiners to expand prior art search. The examiners must search not only the field in which the invention classified, but also analogous arts. This results in increasing pendency, decreases time available to prosecute any particular patent and decreases overall intellectual property validity[714].

(c) It has spawned new intellectual property problems, infringement possibilities and enforcement challenges, such as cybersquatting, trademark infringement etc[715];

(d) It has failed to bridge the chasm between industry and intellectual property creators and has not significantly increased the adaptation of intellectual property by companies[716].

5.4 Copyright Protection in Cyberspace

The observation of Peterson J., in University of London Press V University of Tutorial Press[717] that ' **What is worth copying is prima facie worth protecting'** is probably the best saying in relation to copyright protection in all ages industrial or information.

---

[713] Ryder, Rodney, "Intellectual Property and the Internet", LexisNexis, New Delhi, (2002) at p 5

[714] ibid
[715] ibid
[716] ibid
[717] Cited from Cornish & Llewelyn, Intellectual Property: Patents, Copyright Trademarks and Allied Rights, 5th edition, Sweet & Maxwell, London, 2003

The purpose of copyright law is to improve society through advancement of knowledge. The philosophy underlying Copyright law is to encourage the creators and innovators by granting monopoly rights to them to exploit their works commercially for a definite period and in return it requires the work to be disclosed to the public. . The copyright law aims at balancing the rights of copyright owners with the rights of the public for access to and use of creative works .It provides incentive to authors or creators and limits the author's rights to control and exploit works. If society wants to induce creativity and entrepreneurship, it must provide financial protection for intellectual property so that inventions and the fruits of artistic creativity are forthcoming[718].

Sec.14 of the Copyright Act, 1957 empowers authors of original literary, dramatic, musical, artistic works, computer programmers etc with various rights in relation to their works. They have exclusive right to reproduce their work, make copies, perform their work in public or display, make translation of their work, adaptation of work etc.

History demonstrates that the Copyright law is the most affected one with the introduction of new technologies. Advances in printing and telecommunication technologies have promoted the process of reproduction, distribution and use of copyrighted material for the betterment of the society but at the same time they have posed several problems for the right holders. While the shape of copyright law has always been drawn by the developments in the technological world , the emergence of digital technologies towards the concluding decades of the 20th century as the defining paradigms of new age communications have raised a whole new set of challenges to copyright regimes. All works can now be digitalized whether they comprise texts, images, sound, animation , photograph and once digitalized the various elements are all equal and can be merged, transformed, manipulated or mixed to create an endless variety of new works. Earlier rights of reproduction and distribution affected only tangible physical copies of a work.

---

[718] Bowie E Norman, Digital Rights and Wrongs: Intellectual Property in Information Age, Business and Society Review 110:1 77–96

The ease with which works in digital form can be replicated and transmitted poses a difficult problem for the law to handle. In the existing copyright regime, there is a general perception that making copies for personal or private use is considered fair use[719] and lawful. While the technology of reprography has improved dramatically, in digital domain, "perfect" multiple copies can be generated by the same technology which is employed for the use of digital product. Hence it has become more difficult for the copyright owners to exercise control over replication of their works and to obtain compensation for unauthorized replication. Although the copyright system in the print world has generally focused on sales of copies of copyrighted works, in the digital world the trend is to reap the financial rewards for creating and disseminating intellectual products by charging for access to and use of digital works and limiting rights to use and copy these products. The older technologies of photocopying and taping allowed only mechanical copying by individual consumers, but in limited quantities, requiring considerable time, and of a lower quality than the original. Moreover, the copies were physically located in the same place as the person making the copy. On the internet, in contrast, one can make an unlimited number of copies, virtually instantaneously, without any degradation in quality. The result could be the disruption of traditional markets for the sale of copies of computer software, music, art, books, movies etc.

5. 5 Computer Mediated phenomenon – Software Patents

Modern society relies heavily on computer technology. Without software, a computer cannot operate. Software and hardware work in tandem in today's information society. So it is no wonder that intellectual property protection of software is crucial not only for the software industry, but for other businesses as well[720]. While software has been specifically identified by the Parliament and the courts as deserving of copyright protection, the scope of copyright protection afforded to software has been in flux in recent years. The Copyright Act, 1957

---

[719] A concept in copyright law that allows limited use of copyright material without requiring permission from the rights holders, eg, for scholarship or review, education, research etc
[720] WIPO, Patenting Software, SMEs, available at
http://www.wipo.int/sme/en/documents/software_patents.htm , visited 13 Mar 2003

specifically state that copyright protection does not "extend to any idea, procedure, process, system, method of operation, concept, principle, or discovery" . Copyright protection extends only to specific expression, and not to the ideas behind this expression - commonly referred to as the "idea-expression" dichotomy.

5.5.1 Understanding Computer Software

Sec.2(i) of the Information Technology Act, 2000 defines 'Computer' as any electronic , magnetic, optical or other high speed data processing device or system which performs logical , arithmetic and memory functions by manipulation of electronic , magnetic or optical impulses and includes all input, output, processing , storage, computer software or communication facilities which are connected or related to the computer in a computer system or computer network.

According to Sec.2(ffb) of Copyright Act,1957 'Computer' includes any electronic or similar device having information processing capabilities.

A computer basically consists of electronic components which are supported by electrical devices and mechanical systems. All these electronic, electrical and mechanical components used in a computer are called Computer Hardware. Computer Hardware components are actuated and controlled with the help of computer programs called Computer Software[721].

Computer software is classified into two categories:

1) Application Software – programs used to solve specific problems (tasks) like railway reservation , banking etc[722];

2) System Software – programs used to handle the computer hardware and to execute the application programs. Examples include operating systems (Windows, Linux etc) , compilers, assemblers etc[723];

---

[721] Computer Concepts & C Programming, Vikas Publications, Chennai, 2002, at p20
[722] ibid at p23
[723] ibid at p23

5.5.2 Computer Languages

To communicate with the computer following three languages are used;

1) Machine Language : writing instructions to computer using 0's and 1's (binary numbers) is referred as machine language programming[724].

2) Assembly Language : writing instructions using mnemonics like ADD, SUB etc is referred as Assembly Language programming[725].

3) High Level Language : here, instructions are written using English like language with symbols or digits. Commonly used high level languages are FORTRAN, BASIC, COBOL, PASCAL, C, C++ etc[726].

The complete instruction set written in one of these languages is called Computer Program or Source Code.

In order to execute instructions, (as computer can understand 0's and 1's only) , the source code is translated into binary form by a compiler or interpreter. A compiler is also used to translate source code written in High Level Language into an object program.

5.5.3 Developing Software

For developing software the given task is divided into sub-tasks and algorithms and flow charts are used draw up the blue print (to design the software) for developing the actual source code.

Algorithm is a step-by-step procedure for solving a problem or accomplishing some end especially by a computer[727].

Flowchart is a graphic representation of a program in which symbols represent logical steps and flow lines define the sequence of those steps. These are used to design new programs, and to document existing programs[728].

---

[724] Subramanian N, Introduction to computer Fundamentals, Tata McGraw-Hill, New Delhi, 1993
[725] ibid
[726] ibid
[727] Rajaraman V, Fundamentals of Computer, Prentice Hall of India, New Delhi, 1997
[728] ibid

5.5.4 Legal Definition of Computer Program (Software)

WIPO Model provisions on the protection of computer software ,Geneva ,1978 defines 'Computer Program' as follows ;
"A set of instructions capable, when incorporated in a machine readable medium of causing a machine having information processing capabilities to indicate, perform or achieve a particular function, task or result."

The US Copyright Law at Section 101 defines a computer program as ' a set of statements or instructions to be used directly or indirectly in a computer in order to bring about a certain result.'

Sec.2(ffc) of Indian Copyright Act, 1957 defines 'Computer Program' as a set of instructions expressed in words, codes, schemes or in any other form, including a machine readable medium , capable of causing a computer to perform a particular task or achieve a particular result. This definition seems to be based on WIPO definition. Computer Program and Computer databases are considered as literary works under Sec.2(o) of Copyright Act, 1957.

Explanation (b) to Section 80 HHE of the Income Tax Act, 1961 defines "computer software" to mean any computer programme recorded on any disc, tape, perforated media or other information storage device and includes any such programme or any customised electronic data which is transmitted from India to a place outside India by any means.

From the above it can be concluded that a computer program should be considered as a set of statements or instructions which is capable of causing a machine having information processing capabilities (a computer) to perform a set of functions to achieve a result.

5.5.5 Copyright Protection for Computer Programs

Computer programs or software plays a vital role in the architecture of Internet. It is the software that determines various functional aspects of Internet.

Early in the development of the art of software writing, the originators thereof feared that traditional forms of protection such as patents and copyrights would not give them sufficient protection and relied upon trade secret law. It soon became clear, however, that this was not the best solution to the problem since to establish trade secret protection, one must take some steps to impose a confidential relationship on those who have access to the secret. In a free flowing industry such as the computer software business, this is difficult[729].

Attention has, therefore, returned to the traditional protection of patents and copyrights. However, patent protection cannot be obtained for inventions in this field that do not meet the current test for patentable subject matter. Furthermore, to be patentable the program must be "not obvious". This can be a difficult requirement to fulfill. Furthermore, patent protection requires a fairly prolonged examination by the Patent Office before any rights arise and is thus not the ideal way of dealing with copyists who may be extremely quick off the mark[730].

When a computer program is written out on a piece of paper, it is quite clear that copyright exists in this work in the same way as it would in respect of any other literary work. The first problem with which the courts had to grapple was whether copyright law could be extended to cover computer programs which exist merely in magnetic or electric form or as specific circuits etched on to a silicon chip[731].

In Sega Enterprises V Richards[732], it was held that under the provisions relating to literary works in the Copyright Act, copyright subsisted in the assembly program code of a video game and that the machine code derived from it was either a reproduction or adaptation of the copyright work.

---

[729] Ladas & Parry Guide to Statutory Protection for Computer Software in the United States, available at
http://www.ladas.com/Patents/Computer/Copyright.USA.html , visited on 25 Dec 2005
[730] ibid
[731] ibid
[732] English case reported in Copyright & Industrial Designs by P.Naryanan, 3rd edition, Eastern Law House, 2002

In Apple computer Inc. V Computer Edge Pvt Ltd[733], it was held that a computer program consisting of source code is original literary work. A source code is a program written in any of the programming languages employed by computer programmers. An object code is the version of a program in which the source code language converted or translated into the machine language of the computer with which it is used. It was further held that an object code is an adaptation or mechanical translation of the source code within the meaning of the copyright law and copying of the object code was an infringement of the copyright in the source code.

In United States also it has been held that an object code is entitled to copyright protection in Apple Computer V Fraklin Computer[734].

In India, the words 'schemes or in any other forms' used in Sec.2(ffc) would seem to indicate that the source code and object code of a computer program are entitled to copyright protection.

Copyright Act, 1957 of India provided copyright protection for original works of authorship in literary works . It was the amendment made in 1994 that inserted Sec.2(o), making Computer Programs expressly recognized for copyright protection.

5.5.6 Rise of Software Patents

US was the first country to establish the practice of granting patents to computer programs. The first decision by the Supreme Court on the question of software patenting was called Gottschalk V Benson[735], decided in 1972. Benson developed a method of converting binary coded decimals with which a number can be represented by one or more groups of four zeros and ones, to pure binary notation, which allows any number to be written by a single collection of zeros and ones. The

---

[733] Austrlian case reported in Copyright & Industrial Designs by P.Naryanan, 3rd edition, Eastern Law House, 2002.
[734] 714 F.2d 1240 (3d Cir. 1983), available at http://www.internetlegal.com/impactof.htm, visited 30 Dec 2005
[735] 409 US 63 (1972),
http://caselaw.lp.findlaw.com/scripts/getcase.pl?court=US&vol=409&invol=63, visited 10 Jan 2006

court noted that any existing computer could carry out Benson's procedures and that they could be performed without a computer. Looking back on cases it had decided decades earlier, the Court concluded that Benson's program involved only mathematical calculations and mental steps, and that it did not constitute a patentable process[736].

Six years later, the Court looked at another software program in Parker V Flook[737]. Flook had devised a mathematical algorithm that allowed equipment monitoring of an industrial process to determine whether the temperature and pressure indicated some problem had arisen, that is, whether an "alarm limit" had been reached. Because acceptable temperature and pressure varied depending on the stage of the process, Flook's algorithm varied the alarm limit. The Court refused to grant the patent, determining that Flook's program was an abstract or phenomenon of nature, outside the patent domain.

Not until its third software patent case, Diamond V Diehr[738] in 1981, would the Supreme Court move toward the patenting of computer programs. The patent application in Diehr involved a process for curing rubber within a molding process. Diehr created a system that would constantly measure the temperature inside. This data was sent to a computer that used a well-known mathematical equation to recalculate the time necessary for the rubber to cure based on the temperature readings. When calculated optimum curing time equaled the actual time elapsed, the computer would open the press. This time the Court did not dismiss the invention as a mathematical algorithm. Instead, the Court concluded that Diehr had developed a patentable process[739]. The fact that the process utilized a mathematical algorithm was only part of the relevant inquiry[740]. The similarity between the inventions in Flook and Diehr, and the different results, illustrate the complexity involved in interpreting software patent questions.

---

[736] ibid
[737] 434 US 584 (1978), available at http://caselaw.lp.findlaw.com/cgi-bin/getcase.pl?court=US&vol=437&invol=584, visited on 10 Jan 2005
[738] Diamond v. Diehr, 450 U.S. 175 (1981), available at
http://caselaw.lp.findlaw.com/scripts/getcase.pl?court=US&vol=450&invol=175, visited on 10 Jan 2005
[739] ibid
[740] ibid

5.5.7 Computer Program : Copyright V Patents Debate

The dichotomy and the debate in relation to the protection of computer program by patent or copyright regime seems to never ending. In US, the decision of the US court in Diamond V Diehr[741] set the stage for granting patents to computer programs. European Council has relaxed its initial position by granting patents to computer software by issuing directive on computer-implemented inventions.

5.5.8 Arguments for inclusion of Computer Program under Patents

a) One of the main arguments is that a good idea behind software is not protected as it is in a copyright regime and hence it is easy to create new software with altering the expression part of it. Hence there is no incentive in creating a 'big idea', which is left unprotected[742].

b) The period of software under copyright is around 60 years (now 70 years) and the author's lifetime in most regimes is anachronistic with the productive life of software ranging from couple of years to additional couple of year. It would be prudent to give a shorter but stricter monopoly, which will benefit the creators[743].

c) On the enforcement of the IP regime, copyright regime allows criminal proceedings, which would not be in case of the classification as patent regime where there are only civil proceedings.

d) The copyright of any work is instant and there is no professional or inventive proof needed makes it easy for many to do reverse engineering

---

[741] Diamond v. Diehr 450 U.S. 175 (1981), available at, http://caselaw.lp.findlaw.com/scripts/getcase.pl?court=US&vol=450&invol=175 , visited 10 Jan 2005

[742] Stokes, Simon, Digital Copyright : Law and Practice, Butterworths, UK, 2002

[743] Brett N. Dorny and Michael K. Friedland , Copyrighting "Look And Feel": Manufacturers Technologies V. Cams, Harvard Law Technology Journal,Vol.3 Spring Issue, 1990

of a source code and keep flooding the market with products and may not be a viable proposition of a sustained business model for the industry[744].

e) Many a software in the high-end application in the sectors of satellite communication, aviation, nuclear physics are done at huge costs with no commercial returns per se in the short run. These programmes if not protected by Patents may end up exploited by commercial programmers who can create programmes with alternate expressions without investing in the 'idea'[745].

f) Physical invention has been replaced with digital mode of software and hence one need to revamp the existing patent jurisprudence to accommodate software in the patent regime.

5.5.9 Arguments against Computer Program patenting

a) Patenting of software will lead to a monopoly of 'few ideas' which will not allow the new software to come in as it is happening under the 'copyright regime.'[746]

b) Patenting of software will lead to defensive portfolios of patents, which will block new entrepreneurship and applications and creativity.

c) Placing software in patenting will result in inordinate delay for products to come to the market as the procedural hurdles and other issues will block products.

d) With the software life very short it any way will not benefit by a patents regime giving monopoly for 14 or twenty years. In fact by the time patent is granted the utility of the product may be outdated[747].

e) With the rapid application of software in hitherto unknown fields, speed and adaptations is the key to sustain the industry and hence copyright is more

---

[744] ibid
[745] ibid
[746] Mergers P, Robert, As Many as Six Impossible Patents Before Breakfast: Property rights for Business Concepts and patent System Reform, Berkeley Technology Law Journal, Vol.14:577, 1999
[747] ibid

suited as it allows products to be in the market than waiting for patents to be granted.

f) Mathematical algorithms are not inventions and cannot be considered as inventions but rather a creative use of a subject and hence copyright regime is best-suited one for software[748].

g) As a product which is intangible and can be copied with ease by even a computer illiterate, civil remedies will only throw the baby out of the bath water and hence copyright regime and criminal remedy could only be the deterrent.

h) Software has assumed a mass movement with the advent of open source code model like Linux, which allows more creative minds to be part of the movement, and this will be stopped by the quagmire of patent portfolios and litigations.

5.5.10 Software Patents V Freedom of Speech and Expression

Anyone who has ever written both a program and an essay knows how similar these complex endeavors are. Both require use of all one's skill and knowledge. Both involve continual invention and creativity. Both require constant revision. Both evolve with time, as one's knowledge grows. Both are written in a language which has a vocabulary that can be used in an infinite variety of ways. Although software is often a less direct method of communication than prose, in that there may be many intermediaries between a particular programmer and the end-user of an application which uses a piece of his or her code, the same is true for other forms of expression. Theater goers, for example, don't directly read theater scripts, but see and hear them acted by intermediaries (actors); nonetheless, the scripts are writings[749].

---

[748] ibid
[749] Phil, Salin, Freedom of Speech in Software, http://www.philsalin.com/patents.html visited on 2 Mar 05

Although a program has to be run to be used, before it can be run it has to be written. There are now millions of individuals all over the world who know how to write a computer program. It is an absurdity to expect those millions of individuals to perform patent searches or any other kind of search prior to the act of writing a program to solve a specific problem. If others wish to purchase a program, as with the sale of written prose and written music, absolutely no patent restrictions should be placed on the ability of authors to sell or publish their own writings. Suppression of free thought and speech in software (writing, or publishing) is an evil, even when only a small number of individuals recognize that speech is being restricted, or what the costs will be if this harmful censorship-by-another-name, viz "patent licensure", is now allowed to expand unchecked[750].

In the case of Universal City Studios v.Reimerdes[751] the US court has held that source code of the computer program constitutes Free speech and would be protected under first amendment[752].

5.6 Digital Music: Problems and Prospects

Almost all music is distributed today in digital, rather than analog, form. Until recently, most digital music was sold in containers called Compact Discs (CD). Developed and refined between 1965 and 1985, CD technology swept the consumer market during the late 1980s and the early 1990s, displacing almost completely long-play vinyl albums. In the past few years, a new method of distributing digital music has become increasingly popular: transmission of container less files via the internet, followed by storage on home computers. Music distributed in this manner

---

[750] ibid
[751] Universal City Studios, Inc. v. Reimerdes 111 F.Supp.2d 294 (S.D.N.Y. 2000, available at http://laws.lp.findlaw.com/2nd/009185.html , visited on 12 Mar 2005
[752] Halpern E Stevens, Harmonizing The Convergence Of Medium, Expression, And Functionality: A Study Of The Speech Interest In Computer Software, Harvard Journal of Law & Technology, Volume 14, Number 1 Fall 2000

typically is replayed either through stereo systems attached to the home computers or through portable devices analogous to the 'walkman'[753].

Widespread adoption of the techniques of distributing digital music via the internet either in MP3 format or in some other form would give rise to five important social and economic advantages. They are

(1) Cost saving associated with disintermediation- currently , most of the retail price paid by a consumer for a compact discs goes to the manufacturer of the disc itself, the distributor of the disc, the retail store where she purchased it, or the record company that produced the recording. The composer and the recording artist rarely receive more than 16% of the purchase price. If the music were distributed over the internet by the artist himself, almost all of costs associated with making and distributing discs could be eliminated. The result is that the musicians could earn more or consumers could pay less or both[754].

(2) Elimination of overproduction and underproduction- Under the current system, the record companies must guess how many copies of each CD consumers will demand. Distribution of container less digital files over the internet would eliminate this problem[755].

(3) Convenience and Precision- The many annoyances associated with buying music in retail stores (travel time, the disappointment when the CDs are out of stock etc) would all be eliminated by internet distribution. The less substantial annoyances associated with mail-order purchases of CDs (waiting for delivery, being forced to purchase an entire CD when one is only interested in a few tracks) would also be eliminated. Consumers would get exactly the music they wanted instantly[756].

(4) Increase in the number and variety of musicians- The set of musicians who would like to make their music available to the public and the set that significant numbers of consumers would like to hear are both much larger than the set hired by the recording companies. The opportunities available to new artists and to bands

---

[753] Fisher ,Williams, Digital Music: Problems and Possibilities, Harvard Law School Publications, available at http://www.law.harvard.edu/faculty/tfisher/Music.html , visited on   10 Dec 2005.
[754] ibid
[755] ibid
[756] ibid

that appeal to niche markets would increase rapidly through widespread adoption of the new technology[757].

(5) Semiotic democracy- In most modern capitalist countries, the power to make meaning, to shape culture, has been concentrated in relatively few hands. One of the great cultural benefits of the internet in general lies in its tendency to decentralize this semiotic power. In two respects, internet distribution of digital music would contribute to that decentralization. The first consists of the expansion of the set of musicians who can reach wide audiences and the associated diminution of the cultural power of the record companies. The second of the ease with which consumers of digital music manipulate it, recombine pieces of it, blend it with their own material can become producers[758].

5.6.1 MP3 Music- Delight for Music Consumers, Nightmare for Music Producers

The technology that has made distribution of music over internet convenient and simple is MP3[759], an audio compression file format. Musical files compressed using MP3 occupy approximately 1/12 of the disk space occupied by uncompressed files, enabling them to be transmitted faster and stored more easily. Two groups have embraced MP3 technology especially enthusiastically. First, musicians unable to obtain recording contracts with the major record companies have found that, at modest cost, they can record their material in MP3 format and then make it available over the internet. Second, the net users have discovered that they can obtain on the internet MP3 copies of most of the songs of their favorite musicians. A high percentage of the MP3 recordings available in this manner were prepared without the permission of the owners of the copyrights in the music[760].

---

[757] ibid
[758] ibid
[759] An abbreviation of MPEG Audio-Layer 3. This is a compression algorithm developed by the Fraunhofer Institute in Germany and later standardised by the MPEG (Motion Picture Experts Group) that permits audio files to be highly compressed and yet retain excellent levels of quality. available at www.futuremark.com/community/hardwarevocabulary/, visited on 10 Jan 2006
[760] ibid

The music and recording industry in US has waged war against unauthorized copying on four fronts; against the manufacturers of the machines used to play MP3 files; against the operators of pirate websites; and against the growing group of intermediaries that assist users in locating and obtaining MP3 files. To date, none of these struggles has been decisively resolved. On the first two fronts, the forces embracing the new technology are currently winning; on the third and fourth, the forces seeking to limit uses of the new technology are currently winning. But the outcomes of all four campaigns remain in doubt[761].

One of the earliest cases to be decided by US courts in relation to distribution of illegal MP3 files is A&M Records, Inc., et al. v. Napster, Inc[762]. The court denied Napster Inc.'s ("Napster") motion for partial summary judgment, in which motion Napster sought to limit the damages and other relief that could be awarded against it for alleged direct or contributory copyright infringement by application of the safe harbor provisions of 17 U.S.C. Section 512(a) of the Digital Millennium Copyright Act ("DMCA"). Section 512(a) limits a service provider's liability for copyright infringement by reason of the service provider's "transmitting, routing or providing connections for material through a system or network controlled or operated by or for the service provider ..."[763].

The court held that Napster's role in the transmission of MP3 files by and among the various users of its system was not entitled to protection under Section 512(a) because such transmission does not occur through Napster's system. Rather, although Napster informs the user's computer of the location of a computer on which MP3 files the user seeks are stored, and its willingness to permit the user to download such files, all files transfer directly from the computer of one Napster user through the Internet to the computer of the requesting user. Similarly, any role that Napster plays in providing or facilitating a connection between these two computers

---

[761] Fisher Williams, Digital Music: Problems and Possibilities, Harvard Law School Publications, available at http://www.law.harvard.edu/faculty/tfisher/Music.html , visited on 10 Dec 2005.

[762] A&M Records, Inc., et al. v. Napster, Inc., 239 F.3d 1004 (9th Cir. 2001), available at United States Court for the Ninth Circuit, http://lvalue.com/nap.html , visited 22 Dec 2005
[763] ibid

does not occur through its system. "Although the Napster server conveys address information to establish a connection between the requesting and host users, the connection itself occurs through the Internet."[764]

The court also held that issues of fact existed as to whether Napster was entitled to any protection under the DMCA at all. To be entitled to such protection, a service provider must meet the requirements of section 512(i) of the DMCA, which, among other things, obligates the service provider to "adopt and reasonably implement and inform subscribers and account holders of the service provider's system or network of a policy that provides for the termination in appropriate circumstances of subscribers and account holders of the service provider's system or network who are repeat infringers ...". The court held that issues of fact existed as to whether Napster had appropriately adopted and informed its users of such an effective policy which precluded at this time any relief to Napster under the DMCA[765].

5.6.2 Peer-to-Peer Networking (P2P)

Commentators and courts have universally hailed the Internet as an abundantly fertile field for self-expression and debate. But this acclamation masks sharp disagreement over whether certain Internet activity should be lauded or deplored. A prime example is the unlicensed use of copyright protected material. The explosion of sharing and remixing of popular songs and movies over Internet based peer-to-peer ("P2P") networks like Napster, KaZaA, and Morpheus has evoked sharply discordant reactions. Some commentators embrace the collection, exchange, and transformation of existing works as part and parcel of the individual autonomy, self-expression, and creative collaboration for which we celebrate the Internet. Others denounce those activities as massive piracy of intellectual property. They fear that P2P file swapping poses a mortal threat to the copyright system that sustains

---

[764] ibid
[765] ibid

239

authors, artists, and a multi-billion-dollar industry in the production and dissemination of creative expression[766].

The P2P controversy has degenerated into a steadily intensifying war of words and legal action. The copyright industries have successfully shut down a number of P2P networks — most famously, Napster — and continue to bring lawsuits against others. They have also sought to compel telecommunications and consumer electronics companies to disable unlicensed P2P sharing of copyright protected works. The industries are now targeting individuals who trade large numbers of files as well. Yet, despite this three pronged attack, unlicensed P2P file swapping continues apace[767].

P2P networks are those networks where communication between computers takes place directly without help of the central server[768]. In MGM V Grokster[769], the question before the court was under what circumstances the distributor of a product capable of both lawful and unlawful use is liable for acts of copyright infringement by third parties using the product. Respondents, Grokster Ltd and StreamCast Networks Inc. used to distribute a piece of software which enabled computer users to share electronic files through peer-to-peer networks. The advantage of peer-to-peer networks over information networks of other types shows up in their substantial and growing popularity. Because they need no central computer server to mediate the exchange of information or files among users, the high bandwidth communications capacity for a server may be dispensed with, and the need for costly server storage space is eliminated. Since copies of a file (particularly a popular one) are available on many users' computers, file requests and retrievals may be faster than on other types of networks, and since file exchanges do not travel through a server, communications can take place between any computers that

---

[766] Netanel Weinstock Neil, Impose A Noncommercial Use Levy to Allow Free Peer-To-Peer File Sharing, Harvard Journal of Law & Technology, Vol.17, Number 1 Fall 2003, available at http://jolt.law.harvard.edu/articles/pdf/v17/17HarvJLTech001.pdf , visited on 13 Dec 2005
[767] ibid

[768] Metro-Goldwyn-Mayer Studios Inc., et al. v. Grokster, Ltd., et al. 545 U.S. 913 (2005), available at http://www.law.cornell.edu/supct/html/04-480.ZS.html, visited on 14 June 2006

[769] ibid

remain connected to the network without risk that a glitch in the server will disable the network in its entirety. Given these benefits in security, cost, and efficiency, peer-to-peer networks are employed to store and distribute electronic files by universities, government agencies, corporations, and libraries, among others[770].

MGM argued that Respondents are liable for copyright infringement – direct infringement, contributory infringement and vicarious infringement. Respondents pleaded their actions does not amount to copyright infringement and relied on the principle laid down in Sony Corp. v. Universal City Studios[771]. Further MGM contended that holding of Ninth Circuit Court, which held that Respondents are not vicariously liable, would upset a sound balance between the respective values of supporting creative pursuits through copyright protection and promoting innovation in new communication technologies by limiting the incidence of liability for copyright infringement. The more artistic protection is favored, the more technological innovation may be discouraged; the administration of copyright law is an exercise in managing the trade-off[772].

The tension between the two values is the subject of this case, with its claim that digital distribution of copyrighted material threatens copyright holders as never before, because every copy is identical to the original, copying is easy, and many people (especially the young) use file-sharing software to download copyrighted works. This very breadth of the software's use may well draw the public directly into the debate over copyright policy, and the indications are that the ease of copying songs or movies using software like Grokster's and Napster's is fostering disdain for copyright protection. As the case has been presented to us, these fears are said to be offset by the different concern that imposing liability, not only on

---

[770] ibid
[771] 464 US 417 (1984) available at http://www.law.cornell.edu/copyright/cases/464_US_417.htm , visited on 2 Feb 2006

[772] Metro-Goldwyn-Mayer Studios Inc., et al. v. Grokster, Ltd., et al. 545 U.S. 913 (2005), available at http://www.law.cornell.edu/supct/html/04-480.ZS.html, visited on 14 June 2006

infringers but on distributors of software based on its potential for unlawful use, could limit further development of beneficial technologies[773].

The Court referring to In re Aimster Copyright Litigation[774], 334 F. 3d 643, 645-646 (CA7 2003) observed that the argument for imposing indirect liability in this case is, however, a powerful one, given the number of infringing downloads that occur every day using StreamCast's and Grokster's software. When a widely shared service or product is used to commit infringement, it may be impossible to enforce rights in the protected work effectively against all direct infringers, the only practical alternative being to go against the distributor of the copying device for secondary liability on a theory of contributory or vicarious infringement. One infringes contributorily by intentionally inducing or encouraging direct infringement, and infringes vicariously by profiting from direct infringement while declining to exercise a right to stop or limit it. Although "the Copyright Act does not expressly render anyone liable for infringement committed by another, as laid down in Sony Corp. v. Universal City Studios[775], these doctrines of secondary liability emerged from common law principles and are well established in the law.

In Sony Corp. v. Universal City Studios[776], the Court addressed a claim that secondary liability for infringement can arise from the very distribution of a commercial product. There, the product, novel at the time, was what we know today as the videocassette recorder or VCR. Copyright holders sued Sony as the manufacturer, claiming it was contributorily liable for infringement that occurred when VCR owners taped copyrighted programs because it supplied the means used to infringe, and it had constructive knowledge that infringement would occur. At the trial on the merits, the evidence showed that the principal use of the VCR was for " time-shifting" or taping a program for later viewing at a more convenient time,

---

[773] ibid
[774] 334 F. 3d 643, 645-646 (CA7 2003), available at
http://homepages.law.asu.edu/~dkarjala/cyberlaw/InReAimster(9C6-30-03).htm, visited on 14 Jan 2006
[775] 464 US 417 (1984) available at http://www.law.cornell.edu/copyright/cases/464_US_417.htm , visited on 2 Feb 2006
[776] ibid

which the Court found to be a fair, not an infringing, use[777]. There was no evidence that Sony had expressed an object of bringing about taping in violation of copyright or had taken active steps to increase its profits from unlawful taping[778]. Although Sony's advertisements urged consumers to buy the VCR to " 'record favorite shows' " or " 'build a library' " of recorded programs[779], court found that neither of these uses was necessarily infringing[780].

On those facts, with no evidence of stated or indicated intent to promote infringing uses, the only conceivable basis for imposing liability was on a theory of contributory infringement arising from its sale of VCRs to consumers with knowledge that some would use them to infringe. But because the VCR was "capable of commercially significant non-infringing uses," court held the manufacturer could not be faulted solely on the basis of its distribution[781].

This analysis reflected patent law's traditional staple article of commerce doctrine, now codified, that distribution of a component of a patented device will not violate the patent if it is suitable for use in other ways. The doctrine was devised to identify instances in which it may be presumed from distribution of an article in commerce that the distributor intended the article to be used to infringe another's patent, and so may justly be held liable for that infringement. "One who makes and sells articles which are only adapted to be used in a patented combination will be presumed to intend the natural consequences of his acts; he will be presumed to intend that they shall be used in the combination of the patent.[782]"

In sum, where an article is "good for nothing else" but infringement, the Court held there is no legitimate public interest in its unlicensed availability, and there is no injustice in presuming or imputing intent to infringe. Conversely, the doctrine absolves the equivocal conduct of selling an item with substantial lawful as well as unlawful uses, and limits liability to instances of more acute fault than the mere

---

[777] ibid
[778] ibid, at p 438
[779] Ibid at, p at 459 (*Blackmun, J.,* dissenting)
[780] ibid
[781] ibid
[782] ibid

understanding that some of one's products will be misused. It leaves breathing room for innovation and a vigorous commerce.

The Court did draw the distinction between direct infringement, indirect or induced infringement and vicarious infringement but decided to determine the matter only on induced infringement. The classic case of direct evidence of unlawful purpose occurs when one induces commission of infringement by another, or "entices or persuades another" to infringe, as by advertising (Black's Law Dictionary 790 (8th ed. 2004)). Thus at common law a copyright or patent defendant who "not only expected but invoked infringing use by advertisement" was liable for infringement "on principles recognized in every part of the law.

The rule on inducement of infringement as developed in the early cases is no different today. Evidence of "active steps ... taken to encourage direct infringement," Oak Industries, Inc. v. Zenith Electronics Corp., 697 F. Supp. 988, 992 (ND Ill. 1988)[783], such as advertising an infringing use or instructing how to engage in an infringing use, show an affirmative intent that the product be used to infringe, and a showing that infringement was encouraged overcomes the law's reluctance to find liability when a defendant merely sells a commercial product suitable for some lawful use.

Based on the above analysis the Court held that one who distributes a device with the object of promoting its use to infringe copyright, as shown by clear expression or other affirmative steps taken to foster infringement, going beyond mere distribution with knowledge of third-party action, is liable for the resulting acts of infringement by third parties using the device, regardless of the device's lawful uses.

---

[783] Cornell University Law School, Supreme Court Collection, available at http://www.law.cornell.edu/ , visited on 1 March 2006.

5.7 Linking, Framing and Caching

Some of the copyright issues involved in cyberspace are related to the interaction between websites, service providers and consumers for the purpose of e-business. These include Linking, Framing and caching. In this section how these internet specific activities would infringe copyright are discussed.

In the past several years, the World Wide Web has seen two significant changes:

(1) its popularity and use have exploded, and

(2) it has become a place of substantial commercial activity.

These two characteristics have made the Web a place of increasing legal turmoil. Certain practices by authors of Web sites and pages have been attacked as violative of others' intellectual property rights or other entitlements. These practices include "linking," "framing" and "caching".

5.7.1 Linking

Internet links may create legal liability. Despite the internet's initial 'free linking' ethos, links can be unlawful when they are designed to confuse viewers, to evade court orders or clear statutory prohibition, or promote illegal conduct by others. Linking law, which began with Shetland Times head-line linking case in Scotland in late 1996, now includes several precedents as well as developing worldwide body of opinions on various subjects[784].

"Linking" allows a Web site user to visit another location on the Internet. By simply clicking on a "live" word or image in one Web page, the user can view another Web page elsewhere in the world, or simply elsewhere on the same server as the original page. This technique is what gives the Web its unique communicative power. At the same time, however, linking may undermine the rights or interests of the owner of

---

[784] Sableman, Mark, Linking law Revisited : Internet Linking Law At Five Years, Berkely Technology Law Journal , Volume 16 (2001), Issue 16:3 (Fall 2001)

the page that is linked to[785]. A website consists of several pages. By linking it is possible to transfer the control of browser to the web page of another website. Suppose, for example, that X sets up a homepage for her site. On the homepage she places some advertisements, from which she hopes to make some money. The homepage also contains links to various subordinate pages, which contain content that X believes consumers wish to see. Y then creates his own Web site, which contains links to X's subordinate pages. The net result is that visitors to Y's site will be able to gain access to X's material, without ever seeing X's advertisements which are placed on the Home page. This type of activity is called "**deep linking**." Other problems arise when one site contains links to copyrighted materials contained in another site against the wishes of the copyright owner. Though the person who provides the link may not be making copies himself or herself, judicial view has been that the link provider partially responsible for ensuing copyright infringement[786].

Section 51 of the Copyright Act, 1957 lists the circumstances under which a copyright is said to be violated[787]. Sec.51 (b) (iii) provides that if any person exhibits copyrighted work without authorization in public by way of trade has violated the rights of the owner. This provision of the law would affect deep linking.

---

[785] ibid

[786] Berkmen Center for Internet and Society, Harvard Law School, Intellectual Property in Cyberspace (2000), available at http://cyber.law.harvard.edu/property00/metatags/main.html, visited 22 Jan 2006

[787] Sec.51. When copyright infringed- Copyright in a work shall be deemed to be infringed- (a) when any person, without a licence granted by the owner of the copyright or the Registrar of Copyrights under this Act or in contravention of the conditions of a licence so granted or of any condition imposed by a competent authority under this Act-

(i) does anything, the exclusive right to do which is by this Act conferred upon the owner of the copyright; or (ii) permits for profit any place to be used for the communication of the work to the public where such communication constitutes an infringement of the copyright in the work, unless he was not aware and had no reasonable ground for believing that such communication to the public would be an infringement of copyright; or

(b) when any person- (i) makes for sale or hire, or sells or lets for hire, or by way of trade displays or offers for sale or hire, or (ii) distributes either for the purpose of trade or to such an extent as to affect prejudicially the owner of the copyright, or (iii) by way of trade exhibits in public, or (iv) imports into India, any infringing copies of the work:

Deep linking definitely involves communication to the public of unauthorized work as provided under Sec.2 (ff) of the Copyright Act, 1957. According to Sec.2(ff) Communication to the public means making any work available for being seen or heard or otherwise directly or by any means of display or diffusion other than by issuing copies of such work regardless of whether any member actually sees, hears or otherwise enjoys the work so made available. Thus, we can see an act of deep linking constitutes infringement of copyright. But without deep linking, the internet as we know it today would collapse. One could not have a search engine, for example[788]. Hence these grey areas do need to be addressed.

5.7.2. Legal Issues involved in Linking

It is no surprise that the absolute "free linking" ethos of Berners-Lee[789] and other Internet pioneers have not been adopted by the law. The real business world operates differently than the world of academics, technology enthusiasts, and information-loving individuals. Businesses care about what information is shared, with whom, and in what context—especially when the communications involved interfere with their sales or marketing. They also care about how they are portrayed in relationship to others, especially competitors. Hence, in the context of business and advertising, Internet links may raise issues of, among other things, unfair competition, trademark or copyright infringement, tarnishment, and misappropriation[790].

The laws of unfair competition and intellectual property provide the backdrop for most hyperlink disputes. In particular, the law of unfair competition an umbrella

---

[788] Sableman Mark, Linking law Revisited : Internet Linking Law At Five Years, Berkely Technology Law Journal , Volume 16 (2001), Issue 16:3 (Fall 2001).See also US Ninth Circuit court of appeals decision in Leslie A V Arriba Soft corporation for the significance of search engine for internet. Available at http://www.philipsnizer.com/internetlib_subject.cfm?TopicID=36 visited on 20 Mar 2006

[789] Sir Timothy John Berners-Lee is an English developer and inventor of the World Wide Web in March 1989. With the help of Mike Sendall, Robert Cailliau, and a young student staff at CERN, he implemented his invention in 1990, with the first successful communication between a client and server via the Internet on December 25, 1990. He is also the director of the World Wide Web Consortium (which oversees its continued development), and a senior researcher and holder of the 3 com Founders Chair at the MIT Computer Science and Artificial Intelligence Laboratory (CSAIL).

[790] Sableman, Mark, Linking law Revisited : Internet Linking Law At Five Years, Berkely Technology Law Journal , Volume 16 (2001), Issue 16:3 (Fall 2001) at p 18

term that embraces trademark infringement and dilution, passing off, and false or deceptive advertising provides the legal context for many linking disputes. Several other legal areas— copyright, data protection, and misappropriation have figured in several important Internet linking disputes. This section briefly describes the basic principles of the legal fields on which most unauthorized linking claims are based[791].

5.7.3 Direct Linking

Link law began with a hyperlinked headline on an electronic newspaper in the Shetland Islands of Scotland. The ensuing copyright lawsuit between rival newspapers brought little enlightenment to the concept of links as copyright infringement. A few years later, a parallel lawsuit in California[792], concerning thumbnail photographs as links, brought the copyright theory of link law into sharper focus.

In Shetland Times Ltd., V Dr.Jonathan Wills and another[793], the plaintiff, the Shetland Times operated a web site through which it made available many of the items in the printed version of its newspaper. The defendant also owned a website and operated a web site on which they published a news reporting service. Defendants reproduced verbatim a number of headlines appearing in the Shetland Times. These headlines were hyperlinked to the plaintiff's site. Clicking on the headline took the reader to the internal pages in the plaintiff's site on which related story was found. The Judge agreed that the plaintiff had presented at least a prima facie case of copyright infringement based upon the United Kingdom's law governing cable television program providers. He found that the articles were being sent by the Shetland Times but through the web site maintained by the defendants.

---

[791] ibid at 19

[792] Kelly v. Arriba Soft Corp., 77 F. Supp. 2d 1116 (C.D. Cal. 1999), available at http://pub.bna.com/ptcj/99-560.htm, visited on 24 Jan 2006

[793] Cited in Legal Dimensions of Cyberspace (edt by S K Verma and Ram Mittal) , Indian Law Institute, New Delhi, (2004) at p 119

In the process, the home page of the Shetland Times site was bypassed, significantly diminishing the value of the site to potential advertisers. The court issued an interim interdict barring defendants, without the plaintiff consent, from copying headlines from the plaintiff's news paper on to their website, and creating hyperlinks from those headlines to the location on the plaintiff's site on which the article described in the headline appears.

A much different approach and answer to a similar question came with the decision of a California federal district court in Kelly v. Arriba Soft Corp[794] This case presented essentially the picture equivalent of the Shetland Times headline as hyperlink claim. The defendant, Arriba Soft, offered a specialized Internet search engine for photography on its website. On that site, Arriba Soft provided a traditional search engine with a photographic twist. As the court explained, like other Internet search engines, Arriba Soft's search engine: "allows a user to obtain a list of related Web content in response to a search query . . . . Unlike other Internet search engines, Defendant's retrieves images instead of descriptive text. It produces a list of reduced, 'thumbnail' pictures related to the user's query".[795]

Leslie Kelly, a professional photographer, offered his photographs for sale through an Internet website, and Arriba Soft indexed his site along with other professional photographers' sites. That meant that when searchers used Arriba Soft's "visual search engine" and the search results included Kelly's photographs, the images of those photos would be made available in thumbnail form on the search results page. The thumbnail images in turn linked to Kelly's own website, and hence potentially increased Kelly's business traffic. Kelly claimed in a similar way as the *Shetland Times* had claimed about use of its headlines—that use of his work in the thumbnail link constituted copyright infringement. The thumbnail images in question were, admittedly, copies of Kelly's photographs. The issue was thus posed: Did use of

---

[794] Kelly v. Arriba Soft Corp., 77 F. Supp. 2d 1116 (C.D. Cal. 1999). available at http://pub.bna.com/ptcj/99-560.htm, visited on 24 Jan 2006

[795] ibid

Kelly's photographs as thumbnail markers of links to Kelly's website constitute copyright infringement?[796]

The thumbnails presented a credible case of infringement. While a few words of a headline do not qualify alone as copyrightable material in United States law, the photo thumbnails were simply reduced versions of Kelly's copyrighted photographs. As such, the thumbnails contained all (or at least most) of the creative elements of the photos, such as subject, composition, lighting, and so forth. The only question was whether Arriba Soft's use of the photographs in its visual search engine constituted fair use under section 107 of the Copyright Act of US. Judge Gary Taylor analyzed each of the statutory fair use factors, as well as the "transformative use" factor, and found Arriba Soft's use to be fair[797].

Initially, Judge Taylor found that while Arriba Soft's search engine was commercial, the search engine's commercial purpose was "of a somewhat more incidental and less exploitative nature" than normal. Arriba Soft's website did not exist to exploit the visual impression of the indexed photographs; rather, it served a library like function, as it "cataloged and improved access to images on the Internet." Thus, the first fair use factor—focusing on the commercial or noncommercial use of the copyrighted work favored Arriba Soft. The second factor— the nature of the work favored Kelly, because photographs are artistic works at the core of copyright protection. On the third factor focusing on the amount and substantiality of the copyrighted work used— the court found the use of indexing thumbnails generally fair, because thumbnails are necessary on a visual search engine, and the size reduction mitigates any damage. Because Arriba Soft's search engine had also displayed a larger version of the indexed photographs (a practice it had eliminated by the time of the court's decision), however, the court found the "amount and substantiality" factor to favor Kelly somewhat. Finally, in considering the fourth fair use factor—the effect on the market for plaintiff's products the court found no evidence of harm, and a logical conclusion that the

---

[796] ibid
[797] ibid

search engine would increase traffic to the websites of professional photographers such as Kelly. Thus, the court found that this factor favored fair use[798].

With the fair use score a two-two tie, the Court relied on the "transformative use" analysis of Campbell v. Acuff-Rose Music, Inc[799], to make its final conclusion that Arriba Soft's use was fair. Essentially, the court recognized the usefulness of search engines and their contribution to users and web publishers (like Kelly) alike, and found that Arriba Soft's "visual search engine" had transformed Kelly's images into something new. The court held that the photo cataloging and thumbnail displaying functions of Arriba Soft's visual search engine, which "swept up" plaintiff's images along with two million other photographs in its ordinary operation, fulfilled an "inherently transformative" function. This transformative aspect of the visual search engine—"a new use and a new technology" weighed more heavily with the court than the fact that Arriba Soft copied the photographs. In essence, the usefulness of Internet search engines was the determinative factor in the fair use analysis in Kelly, leading to the court's conclusion that Arriba Soft could use thumbnail images of copyrighted works in its search results display[800].

Although the Kelly analysis could be questioned or confined to the unique facts of that case, the decision provides guidance for other copy-right linking cases. The decision wisely permits use of the content indexes and links that are typically used and needed in Internet searching and navigation. This result seems consistent with fair use principles, since the indexing material does not replace the full copyrighted works and it usually facilitates navigation to the owners of those works. It also accords with precedent, such as long established acceptance of catalogs, summaries, and reviews as fair use. If *Kelly* is followed when future linking claims based on copyright are asserted, the fair use doctrine is likely to protect normal indexing and summarizing use of Internet content as hyper-links[801].

---

[798] ibid
[799] 510 US 569 (1994), available at http://supct.law.cornell.edu/supct/html/92-1292.ZS.html, visited on 23 Jan 2006
[800] Supra Note 794
[801] Supra Note 794

5.7.4 Deep Linking

Perhaps the most curious of all anti-linking theories is the one that holds "deep linking" unlawful. While this theory seems to loom large in popular discussions, it does not yet have legal support in the United States, and courts have addressed the theory with skepticism[802].

Most websites have a central "home" page to which all subsidiary pages are linked. Website publishers probably expect users to visit their site through this home page "front door," and to move around the website using the website's own links to subsidiary pages. With this expectation, many website publishers post introductory material—possibly including third party paid banner advertisements, and special teasers and highlights relating to their own site on that home page. Website publishers expect that most website visitors will encounter those advertisements or special highlights before going further into the website's subsidiary pages[803].

In practice, however, anyone who reaches a subsidiary page may record the URL of that page and use it as a hyperlink, thus enabling others to bypass the website's front door and go to the subsidiary page of interest. Such links are known as "deep linking" because they link directly to a subsidiary page "deep" within a website. Is such linking unlawful? The Ticketmaster ticket selling agency asserted that such linking was unlawful in two highly publicized cases[804].

In Ticketmaster Corp V Microsoft Corp[805], the plaintiff, Ticketmaster Corporation sued Microsoft's practice of linking, without permission, deep within its site rather to the home page, and claimed, inter alia, that Microsoft effectively diverted advertising revenue that otherwise would have gone to the plaintiff. Ticketmaster Corporation had also entered into contract with other firms whereby those firms had agreed to pay link to the Ticketmaster site. Free linking by Microsoft to the

---

[802] Sableman Mark, Linking law Revisited : Internet Linking Law At Five Years, Berkely Technology Law Journal , Volume 16 (2001), Issue 16:3 (Fall 2001) at p 20

[803] ibid at p 21
[804] ibid
[805] Legal Dimensions of Cyberspace (edt by S K Verma and Ram Mittal) , Indian Law Institute, New Delhi, (2004) at p 119

plaintiff's site could have devalued those contractual relationships. Ticketmaster had also contracted to give MasterCard prominence at its site. Microsoft's bypassing of the home page threatened the ability of Ticketmaster to comply with that contract. Allowing such a free link undercut Ticketmaster's flexibility both in designing its site and in its marketing efforts and arrangements with other sites. During the pendency of the court proceedings the parties entered into a settlement agreement whereby Microsoft agreed not to link to pages deep within the Ticketmaster site and agreed that the links will point visitors interested in purchasing tickets to the ticketing service's home page[806].

Ticketmaster was back in court a few years later, when it learned that a rival agency, Tickets.Com, Inc., was also linking to Ticketmaster's subsidiary pages. In Ticketmaster Corp. v. Tickets.Com, Inc[807]., Ticketmaster claimed that deep linking constituted both copyright infringement (because the information derived from Ticketmaster's website) and unfair competition (because customers would associate Tickets.com with Ticketmaster). In a preliminary decision, the court explained that Tickets.com simply linked to Ticketmaster (or some other exclusive ticket broker) for events for which Tickets.com could not itself sell tickets[808]. Tickets.com provided its customers with a "Buy this ticket from another on-line ticketing company" link, which automatically transferred the customer to the relevant interior webpage of Ticketmaster, bypassing the home page. Since this interior page contained the Ticketmaster logo, the court concluded that a customer must know he or she was dealing with Ticketmaster, not Tickets.com. In granting, in part, Tickets.com's motion to dismiss the complaint, the court expressed strong skepticism about the deep linking theory[809].

First, the court expressly rejected the copyright theory. Ticketmaster alleged that Tickets.com copied facts and used a deep linking hyperlink. Facts are not protected

---

[806] ibid
[807] 54 U.S.P.Q.2d (BNA) 1344 (C.D. Cal. Mar. 27, 2000), available at http://pub.bna.com/ptcj/ticketmaster.htm, visited on 24 Apr 2006

[808] ibid
[809] ibid

by copyright, and the hyperlink simply transferred the user to the plaintiff's page. Next, although the court did not dismiss the unfair competition claims, it brushed off the possibility that merely posting a deep link could itself constitute unfair competition: "The court concludes that deep linking by itself (i.e., without confusion of source) does not necessarily involve unfair competition." Perhaps most significantly, in dicta the court analogized hyperlinks to traditional indexing techniques, thus suggesting that they are benign and indeed helpful, and thus hardly tortious. The court stated: "The customer is automatically transferred to the particular genuine webpage of the original author. There is no deception in what is happening. This is analogous to using a library's card index to get reference to particular items, albeit faster and more efficiently."[810]

From the above two cases the law of linking may seem to be confusing, but I am of the opinion that to protect the interest of cyberspace entities , especially their rights in copyright and trademark, deep linking should be prohibited and it should amount to circumvention when web sites deep link into others.

5.7.5 Framing & In-lining

Framing is a way of constructing a web page. The related practice of "framing" may also serve to undermine the rights of Web site owners. The use of "frames" allows a Web page creator to divide the Web browser window into several separate areas. The programmer of the Web page can dictate what goes into each frame. Commonly, a Web site designer creates a page that at all times displays one frame containing the name of the Web site and other identifying information. The other frames are then controlled by the user. For example, a Web site employing frames might always show the original Web site's graphic logo on the top of the page while allowing the user to view the other Web site in a different frame. The legal implications of this are complex. In the example just given, a Web surfer might easily be confused concerning the relationship between the actual site (victim) and

---

[810] ibid

the framing site. Moreover, the framing site might be unfairly deriving traffic from the actual site (victim) legally protected work[811].

In Washington Post Co., V Total News Inc[812]., the Washington Post filed a complaint against an online news site, Total News, the publisher of the web site www.totalnews.com. Total News, an aggregator of web news sources, employed frame technology to display news sites from around the web. Total News had created pages with frames that contained hyperlinks to other news web sites, such as Washington Post, CNN, USA Today etc. Web users, therefore, could use www.totalnews.com to access articles from various sources. The Total news web site generated its revenue from advertising, which it placed in a static border frame. Clicking hyperlink to 'Washington Post' within the Total News Web Page displayed the content of the Washington Post page within a frame that was surrounded by Total News' URL, logo, banner, advertisements and information. Plaintiff claimed that defendants' action of framing was the internet equivalent of pirating copyrighted material. They also alleged that misappropriation, trademark infringement and trademark dilution. The plaintiff complained that Total News has designed a parasitic web site that republishes the news and editorial content of others web sites in order to attract both advertisers and users resulting in infringement of their copyright. But the matter was finally settled out of court between the parties.

Under Indian Copyright Act, 1957, Sec.14 (a) (vi), the right of adaptation is conferred on the owner of the copyrighted work. The framing site could take some elements from the framed site's multimedia settings and create its own, thereby affecting the right of making a derivative work of the framed site since taking some elements from the multimedia setting and combining them with some other could well fit into the definition of adaptation. Hence, we can say that framing using internet technology infringes the rights of the creators.

---

[811] Ryder, Rodney, "Intellectual Property and the Internet", LexisNexis, New Delhi, (2002), at p 128
[812] No. 97 Civ. 1190 (PKL) (SDNY), available at
http://www.issuesininternetlaw.com/cases/washington.html, visited 23 Jan 2006

5.7.6 Caching

Caching involves the storing of Web pages either in a computer's local RAM (Random Access Memory), or at the server level. Caching web pages on a computer's local memory allows us to navigate back and forth through pages we have visited in the past without having to download the pages each time we return to them. Caching at the server level, also known as "proxy caching," is used by several of the more popular Internet service providers such as AOL (America on Line), Prodigy, and Compuserve[813]. This kind of caching may amount to copyright infringement. But it is impossible to have web page operations without caching and technically may not be feasible. Therefore there is a need to declare expressly that caching of web pages do not constitute copyright infringement[814].

5.8 Resolving Link Law Disputes – Some Principles

New technologies always lead to predictions of dire technological harm, and corresponding cries for new legal controls. It happened with the telegraph, the so-called "Victorian Internet" of the late nineteenth century. It happened with radio and television. It happened even quite recently with such benign technologies as the telephone and the facsimile.

Accordingly, we need focus on the early Internet link law cases, especially to the extent that they appear to restrict or prohibit use of Internet linking technologies without adequate policy justification. If the history of broadcasting is any guide, a new communications technology is most likely to blossom in the absence of strict regulation. Just as hard cases make bad law, cutting-edge cases, decided when a technology appears new and mysterious, can make questionable precedents. Moreover, the truism that courts many times reach the right result for the wrong

---

[813] Berkmen Center for Internet and Society, Harvard Law School, Intellectual Property in Cyberspace (2000), http://cyber.law.harvard.edu/property00/metatags/main.html, visited 23 Dec 2005

[814] However, Section 512(b) of DMCA limits the liability of service providers for the practice of retaining copies, for a limited time, of material that has been made available online by a person other than the provider, and then transmitted to a subscriber at his or her direction. The service provider retains the material so that subsequent requests for the same material can be fulfilled by transmitting the retained copy, rather than retrieving the material from the original source on the network.

reason is often borne out in novel situations, where judges must proceed to decision points without the comforting aid of many precedential pointers, or even a firm grip on the technology and how it may develop. In developing sound link law policies, we need to heed early link law cases, without being tied to all of their narrow conclusions.

Against this background, several principles for Internet linking controversies may be suggested:

(1) Recognize a presumptive right to make reference links:- HREF[815] links seem presumptively allowable in almost all situations. A hyperlink is, in one analyst's words, "an automated version of a scholarly footnote or bibliographic reference; it tells the reader where to find the referenced material." While such links were held actionable in the initial Shetland Times decision, that decision seems wrong as a matter of United States copyright law. It also appears unnecessary to vindicate the unfair competition interests that seemed to trouble the trial court. Where there is concern that a reference link threatens to confuse consumers or appropriate business opportunities, these perils can usually be avoided by adequate disclosures and non-deceptive practices by the linking party. A fair, adequate disclosure by the Shetland News that its link will take the reader to the Shetland Times website should have been sufficient in that case[816]. Fair disclosure still may not cover the losses that may happen due to linking.

Sometimes even reference hyperlinks may lead to liability. One may easily use a simple hyperlink to libel another, or to tarnish a trademark, for example, and hence there can be no immutable rule that hyperlinks are always allowable. The principle should simply be that a linkage itself is presumptively all right, and restrictions should be imposed only when the circumstances show a clear abuse that would be actionable in a non-Internet situation.

(2) Study actual consumer understandings and recognize web user intelligence and sophistication as appropriate:- Trademark and unfair competition laws focus on

---

[815] A hyperlink (often referred to as simply a link), is a reference or navigation element in a document to another section of the same document; available at www.en.wikipedia.org/wiki/Href ,visited on 3 Nov 2005

[816] Sableman Mark, Linking law Revisited : Internet Linking Law At Five Years, Berkely Technology Law Journal , Volume 16 (2001), Issue 16:3 (Fall 2001) at p 60

consumer understandings. Whether a particular use of a mark constitutes infringement depends on how consumers will react; specifically, whether they are likely to be confused. Even dilution laws, which protect trademarks beyond the area of "confusion," focus essentially on states of mind: whether use of a mark will "blur" or "tarnish" the image of the mark in the minds of the relevant consumers. False advertising and unfair competition law also depend on how consumers understand certain information put forth by one competitor about another. In such cases, consumer surveys are often needed to determine consumer perceptions and how consumers' overall knowledge and instincts interact with the advertising or statements at issue[817].

While the law's focus should be on actual consumer understandings, courts have become accustomed to assume at times that, at least in the general product marketplace, consumers do not use a terrible amount of thought or intelligence. The image of unthinking and simplistic consumer behavior is widespread, and goes back at least to Judge Learned Hand's observation that buyers tend to quickly glance at package labels without carefully studying them. Some of the key link law cases can be seen as hinging on somewhat paternalistic views of Internet users. The metatag cases that found infringement, for example, are premised on Internet users as being easily confused about sponsorship and associations.

Courts should not assume any particular level of sophistication of Internet users. Rather, they need to require litigants to develop specific evidence about the understandings and behavior of Internet users. Internet users may well turn out to be far more sophisticated and capable of understanding the significance of links than many courts have thus far credited. After all, they have the ability to turn on a computer and the daring to attempt to navigate the world's largest collection of information. Actual evidence of consumer understandings may be especially important in instances, such as framing and inlined links, where at present one can only speculate as to typical user perceptions. So far, although some litigants have

---

[817] Ficsor, Mihaly , The Law of Copyright and the Internet, Oxford University Press, New York, 2002, at p 359

attempted to survey Internet users, there is a paucity of empirical evidence regarding the psychology and understanding of Internet users[818].

(3) Recognizing the unique nature and value of information linking technologies:- Lawyers and judges live by the analytical tools of precedent and analogy, and where precedents are lacking, as in the case of new technologies, they rely on analogies. The Internet, for example, has been analogized to everything from a New England town meeting to a dance hall to a dark alley. So, not surprisingly, linking technologies have been analogized to various kinds of non-technological links and associations, including the familiar links, endorsements, and associations known to the law of unfair competition. While the term "link" suggests these analogies, they may not be the proper analogies. If indeed an Internet "link" is no more than an automated footnote or a digitized Dewey decimal reference, then the unfair competition analogy is not valid, and such an analogy inhibits sound analysis[819].

Internet linking technologies need to be examined afresh, without the prejudgment of forced analogies. In particular, courts need to examine the unique benefits and possibilities of these new technologies, as well as offenses alleged to have been committed with them. In such a "big picture" examination, perhaps even new terminology is needed. Professor Dan Burk has aptly characterized the issue in many link law disputes as that of "control over information referencing." Perhaps not surprisingly in view of this characterization of the issue, Professor Burk has suggested that "intellectual property law should optimally be interpreted so as to forestall future monopolization of information tagging systems." Whatever the ultimate policy—or, more likely, policies—relating to linking disputes, we will all be better served if courts undertake to understand and consider the overall potentialities and benefits of the technology under examination[820].

(4) Recognizing the right to create, use and exploit electronic searching of an open electronic network :- Just as telephone technology led to the telephone book, the Internet has caused the creation of search engines. As a practical matter, navigation of the web would be difficult or impossible without search engines. Yet just as

---

[818] ibid at p 361
[819] ibid at p 362
[820] ibid at p 363

telephone directories could conceivably be faulted as invasions of privacy, search engines and how they are used and exploited can be, and have been, faulted on numerous grounds. As we have seen, linking claims can arise from website owners' use of metatags to attract search engines, and from search engine operators' own sale of banner advertisements[821].

These acts of use and exploitation of electronic searching capabilities should not be viewed in isolation. The Internet is an electronic network, where electronic searching—and hence electronic tagging is necessary and expected. Because of the vastness of the Internet, and its decentralized openness allowing practically anyone to add new content, effective computer based search tools are needed. No one who enters into an open computer network ought to be surprised by the existence, capabilities or use of electronic searching. Nor should anyone, even one who remains outside the network, be shocked that words of trade and commerce, including trademarks, show up in Internet communications as targets and outputs of search engines. In other words, a web user's utilization of search technology should be no more suspicious than a sign painter's use of a paintbrush; what matters is not the technology but what is done with it. Mere search engine use of the trademarks of another—as metatag targets or banner advertisement prompts, for example should not be verboten any more than use of trademarks in labels, coupons, or comparative print advertisements. Abuses, if they occur, can always be distinguished and dealt with appropriately[822].

Just as media are treated more deferentially than other speakers, and just as common carriers like telephone companies are given immunity from content restrictions, courts may need to provide special protections for search engines. Certainly an automatically generated search engine list of links to illegal content should be treated differently than a list of links created by a party that deliberately seeks to direct traffic to the illegal sites. While this problem may be handled in part by the application of the traditional element of contributory infringement that requires knowledge by the alleged contributory infringer, it may be necessary to create a

---

[821] ibid at p 363
[822] ibid at p 364

search engine exemption or privilege in some situations. Courts already seem cognizant of the critical need for search engines, indexes, and links associated with such search tools[823].

(5) Use technology rather than law to close doors on any open network:- Where web publishers desire to control access to their otherwise unrestricted websites such as by prohibiting deep links legal barriers should not be the preferred method. Rather, web publishers should be expected to utilize all practical and available technological tools to achieve their objectives before they seek innovative legal rulings, which will inevitably carry broad effects[824].

Deep linking, for example, can be addressed with the help of technology by various means, including requiring password access, blocking requests or links except from certain pre-approved sites, use of dynamic (i.e., frequently changing) URLs for subsidiary pages. If web publishers use these rather than legal methods to control or restrict deep links, they can satisfy their objectives without causing distortions to the law or hardships or restrictions on the broad Internet community. The same principles ought to apply to problems be-sides deep linking as well[825].

(6) Study issues raised by framing or inlining, and encourage licensing where websites incorporate off-site materials:- Framing and inlining technologies raise more concerns than simple reference hyperlinks. Both techniques raise serious issues of the creation of derivative works under copyright law. In image inlining, when A takes B's copyrighted image and places it on A's website—perhaps as an integrated element of a composite design such as a collage—A seems to have adapted B's work and hence violated B's exclusive right to make derivative works. When A uses framing technology to frame portions of B's web content on A's website, the derivative work issue may arise, although one does not create a derivative work by putting a frame (e.g., a picture frame) around a copyrighted work[826].

---

[823] ibid
[824] ibid at p 365
[825] ibid
[826] ibid at p 366

The non-copyright issues arising from framing and inlining need more study. The Total News complaint artfully highlighted some serious potential legal concerns with framing, but due to the particular relative sizes of the litigants (major media companies against a small web pioneer) and the early settlement utilizing a linking license, these innovative theories never underwent real testing. In particular with respect to the unfair competition theories in such a case, the facts regarding consumer perceptions are all important. Do consumers believe when they view a framed site that the framed site is associated with the framing site? Or do viewers see a framed site for what it is, and easily navigate directly to the framed site when they so desire? Similarly the issues of advertising expectations and losses need factual development before we settle on legal policies for these situations[827].

(7) Consider Internet consequences in analyzing proposed legislation:- Just as the Shetland Times case foreshadowed linking disputes in the United States, foreign link law disputes continue to preview the kind of disputes and legal claims that may develop in the United States. Several recent European cases, for example, warn that we may see future deep linking claims based on database rights if the United States enacts database protection legislation similar to that in the European Union. For that the possibility of opening up more deep linking claims in connection with proposed legislation like database protection. As our society walks down the path of greater recognition of proprietary rights, it must take care that it does not in so doing unduly restrict useful tools and techniques like Internet linking[828].

(8) Maintain flexibility to permit adaptation to technological advances:- Laws must be adaptable to evolving technologies. The Internet is changing and evolving rapidly and consequently courts need to be careful not to promulgate doctrines narrowly tailored to today's technology, which may be gone tomorrow. HTML, today's "language of the web," may be replaced before long with eXtensible Markup Language ("XML"), a new computer language that could dramatically affect the way links operate, and which might empower both linker and linkee alike to deal more directly with the links of concern to them. Courts should be particularly

---

[827] ibid at p 366
[828] ibid at p 367

cautious about intervening in areas where new technology may empower private problem solving[829].

5.9 Digital Millennium Copyright Act (DMCA)

One of the earliest attempts made in the history of cyberspace to protect the interest of the copyright holders in the digital era can be traced to the enactment of DMCA by US. On October 12, 1998, the U.S. Congress passed the Digital Millennium Copyright Act (DMCA), ending many months of turbulent negotiations regarding its provisions. The Act is designed to implement the treaties signed in December 1996 at the World Intellectual Property Organization (WIPO) Geneva conference[830], but also contains additional provisions addressing related matters[831].

Some of the important features of the DMCA are as follows

a) Makes it a crime to circumvent anti-piracy measures built into most commercial software[832]

b) Outlaws the manufacture, sale, or distribution of code-cracking devices used to illegally copy software[833].

c) Does permit the cracking of copyright protection devices, however, to conduct encryption research, assess product interoperability, and test computer security systems[834].

---

[829] ibid at p 368

[830] WIPO has made two treaties for the protection of copyright holders - Two treaties were concluded in 1996 at the World Intellectual Property Organization (WIPO) in Geneva. One, the **WIPO Copyright Treaty (WCT)**, deals with protection for authors of literary and artistic works, such as writings and computer programs; original databases; musical works; audiovisual works; works of fine art and photographs. The other, the **WIPO Performances and Phonograms Treaty (WPPT)**, protects certain "related rights" (that is, rights related to copyright): in the WPPT, these are rights of performers and producers of phonograms.

[831] The UCLA Online Institute for Cyberspace Law and Policy, The Digital Millennium Copyright Act available at http://www.gseis.ucla.edu/iclp/dmca1.htm , visited 10 Jan 2005

[832] Sec.1201, Digital Millennium Copyright Act, 1998
[833] ibid
[834] Sec.1201(c)(1) , Digital Millennium Copyright Act, 1998 (Title I)

d) Provides exemptions from anti-circumvention provisions for nonprofit libraries, archives, and educational institutions under certain circumstances[835].

e) In general, limits Internet service providers from copyright infringement liability for simply transmitting information over the Internet[836].

f) Service providers, however, are expected to remove material from users' web sites that appears to constitute copyright infringement.

g) Limits liability of nonprofit institutions of higher education, when they serve as online service providers and under certain circumstances for copyright infringement by faculty members or graduate students[837].

h) Requires that "webcasters" pay licensing fees to record companies[838].

i) Requires that the Register of Copyrights, after consultation with relevant parties, submit to Congress recommendations regarding how to promote distance education through digital technologies while "maintaining an appropriate balance between the rights of copyright owners and the needs of users."[839]

j) States explicitly that "nothing in this section shall affect rights, remedies, limitations, or defenses to copyright infringement, including fair use..."

Digital networked environments pose particularly severe challenges for owners of intellectual property rights because digital networks make it so simple for members of the public to make multiple copies of those works and distribute them to whomever they choose at virtually no cost. Left unregulated, this activity would undermine the incentives of authors and publishers to invest in the creation and distribution of creative works, for the first distribution of a digital copy to the public

---

[835] Sec.1201(d), Digital Millennium Copyright Act, 1998 (Title I)

[836] Sec.1201(c)(2), Digital Millennium Copyright Act, 1998 (Title I)

[837] Sec 512 (e) Title II of Digital Millennium Copyright Act, 1998

[838] Title IV, Sec.112, Digital Millennium Copyright Act, 1998

[839] Title I, Sec.104, Digital Millennium Copyright Act, 1998

would enable those who receive it to set themselves up as alternative publishers of the work, able to undercut the first publisher's price because they need not recoup any development costs[840].

5.10 Trademarks and Domain Names in Cyberspace

A trademark is a name, word, symbol, or device used by a manufacturer of goods or a supplier of services to designate products sold and to distinguish them from goods or services sold by others. In the case of goods, the mark must be affixed to the goods, or to packaging or point of sales displays. In the case of services, the mark must be used so as to designate the services, usually in advertising referring to the services.

The problem with trademarks on the Internet often is whether trademark use has occurred or not. In the "real" world, we can slap a label on a product or put a sign on a building, but in the on-line context, the use of the trademark may be as ephemeral as a momentary appearance on a computer screen[841].

In Playboy Enterprises v. Frena[842],839 F Supp 1552 (MD Fla 1993), the court found trademark infringement when a subscription computer bulletin board owner distributed Playboy photographs owned by Playboy Enterprises, Inc., that contained the "PLAYBOY" and "PLAYMATE" trademarks. The court also found unfair competition and violation of trademark law based upon the bulletin board owner obliterating some Playboy trademarks and putting its advertisement on Playboy photographs. The court found that these acts of the defendant made it appear that Playboy had authorized use of the photographs on the bulletin board[843].

---

[840] Samuelson ,Pamela, "Legally Speaking: The NII Intellectual Property Report", available at http://www.eff.org/IP/?f=ipwg_nii_ip_report_samuelson.comments.txt , visited on 21 Dec 2005
[841] Jere M. Webb ,Trademarks, Cyberspace, and the Internet, available at http://www.gseis.ucla.edu/iclp/jmwebb.html , visited on 7 Jul 05.

[842] The Internet Law Page, Playboy v Frena available at http://floridalawfirm.com/iplaw/playb2.html
[843] ibid

Similarly, in Sega Enterprises, Ltd. v. Maphia[844], 857 F Supp 679 (ND Cal 1994), the court enjoined a computer bulletin board owner, based on copyright and trademark infringement, from uploading and downloading unauthorized copies of Sega's video games. Sega's trademarks appeared on the copied games and on file descriptions on the bulletin board[845].

The expanded usage of the Internet for commercial purposes has resulted in greater importance and significance of name recognition on the Internet. An identifying address on the Internet, the "domain name", creates an expectation about who and what is located at that address. Because a domain name may suggest identity, quality and content, it may be closely related to or function as a trademark[846]. A domain name is the human friendly address of a computer that is usually in a form easy to remember or identify – www.abc.com.

The Internet domain name registration policy of first come/first served has resulted in hundreds of controversies surrounding ownership of a particular name , including a number of well-known instances where individuals have registered names based on a corporation's trademark or where corporations have registered names based upon a competitor's trademark[847].

Controversy and confusion result especially where well-known trademarks have been registered by unrelated third parties for the purpose of re-selling them to the rightful owner or using them for their own purposes. This has been come to known as "Cybersquatting". That is, deliberate registration of trade names or trademarks of another company or individual in bad faith.

Panavision International V Deniss Toeppen[848] , a case filed in United States of America, is a classical case of cybersquatting. When Panavision , the owner of

---

[844] David Loundy's E-law, Available at http://www.loundy.com/CASES/Sega_v_MAPHIA.html
[845] ibid
[846] Rich L Lylod , "Trademark Protection in Cyberspace", http://www.publaw.com/cyber.html visited on 9 Jul 2005
[847] ibid
[848] Cited in Rawell Sanjiv and Kudrolli Shakeel, "Legal Issues in E-commerce", Management Review, (Sep 2000) . See also Findlaw, available at http://laws.lp.findlaw.com/9th/9755467.html

several federally registered trade mark including 'Panavision' attempted to establish a website under its own name, it discovered that Toeppen had registered 'panavision.com' as its domain name. Therefore, the company was unable to register and use its trademark as an internet domain. When Panavision notified Toeppen, he demanded $13,000 to discontinue his use of the domain name. Panavision refused Toeppen's demand and filed an action for infringement. The court granted an injunction order restraining Toeppen from using 'panavision' for business purposes and further directed him to transfer the domain name to Panavision International.

In India too, there have been two reported cases of domain name/trademark disputes so far . In the case of Yahoo Inc V Akash Arora[849] , the Delhi High Court protected the international reputation of Yahoo and restrained Arora from using 'Yahooindia.com'. The Mumbai High Court went a step further and in the case of Rediff Communication V Cyber Booth[850], held that a domain name is a valuable corporate asset requiring protection.

In India, we do not have a specific legislation which prevents cybersquatting as in US, where cybersquatting is regulated by Anti-cybersquatting Consumer Protection Act, 1999. But the definition of "mark" and "trademark" given by Trademarks Act, 1999 under Sec.2 (1) (m) and Sec.2 (1) (z) are wide enough to cover the issues of domain name. It may be noted that a "mark" is used, rightly or wrongly, if it is used in printed or other visual representation as per Se.2 (2) (b). It can not be doubted that a domain name corresponding a mark is definitely used both in the printed form (electronic form) and by the visual representation. Thus, the provisions of the Trademark Act, 1999 can be safely invoked to fix the liability in cases involving domain names.

---

[849] 1999 PTC 201
[850] 2000 PTC 209

5.10.1 Metatags – Use of Indexing Words

Meta tag misuse may generate less obvious but equally serious problems to trademark holders. Web sites are written in the HTML (Hyper Text Markup Language) language. This language is nothing more than a list of "tags" that can be used to format and arrange text, images, and other multimedia files. "Meta tags" are tags that have no *visible* effect on the Web page. Instead, they exist in the source code for a Web page to assist search engines (for example Google search engine) in ascertaining the content of the page. Problems arise when companies include in their own Web sites Metatags containing the names or descriptions of other companies. Suppose, for example, that Coca Cola used the keyword "Pepsi" in its Metatags. Web surfers who used search engines to obtain information about "Pepsi" would then be directed to Coca Cola's Web site[851].

5.11 ICANN and UDRP

Internet Corporation on Assigned Names and Numbers (ICANN) has taken up the responsibility of resolving domain name disputes. The ICANN's domain name resolution policy has sought to address the issue of cybersquatting through a mechanism of online arbitration. The World Intellectual Property Organization's (WIPO) Arbitration center has passed orders in more than a hundred cases directing cybersquatters to transfer the disputed domain names to their true owners. Bennet and coleman was the first in India to have got back its trademarks and the well known names "thetimesoindia.com" and the "theeconomictimes.com" from the cybersquatters. It may be noted here that the online dispute resolution mechanism is limited in its scope to cybersquatting.

---

[851] Berkmen Center for Internet and Society, Harvard Law School, Intellectual Property in Cyberspace (2000), http://cyber.law.harvard.edu/property00/metatags/main.html, visited 10 Jan 2005

Uniform Domain Name Resolution Policy[852] (UDRP) has laid down three substantive conditions which define what the complainant must show in case cybersquatiing;

(1) The domain name must be identical or confusingly similar to a trade mark in which the complainant has rights;

(2) The respondent must have rights or legitimate interest in the domain name; and

(3) The domain name must have been registered and be used in bad faith

While these principles are a reflection of a shared approach in most legal systems to deliberately wrongful misrepresentation of indications of source, it does not follow the precise rules of any one legal system. Fundamentally that is because the comparison which has to be made is in essence different. In a dispute over the use of trade marks or names, the claimant is usually concerned to show misrepresentation relating to the defendant's use of the mark on the same or similar goods or services. But a domain name is not tied to trade in anything in particular or indeed to any obligation to use it.

The boldest cyber-squatters offer no apology for acquiring the domain name simply in order to sell it to the enterprise or person whose name is being taken in vain. Others may offer an excuse from a range of ingenious justifications. Deciding how far these must be treated as genuine is a recurrent reason how UDRP adjudication can be far from straightforward[853].

First, the claimant's right to a mark and confusion with it. It is accepted that the right may arise through protection of a trading reputation as well as by registration. But a panel may look carefully at claims where the mark is, for instance, descriptive. Evidence for this, which complainant may be unwilling to reveal, may

---

[852] See Internet Corporation for Assigned Names and Numbers for complete document, available at http://www.icann.org/udrp/udrp.htm , visited 20 Jan 2005
[853] Cornish William and Llewelyn David, Intellectual Property: Patents, Copyright, trademarks and Allied Rights, 5th Edition, Sweet and Maxwell, London, 2003

appear from the fact that applications to register the mark have not been made or not progressing. The claimant may succeed where a case of unfair competition or passing off can be shown to exist, for example, from unfair competition or passing off can be shown to exist, for example, from long established or heavily advertised trade or other activity. It is over such matters that the scheme is at its most eclectic: the result is supra-national body of precedent which is rapidly burgeoning[854].

It is also accepted that such "common law rights" may be those of celebrities, such as pop stars, authors and sportsmen, since they will at least have rights in the primary goods or services which they are involved in offering. It is sometimes said that this goes further than, for instance, English law, which has been reluctant to protect a celebrity's ability to endorse the goods or services of others. But that is to forget that a domain name is not tied to the making and marking of particular goods and services. Most of the celebrities who have succeeded under the UDRP have a "trade" connection with the primary goods (books, records, films) or services (signing, modeling, footballing) which make them famous. Whether the same can be said of municipal authorities or other public bodies which claim rights in the name of their town or region is much more questionable, even if they hold a mark registration. One issue is who should b allowed to succeed (particularly in securing a transfer of the domain name) when there are several potential complainants[855].

As to probability of confusion, the global character of the Internet poses various problems. Who are the public who are likely to be confused by a domain name? It has been held to be any group of substantial size within a country as well as a region or language group. The issue has arisen particularly over "gripe sites" for airing complaints about well-known enterprises and individuals. Any American knows that "walmartsucks.com" is unlikely to lead to an official Walmart site, but will Greeks, Ethiopians or Phillippinos?[856]

---

[854] ibid at p 818
[855] ibid at p 819
[856] ibid

Secondly, a right or legitimate interest of the respondent in the name. The UDRP states that the respondent can make this out by showing (i) that he has used the domain name, or made genuine preparations to use it, for a genuine website; (ii) that he or it is commonly known by the name; or (iii) that he is making a legitimate non-commercial or fair use of the domain name, without intent, for commercial gain, to divert Internet users or tarnish the complainant's mark. Justifications under one or other of these heads play prominent parts in contested UDRP cases, but they need to be more than unsupported assertions. Some of the submissions are dismissed as disingenuous or fantastic. This may well be the fate of assertions that the name is the nickname of the respondent or a family member, or is the name of some event, individual or character associated somehow with them. The same may happen when a claim to be running a business is not shown to have any substance[857].

Where the respondent asserts an intention to set up a site commenting on the complainant by way either of adulation (a fan club) or of criticism (a commercial gripe site, political opposition), it is particularly important to recognize any genuine claim to freedom of expression, given its status as a human right. Claims of that kind deserve very careful attention. They can scarcely be sustained where a respondent has collected an array of domain names, which he is offering to be targeted enterprises in order to save them from the domain falling into the hands of someone else that might actually set up a site for spoofs, parodies, complaints, exposes or denunciations[858].

Thirdly, bad faith both in registering and using the name. Here the policy makes explicit that "use" has a broad meaning. It covers situations where (i) the domain name has been obtained primarily for the purpose of selling it to the complainant or a competitor for a sum exceeding out-of-pocket costs; (ii) where the registration is in order to prevent the complainant from reflecting its mark in that domain name or to disrupt its business; and (iii) where it was registered in order to try to divert

---

[857] ibid at p 820
[858] ibid

271

Internet users to the respondent's website by creating a likelihood of confusion. Each of these types of use has in turn been read inclusively. Under (i) advertising the domain as being for sale on an auction website can satisfy the condition. Under (ii) it is not necessary to show that the complainant has been deprived of all possible domains. Evidence that it has appropriated many of them merely reinforces the proof of mala fides[859].

Under (iii) there is a difficult question: when, in the process of discovering a website, then clicking on to it and scrolling its pages, can sufficient probability of confusion be said to arise? A search engine looking for the main word in the gTLD may produce a great splay of sites. Internet users soon learn that many of them will not be an "official" site. Their true nature will generally be clear from the home page at the site itself, or sometimes only by moving further into the site. If users are led by the name to what turns out to be a comment site which is judged to be a legitimate outlet for opinion, this cannot be a bad faith holding of the name. On the other hand, if the site proves to be a sales outlet for other goods than the complainant's, the temporary uncertainty between finding the site and perusing it is likely to be treated as showing bad faith. Here too there are uncertainties and inconsistencies at work[860].

UDRP jurisdiction has been heavily used in its early years: WIPO alone has handled some 20,000 cases in just over three years. Across the world established businesses have readily accepted the results. Of a handful of critical analyses, some raise issues of real concern particularly that some panelists have been unduly ready, either to accept the complainant's account of the situation or to stretch the terms of the policy beyond any acceptable limits. It is true that the only means of questioning a decision is to bring proceedings in an appropriate national court, and that has happened only on a handful of occasions. The phenomenon of "reverse high jacking" has been acknowledged as a hazard: inevitably some complaints will

---

[859] ibid at p 821
[860] ibid

272

turn out to be illegitimate attempts, based on fabricated evidence or wholly unjustified assertions, to oblige domain holders to pay up or suffer transfer. Panels have been given power to declare against a complainant. Respondents rarely seek to have them exercise their powers and much more rarely still is a finding against a complainant successful[861].

On balance, however, the confidence which the policy has generated seems justified. The jurisdiction deserves comparison with the other "internal" solution to disputes which the Internet is generating: the Notice and Take Down procedures for controlling improper content on the Internet by requiring site closure or changes through the intervention of the Host Service Provider. In the US at least this is proving one method of mass action against copyright and other infringement which is affecting the balance of power between right-owners and their opponents. It too is capable of over-enthusiastic application: for instance where a site is closed down even through it makes legitimate material available as well as material that infringes copyright (or is defamatory or pornographic, etc)[862].

The two schemes use the Internet to police its operation, with effects for the system across the globe. Both open prospects of mass action which cannot be expected of litigation through national court systems. They affect very different sorts of Internet operator: Notice and Take Down is typically aimed at free sharing: the P2P site which provides access to music, films and the like without having to pay the right-owner's subscription to an authorized service. The root intention is not to make money (though that may become an indirect motivation). Many free sharers find it simplest to submit to the take down and to set up again under a new name. The domain name appropriator, on the other hand, is in the business of selling particular names and will have no chance of regaining his asset if it is transferred away to a person entitled to object to a bad faith operation. That is why the UDRP and like jurisdictions are in practice so much more contentious and why the need to oversee

---

[861] ibid at p 822
[862] ibid

the fairness of the adjudicative process will remain important as long as this form of name squatting persists[863].

5.12 Patent Misuse in Cyberspace

Internet is software driven. Software enables the networking of computers and the actual transmission of data. Controversy as to whether computer software should be protected under copyright law or patent law is not yet resolved and still remains as an elusive concept for intellectual property lawyer.

Patents are granted to inventions which are new, novel and useful[864]. Traditionally, patents have been associated with more industrial or scientific innovations, such as machinery, manufacturing process, computer chips and pharmaceuticals. A patent grants its owner the right to exclude others from making, using, selling, or offering to sell the patented invention. However, as technology changes, so do the patent laws available to protect it.

Two important issues concerned with patents and have created controversy over the cyberspace are software patents and business method patents. Sec.3 (k) of the Indian Patent Act, 1970 expressly excludes patenting of business methods and computer programs per se from the subject matter of patentability. Hence in India patents are not available to computer programs per se and business methods either in the real word or in the cyberspace. But countries like United States of America and Japan have already started granting patents for business methods and granting patents for computer software has become well established practice in these countries.

---

[863] ibid
[864] Art.27.1, WTO Agreement on trade Related Aspects of Intellectual property Rights- patents shall be available for nay inventions, whether products or processes, in all fields of technology, provided they are new , involve an inventive step and are capable of industrial applications.

In Amazon.com V Barnesandnoble[865], Amazon.com filed a patent application with USPTO (United States Patent and Trademark Office) for a business method; "Method and system for placing a purchase order via a communications network". In its patent application, Amazon.com claimed as its invention a business methodology for placing an order, whereby in response to only a single action performed by a consumer (such as click of a mouse), a requested item may be ordered. Additional information necessary to complete the order, such as credit card number and shipping address, is obtained from information previously received from the consumer and stored in a database by the vendor. This patent was dubbed as "1-click" patent because users of the invention need click only once with the mouse on a hyperlink to complete the purchase of an item. When BarnesandNobel, followed the same method for its operations, the court granted interim injunction and restrained the BarnesandNobel from using the "1-click" method of operation[866].

Some commentators have criticized the "1-click" patent as an example of a patent system gone astray. These critics contend that the patent system has been stretched too far with the allowance of business method[867] patents, and that even if business methods are worthy of patent protection, the US patent and Trademark Office is not equipped to handle the examination of patent applications for this type of innovation. At the same time, others herald the patenting of business methods as a natural progression in an ever changing technology driven world. As it so often happens, the truth probably lies somewhere between[868].

Regardless, few will dispute that business method patents, as well as software patents in general, are having a profound impact on how software and internet companies are conducting business. Technology companies that just a few years go

---

[865] U.S. Federal Circuit Court of Appeals, Findlaw, available at http://laws.findlaw.com/fed/001109.html , visited 21 Jan 2005

[866] Isenbourg Doug, "The Giga Law, Guide to Internet Law", Random House Trade Paperback Edition, New York,(2002)
[867] Sec.3(k) of the Patent act, 1970 excludes patenting of business methods in India.
[868] Isenbourg Doug, "The Giga Law, Guide to Internet Law", Random House Trade Paperback Edition, New York, (2002) at p112

would not have ever considered the impact of patent protection – either offensively or defensively- are now devoting many resources to ensuring they are protected , and minimizing the possibility of infringing third party patent rights[869].

5.13 Conclusion

Information and Communication Technologies gives rise to a variety of legal problems. The problems themselves are not novel in their character. But they deserve special treatment, because of the environment in which they take their birth and the nature of the machinery used in the environment and the means employed for recording the information in question.

The digital dilemma is that the information technology that is making more current information available more quickly and completely also has the potential to demolish the balancing of public good and private interest that has emerged from the evolution of intellectual property law.

The relationship of copyright to new technologies that exploit copyrighted works is often perceived to pit copyright against progress. Historically, when copyright owners seek to eliminate a new kind of dissemination, and when courts do not deem that dissemination harmful to copyright owners, courts decline to find infringement. However, when owners seek instead to participate in and be paid for the new modes of exploitation, the courts, and law making bodies, appear more favourable to copyright control over that new market. Today, the courts and the legislatures regard the unlicensed distribution of works over the internet as impairing copyright owners; ability to avail themselves of new markets for digital communication of works; they accord control over those markets to copyright owners in order to promote wide dissemination. Copyright control by authors, particularly those excluded by traditional intermediary-controlled distribution

---

[869] ibid at p113

systems, may offer the public an increased quantity and variety of works of authorship[870].

Legal, economic and public policy research should be undertaken to determine the extent to which intellectual property rights have to be protected in cyberspace. Appropriate modifications in existing intellectual property law have to be made and if necessary new legislations must be enacted to meet the challenges posed by this new technology. Internet being a borderless medium is responsible for the 'death of distance'[871] among nations which has created international jurisdictional problems, international conventions/treaties seem to be more appropriate to protect and promote the interest of the cyberspace entities.

---

[870] Ginsburg c Jane, Copyright and Control over New Technologies of Dissemination, Columbia Law Review, Vol.101, N0.7 (Nov.2001), p 1613-1647
[871] Cairncross Frances, Death Of Distance, Harvard Business Review Publications, 1997

Chapter 6

JURISDICTION

The Internet has no territorial boundaries. To paraphrase Gertrude Stein, as far as the Internet is concerned, not only is there perhaps 'no there there,' the 'there' is everywhere where there is Internet access.

Nancy Gertner[872]

6.1 Introduction

Enforcement of human rights of cyberspace entities is crucial and without enforcement mechanism the exercise of human rights in cyberspace becomes meaningless. The question to be asked of any law or regulation that purports to govern activity on the Internet is not whether it is applicable, but rather whether it is enforceable? Though it may be vogue to call for regulation, the primary question that should govern whether or how a regulation should be framed is not whether it is applicable- it will almost certainly be so. The question must be whether the regulation is needed, and if so, whether it is enforceable in a coherent and satisfactory manner that satisfactory mechanism yields fruits. If regulations are not needed or do not prove to be enforceable due to the jurisdictional or substantive issues then there is a threat that users of the internet will hold them in contempt[873].

This distinction between applicability and enforceability is fundamental to the future development of Internet law. It is a comparatively easy task for a legislator to draft a law which applies to a particular activity undertaken via the Internet, but much more difficult to frame the law so that it is enforceable in practice. Laws which are unenforceable have two major defects; not only do they fail to deal with the

---

[872] Judge who delivered the judgment in Digital Equipment Corp. v. Altavista Technology, Inc., 1997 , 960 F. Supp. 456, 462 (D. Mass. 1997), available at
http://www.techlawjournal.com/courts/drudge/80423opin.htm , visited on 12 Dec 2003
[873] Lars Davies, A Model for Internet Regulation?- Constructing a Framework for Regulating Electronic Commerce, Society for Computers and Law, London, 1999, available at www.scl.org ,visited on 1 Jun 2003

mischief which the law seeks to remedy, but the knowledge that they are unenforceable weakens the normative force of other laws[874].

In relation to the enforceability of law and regulations, it is important to recognize that compliance with law is not solely dependent on that law's enforcement through the courts. In the vast majority of the instances, the law is complied with because of its normative force, that is, because it is law[875]. Thus most citizens refrain from criminal behaviour because they wish to act lawfully, not because of a fear of prosecution and similarly private law matters such as contracts, the parties adhere to their bargains because that is what they have agreed. However, the ultimate enforceability of a law is important if it is to have normative force. For this reason, a system of law regulation, which is so contradictory that it is in practical terms, impossible to obey is treated here as unenforceable. Because it is impossible or excessively burdensome to act in accordance with the law it loses normative force and ceases to be treated by citizens and businesses as binding on them.

The first problem one would face in enforcement of his right is in relation to jurisdiction of courts and the applicability of procedural and substantive law for the dispute to be resolved. Cyberspace having multijurisdcitionality as its main feature poses several challenges to legal community for the enforcement of basic rights. Interestingly it is human rights issues involving free speech in Yahoo! France case and defamation in Gutnick case highlighted the jurisdictional problems created by cyberspace activities.

6.2 Jurisdiction

Jurisdiction refers to the power of a state to govern persons, property and situations. A number of different categories and types of jurisdiction should be identified from the outset. It is necessary to distinguish between prescriptive jurisdiction, which

---

[874] Reed Chris, Internet Law- Text and Materials, 2nd Edition, Universal Law Publishing Co.,Delhi,2004
[875] Kelsen , Hans, Pure Theory of law, 2nd Edition, Unviversity of California, Berkeley, 1967, at pp 35-47

indicates the power to prescribe rules, and enforcement jurisdiction, which refers to the power to enforce rules.

International law concerns itself with the propriety of the exercise of jurisdiction. Jurisdiction has primarily and historically been exercised on a territorial basis, but there are occasions when states exercise jurisdiction over people or things outside their own territory. Governmental power gave rise to three types of jurisdiction: prescriptive jurisdiction, adjudicative jurisdiction and enforcement jurisdiction[876]. Prescriptive jurisdiction is the power to apply legal norms to conduct; adjudicative jurisdiction is the power of tribunals to resolve disputes; and enforcement jurisdiction is the power of the jurisdiction to enforce[877].

In addition to jurisdiction exercised on a territorial basis there are a number of other relevant principles, which have been identified, and which have received varying degrees of international acceptance. The commentary on the Harvard Research Draft Convention on Jurisdiction with respect to Crime in 1935 identified five general heads of jurisdiction, namely:

(a) The territorial principle

(b) The passive personality principle

(c) The nationality principle

(d) The protective principle ; and

(e) The universality principle

The heads of traditional jurisdiction may be briefly defined as follows;

(a) **Territorial principle**: The ability of a state to exercise jurisdiction over actions, events and things within its territory is an essential attribute of sovereignty and the territorial principle has received universal recognition. According to this principle, events occurring within a state's territorial boundaries and persons within that territory, albeit temporarily, are subject to local laws and the jurisdiction of the local

---

[876] Perritt H Henry, Jr, Jurisdiction and the Internet: Basic Anglo/American Perspectives, Internet Law Forum, July 26, 1999, available at http://www.ilpf.org/confer/present99/perrittpr.htm , visited on Feb 26, 2002
[877] ibid

courts. The principle has practical advantages in terms of availability of witnesses[878].

(b) **Passive Personality**: Under this principle, jurisdiction is claimed on the basis of the nationality of the actual or potential victim. In other words, a state may assert jurisdiction over activities which, although committed abroad by foreign nationals, have affected or will affect nationals of that state[879].

(c) **Nationality Principle**: Most civil law system claim a wide jurisdiction to punish crimes committed by their nationals, even on the territory of a foreign state. Those states which make little use of the nationality principle do not appear to protest about its use elsewhere. Although a state may not enforce its laws within the territory of another state, it can punish crimes committed by nationals extra-territorially when the offender returns within the jurisdiction. Jurisdiction based on nationality is less usual in common law countries, although there may be exceptions with regard to serious offences[880].

(d) **Protective or security Principle**: Under this principle, a state can claim jurisdiction over offences committed outside its territory, which are considered injurious to its security, integrity or vital economic interests. The principle remains ill defined and there are uncertainties about how far it can extend. There remains a considerable danger of abuse. Nevertheless, a large number of states have used the principle to a greater or lesser extent. Generally speaking the protective personality principle is most often used in cases involving currency, immigration and economic offences[881].

(e) **Universality Principle**: It has been seen that so far all the bases of jurisdiction have in some way involved a connection with the state asserting jurisdiction; events

---

[878] Brian Fitzgerald and Anne Fitzgerald, Cyberlaw- Cases and Materials on the Internet, Digital Intellectual Property and Electronic Commerce, LexisNexis, Butterworths,, Australia, 2002 at p 121
[879] ibid at p 122
[880] ibid
[881] ibid

have taken place within the territory of the jurisdictional state or they have been committed by or against nationals or in some other way impinge on the interests of the state claiming jurisdiction. International law further recognizes that where an offence is contrary to the interests of the international community, all states have jurisdiction irrespective of the nationality of the victim and perpetrator and the location of the offence. The rationale behind the universality principle is that repression of certain types of crime is a matter of international public policy[882]. Human rights being universal rights, their violations in cyberspace would be contrary to the interests of the international community.

The non-geographic character of the net makes it very difficult to apply current, territorially based rules to activities online[883]. Sovereign countries may have monopoly on the lawful use of physical force but they cannot control online actions whose physical location is irrelevant or cannot even be established. Majority Jurisdictional issues that have been raised are related to legal disputes in the areas of trademarks, domain names, defamation, free speech, copyright etc.

6.2.1 Personal Jurisdiction, Multimedia and Broadcasting

In evaluating the ability to obtain personal jurisdiction over a defendant due to operation of a Web site, a parallel can be drawn to print publications. Print publications, like Web sites, come into contact with several jurisdictions, based on conduct that occurs primarily in one location. Print publications are created by conduct concentrated at the location of the author and publisher. The activity creating a Web site occurs in the state in which the Web site is developed, and the location of the Web server. However, like a broadly distributed magazine or broadcast, a Web site is accessible everywhere[884].

---

[882] ibid
[883] David R Johnson and David G Post, Law And Borders-Rise of Law in Cyberspace, 48 Stanford Law Review 1367 (1996)
[884] Warren E. Agin of Swiggart & Agin, L.L.C., Coping with Personal Jurisdiction in Cyberspace ABA Subcommittee on Internet Law Liability Report #3, available at http://library.findlaw.com/2000/Dec/20/126993.html, visited on 5 Mar 2005

The United States Supreme Court has held that a state can exercise personal jurisdiction over a publisher accused of publishing libelous material about a resident of that state when the publisher targets its economic activity at that state. In Keeton v. Hustler Magazine, Inc[885] the United States District Court for the District of New Hampshire was able to exercise personal jurisdiction over an Ohio corporation because the defendant's magazine circulation in the state of New Hampshire created minimum contacts with that state. Jurisdiction was appropriate because of the State's interest in discouraging libel by the defendant against its citizens[886].

In a companion case, Calder v. Jones[887], the Supreme Court held that a California court could exercise personal jurisdiction against an author and editor, both resident in Florida, who had libeled a California resident in an article published in the National Enquirer newspaper. The court determined that the defendants had purposefully targeted their libelous activity at California by publishing their article containing libelous material about a California resident in a magazine which they knew was sold and circulated in California and "must reasonably anticipate being haled into court" in California[888].

In these cases, the tortious act is the knowing publication in the state attempting to exercise personal jurisdiction over the defendant. The results differ if the tortious act is unrelated to the act of publication. If, instead of publishing an article in a magazine or newspaper circulated in the forum state, the defendant submits advertising to a nationally circulated magazine or newspaper, the fact of that advertising is generally not sufficient to create jurisdiction, unless the claim arises from the advertising. For example, in IDS Life Insurance Company v. SunAmerica,

---

[885] Keeton v. Hustler Magazine, Inc., 465 U.S. 770, 104 S. Ct. 1473 (1984), available at http://caselaw.lp.findlaw.com/scripts/getcase.pl?court=US&vol=465&invol=770, visited on 23 Feb 2003
[886] ibid
[887] Calder v. Jones, 465 U.S. 783, 104 S. Ct. 1482 (1984) available at http://caselaw.lp.findlaw.com/scripts/getcase.pl?navby=search&court=US&case=/us/465/783.html, visited on 20 May 2004
[888] ibid

Inc[889], the defendant advertised in nationally circulated newspapers and magazines and on national television, and maintained an Internet Web site. The District Court for the Northern District of Illinois held that such advertising did not involve systematic and continuous contact with the forum state, Illinois, and concluded that it did not have personal jurisdiction over the defendant[890]. In another case, Gaingolo v. Walt Disney World Co[891], a district court judge noted that allowing national advertising to make a defendant subject to suit wherever the advertisement appeared would "substantially undermine the law of personal jurisdiction[892]."

6.3 Evolution of Internet Jurisdiction – Case Law Development

While Internet jurisdiction creates significant challenges, courts have not enjoyed the luxury of considering the issue from an abstract, theoretical perspective. Since 1996, courts in the United States have regularly faced litigation that includes an Internet jurisdiction component. As courts grapple with the issue, the jurisprudence has shifted first toward the Zippo passive versus active test, then more recently towards an effects based test with elements of targeting analysis[893].

In International Shoe Co. v. Washington, the US Supreme Court outlined the contemporary basis for jurisdiction[894]. In this case the Court held that, a court could exercise personal jurisdiction over a nonresident defendant if that defendant has "certain minimum contacts with [the forum] such that the maintenance of the suit does not offend 'traditional notions of fair play and substantial justice.'[895] The minimum contacts standard serves two purposes: protecting defendants from

---

[889] DS Life Insurance Company v. SunAmerica, Inc., 958 F. Supp. 1258 (N.D. Ill. 1997), available at http://laws.findlaw.com , visited on 2 Mar 2003
[890] The court stated, in reaching its decision that "It cannot plausibly be argued that any defendant who advertises nationally could expect to be haled into court in any state, for a cause of action that does not relate to the advertisements."
[891] Gaingolo v. Walt Disney World Co., 753 F. Supp. 148 (D.N.J. 1990), available at http://laws.findlaw.com, visited on 2 Mar 2003
[892] ibid
[893] Geist ,A Michael, Is There A There There? Toward Greater Certainty For Internet Jurisdiction, Berkeley Technology Law Journal, Vol.16, Issue 16:3, Fall 2001
[894] 326 U.S. 310, 316 (1945) available at http://lwas.findlaw.com/us/326/310.html, visited on 15 May 2003
[895] ibid

burdensome litigation and ensuring that states do not reach too far beyond their jurisdictional limits[896].

Minimum contacts have been defined as "conduct and connection with the forum . . . such that the defendant should reasonably anticipate being haled into court there."[897]   A defendant's contacts are sufficient to satisfy the minimum contacts standard where they are "substantial" or "continuous and systematic," such that the defendant "purposefully availed itself of the privilege of conducting activities within the Forum State, thus invoking the benefits and protections of its laws."[898] The plaintiff has the burden of showing that the defendant took action "purposefully directed" at the forum and that the cause of action arises from this action.[899] A defendant "purposefully avails" himself of jurisdiction when "the contacts proximately result from actions by the defendant himself that create a 'substantial connection' with the forum State.'[900]

In determining whether the exercise of jurisdiction comports with notions of fair play and substantial justice, a court must balance several factors. These factors are: (1) the extent of a defendant's purposeful interjection; (2) the inconvenience to the defendant of defending in that forum; (3) the extent of conflict with the sovereignty of the defendant's state; (4) the forum state's interest in adjudicating the dispute; (5) the interstate judicial system's interest in the efficient resolution of conflicts; (6) the plaintiff's interest in obtaining convenient and effective relief; and (7) the existence of an alternative forum[901].

---

[896] World-Wide Volkswagen Corp. v. Woodson, 444 U.S. 286, 291 (1980) available at http://laws.findlaw.com/us/444/286.html , visited on 25 June 2003

[897] ibid
[898] Hanson v. Denckla, 357 U.S. 235, 253 (1958) available at http://supreme.justia.com/us/357/235/case.html, visited on 23 June 2003

[899] Supra Note 887,Calder v. Jones, 465 U.S. 783, 789 (1984) (upholding jurisdiction where conduct was allegedly calculated to cause injuries in the forum state and the cause of action arose from this conduct).

[900] Burger King v. Rudzewicz, 471 U.S. 462, 475 (1985) available at http://supreme.justia.com/us/471/462/case.html, visited on 23 June 2003

[901] ibid

One of the earliest US case in which applications of these principles to the Internet traces back to 1996 and applied by a Connecticut District court in Inset Systems, Inc. v. Instruction Set, Inc.,[902]. In this instance, Inset Systems, a Connecticut company, brought a trademark infringement action against Instruction Set, a Massachusetts company, arising out of its use of the domain name "Inset.com."[903] Instruction Set used the domain name to advertise its goods and services on the Internet, a practice to which Inset objected since it was the owner of the federal trademark "Inset."[904] The legal question before the court was one of jurisdiction. Did Instruction Set's activity, the establishment of a website, properly bring it within the jurisdiction of Connecticut under that state's long-arm statute? Did Inset's conduct meet the minimum contacts standard outlined by the United States Supreme Court in World-Wide Volkswagen?[905].In this case the court concluded that it could properly assert jurisdiction, basing its decision on Instruction Set's use of the Internet[906]. Likening the Internet to a continuous advertisement, the court reasoned that Instruction Set had purposefully directed its advertising activities toward Connecticut on a continuous basis and therefore could reasonably have anticipated being sued there.[907]

The court's decision was problematic for several reasons. First, its conclusion that creating a website amounts to a purposeful availment of every jurisdiction distorts

---

[902] Inset Sys., Inc. v. Instruction Set, Inc., 937 F. Supp. 161 (D. Conn. 1996) available at http://cyber.law.harvard.edu/property00/jurisdiction/insetedit.html, visited 24 June 2003

[903] Internet domain names, which have become a ubiquitous part of commercial advertising, enable users to access websites simply by typing in a name such as "www.inset.com" in their web browser. The "www" portion of the address identifies that the site is part of the World Wide Web; the "Inset" portion is usually the name of a company or other identifying words; and "com" identifies the type of institution, in this case a company. Domain names, the subject of several other litigated cases, are administered in the United States by a government appointed agency, Network Solutions Inc. (NSI) and are distributed on a first come, first served basis. *See* Cynthia Rowden & Jeannette Lee, Trademarks and the Internet: An Overview, Nov. 4, 1998, available at http://www.bereskinparr.com/art-pdf/TM&InternetOverview.pdf. visited on 23 Apr 2003

[904] Supra Note 902, Inset Sys., Inc. v. Instruction Set, Inc., 937 F. Supp. 161
[905] World-Wide Volkswagen Corp. v. Woodson, 444 U.S. 286, 291 (1980) available at http://laws.findlaw.com/us/444/286.html, 13 July 2003
[906] Supra Note 902, Inset Sys., Inc. v. Instruction Set, Inc., 937 F. Supp. 161

[907] ibid

the fundamental principle of jurisdiction[908]. Second, the court did not analyze the Internet itself, but merely drew an analogy between the Internet and a more traditional media form, in this case a continuous advertisement[909]. If the court was correct, every court, every-where, could assert jurisdiction where a website was directed toward its forum. This approach would stifle future Internet growth, as potential Internet participants would be forced to weigh the advantages of the Internet with the chances of being subject to legal jurisdiction throughout the world. Third, the court did not assess Instruction Set's actual activity on the Internet[910]. The mere use of the Internet was sufficient for the court to hold that jurisdiction was established[911]. In fact, the court acknowledged that Instruction Set did not maintain an office in Connecticut nor did it have a sales force or employees in the said state[912]. This principle would affect the interest of cyberspace entities severely restricting their free speech as standards of free speech scrutiny vary from country to country.

In Bensusan Rest. Corp. v. King[913], a New York district court created an important exception to the rule created in Inset Systems[914]. The Blue Note was a small Columbia, Missouri club operated by the defendant (King). King promoted his club by establishing a website that included information about the club, a calendar of events, and ticketing information[915]. New York City was also home to a club named The Blue Note, this one operated by the Bensusan Restaurant Corporation, who owned a federal trademark in the name[916]. King was familiar with the New York Blue Note as he included a disclaimer on his website that stated: "The Blue Note's

---

[908] Supra Note 902,Inset Sys., Inc. v. Instruction Set, Inc., 937 F. Supp. 161, 165

[909] Geist A Michael,, Is There A There There? Toward Greater Certainty For Internet Jurisdiction , Berkeley Technology Law Journal, Vol.16, Issue 16:3, Fall 2001

[910] ibid at p 25

[911] ibid at p 26

[912] ibid at p 26

[913] 937 F. Supp. 295 (S.D.N.Y. 1996), available at http://caselaw.lp.findlaw.com/scripts/getcase.pl?court=2nd&navby=docket&no=969344 , visited on 15 Aug 2003

[914] Supra Note 902

[915] Supra Note 913,Bensusan Rest. Corp. v. King, 937 F. Supp. 295 (S.D.N.Y. 1996)

[916] ibid

Cyberspot should not be confused with one of the world's finest jazz clubs, the Blue Note, located in the heart of New York's Greenwich Village..."[917]

Within months of the establishment of King's Blue Note website, Bensusan brought a trademark infringement and dilution action in New York federal court[918]. Once again, the court faced the question of personal jurisdiction in a trademark action arising out of activity on the Internet. Unlike the Inset systems line of cases, however, the court considered the specific uses of the website in question. It noted that King's website was passive rather than active in nature, that is, several affirmative steps by a New York resident would be necessary to bring any potentially infringing product into the state[919]. Specifically, tickets could not be ordered online, so that anyone wishing to make a purchase would have to telephone the box office in Missouri, only to find that the Missouri club did not mail tickets[920]. The purchaser would have to travel to Missouri to obtain the tickets[921]. Given the level of passivity, the court ruled that the website did not infringe Bensusan's trademark in New York[922]. The court observed that "the mere fact that a person can gain information on the allegedly infringing product is not the equivalent of a person advertising, promoting, selling or otherwise making an effort to target its product in New York."[923]

The decision in Bensusan case, which the Court of Appeals for the Second Circuit affirmed in September 1997[924], provided an important step toward the development of deeper legal analysis of Internet activity. Although the decision did not attempt to reconcile the *Inset* line of cases, it provided the groundwork for a new line of

---

[917] ibid
[918] ibid
[919] ibid
[920] ibid
[921] ibid
[922] ibid
[923] ibid
[924] Supra Note 913,Bensusan Rest. Corp. v. King, 126 F.3d 25, 29 (2d Cir. 1997)

cases[925]. By the end of 1996, however, the majority of Internet related decisions evidenced little genuine understanding of activity on the Internet. Rather, most courts were unconcerned with the jurisdictional implications of their rulings and instead favored an analogy based approach in which the Internet was categorized en masse[926]. This analogy-based approach by courts was ignoring the fact that Internet technology has offered a great platform for expressing one's view in an inexpensive way. In all these cases courts were interested in resolving jurisdictional problems and were unable to consider the rights of the cyberspace entities.

6.4 The Rise and fall of Zippo Test – Passive versus Active Test

A new approach to internet jurisdiction emerged with the decision of Pennsylvania district court decision in Zippo Manufacturing Co. v. Zippo Dot Com, Inc[927].It was with this decision that courts gradually began to appreciate that activity on the Internet was as varied as that in real space, and that all encompassing analogies could not be appropriately applied to this new medium. This realization again reinforces Lawrence Lessig argument for separate study for cyberlaw. In the above case, Zippo Manufacturing was a Pennsylvania based manufacturer of the well-known "Zippo" brand of tobacco lighters[928]. Zippo Dot Com was a California based Internet news service that used the domain name "Zippo.com" to provide access to

---

[925] For example in Hearst Corp. v. Goldberger, 15 (S.D.N.Y. Feb. 26, 1997), available at http://www.internetlibrary.com/cases/lib_case172.cfm , visited on 2 Feb 2003, the court relied heavily upon the Bensusan analysis in refusing to assert personal jurisdiction in a trademark infringement matter involving the domain name "Esqwire.com."In this case the court carefully reviewed Internet case law to that point, noted its disagreement with decisions such as Inset Systems etc cautioned that:

"Where, as here, defendant has not contracted to sell or actually sold any goods or services to New Yorkers, a finding of personal jurisdiction in New York based on an Internet website would mean that there would be nationwide (indeed, worldwide) personal jurisdiction over anyone and everyone who establishes an Internet website. Such nationwide jurisdiction is not consistent with traditional personal jurisdiction case law nor acceptable to the court as a matter of policy."

[926] Geist A,Michael , The Reality of Bytes: Regulating Economic Activity in the Age of the Internet, 73 WASH. L. REV. 521, 538 (1998).

[927] 952 F. Supp. 1119, 1126 (W.D. Pa. 1997) available at http://people.hofstra.edu/peter_j_spiro/cyberlaw/zippo.htm , visited on 17 Sep 2003

[928] ibid

Internet newsgroups[929]. Zippo Dot Com offered three levels of subscriber service—free, original, and super[930]. Those subscribers desiring the original or super level of service were required to fill out an online application form and submit a credit card number through the Internet or by telephone[931]. Zippo Dot Com's contacts with Pennsylvania occurred almost exclusively on the Internet because the company maintained no offices, employees, or agents in the state[932]. Dot Com had some success in attracting Pennsylvania subscribers; at the time of the action, approximately 3,000, or two percent of its subscribers, resided in that state[933]. Once again, the issue before the court was one of personal jurisdiction arising out of a claim of trademark infringement and dilution[934].

Rather than using Internet analogies as the basis for its analysis, the court focused on the prior, somewhat limited Internet case law[935]. The court, which clearly used the *Bensusan* decision for inspiration, determined that, although few cases had been decided, the likelihood that personal jurisdiction can be constitutionally exercised is directly proportionate to the nature and quality of commercial activity that an entity conducts over the Internet[936].

The court proceeded to identify a sliding scale based on Internet commercial activity:
"At one end of the spectrum are situations where a defendant clearly does business over the Internet. If the defendant enters into contracts with residents of a foreign jurisdiction that involve the knowing and repeated transmission of computer files over the Internet, personal jurisdiction is proper. At the opposite end are situations

---

[929] ibid
[930] ibid
[931] ibid
[932] ibid
[933] ibid
[934] ibid
[935] In Zippo case the court relied on court was Compuserve Inc. v. Patterson, 89 F.3d 1257 (6th Cir. 1996). Although the *Zippo* court refers to the decision as an Internet case, in fact, the activity in question did not involve the use of the Internet. Rather, Patterson used Compuserve's proprietary network to dis-tribute certain shareware programs. Accordingly, Patterson's contacts with Ohio, Compuserve's headquarters and the location of the litigation, were confined to an offline contractual agreement and the posting of shareware on a Compuserve server that was avail-able to users of its proprietary network (not Internet users at large).

[936] 952 F. Supp. 1119, 1126 (W.D. Pa. 1997) available at http://people.hofstra.edu/peter_j_spiro/cyberlaw/zippo.htm, visited on 17 Sep 2003

where a defendant has simply posted information on an Internet Web site, which is accessible to users in foreign jurisdictions. A passive Web site that does little more than make information available to those who are interested in it is not grounds for the exercise of personal jurisdiction. The middle ground is occupied by interactive Web sites where users can exchange information with the host computer. In these cases, the exercise of jurisdiction is determined by examining the level of interactivity and commercial nature of the exchange of information that occurs on the Web site."[937]

Although the court may have conveniently interpreted some earlier cases to obtain its desired result, its critical finding was that the jurisdictional analysis in Internet cases should be based on the nature and quality of the commercial activity conducted on the Internet. There is a strong argument that prior to Zippo, jurisdictional analysis was based upon the mere use of the Internet. Courts relying solely on the inappropriate analogy between the Internet and advertisements developed a legal doctrine poorly suited to the reality of Internet activity. In the aftermath of the Zippo decision, Internet legal analysis underwent a significant shift in perspective[938].

The test laid down by the court in Zippo fails on many counts. First, the majority of websites are neither entirely passive nor completely active. Accordingly, they fall into the "middle zone," that requires courts to gauge all relevant evidence and determine whether the site is "more passive" or "more active." With many sites falling into this middle zone, their legal advisors are frequently unable to provide a firm opinion on how any given court might judge the interactivity of the website.

Second, distinguishing between passive and active sites is complicated by the fact that some sites may not be quite what they seem. For example, sites that feature content best characterized as passive, may actually be using cookies or other data collection technologies behind the scenes without the knowledge of the individual

---

[937] ibid
[938] Geist A Michael , Is There A There There? Toward Greater Certainty For Internet Jurisdiction , Berkeley Technology Law Journal, Vol.16, Issue 16:3, Fall 2001 at p 27

user[939]. Given the value of personal data, its collection is properly characterized as active, regardless of whether it occurs transparently or surreptitiously[940]. Similarly, sites such as online chat rooms may appear to be active, yet courts have consistently characterized such sites as passive[941].

Third, it is important to note that the standards for what constitutes an active or passive website are constantly shifting. When the test was developed in 1997, an active website might have featured little more than an email link and some basic correspondence functionality. Today, sites with that level of interactivity would likely be viewed as passive, since the entire spectrum of passive versus active has shifted upward with improved technology. In fact, it can be credibly argued that owners of websites must constantly reevaluate their positions on the passive versus active spectrum as web technology changes[942].

Fourth, the Zippo test is ineffective even if the standards for passive and active sites remain constant. With the expense of creating a sophisticated website being high, few organizations will invest in a website without anticipating some earning potential. Since revenue is typically the hallmark of active websites, most new sites are likely to feature interactivity, and therefore be categorized as active sites. From a jurisdictional perspective, this produces an effect similar to that found in the *Inset* line of cases—any court anywhere can assert jurisdiction over a website because virtually all sites will meet the Zippo active benchmark[943].

In light of the ever changing technological environment and the shift toward predominantly active websites, the effectiveness of the *Zippo* doctrine is severely undermined no matter how it develops. If the test evolves with the changing

---

[939] Kang ,Jerry , Information Privacy in Cyberspace Transactions, 50 STAN. L. REV. 1193, 1226-29 (1998).

[940] Supra Note 921,Zippo Mfg. Co. v. Zippo Dot Com, Inc., 952 F. Supp. 1119, 1126 (W.D. Pa. 1997)

[941] Barrett v. Catacombs Press, 64 F. Supp. 2d 440 (E.D. Pa. 1999) , available at http://www.findlaw.com, visited on 18 May 2003

[942] Geist A Michael , Is There A There There? Toward Greater Certainty for Internet Jurisdiction, Berkeley Technology Law Journal, Vol.16, Issue 16:3, Fall 2001 at p 39

[943] ibid at p 45

technological environment, it fails to provide much needed legal certainty. On the other hand, if the test remains static to provide increased legal certainty, it risks becoming irrelevant as the majority of websites meet the active standard.[944]Therefore, we need to look for alternative tests.

The limitation of the Zippo doctrine was highlighted in Millennium Enterprises, Inc. v. Millennium Music L.P.,[945] a case in which the court found insufficient commercial effects and therefore declined to assert jurisdiction. The defendant, a South Carolina corporation, sold products both offline and on the web. The plaintiffs, an Oregon based corporation, sued the defendants in Oregon district court for trademark infringement. The defendant filed a motion to dismiss for lack of personal jurisdiction[946]. After canvassing numerous Internet jurisdiction cases decided in the Ninth Circuit, as well as Zippo, the court stated:

"The middle interactive category of Internet contacts as described in Zippo needs further refinement to include the fundamental requirement of personal jurisdiction: that is, "deliberate action" within the forum state in the form of transactions between the defendant and residents of the forum or conduct of the defendant purposefully directed at residents of the forum state. This, in the court's view, is the "something more" that the Ninth Circuit intended in Cybersell and Panavision cases.[947]

6.5 The Effects-doctrine for Internet Jurisdiction

Another important doctrine used by US courts for the determination of personal jurisdiction is known as effects doctrine.

In the application of "effects doctrine" to the cases, the US Supreme Court asserted jurisdiction on the principle that the defendant knew that his action would be injurious to the plaintiff, therefore he must reasonably anticipate being haled into court where the injury occurred. The "effects" cases are of particular importance in

---

[944] ibid at p 64
[945] 33 F. Supp. 2d 907 (D. Or. 1999), available at
http://www.internetlibrary.com/cases/lib_case178.cfm , visited on 20 May 2004
[946] ibid
[947] ibid

cyberspace because conduct in cyberspace often has effects in various jurisdictions[948].

Under this "effects" test approach, rather than examining the specific characteristics of a website and its potential impact, courts focused their analysis on the actual effects that the website had in the jurisdiction. Indeed, courts are now relying increasingly on the effects doctrine established by the United States Supreme Court in Calder v. Jones[949].

The effects doctrine holds that personal jurisdiction over a defendant is proper when: a) the defendant's intentional tortious actions b) expressly aimed at the forum state and c) cause harm to the plaintiff in the forum state, which the defendant knows is likely to be suffered[950]. In Calder case, a California entertainer sued a Florida publisher for libel in a California district court[951]. In ruling that personal jurisdiction was properly asserted, the Court focused on the effects of the defendant's actions[952]. Reasoning that the plaintiff lived and worked in California, spent most of her career in California, suffered injury to her professional reputation in California, and suffered emotional distress in California, the Court concluded that

---

[948] Kesan Jay, Personal Jurisdiction in Cyberspace: Brief Summary of Personal Jurisdiction Law, Learning Cyberlaw in Cyberspace available at http://www.cyberspacelaw.org/kesan/kesan1.html , visited on Mar 22, 2004

[949] 465 U.S. 783 (1984) available at
http://caselaw.lp.findlaw.com/scripts/getcase.pl?navby=search&court=US&case=/us/465/783.html, visited on 23 May 2004.In this case the actress Shirley Jones who worked and lived in California brought a libel suit in California against a reporter and executive for the National Enquirer. The defendant had only been to California twice, and neither of these visits was connected in any manner with the Jones claim of libel. However, the court held that because Jones caused the story to the published which he knew would have a "potentially devastating impact . . the brunt of that injury would be felt by [plaintiff] in the state in which she lives and work and in which the National Enquirer has its largest circulation," the defendant must "reasonably anticipate being haled into court there." 465 U.S. at 784, 104 S.Ct. at 1484. The court in Calder emphasized was this was a case of an intentional tort that was highly foreseeable to cause damage in California. The court also found significant that the effects of the article were centered in California, both in the content of the story as well as where the harm would be suffered. Thus the Calder case is considered a classic effects case, because jurisdiction was based on the effects of the defendants conduct

[950] ibid
[951] ibid
[952] ibid

294

the defendant had intentionally targeted a California resident and thus it was proper to sue the publisher in that state[953]. Thus in effect doctrine court considered the effects created on defendant to assert personal jurisdiction over the plaintiff.

The application of the Calder test can be seen in the Internet context in Blakey v. Continental Airlines, Inc.,[954] an online defamation case involving an airline employee. The employee filed suit in New Jersey against her co-employees, alleging that they published defamatory statements on the employer's electronic bulletin board, and against her employer, a New Jersey-based corporation, alleging that it was liable for the hostile work environment arising from the statements[955]. The lower court granted the co-employees' motion to dismiss for lack of personal jurisdiction and entered summary judgment for the employer on the hostile work environment claim[956].

In reversing the ruling, the New Jersey Supreme Court found that defendants who published defamatory electronic messages with the knowledge that the messages would be published in New Jersey could properly be held subject to the state's jurisdiction[957]. The court applied the effects doctrine and held that while the actions causing the effects in New Jersey were performed outside the state, this did not prevent the court from asserting jurisdiction over a cause of action arising out of those effects[958].

The broader effects based analysis has moved beyond the defamatory tort action at issue in Calder case to a range of disputes including intellectual property and commercial activities. On the intellectual property front, Nissan Motor Co. Ltd. v.

---

[953] ibid
[954] 751 A.2d 538 (N.J. 2000) , available at http://lawlibrary.rutgers.edu/courts/supreme/a-5-99.opn.html, visited on 10 June 2004

[955] ibid
[956] ibid
[957] ibid
[958] ibid

Nissan Computer Corp[959] typifies the approach. The plaintiff, an automobile manufacturer, filed a complaint in a California district court against a Massachusetts based computer seller. In the complaint there was an allegation that the defendant altered the content of its "nissan.com" website to include a logo that was similar to the plaintiff's logo and links to automobile merchandisers and auto related portions of search engines. In considering the defendant's motion, the court relied on the effects doctrine, ruling that the defendant had intentionally changed the content of its website to exploit the plaintiff's goodwill and to profit from consumer confusion[960]. Moreover, since the plaintiff was based in California, the majority of the harm was suffered in the forum state[961]. The court rejected the defendant's argument that it was not subject to personal jurisdiction because it merely operated a passive website[962]. Although the defendant did not sell anything over the Internet, it derived advertising revenue through the intentional exploitation of consumer confusion. This fact, according to the court, satisfied the decision in *Cybersell* and the requirement of "something more," . The court held that the defendant's conduct was deliberately and substantially directed toward the forum state[963].

Courts have also refused to assert jurisdiction in a number of cases where insufficient commercial effects were found. For example, in People Solutions, Inc. v. People Solutions, Inc.[964], the defendant, a California based corporation, moved to dismiss a trademark infringement suit brought against it by a Texas based corporation of the same name. The plaintiff argued that the suit was properly brought in Texas because the defendant owned a website that could be accessed and viewed by Texas residents[965]. The site featured several interactive pages that

---

[959] 89 F. Supp. 2d 1154 (C.D. Cal. 2000) ,available at
http://www.internetlibrary.com/cases/lib_case292.cfm, visited 25 June 2004

[960] ibid
[961] ibid
[962] ibid
[963] ibid
[964] Quoted from Michael A. Geist , Is There A There There? Toward Greater Certainty for Internet Jurisdiction, Berkeley Technology Law Journal, Vol.16, Issue 16:3, Fall 2001 at p 30

[965] ibid at p 31

allowed customers to take and score performance tests, download product demonstrations, and order products online[966].

The court characterized the site as interactive but refused to assert jurisdiction over the matter[967]. Relying on evidence that no Texans had actually purchased from the website, the court held that "personal jurisdiction should not be premised on the mere possibility, with nothing more, that defendant may be able to do business with Texans over its website."[968] Instead, the plaintiff had to show that the defendant had "purpose-fully availed itself of the benefits of the forum state and its laws."[969]

Effects doctrine has its own limitations and hence cannot be applied to cyberspace under all circumstances. A country cannot enforce conduct occurring outside its borders without the willingness of other countries to cooperate or the ability to exercise its own coercive power to extraterritorially enforce its laws. To do so would create inter-sovereign conflict and technology enabled countries may be able to extend their enforcement jurisdiction beyond persons, things or activities that are present in the enforcing jurisdiction[970].

6.6 The Yahoo! France Case

The Yahoo case serves as an example of a nation struggling to exercise its laws in cyberspace[971]. Yahoo Inc., a California based company, provides internet users with access to online resources, including various communication tools, online forums, shopping services, personalized content and branded programming through its network properties. 'Yahoo auctions', is one of the applications offered through the service; it allows users to communicate through the use of service[972], to buy and sell

---

[966] ibid at 31
[967] ibid
[968] ibid
[969] ibid
[970] Adria,Allen , Internet Jurisdiction Today, Northwestern Journal of International Law & Business, Fall 2001, 82, 1

[971] See generally , Nazis, Libel, Porn- The Web's Legal Minefield, Reuters, Aug 11, 2000, available at http://www.zenet.com/intweek/stories/new/0,41586,261456,00.html, visited 10 Oct 2003
[972] Yahoo! Terms of Service, available at http://www.docs.yahoo.com/info/terms, visited on 4 Feb 2002

items in an online auction[973]. Auction items range from baseball collections, to antiques, to electronics, to automobiles and, until, recently to Nazi memorabilia[974].

Few cyber law cases have attracted as much attention as the *Yahoo! France* case, in which a French judge ordered the world's most popular and widely visited website to implement technical or access control measures blocking auctions featuring Nazi memorabilia from French residents[975]. Yahoo! reacted with alarm, maintaining that the French court could not properly assert jurisdiction over the matter[976]. Yahoo! noted that the company maintains dozens of country-specific websites, including a Yahoo.fr site customized for France that was free of Nazi-related content. These country specific sites target the local population in their local language, and endeavor to comply with all local laws and regulations[977].

The company argued that its flagship site, Yahoo.com, primarily targeted a United States audience. Since United States free speech laws protect the sale of Nazi memorabilia, the auctions were entirely lawful[978]. Moreover, the Yahoo.com site featured a terms of use agreement, which stipulated that the site was governed by United States law[979]. Since the Yahoo.com site was not intended for a French audience, and users implicitly agreed that United States law would be binding, the company felt confident that a French judge could not credibly assert jurisdiction over the site.

---

[973] An auction is a public sale in which the price is determined by bidding, and the item is sold to the highest bidder. A potential buyer participates by bidding on an item that the seller has listed. The person who has offered the highest bid at close of auction wins the right to purchase the item at that price. What is an Auction? Yahoo! Auctions Tour, at http://www.auctions.yahoo.com.phtml/auc/us/tour/0-1-whatis.html, visited on 21 Feb 2003

[974] See Yahoo! Auctions , available at http://www.list.auctions.yahoo.com, visited on 21 Feb 2003

[975] *See* Jim Hu & Evan Hansen, Yahoo Auction Case May Reveal Borders Of Cyberspace, CNET NEWS.COM, Aug. 11, 2000, at http://news.cnet.com/news/0-1005-200-2495751.html , visited o 11 Sep 2005 ("A warning to Internet companies doing business abroad: Local governments may have the power to impose restrictions even if your servers are in the United States.");

[976] ibid

[977] *See* Yahoo! Terms of Service, *at* http://docs.yahoo.com/info/terms , visited on 26 Nov 2003.

[978] Brendon Fowler et al., Can You Yahoo!? The Internet's Digital Fences, 2001 DUKE L. & TECH. REV. 12, 1, available *at* http://www.law.duke.edu/journals/dltr/articles/-2001dltr0012.html ,Visited on 25 Feb 2003

[979] See Yahoo! Terms of service at http://docs.yahoo.com/info/terms

Judge Jean-Jacques Gomez of the County Court of Paris disagreed, ruling that the court could assert jurisdiction over the dispute since the content found on the Yahoo.com site was available to French residents and was unlawful under French law[980]. Before issuing his final order, the judge commissioned an international panel to determine whether the technological means were available to allow Yahoo! to comply with an order to keep the prohibited content away from French residents. The panel reported that though such technologies were imperfect, they could accurately identify French Internet users at least seventy percent of the time[981]. Based on this report, Judge Gomez ordered Yahoo! to ensure that French residents could not access content that violated French law on the site. Failure to comply with the order would result in fines of 100,000 francs per day after a three month grace period[982].

Soon after, Yahoo! removed the controversial content from its site, but the company proceeded to contest the validity of the French court's order in a California court. In November 2001, the California court ruled in favor of Yahoo!, holding that the French judgment was unenforceable in the United States[983].

Yahoo argued and continues to argue that the auction sites involved in the Yahoo case were aimed at the American market and the US First amendment governing freedom of speech prevented it from shutting them down[984]. Though Yahoo later removed Nazi artifacts from its internet auction sites, it had decided not to drop its US suit over French ruling[985].

---

[980] The sale of Nazi items violates Article R645-1 of the French Penal Code. For translation of Article R645-1 of the French Penal Code see http://www.laores.net/html/codpen.html, visited on 25 Oct 2003

[981] UEJF et LICRA v. Yahoo! Inc. et Yahoo France, T.G.I. Paris, Nov. 20, 2000, N° RG: 00/05308 quoted from Michael A. Geist , Is There A There There? Toward Greater Certainty for Internet Jurisdiction, Berkeley Technology Law Journal, Vol.16, Issue 16:3, Fall 2001

[982] ibid

[983] Yahoo!, Inc. v. LICRA, C-00-21275 JF, 2001 U.S. Dist. LEXIS 18378 (N.D. Cal. Nov. 7, 2001), available at www.findlaw.com , visited on 20 Jan 2003

[984] Lawsuit Accuses Yahoo of justifying war crimes, REUTERS, 22 Jan. 2003 available at http://news.cnet.com/news/0-1007-200-4560537.html, visited 2 Mar 2003

[985] Lori Enos, Holocaust Survivors sue Yahoo! Over Nazi Auctions, E-commerce Times, 23 Jan 2003, available at http://www.ecommercetimes.com/perl/story/6923.html, visited 24 Feb 2003

Further Yahoo contended that Judge Gomez's order violates the First Amendment and the Communication Decency Act's (CDA) immunization of ISPs from liability to third party content[986]. The fact that Yahoo decided to remove Nazi items from its auction sites, thus appeasing the plaintiffs and the court order in the Yahoo case, does not mean that Yahoo has backed down from its original position: Yahoo will fight the ruling that threatens to pin "frontier-free internet back beyond international boundaries."[987]

The French government found Yahoo guilty of violating French law. In doing so, the French court took the position that 'no one should gain or lose rights merely by going online'[988]. According to this view, 'if Nazi artifacts cannot be sold offline, they should not be sold online'[989]. All existing legislation applies to internet users and a racist message circulated on the web is an offense just as it would be in a newspaper or on radio or television[990]. Because internet users in France have access to Yahoo's US site, indeed all websites, they must follow French law[991]. The problem that arises from this "when-in-Rome"[992] perception of internet jurisdiction is that it could lead to the conclusion that any court anywhere in the world has adjudicative jurisdiction over the author, publisher or provider of a web page[993]. Unlike traditional jurisdictional problems that might involve two or three conflicting jurisdictions, cyberlaw jurisdictional theorists are faced with the reality that a simple

---

[986] ibid

[987] Hate Foes Praise Yahoo Move, REUTERS, 3 Jan 2003 available at, http://www.wirednews.com/news/politics/0,1283,4095,00.html, visited on 25 Feb 2003

[988] Ariel Tam, Online Free of Speech is not So Free, ZDNet ASIA, Jan 22, 2001, available at http://www.ZDNET.com/zdnn/stories/news/0,4586,2677192,00.html, visited on 4 Feb 2002

[989] ibid

[990] David McGuire, Yahoo Decision Won't End Online Speech Debate, NEWSBYTES, 4 Jan 2002, available at http://www.newsbytes.com/news/01/16002.html, visited on 5 Feb 2002

[991] Pimm Fox, News Analysis: Can French Law be Imposed on an Internet Company? COMPUTERWORLD, Nov.28, 2000 , available at http://www.computerworld.com/cwi/s, visited on 4 Feb 2002

[992] The "when-in-Rome" rule refers to the concept that a country can have jurisdiction overall websites merely because they are accessible from the country

[993] Peritt H Henry, Jr., Jurisdiction and the Internet: Basic Anglo/American Perspectives Projects in the coming 2000's, Internet law and Policy Forum, available at http://www.ilpf.org/confer/present99/perrittpr.htm visited Feb 16, visited on 23 July 2003

web page could be subject to jurisdiction by all of the nearly three hundred sovereigns around the world[994].

If we were to apply traditional jurisdictional principles to the Yahoo case, the case satisfies many of the bases for French perspective jurisdiction. According to the facts of the Yahoo case, France has the authority to prescribe its laws on cyberspace. First, subjective territoriality exists because Nazi items, in violation of Article R645-1, were being offered in France[995]. Second, objective territoriality is satisfied because, even if it was determined that the sale of Nazi items took place either in cyberspace, or the location of the seller, the primary effect of the transaction was felt in France[996]. Third, France has jurisdiction over French citizens that are buying Nazi memorabilia[997]. Fourth, the passive nationality theory applies because the victims of a breach of Article R645-1 are thought to be French citizens, some of which are holocaust survivors, offended by the sale of Nazi artifacts[998].Fifth, the victim in the Yahoo! case could be viewed not only as French citizens, but also as France itself, giving France jurisdiction to prescribe its laws over the internet based on the protective principle theory[999]. Finally, though it is not applicable to this case, universal interest jurisdiction could be expanded to Internet law to deal with such areas as internet piracy, computer hacking and viruses[1000].

The traditional model of international jurisdiction would validate the French Tribunals order in the Yahoo! case. A conclusion, such as this, could have far reaching implications for the development of the internet and the future of cyber law. Internet jurisdiction is a subject of increasing debate. Opinions worldwide are "split between civil libertarians who want to uphold the freedom of internet speech

---

[994] Menthe Darrel, Jurisdiction in Cyberspace: A theory of International Spaces, 4 Mich.Telecom.Tech.L.Rev. 69(1998) available at http://www.mttlr.org/volfour/menthe.html, visited on Feb 25, 2004
[995] The sale of Nazi items violates Article R645-1 of the French Penal Code. For translation of Article R645-1 of the French Penal Code see http://www.laores.net/html/codpen.html, visited on 25 Oct 2003
[996] Menthe Darrel, Jurisdiction in Cyberspace: A theory of International Spaces, 4 Mich.Telecom.Tech.L.Rev. 69(1998) available at http://www.mttlr.org/volfour/menthe.html, visited 25 on Feb 2004

[997] ibid
[998] ibid
[999] ibid
[1000] ibid.

at all costs and lawyers and governments trying to find practical compromise that respects the open nature of the web whilst protecting vulnerable people."[1001] The internet's extraordinary growth and distinct ability to make information available to anyone, anywhere in the world with Internet access, has taken traditional national sovereignty by surprise[1002]. While nations are trying to maintain sovereignty in cyberspace, companies, such as Yahoo, fear that the Yahoo case will be used as precedent, forcing web sites to "self-police all online content and activities and make them comply with any number of laws from any country or community."[1003]

6.7 Tackling Internet Jurisdictional Problems

Goldsmith asserts that regulation of cyberspace is both feasible and legitimate from the perspective of traditional jurisdiction and choice of law[1004].He claims that enforceability will operate for cyberspace in the same way as in real space. Rather than being simultaneously subjects to all national regulations, internet users will have to concern themselves with countries that are able to enforce their laws across geographic boundaries[1005]. In the Yahoo case, the California based corporation has a subsidiary company operating in France, which could be used by France to enable enforcement of French law. However, as seen by the expert's proposal in the Yahoo case, as technology increases, the threat of liability will lesson[1006]. As we have seen in Napster case, court order was enforced but in the Grokster case court order can not be enforced because of lack of physical location.

[1001] Adria, Allen , Internet Jurisdiction Today, Northwestern Journal of International Law & Business, Fall 2001, 22, 1
[1002] See generally Reno V ACLU, 521 US 844(1997)
[1003] Kenneth N Cukier, Virtual Exceptionalism: Cyberspace Meets Sovereignty, Wall Street Journal, Aug 6, 2000 at page 6
[1004] Goldsmith L Jack., Against Cyberanarchy, 65 U.Chi.L.Rev 1199 (1998), available at http://eon.law.harvard.edu/property00/jurisidction/cyberanarchy.html, visited on 20 Feb 2004. Though Goldsmith argues that regulation from the perspective of jurisdiction and choice of law is "legitimate and feasible", he does not argue that it is a good idea, and does not take a position on the merits beyond their jurisdictional legitimacy. Further, Goldsmith does not rule out the fact that the new cyberspace will lead to changes in governmental regulation in the same way that the radio , television and satellite gave way to social and regulatory change.
[1005] ibid
[1006] ibid, "The threat of liability will lessen as content providers continue to gain means to control information flows" at, 1221

Skeptics overstate the challenges posed on traditional international jurisdiction by the Internet[1007]. First, the practical problems of jurisdiction will diminish when the substantive content of law in different sovereigns is the same. When harmonization is not an option, the problems may be complex and genuine[1008]. However, Goldsmith asserts that they are not unique to cyberspace. Though the new medium is 'richer, more complex and much more efficient, it is not different than other forms of transnational communication[1009]. Transactions over the internet either involve real people in one territorial jurisdiction transacting with real people in other territorial jurisdictions, or engaging in activity that causes real world effects in another territorial jurisdiction[1010].

6.7.1 Targeting Test for Internet jurisdiction

Targeting test can be used to resolve internet jurisdictional problems. It focuses on three factors: contract, technology and actual or implied knowledge[1011].

A targeting approach is not a novel idea. Several United States courts have factored targeting considerations into their jurisdictional analysis of Internet-based activities. For example, in Bancroft & Masters, Inc. v. Augusta National Inc[1012]., a dispute over the "masters.com" domain name, the Ninth Circuit considered targeting to be the "something more" required when applying an effects based analysis:

> We have said that there must be "something more," but have not spelled out
> what that something more must be. We now conclude that "something
> more" is what the Supreme Court described as "express aiming" at the
> forum state. Express aiming is a concept that in the jurisdictional context
> hardly defines itself. From the available cases, we deduce that the
> requirement is satisfied when the defendant is alleged to have engaged in

---

[1007] ibid at p 1240
[1008] ibid
[1009] ibid
[1010] ibid
[1011] Geist A Michael A. , Is There A There There? Toward Greater Certainty for Internet Jurisdiction, Berkeley Technology Law Journal, Vol.16, Issue 16:3, Fall 2001 at p 56
[1012] 223 F.3d 1082 (9th Cir. 2000) available at http://caselaw.lp.findlaw.com/cgi-bin/getcase.pl?court=9th&navby=case&no=9915099, visited 6 Jan 2005

wrongful conduct targeted at a plaintiff whom the defendant knows to be a
resident of the forum state.[1013]

Targeting based analysis has also become increasingly prevalent among
international organizations seeking to develop global minimum legal standards for
e-commerce. The OECD Consumer Protection Guide-lines refer to the concept of
targeting, stating that "business should take into account the global nature of
electronic commerce and, wherever possible, should consider various regulatory
characteristics of the markets they target."[1014]

Similarly, a recent draft of the Hague Conference on Private International Law's
Draft Convention on Jurisdiction and Foreign Judgments includes provisions related
to targeting[1015]. During negotiations over the e-commerce implications of the draft
convention in Ottawa in February 2001, delegates focused on targeting as a means
of distinguishing when consumers should be entitled to sue in their home
jurisdiction. Version 0.4a of Article 7 (3)(b) includes a provision stating, "activity
by the business shall not be regarded as being directed to a State if the business
demonstrates that it took reasonable steps to avoid concluding contracts with
consumers habitually resident in that State."[1016]

Targeting also forms the central consideration for securities regulators assessing
online activity. As the United States Securities and Exchange Commission stated in
its release on the regulation of Internet based offerings:

> "We believe that our investor protection concerns are best ad-dressed
> through the implementation by issuers and financial service providers
> of precautionary measures that are reasonably de-signed to ensure

---

[1013] ibid

[1014] Organization for Economic Cooperation and Development, Recommendation of the OECD
Council Concerning Guidelines for Consumer Protection in the Context of Electronic Commerce, at
5, at http://www.oecd.org/dsti/sti/it/consumer/prod/-CPGuidelines_final.pdf, visited 26 Nov 2004

[1015] Hague Conference on Private International Law, Preliminary Draft Convention on Jurisdiction
and Foreign Judgments in Civil and Commercial Matters, Oct. 30, 1999, available at
http://www.hcch.net/e/conventions/draft36e.html, visited on 2 Jul 2003

[1016] ibid

that offshore Internet offers are not targeted to persons in the United States or to U.S. persons"[1017]

The American Bar Association Internet Jurisdiction Project, a global study on Internet jurisdiction released in 2000, also recommended targeting as one method of addressing the Internet jurisdiction issue[1018]. It was noted in the report:

"Entities seeking a relationship with residents of a foreign forum need not themselves maintain a physical presence in the forum. A forum can be "targeted" by those outside it and desirous of benefiting from a connecting with it via the Internet . . . . Such a chosen relationship will subject the foreign actor to both personal and prescriptive jurisdiction, so a clear understanding of what constitutes targeting is critical"[1019].

It is the ABA's last point that a clear understanding of what constitutes targeting is critical that requires careful examination and discussion. Without universally applicable standards for assessment of targeting in the online environment, a targeting test is likely to leave further uncertainty in its wake. For example, the ABA's report refers to language as a potentially important determinant for targeting purposes. That criterion overlooks the fact that the development of new language translation capabilities may soon enable website owners to display their site in the language of their choice, safe in the knowledge that visitors around the world will read the content in their own language through the aid of translation technologies[1020].

[1017] ibid

[1018] *See* American Bar Association, Achieving Legal and Business Order in Cyber-space: A Report on Global Jurisdiction Issues Created By the Internet , available at www.abanet.org, visited on 2 Feb 2003

[1019] ibid
[1020] ibid

6.8 Components of Targeting Test

Targeting as the litmus test for Internet jurisdiction is only the first step in the development of a consistent test that provides increased legal certainty. The second, more challenging step is to identify the criteria to be used in assessing whether a website has indeed targeted a particular jurisdiction. This step is challenging because the criteria must meet at least two important standards. First, the criteria must be technology neutral so that the test remains relevant even as new technologies emerge. This would seem to disqualify criteria such as a website language or currency, which are susceptible to real time conversion by newly emerging technologies. In the case of real time conversion language, a Greek website, which might otherwise be regarded as targeting Greece, could be instantly converted to English, and therefore rendered accessible to a wider geographic audience[1021].

Second, the criteria must be content neutral so that there is no apparent bias in favor of any single interest group or constituency. Several business groups are currently lobbying for a "rule of origin" approach under which jurisdiction would always rest with the jurisdiction of the seller[1022]. Consumer groups, meanwhile, have lobbied for a "rule of destination" approach that ensures that consumers can always sue in their home jurisdiction[1023]. The origin versus destination debate has polarized both groups, making it difficult to reach a compromise that recognizes that effective consumer protection does not depend solely on which law applies, while also acknowledging, as the court did in Stomp Inc. v. Neato L.L.C[1024]., that business must shoulder some of the risk arising from e-commerce transactions.

[1021] Geist A Michael A., Is There A There There? Toward Greater Certainty for Internet Jurisdiction, Berkeley Technology Law Journal, Vol.16, Issue 16:3, Fall 2001 at p 64

[1022] See for example,, Global Business Dialogue on Electronic Commerce, available *at* http://www.gbde.org, visited 26 Nov. 2005

[1023] See, for example., Consumers International, *at* http://www.consumersinternational.org , visited on 16 Oct. 2005

[1024] 61 F. Supp. 2d 1074, 1080-81 (C.D. Cal. 1999) available at http://www.ecjlaw.com/CM/InternetandTechnologyLawReporter/InternetandTechnologyLawReporte

To identify the appropriate criteria for a targeting test, we must ultimately return to the core jurisdictional principle, foreseeability. Foreseeability should not be based on a passive versus active website matrix. Rather, an effective targeting test requires an assessment of whether the targeting of a specific jurisdiction was itself foreseeable. Foreseeability in that context depends on three factors: contracts, technology, and actual or implied knowledge. Forum selection clauses found in website terms of use agreements or transactional clickwrap agreements allow parties to mutually determine an appropriate jurisdiction in advance of a dispute. They therefore provide important evidence as to the foreseeability of being haled into the courts of a particular jurisdiction. Newly emerging technologies that identify geographic location constitute the second factor. These technologies, which challenge widely held perceptions about the Internet's architecture, may allow website owners to target their content to specific jurisdictions or engage in "jurisdictional avoidance" by "de-targeting" certain jurisdictions. The third factor, actual or implied knowledge, is a catch-all that incorporates targeting knowledge gained through the geographic location of tort victims, offline order fulfillment, financial intermediary records, and web traffic[1025].

Although all three factors are important, no single factor should be de-terminative. Rather, each must be analyzed to adequately assess whether the parties have fairly negotiated a governing jurisdiction clause at a private contract level, whether the parties employed any technological solutions to target their activities, and whether the parties knew, or ought to have known, where their online activities were occurring. While all three factors should be considered as part of a targeting analysis, the relative importance of each will vary. Moreover, in certain instances, some factors may not matter at all. For example, a defamation action is unlikely to

---

r206.asp , visited on 24 Feb 2004; See generally for clickwrap contracts, Rowland, Diane, Information Technology Law, Cavendish Publishing Ltd, London, 1997

[1025] Geist A Michael , Is There A There There? Toward Greater Certainty for Internet Jurisdiction, Berkeley Technology Law Journal, Vol.16, Issue 16:3, Fall 2001 at p 60

involve a contractual element, though evidence from the knowledge factor is likely to prove sufficient to identify the targeted jurisdiction[1026].

It is important to also note that the targeting analysis will not determine exclusive jurisdiction, but rather identify whether a particular jurisdiction can be appropriately described as having been targeted. The test does not address which venue is the most appropriate of the jurisdictions that meet the targeting threshold[1027].

Contract is the first of the three factors for the recommended targeting test considers whether either party has used a contractual arrangement to specify which law should govern. Providing parties with the opportunity to limit their legal risk by addressing jurisdictional concerns in advance can be the most efficient and cost effective approach to dealing with the Internet jurisdiction issue. The mere existence of a jurisdictional clause within a contract, however, should not, in and of itself, be determinative of the issue, particularly when consumer contracts are involved. In addition to considering the two other targeting factors, the weight accorded to an online contract should depend upon the method used to obtain assent and the reasonableness of the terms contained in the contract.

Courts in the United States have upheld the per se enforceability of an online contract, commonly referred to as a click-wrap agreement[1028]. These agreements typically involve clicking on an "I agree" icon to indicate assent to the agreement. Given their ubiquity, it should come as little surprise to find that courts have been anxious to confirm their enforceability. For example, in the 1999 Ontario case of Rudder v. Microsoft Corp.,[1029] the court upheld a forum selection clause contained in an electronic ISP Terms of Service Agreement. The court feared that not upholding the clause would not only fail to advance the goal of "commercial

---

[1026] ibid
[1027] ibid
[1028] Gringras , Clive, The Laws of the Internet, Butterworth, London, 1997

[1029] Rudder V Microsoft , NO. 97-CT-046534CP,Ontario Superior Court Of Justice, available at http://aix1.uottawa.ca/~geist/microsoft.htm , visited on 24 Feb 2004; But contrary to this Indian courts have taken the view that the parties to the suit cannot confer jurisdiction on courts. Either it must be through the Constitution or statutory enactment.

certainty," but would also move this type of electronic transaction into the realm of commercial absurdity. The court further feared that it would lead to chaos in the marketplace, "render ineffectual electronic commerce and undermine the integrity of any agreement entered into through this medium."[1030]

Contracts must clearly play a central role in any determination of jurisdiction targeting since providing parties with the opportunity to set their own rules enhances legal certainty. As the cases decided by US courts suggest, however, contracts do not provide the parties with absolute assurance that their choice will be enforced, particularly in a consumer context. Rather, courts must engage in a detailed analysis of how consent was obtained as well as consider the reasonableness of the terms. The results of that analysis should determine what weight to grant the contractual terms when balanced against the remaining two factors of the proposed targeting analysis.

Technology as the second targeting factor focuses on the use of technology to either target or avoid specific jurisdictions. Just as technology originally shaped the Internet, it is now reshaping its boundaries by quickly making geographic identification on the Internet a reality[1031]. The rapid emergence of these new technologies challenges what has been treated as a truism in cyber law- that the Internet is borderless and thus impervious to attempts to impose on it real space laws that mirror traditional geographic boundaries[1032].

Courts have largely accepted the notion that the Internet is borderless as reflected by their reluctance to even consider the possibility that geographic mapping might be

---

[1030] ibid

[1031] Software companies like Infosplit and NetGeo claims to have the ability to accurately pinpoint the location of any IP address using a proprietary set of techniques and algorithms. The technology provides instant and precise geographic identification and page routing in a process invisible to the web user. The companies maintain that its technology accurately determines the country of origin with 98.5% accuracy, the state or province with 95% accuracy, and the city with 85% accuracy, and that it can even accurately determine user location for users of national or global ISPs such as AOL. *See* Infosplit, *at* http://www.infosplit.com , visited Nov. 26, 2004 and NetGeo, *at* http://www.netgeo.com , visited 26 Nov. 2004.

[1032] David R. Johnson & David G. Post, *Law and Borders: The Rise of Law in Cyberspace*, 48 STAN. L. REV. 1367 (1996).

possible online. In American Libraries Association v. Pataki[1033], a Commerce Clause challenge to a New York state law targeting Internet content classified as obscene, the court characterized geography on the Internet and observed as follows;

> "The Internet is wholly insensitive to geographic distinctions. In almost every case, users of the Internet neither know nor care about the physical location of the Internet resources they access. Internet protocols were designed to ignore rather than document geographic location; while computers on the network do have "addresses," they are logical addresses on the network rather than geographic addresses in real space. The majority of Internet addresses contain no geographic clues and, even where an Internet address provides such a clue, it may be misleading"[1034].

Although the court's view of the Internet in the above case may have been accurate in 1997, the Internet has not remained static. Providers of Internet content increasingly care about the physical location of Internet resources and the users that access them, as do legislators and courts who may want real space limitations imposed on the online environment[1035]. A range of companies have responded to those needs by developing technologies that provide businesses with the ability to reduce their legal risk by targeting their online presence to particular geographic constituencies. These technologies also serve the interests of governments and regulators who may now be better positioned to apply their offline regulations to the online environment[1036].

Given the development of new technologies that allow for geographic identification with a reasonable degree of accuracy, a targeting test must include a technology component that places the onus on the party contesting or asserting jurisdiction to demonstrate what technical measures, including offline identifiers, it employed to

---

[1033] American. Libraries Ass'n v. Pataki, 969 F. Supp. 160 (S.D.N.Y. 1997) , available at www.findlaw.com , visited on 24 Feb 2004;

[1034] ibid

[1035] Bob Tedeschi, E-commerce: Borders Returning to the Internet, N.Y. TIMES, Apr. 2, 2001 visited on 24 Feb 2004

[1036] Goldsmith L Jack & Sykes O,Alan s, The Internet and the Dormant Commerce Clause, 110 YALE L.J. 785, 810-12 (2001).

either target or avoid a particular jurisdiction. The suitability of such an onus lies in the core consideration of jurisdiction law—that is, whether jurisdiction is foreseeable under the circumstances. Geography identifying technologies provide the party that deploys the technology with a credible answer to that question at a cost far less than comparable litigation expenses. Since parties can identify who is accessing their site, they can use technical measures to stop people from legally risky jurisdictions, including those jurisdictions where a site owner is reluctant to contest potential litigation or face regulatory scrutiny. Fair and balanced targeting jurisdiction test demands it as a requirement.

Actual or implied knowledge of parties is the third and last factor that can be used to identify the jurisdiction based upon targeting. This factor assesses the knowledge the parties had or ought to have had about the geographic location of the online activity. Although some authors have suggested that the Internet renders intent and knowledge obsolete by virtue of the Internet's architecture[1037], the geographic identification technologies available nowadays do not support this view. This factor ensures that parties cannot hide behind contracts and/or technology by claiming a lack of targeting knowledge when the evidence suggests otherwise.

The relevance of a knowledge based factor extends beyond reliance on contracts that the parties know to be false. In an e-commerce context, the knowledge that comes from order fulfillment is just as important. For example, sales of physical goods such as computer equipment or books, provide online sellers with data such as a real space delivery address, making it relatively easy to exclude jurisdictions that the seller does not wish to target. Courts have also begun to use a knowledge based analysis when considering jurisdiction over intellectual property disputes. In

---

[1037] *See, e.g.,* Martin H. Redish, Of New Wine and Old Bottles: Personal Jurisdiction, The Internet, and the Nature of Constitutional Evolution, 38 JURIMETRICS J. 575 (1998). Redish notes: The most effective defense of an Internet exception to the purposeful availment requirement is not that state interest should play an important role only in Internet cases, but rather that the technological development of the Internet effectively renders the concept of purposeful availment both conceptually incoherent and practically irrelevant. An individual or entity may so easily and quickly reach the entire world with its messages that it is simply not helpful to inquire whether, in taking such action, that individual or entity has consciously and carefully made the decision either to affiliate with the forum state or seek to ac-quire its benefits.

Starmedia Network v. Star Media, Inc.,[1038], the court asserted jurisdiction over an alleged out-of state trademark infringer, noting that:

> "the defendant knew of plaintiff's domain name before it registered 'starmediausa.com' as its domain name. Therefore, the defendant knew or should have known of plaintiff's place of business, and should have anticipated being haled into New York's courts to answer for the harm to a New York plaintiff caused by using a similar mark."[1039]

But the application of the knowledge principle is more complex when the sale involves digital goods for which there is no offline delivery; the seller is still customarily furnished with potentially relevant information.

Under the three-factor targeting test, it is important to note that no single factor is determinative. Analysis will depend on a combined assessment of all three factors in order to determine whether the party knowingly targeted the particular jurisdiction and could reasonably foresee being haled into court there. In an e-commerce context, the targeting test ultimately establishes a trade-off that should benefit both companies and consumers. Companies benefit from the assurance that operating an e-commerce site will not necessarily result in jurisdictional claims from any jurisdiction worldwide. They can more confidently limit their legal risk exposure by targeting only those countries where they can comply with domestic law.

6.9 Conclusion

Enjoyment of human rights in cyberspace will become ineffective, if they cannot be suitably enforced in the real world. Enforcement of the right actually determines the importance accorded to such rights by the State. In this regard enforcement mechanism for human rights assumes greater significance. Even though there are difficulties in determining jurisdiction and other related problems the assurance that

---

[1038] 2001 WL 417118 (S.D.N.Y. ,2001), available at
http://209.85.175.104/search?q=cache:6irthx4qlc4J:www.nysd.uscourts.gov/courtweb/pdf/D02NYS C/01-04910.PDF+starmedia+network+v+star+media+inc&hl=en&ct=clnk&cd=1&gl=in , visited on 2 Feb 2004

[1039] ibid

netizens claims and rights will be enforced in cyberspace, would promote the interest of the network community. Promotion and protection of human rights of the cyberspace entities would usher a new era in the information age.

Resolving jurisdictional problems assumes greater significance for the enforcement of human rights in cyberspace. For most human rights violations, plaintiff must have an opportunity to institute the proceedings against defendant in his place. The 'destination theory' is more favored for finding the jurisdiction in human right violations.The establishment of European Human Rights Court which enforces human rights violations in EU member countries provides us the basis for establishing a international human rights court for the enforcement of human rights violations in cyberspace.

Multiple bases for the assertion of personal and prescriptive jurisdiction obviously lead to multiple fora with internationally and constitutionally proper jurisdiction over actors and their conduct. Jurisdictional principles can inform business decision making; knowledge that certain uses of technology may result in a distant court asserting jurisdiction and judging conduct under its own law, rendering a judgment a business' home forum would enforce, may determine what uses of technology a business undertakes. But jurisdictional principles can only acknowledge the reality that multiple laws, enforceable by multiple courts, may apply to the same conduct; it can not resolve whatever economic dislocations are caused by that reality[1040].

However, no regime of regulation or of dispute resolution has ever pretended to be the sole source to which parties turn to ease business intercourse. In every culture and in every time, private arrangements as well as governmental activity have attempted to reduce the occasions of conflict necessitating the exercise of judicial decision-making. The economic world of Cyberspace at the beginning of the 21st century is no different. Trade depends on confidence: confidence on the part of the buyer that goods or services will conform to legitimate expectations, and confidence

---

[1040] Achieving Legal and Business Order in Cyberspace: A Report on Global Jurisdiction Issues Created by the Internet Report of the American Bar Association ("ABA") Jurisdiction in Cyberspace Project empanelled in 1998 under the title, "Transnational Issues in Cyberspace: A Project on the Law Relating to Jurisdiction." , available at www.abanet.org , visited on 14 Mar 2003

on the part of the seller that payment will be prompt and complete. Such confidence, in the interests of all parties, is fostered by industry self-regulation that reflects an honest attempt to identify and resolve potential conflicts before they arise. The forms of such regulation are many and are being actively explored as e-commerce becomes an increasingly important segment of the global economy. They include voluntary codes of conduct, the provision of private arbitration for the resolution of disputes, escrow accounts, agreements between buyers, sellers and credit card companies etc.

Beyond private ordering[1041] the harmonization of substantive laws across state and national lines can obviate at least one of the jurisdictional issues, that of prescriptive jurisdiction. To the extent the law of all fora related in any way to the dispute is the same, it matters little which is applied. In many instances, of course, such harmonization will be exceedingly difficult; different states, with different understandings of the needs and rights of those they protect, will argue for very different results with respect to such things as consumer protection, gambling, libel etc. On the other hand, there is likely to be agreement that fraud in an offering of securities is to be prevented. The greater the common understanding, even if laws are not identical, the greater is the likelihood that differences will matter little to the parties; compliance with both will flow more easily from compliance with one.[1042]

[1041] Private ordering is designed, of course, to avoid the need for litigation, but as cases considering the validity of contractual choice of forum and law clauses demonstrate, the judiciary can only remain uninvolved if both parties choose it to remain so.

[1042] States that share such common understandings may also be more willing to defer to contractual choices of a sharing state's law. *See* David R. Johnson, Susan P. Crawford, and Samir Jain, Deferring to Contractual Choices of Law and Forum to Protect Consumers (and vendors) in Ecommerce, available at http://www.kentlaw.edu/cyberlaw/docs/drafts/crawford.html, visited 23 Mar 2003

Chapter 7

CONCLUSION

Internet technology highlights many ambiguities with respect to human rights and available legal protections and the difficulties of their enforcement due to technological inadequacies and human frailties. The future of digital rights management, for instance, depends on choices with respect to the evolution of the copyright law and its interpretation. Jon Bing[1043] emphasizes the interdependence of the evolution of digital technologies, the law as a means of regulation and control, and the potential for inconsistencies between the interpretation of the law and its implementation in computerized code. Once regulations and rules are automated, they are extremely difficult to subject to judicial review. Following Lawrence Lessig's[1044] argument that the code of cyberspace becomes the regulator and this might create situation of 'technology [is] implementing the law'. Increasing diversity in the bundles of rights offered to users of protected information is likely and differences in the negotiating power of right holders and users may lead to a need for new forms of consumer protection. Software agents might become negotiators of legal positions and be guided by formalisms in the software code that may not be consistent with the real world position.

Cyberspace regulation continues to mean different things to different people. For many stake holders, particularly in the libertarian atmosphere of the online world, the mere mention of the word regulation is enough to generate extremely negative reactions. For others, cyberspace regulation generates images of a return to a simpler and more circumscribed lifestyle, when human action seemed much more predictable and when people could more easily rely on certain time tested principles to guide their daily affairs. Those holding such a view do not threatened by

---

[1043] Bing John, Code Access and Control, Human Rights in the Digital Age, (Ed by Mathias Klang & Andrew Murray) The GlassHouse Press, London, 2005 at p 203-211
[1044] Lessig, Lawrence, Code and other laws of Cyberspace, Basic Books, New York, 1999

government action in cyberspace, rather by lawbreakers and anarchists who might use this new communications medium to further their own nefarious ends. On some level, particularly for certain problem areas as far as human rights are concerned; the internet itself is seen as the enemy here. Regulation is viewed as a panacea, and the government is perceived as not doing enough. But regulation will solve all the problems of cyberspace entities is a distant dream. Yet these opposing positions are constantly being eroded by emerging events and changing realties. Those who maintain libertarian positions may be confronted by a new problem that leads them to argue for some sort of regulatory solution. And those who have been lobbying for additional, restrictive law may find themselves in the surprising position of responding to a new issue by arguing that things should simply be left alone.

Architectural considerations, as we have seen in Chapter 1, further complicate this picture. No matter what view of cyberspace one adopts, it must be recognized that on some level this is not a physical reality, but an audio visual representation created and made possible by software code. Any discussion of regulation issues in this area can therefore lead quickly to central questions regarding appropriate analogies. For example, it has been argued that every communication taking place in a networked environment should be viewed as analogous to a phone conversation, and that both e-mail and World Wide Web are nothing more than graphic representation of the conversation created through the magic of software code. According to this view, the regulation question is very simple. All the rules we need are those that have already been worked out for telephones.

But this view is typically countered by noting that digital technology has enabled online users to accomplish many things in a networked environment that were simply not possible on a traditional phone, such as taking virtual tours of museums, viewing live scenes from distant locations and creating digital copies of other people's work. In addition, on some level, an online presence can quickly become very much akin to an offline presence. Establishing interactive business in cyberspace, for example, is in many ways no different than opening a new commercial enterprise in the building down the street. Which rules should apply?

Those for telemarketing or those for brick-and-mortar operations ? And how should the unique, code based aspects of online communication be factored in? Should speed, scale and a greater level of anonymity make any difference in the end? Or can it be expected at some point new software code will adjust for speed, scale and anonymity?

In the light of these complications and inconsistencies, many people are beginning to gravitate away from all-or-nothing positions regarding regulation. Yet the continued rhetoric accompanying these debates has led to the persistence of certain overarching generalizations regarding the current state of affairs. In the aftermath of the Feb 2000 denial-of service attacks[1045] against major commercial websites, for example, the media was filled with comments purporting to explain the parameters of governmental control. Major newspapers declared that the Internet is neither owned nor regulated by the government. Security experts described the online world as "an open system without set standards of regulation". Former President of America Clinton, in a Cyber Security Summit observed that 'one of the reasons the Internet has worked so well is that it has been free of government regulation'.

The fact that promotion and protection of human rights is the primary responsibility of the States in the physical world an they do so in the interest of society but governments will be interested in promoting human rights in cyberspace only when they can have certain control over the activities of the cyberspace entities. This is where the actual problem lies in protecting and promoting human rights in cyberspace.

Human rights are universal, inviolable and inherent in every human being. These rights have to be promoted and protected both in the virtual world like cyberspace and physical world. Internet technologies empower every user to express his views

---

[1045]See CNN.com, Cyber attacks batter web Heavyweights, available at http://archives.cnn.com/2000/TECH/computing/02/09/cyber.attacks.01/index.html , visited on 24 Nov 2004; Denial of Service (DoS) attacks are attacks on compputer networks , which cause networked computers to disconnect from the network or just outright crash. For example, a teenager using very simple DoS tools managed to cripple the web sites of large companies like Yahoo and Amazon during a series of attacks in February 2000. These attacks are sometimes also called "nukes", "hacking", or "cyber-attacks".

and opinions freely in an inexpensive way. The most democratic right of all, freedom of speech and expression, now offers a way to participate in democratic process for all of us. Right to privacy, most valued right by civilized men, if not properly protected faces the danger of being abused by other entities of the cyberspace. For an economic human right like copyright, the internet offers both opportunities and threats to the owners of creative works. If these basic human rights are not enforced, then their exercise in cyberspace becomes meaningless. And this is where the jurisdictional problems created by internet technologies have to be appropriately resolved.

It is quite obvious that there is a potential clash between laws protecting human rights and the principle on which the Internet works i.e. unrestricted flow of information across national boundaries. The most important human rights affected by internet communication include free speech, privacy, right to reputation and economic rights like copyright.

An absolute right to free speech means that those whose privacy and reputation is infringed by that speech have no remedy. An absolute right to privacy restricts free speech of others. Even within a single jurisdiction, the law must balance two rights by placing restrictions on each. Internet being a global media, the balancing of these human rights assumes greater significance and becomes global in nature.

Once information crosses national borders, as is almost inevitable with internet communications, additional conflicts arise. Because the rights of privacy and free speech are not absolute most states impose limitations on them, either for the protection of other citizens or to preserve elements of the national and economic interest[1046]. These limitations widely vary from State to State, as legislators and

---

[1046] For examples, European Convention for Protection of Human Rights and Fundamental Freedoms, 1950, Art.8 (right to respect for private life): '2. There shall be no interference by a public authority with the exercise of this right except such as is in accordance with the law and is necessary in a democratic society in the interests of national security, public safety or the economic well being for the protection of the rights and freedoms of others'; and Art.10 (freedom of expression) :'2. The exercise of these freedoms, since it carries with it duties and responsibilities , may be subject to such formalities , conditions, restrictions or penalties as are prescribed by law and are necessary in a democratic society, in the interest of national security, territorial integrity or public safety, for the prevention of disorder or crime, for the protection of health or morals, for the protection of the

courts take differing views of the necessary balance to be struck. Because, say, a webpage is accessible from all jurisdictions, an author will only be able to comply with the differing national limitations by complying with the most stringent limitations on his freedom of speech and similarly may need to observe the highest privacy standards.

In practice those limitations which protect individual interests by giving the affected person a right of action will rarely have substantially restrictive effects. The normal remedy is one of damages and cross-border litigation is likely only for the most serious infringements. More serious are the limitations which be enforced by national authorities , whose actions will in many cases have an extraterritorial effect as we have seen in LICRA V Yahoo Inc., decided by French court and Dow Jones V Gutnick, decided by an Australian court.

Freedom of speech and expression is the most admired right in cyberspace. The internet has provided a great platform for exercising this basic human right in an unprecedented way. Through blogs and websites almost every net user has become author. Technological change presents new possibilities for freedom of expression, shows the value of free speech in a different light, and makes particular features of freedom of speech particularly salient. These features include interactivity, mass participation, nonexclusive appropriation, and creative transformation. This in turn leads us to a new conception of the purposes of freedom of speech, which we can call the promotion of a democratic culture. However, these same technological changes also create new forms of social conflict, as business interests try to protect new forms of capital investment. This leads, in turn, to attempts to protect and expand rights in intellectual property and in the control of telecommunications networks. These rights claims clash with freedom of speech values in ever new ways; and the attempt to protect property rights in capital investment leads to competing visions of what freedom of speech is and what it is not.

---

reputation or rights of others, for preventing the disclosure of information received in confidence or for maintaining the authority and impartiality of the judiciary'.

Finally, as technological innovation alters the social conditions of speech, the technological and legal infrastructure that supports the system of free expression becomes fore grounded. As a result, free speech values must be articulated and protected in new ways, in particular, through the design of technology and through legislative and administrative regulation of technology, in addition to the traditional focus on judicial doctrines that protect constitutional rights.

As the world changes around us, as the possibilities and problems of new technologies are revealed, our conception of the free speech principle begins to change with them. Our sense of what freedom of speech is, why we value it, and how best to preserve that which we value, reframes itself in the changing milieu. And as we respond to these changes, retracing our steps and rethinking our goals, we eventually come to understand what the free speech principle is about, and more importantly, what it always was about but only now can be adequately expressed. That experience is not the experience of making something new. It is the experience of finding something old, of recognizing principles and commitments already dimly understood which suddenly are thrown into sharper focus by the alteration in our circumstances and living styles.

Free speech should be free in cyberspace. American courts have been leading the world when it comes to free speech issues. But the standard of scrutiny varies from country to country. Applying American standards of free speech scrutiny may be difficult for other countries, especially when religious matters are involved. So the ideal way may be to apply the standards used in defendant community. In this regard individuals and other entities must have consensus that there is no absolute right and free speech is no exception. The best way of regulation seems to be self-regulation. Many chat room activities and blogging activities are being regulated by the groups themselves. Whenever an offending statement appears, the maker is being warned and sometimes removed from the group. But here again there may arguments of bias. There are no standards to measure and declare whether a particular statement made by the netizen is offensive or not?. This is subjective and not quite easily resolved. As far as indecent or obscene material is concerned, Miller test formulated by US Supreme Court merits high as the test prescribes contemporary standard as a test for indecency or obscenity. More interestingly US District court has taken the view that Free speech right is available only against government and not private persons[1047]. This may cause lot of concern for free speech activists in cyberspace as most of the actors in cyberspace are private persons. Government of China is ordering to censor the content to private companies like Google and Yahoo. This kind of regulations poses difficult problems for the netizens free speech right. Right to speak anonymously must be regarded as part of free speech right .And free speech should not be allowed to be abused in cyberspace. Right to reputation of persons must be suitably protected and threatening and hate speech must be prevented. These things are possible only if certain restrictions on are imposed on free speech. The balancing of free speech with other fundamental rights is delicate and maintaining harmony is difficult, but policy makers must make an effort to achieve the right balance among these human rights.

Privacy being a basic human right, we must recognize that a vision protective of information privacy in cyberspace will be singularly hard to maintain. Cyberspace's essence is the processing of information in ways and at speeds unimaginable just years ago. To retard this information processing juggernaut in the name of privacy seems anti-technology, even anti-progress. It cuts against the hackneyed cyber-proclamation that information wants to be free. Nevertheless, this intentional application of friction to personal information flows is warranted. If profit seeking organizations are instituting such friction in the name of intellectual property, individuals should not be chastised for doing the same in the name of privacy. Historically, privacy issues have been an afterthought. Technology propels us forward, and we react to the social consequences only after the fact. But the amount of privacy we retain is to use a decidedly low-tech metaphor a one-way ratchet. Once we ratchet privacy down, it will be extraordinarily difficult to get it back.

[1047] America Online Inc., V Cyber Promotions Inc., United States District Court, E.D., Pennsylvania, 1996, 948 F.Supp.436

More disturbingly, after a while, we might not mind so much. It may dawn on us too late that privacy should have been saved along the way.

Protection of privacy interests of netizens is actually is in their hands. If netizens refuse to disclose their personal data, marketers have to employ technical measures which can be legally prevented. But netizens in US and other developing countries are willingly participating in personal data commodification. We need to have international treaties to share the personal data of netizens of various countries. The safe harbor treaty between US and EU is one such example. The way US looks at personal data, as contractual obligations, is highly inadequate for cyberspace transactions. EU model of treating informational privacy as human rights quite suitable for cyberspace transactions.

Both intellectual property rights and human rights deal with the same fundamental equilibrium. On the one hand there is a need to define the scope of the private exclusive right that is given to authors an incentive to create and as recognition of their creative contribution to society broadly enough to enable it to play its incentive and recognition function in an appropriate and effective way, whilst on the other hand there is the broader access to the fruits of author's efforts. Both intellectual property law and human rights try to get the private public rights balance and as such there is no conflict. Both areas of law however not define that balance in exactly the same way in all cases. There is therefore compatibility between them, rather than a consensus. In cyberspace most rampantly violated right is this human right, copyright.

The growth of Internet, especially the WWW has created a new cyberspace for copyrights exploitation. The analysis of copyrights in cyberspace reveals a mixed result of new opportunities and threats. Cyber technology had offered new ways of commercialization or exploitation of copyrights by business firms and individuals.

These new ways have enabled greater scope for global expansion and market reach around the world, promising huge potential for generation of revenue or other means of returns. However, these new opportunities pose parallel threats many of which even undermine the very rights of the copyright holders. The magnitude of threats is unprecedented with the technological feasibility making it possible not only for easier piracy but also for easier distribution of such pirated works to masses by a click of a button. Such threats often outweigh the opportunities offered by the cyberspace, and this calls for increasing regulation of cyberspace to protect copyrights. The present cyber anarchy has created a range of legal challenges to regulators. The ubiquitous nature of Internet has made many of these challenges international in nature, calling in international copyright regimes for greater regulation of cyberspace. The cyberspace, as such is unregulated and various transactions carried out in the Internet surpass the national regulatory controls. The technological feasibility to surpass national governments or regulation causes doubts as to the effectiveness of any single domestic regime or a select group of domestic regimes to regulate the cyberspace. Moreover, many of the domestic copyright regimes are relatively new ones and as such may be   ill-equipped to address copyright in cyberspace. This calls for increased international   co-operation for the regulation of cyberspace including the protection of copyrights.

Many of the new forms of transactions in cyberspace are highly technology oriented and any legal efforts to regulate the same have to go hand in hand with the technological growth. Law and technology, needs to be combined for effective solutions for many of the cyberspace challenges including those related to copyrights. In the context of copyrights many legal principles need to be developed or settled to determine the legality of the transaction in question. Many such pertinent questions related to copyrights in cyberspace have to be clearly settled at an international level. Lack of internationally agreed principles relating to copyrights in cyberspace gives room for divergent domestic standards. The continued evolution of cyberspace and the rapid growth of cyber technology create a state of flux, prompting a delay in legal response. There are also debates as to the potential of existing international regimes versus the need to create new regimes to address copyrights in cyberspace. Also mindful are the need to balance the conservation of online technological advantages versus the urge to regulate copyrights in cyberspace. The urge to develop regulatory regimes of copyrights in cyberspace is also hindered by the digital divide existing between the developed and the developing world. The entire complex set of cyber copyright issues indicates a range of potential challenges in developing international principles to protect copyrights in cyberspace.

It is quite difficult to apply traditional intellectual property law in cyberspace. And it is more difficult in case of copyright protection. Though technology empowers copyright holders to protect their works it defeats the fair use purposes. Right of the authors to regulate the access and use to their work through digital rights management is quite unacceptable. However, norms that would balance the interests of the user and author are highly desirable. Even then requirement of international institute to protect and enforce copyright enforcement have become inevitable.

The most significant recurring theme is the challenge to our concept of jurisdiction. Legal systems have created an enormous body of doctrine governing the relationship between the territory of the nation state and the legal right to exercise jurisdiction. Although the Internet has not rendered the concept of nation state redundant, the fact that actions in ether[1048], of an unknown person in an unknown location, can bring about the most tangible of consequences renders the connections between territory and jurisdiction less relevant than in the past. The difficulty lies not only in the fact that no solution has yet been found to the problem, but also in that no solution has even appeared on the conceptual horizon.

Does the issue of jurisdiction hold more relevance for legal theory than practice? Legal theorists delight in musing over conundrums and technicalities. Often in

---

[1048] The air, when it is thought of as the place in which radio or electronic communication takes place.

practice, however, these intellectual puzzles rarely influence practical reality. Recent examples of international cooperation in law enforcement might demonstrate that, in some cases, the problems of jurisdiction are surmountable when need be. However, for every high-profile case such as the Mellisa Virus[1049], there are innumerable cases of illegal or improper conduct that might affect the proper exercise of human rights in cyberspace, simply cannot, as yet, be regulated. Whether and how the global society solves the problems of jurisdiction will be a key element in the development of the true Internet jurisdiction.

The topic of jurisdiction leads directly to the drive for the harmonization and globalization of laws. All too often broad aspirations for harmonized laws are expressed in the hope that this might be the panacea for the Internet age. When examining this issue in the future, we should be aware that the espousing rhetoric of harmonization in much more convenient than actually producing it. There are certainly benefits to be gained from international cooperation indeed; to avoid such developments would be to take the stance of Ostrich. Many normative developments applicable to the internet begin their journey to national implementation in the realm of international negotiations and policy discussion. Nevertheless, expressions of international cooperation and aspirational international instruments should be regarded with a healthy skepticism.

In turn, the driver for harmonization highlights the increasing importance of international organizations, including the United Nations, the European Union, Organization for Economic Cooperation and Development, and the World Trade Organization, to name but a few. Each society's normative frameworks provide the benchmark for regulatory stance. The vector sum of various lobby groups produces the final outcome. As the subject of normative debate increasingly international, so too do lobby groups. International organizations are frequently co-opted to represent the interests of large international players. These players might be governmental,

---

[1049] A computer virus which was propagated through macros of Microsoft word 97 and 2000 documents. If launched this macro virus will attempt to start Microsoft outlook to send copies of the infected document via e-mail up to 50 people in outlook's address book as an attachment. See for details http://www.melissavirus.com/

corporate or otherwise. For example, it is clear that the United States policy on encryption has influenced both the polices of other nation sates and those of international organizations.

Experience thus far addressing the challenges posed by the internet community in the European Union (EU) and United States (U.S.) suggests that existing law can sometimes be applied with relative ease to Internet activities and that existing law can sometimes be adapted to reach Internet activities. However, in some instances, new laws seem to be needed. When old laws do not fit and cannot easily be adapted, it may be necessary to go back to first principles and consider how to accomplish societal objectives in the new context of the Internet. Decisions about the law of Internet, whether carried out by judges, legislatures, or regulators, will have an important impact on the kind of information economy that will emerge. The EU is to be commended for realizing that regulating the Internet is about more than information infrastructure and economics. Deciding how to regulate the Internet is also about constructing an information society in which social and cultural values can be preserved.

7.1 Recommendations

Thus, in the light of the analysis set forth in this research work, we conclude and recommend by reviewing certain basic principles that can inform any future oriented   approach to cyberspace regulation for the promotion and protection of human rights;

(1) When addressing human right issues, entire range of regulatory approaches have to be considered including litigation, legislation, policy changes, administrative agency activity, international cooperation, architectural changes, private ordering and self-regulation. In cyberspace, it is reasonable to assume that a creative combination of approaches will be more effective than any single regulatory strategy.

(2) In order to ensure that the Internet retains its ability to serve as a dramatic and unique marketplace of ideas, it is essential that regulatory frame work

must continue to respect the autonomy of individuals and groups in the online world. Internet started as a free medium of communication and its true nature must be maintained. This guarantees the fair exercise of basic human rights in cyberspace.

(3) The status quo, however, should not necessarily be viewed as inviolable. Certain aspects of the online world can and should be changed. And solutions can be crafted for individuals to exercise their rights which will not impact on other cyberspace entities. For example, exercise of individual netizens rights should not affect the rights of the commercial organizations to their detriments. For example commercial organizations right to send unsolicited mails to market their products should not harmed by over-protecting the rights of individuals. We need to be careful about all-or-nothing arguments that view any change in the law for particular situation as the first step down a slippery slope. Restricting the rights of cyberspace entities does no mean that there would be prohibition on the rights of these entities.

(4) Care must be taken to avoid viewing cyberspace regulation issues in a vacuum and the classification of problematic activity into one of four categories is an important first step in this process. By determining whether certain online behaviour constitutes dangerous conduct, fraudulent conduct, unlawful anarchic conduct or inappropriate conduct, patterns can be identified and helpful signposts can be pinpointed within a larger context. In addition, such an approach recognizes that Internet related problems can be as varied as the range of issues that must be addressed by legislators and policymakers in the offline world.

(5) If we are committed to maintaining the present day version of the Internet, then consensus among the various stakeholders will be an essential component of any effective problem solving approach. Under current conditions, given the highly participatory nature of the online activity and the distributed, anarchic design of cyberspace itself, there are hosts of ways to get around most restrictions that may be imposed. In addition, new

architectural changes can often be countered by other code based solutions. Thus a proposed regulatory approach may not be possible unless those that have the ability to resist agree to go along with the plan. And the list of such persons and entities would include not just the government regulators , but also Internet advocacy groups, virtual communities and individual netizens. In this regard it is pertinent to note the role played by organizations like ACLU[1050] and EFF[1051] , in protecting the free speech in cyberspace when they challenged the provisions of Communications Decency Act.

(6) Any decision regarding how to regulate human rights must necessarily begin with the clear understanding of the nature of this new medium, Internet and the challenges and opportunities raised by it. Certain conduct may be no different in cyberspace than it is in the offline world, while other conduct may be so dependent on speed, scale and anonymity that it may require a very new regulatory approach.

(7) The inherent limits of our legal system must always be addressed and taken into account to address the problems of the online world. Human Rights prevail universally only if the rule of law prevails universally. Introduction of computer viruses to the internet is possible from any country. As we have found in the case of 'I Love You', (where Philippines has law punish the offender), a country may be lacking laws regulate unlawful activities in cyberspace. However, both the existing rules and any prospective new strategies that might be developed under the traditional national law model should invariably considered first. Statutes, case decisions and administrative agency activity have already made a difference in certain key areas in US. And while no enforcement operation is ever completely successful, a rule that modifies the behaviour of most people can indeed constitute a reasonable solution in the end.

(8) From the global perspective, it is important to have an international institute which works with the national agencies. National laws may have value in

---

[1050] www.aclu.org
[1051] www.eff.org

some areas that are typically regulated on that level, but given the ease with which borders can be crossed in cyberspace, a legal structure that can impact a larger geographic entity will often be more effective.

(9) Even though the US has continued to dominate both access to cyberspace and the nature of online content, the Internet must inevitably be viewed at least on some level as a global communications medium. Given the fact that any particular moment persons may be connected to the internet from anywhere in the world and through servers located across the globe, international agreement and cooperation has become an essential component of any regulatory strategy. As the Internet continues to foster globalization and as nations move toward the identification of international baselines for certain key areas of the law, the prospects for international cooperation are good here.

(10)   Code based change at various levels of the Internet architecture has emerged as potentially the single most powerful regulatory strategy available. Especially when combined with one or more of the other models, software solutions can have a dramatic impact in a setting that is in fact comprised solely of binary code. Yet even as caution must be exercised in this area so that the essential nature of cyberspace does not change, it must be recognized that code based changes in the online world have often been successfully countered by other code based changes. That means technology can be used circumvent other technologies.

(11)   Private ordering continues to be set forth as a viable regulatory option by many stake holders and its potential effectiveness either by itself or in creative combination with other approaches should not be overlooked. It is in fact useful to identify two types of private ordering. The first, private architectural adjustment through the use of filtering, firewalls and other security measures- can serve a protective function for individuals and groups against unlawful or inappropriate activity. The second, private rule-making by networks, content providers and institutions, will typically dictate what others can and cannot do. While the former is appropriately viewed as

subcomponent of the broad architectural change model, the latter can generally be seen as a type of self-regulation.

(12)   Whatever strategies or combination of strategies that are ultimately adopted, regulators must set forth guidelines that are clear, direct and understandable. Intellectual property laws, for example, have proven notoriously difficult for the average online user to comprehend and we should see that simple and straightforward rules are formulated for the benefit of all.

(13)   In addition, regulatory approaches must be realistic. While this may seem inherently obvious, we have noted, for example, that the law has not truly come to grips with private personal copying since the advent of the Xerox machine and the widespread availability of audio taping and videotaping technology. Certain adjustments have been made, but most of the personal day-to-day copying that takes place in the privacy of an individual's own home remained subject to the vagaries of conflicting legal interpretation.

(14)   As a related corollary, the importance of the implicit social contract in cyberspace must also be taken into account. Clear and realistic rules are an important beginning, but it must also be recognized that, on some level, our legal system is often based upon an implicit social contract. People must want to follow the law, and if they decide they no longer wish to d so, the implicit social contract breaks down. Particularly in certain cyber spaces, where law breaking is still very easy, steps must be taken to foster a spirit of cooperation between and among all online users.

(15)   To this end, regulators must recognize and build on existing social norms. While there has been much debate in the legal and policy literature regarding the extent to which Internet norms can be pinpointed, most commentators agree that – at least for specific areas of the law and in particular cyber spaces – identifiable traditions and clear community standards exist. Examples of generally accepted activity that may have already influenced the development of the law in this regard include linking

without permission , a commitment to libertarian view of free speech rights, an ongoing consensus regarding a perceived right to remain anonymous and a broad acceptance of file sharing technology to create new digital copies of previously protected works. It is pertinent to note here that all these accepted norms in cyberspace among the entities constitute basic human rights in the physical world.

(16)   In India regulatory norms related to privacy, defamation, copyright and trademarks need to be modified to meet the challenges posed by the Internet. There is no express provision guaranteeing right to privacy in Constitution or in any statutory enactment. Law relating to defamation is regulated under IPC and common law and our copyright law fails to take care of the new legal situations created by the Internet. Another way of dealing with the issues associated with cyberspace regulation may be considered under Information Technology Act, 2000, (IT Act) with suitable amendments. It is an enabling act and aims at promoting e-commerce. It provides no solutions to matters like privacy, defamation and copyright. IT Act may be suitably amended to include provisions for regulating privacy, defamation, copyright and trademarks.

(17)   India may consider to have a separate legislation to control and regulate the collection and dissemination of personal data of netizens and in this regard it may adopt the data collection principles of OECD or it may follow the EU guidelines on data collection. Personal data now being treated as commodity and has become a billion dollar industry, this seems to be the appropriate approach.

(18)   Copyright Act, 1957 must be suitable amended to meet the challenges of Internet medium and especially this must be done in the area of Digital Rights Management (DRM). As DRM may tilt the balance in favour of right holder, Sec.52 and Sec.53 have to be amended in such way that the copyright balance is maintained even in digital environment.

(19)   Even though trademark law seems to be adequate to deal with the domain name problems in cyberspace, sometimes applications of the

provisions of the Trademark Act, 1999 may not be suitable to regulate cybersquatting and domain name abuse in cyberspace. The standards of interpretation that is used in the real space for trademarks may not be suitable for domain names of cyberspace.

(20)   Keeping in view the concerns I have expressed about privacy, defamation, copyright, trademark and other grey areas of cyberspace and in order to avoid ambiguity and varied interpretation by judiciary these issues must be covered under a separate enactment , say, Internet Act or Cyberspace Transaction Act

(21)   Ultimately, in the area of cyberspace regulation, there is no magic formula and quick fix. Particularly for certain intractable problems, solutions simply may not be imminent. In these cases, it is important to identify combinations of approaches that may serve to move things in the right direction. Compromises that may seem unacceptable now could become central features of such new approaches under one or more of the three major regulatory models – traditional national law, international agreement and code based change.

The Internet today is one of the great achievements of the modern era, and any attempt to adjust its realities for regulatory purposes must proceed slowly and with great caution. Perhaps the most important of all the inherent limits of our legal system is the rule of unintended consequences. Especially in light of the fact that cyberspace technology will inevitable continue to change, it is essential that we seek to avoid modifications that may have unanticipated effects.

Given the dramatic innovations we witnessed over the past fifteen years it is particularly difficult to predict how cyberspace might look down the road. Most agree that wireless access will become more prevalent, and that a range of smaller and lighter information appliances will enable people to connect more easily to networked environment. Indeed, if anything is certain, is the fact that we will continue to become even more interconnected in the future.

Beyond these basic certainties, however, a range of predictions abound. Prognosticators focusing on the technology have set forth dazzling scenarios that expand the limits of human potential. Those who focus on lifestyle envision an Internet that is so much part of our daily affairs that we no longer think of it as something separate and apart. At that point, many argue, there will be no such thing as cyberspace law because the online world will be virtually indistinguishable from the offline world. There will be no member separate Internet specialization in law and public policy, because every member of the legal profession will be an Internet lawyer and everyone engaged in public policy will be an Internet policy maker.

It does not matter how future internet technologies impact on our society in relation to social, cultural, economic and legal systems, the regulatory mechanism must provide for the promotion and protection of human rights. In the history of our civilizations the internet technologies have created a capacity in such a way that all of us are equal in at least expressing our views and opinions. Regulators should worry how technologies are being used by people rather than how these technologies work.

CPSIA information can be obtained
at www.ICGtesting.com
Printed in the USA
LVHW011814220523
747709LV00020B/192

9 781805 299950